DOMESTIC CAUSES OF AMERICAN WARS

Economic & Political Triggers

IVAN ELAND

Clarity Press, Inc.

©2025 Ivan Eland

ISBN: 978-1-963892-18-5
EBOOK ISBN: 978-1-963892-19-2

In-house editor: Diana G. Collier
Interior book design: Becky Luening

Library of Congress Control Number: 2025939457

Clarity Press, Inc.
2625 Piedmont Rd. NE, Ste. 56
Atlanta, GA 30324, USA
https://www.claritypress.com

Praise for *Domestic Causes of American Wars*

"Ivan Eland's *Domestic Causes of American Wars* will not make it onto the bedside tables of America's politicians, foreign policy gurus, and corporate bosses. That is because he documents their all too often unseemly roles in foisting America's involvement in our declared and undeclared wars and a multitude of military adventures. The domestic political and self-interested economic origins of these conflicts, starting in the 18th century and running up to today, come with frequently ruinous outcomes, sometimes for the politicians who start them but more often for the whole country. Read it."

WINSLOW WHEELER, key staff member on the Senate Budget Committee

"Ivan Eland's book is a must read for both students and practitioners of foreign policy. It provides a thorough historical analysis that demonstrates that in the vast majority of cases, the reasons for U.S. military action have less to do with actual threats to national security and are more for domestic political reasons—a reality the foreign policy and defense establishment refuses to acknowledge. Knowing this reality, Eland makes the compelling case that the United States can adopt a more sensible restrained foreign policy and less costly defense posture—to the benefit of national security and economic prosperity. That would be truly America first."

CHARLES PEÑA, Non-Resident Fellow at Defense Priorities and former Director of Defense Policy Studies at the Cato Institute+

"Ivan Eland's *Domestic Causes of American Wars* is two excellent books in one. He carefully makes the case that the wars we have been in since the 1780s were unnecessary and were often motivated by domestic considerations. He also documents the ways we have lost our liberties during and after most of these wars. Read and learn."

DAVID R. HENDERSON, Research Fellow, Hoover Institution

"Once you start reading *Domestic Causes of American Wars: Economic and Political Triggers,* it will be difficult to put it down. In each chapter, Eland demolishes widely accepted conventional interpretations using devastating logic and careful research. He exposes an all too consistent pattern from the 1790s to the present. Repeatedly, he finds that narrow personal and opportunistic motivations, rather than lofty principles, have dominated the decisions of politicians to wage war. A tour de force."

DAVID T. BEITO, Professor Emeritus of History, University of Alabama

More Praise

"In Ivan Eland's latest book, he investigates the histories of most of the wars and military operations during the history of the American Republic. He concludes that they were all, to varying degrees, not only unnecessary for national security, but frequently harmful to it, besides often presenting dangerous challenges to the constitutional order, especially to civil liberties. Far from being caused by real threats to the security of the United States, Eland argues that historically America has gone to war largely due to the electoral calculations of politicians and the (real or imagined) economic benefits to businesses. This interesting, bold, and provocative book should be of great interest to historians, political scientists, and all students of the history of American foreign policy."

DR. PETER C. MENTZEL, Senior Fellow, Liberty Fund

CONTENTS

SECTION V.
POST-COLD WAR

CONCLUSION

>> CHAPTER 1 <<

THE WARPING OF THE AMERICAN MIND

Most Wars in U.S. History Were Not Needed to Protect National Security

Domestic economic and political factors have been an important cause of most major U.S. wars.[1] Personal and political costs to politicians usually decide whether most wars happen.[2] Bueno de Mesquita best summed up the general phenomenon: "International relations is, simply put, a venue for politicians to gain or lose domestic political advantage."[3] Similarly, another academic study concluded that American wars are usually undertaken for domestic political reasons, not out of national security necessity. In national security terms, most U.S. wars were risky and may have even been counterproductive. This book will examine the origins of major American wars, looking for lesser-known domestic causes, which were often decisive in provoking or causing war.

When most historians look back at the casus belli of American wars, they focus on the "threats" that led to conflicts. But history does not support this claim. Even early in its history, the continental United States, with its enviable geographic isolation, was so far away from the world's center of conflicts and foreign powers that it was difficult for any major adversary to project any use of effective military power against it. Later, in the mid-twentieth century, the United States was the first nation to develop a large arsenal of nuclear weapons, which made it suicidal for any nation to attack or invade it. This intrinsic natural security and later devastating weaponry raise doubts that most U.S. wars have had much national security value or were initiated to protect the U.S. people and mainland from harm.

At America's founding, even most European powers with overseas empires or territories and powerful navies posed only a limited threat to

Americans, who are protected by two huge oceans, extensive shorelines, and a vast, rugged interior. Over time, because overseas threats became manageable, Americans focused on their "manifest destiny" to extend the U.S. government's rule to the North American West Coast. This domestic-focused and self-serving doctrine devised by American elites entailed displacing the weakened or distracted the European powers, Spain and France, which then held territory in the Western hemisphere; annihilating the technologically inferior native peoples, who also succumbed in vast numbers to European-introduced diseases; and taking advantage of two empires, Britain and Russia, whose home countries were far away from contested North American land.

After the closing of the frontier in the American West in 1890, the American government began eyeing lands across the water. This led, during the Spanish-American War in 1898, to its displacing a weakened Spanish Empire in Cuba, the Philippines, Puerto Rico, and Guam, while annexing the strategic naval outpost of Hawaii. President Woodrow Wilson wanted to be a player in planning the world's future after World War I, so he exaggerated the threat of Kaiser Wilhelm II's Germany to the United States, leading to the fateful U.S. entry into World War I. These U.S. military actions during the first century and a quarter of the nation's existence had little to do with an existential threat to the country's territory, people, or cultural way of life, and more to do with economics and politics. And such has been a common theme throughout U.S. history. Domestic factors even played a role in why President Franklin Roosevelt deceptively entered the United States into World War II.

Since the middle of the twentieth century, Americans have fought major wars to support the U.S.'s great power hegemony and have built a permanent peacetime defense industry (military-industrial-congressional complex) to supply a large standing military for the sole use of the commander in chief. The need to feed and maintain this complex has also been a leading cause of expensive, otherwise unnecessary wars. The post–World War II interdependent global economic order, which the United States sponsored, does not need a military superpower to ensure global security, stability, and open sea lanes and skies. Across the millennia, countries have had economic incentives to promote commercial relations without need of a superpower guardian; countries have traded despite political and economic instability, wars, and even while actively fighting each other. The mercantilist proposition of a hegemonic commercial babysitter has always been self-serving, flawed, dangerous, and expensive.

Melvin Small, a Wayne State University historian, has summed up the history of these unnecessary U.S. wars succinctly:

> The United States fought in six major international wars from 1783 to Vietnam—the War of 1812, the Mexican-American War of 1846, the Spanish-American War of 1898, World War I, World War II, and the Korean conflict. Our entry into these wars was unnecessary. In all cases, our national security was not threatened sufficiently to justify the call to arms.[4]

Small has said that a country should go to war only if attacked or if an attack is imminent. He has also argued that war could be justified if a nation's vessels, military bases, or formal allies (mutual security agreements) were attacked—but he categorically rejected war to defend the balance of power, to secure overseas markets, or to uphold international norms. He added that he could not find any war in modern history that began for strictly moral goals.[5]

Small's analysis is compelling. One could take it further and ask if the United States, with a tradition started by Presidents George Washington and Thomas Jefferson of avoiding permanent and entangling alliances, needs *any* foreign military bases or formal alliances? The United States did not have them until the Cold War. Ironically, it created those alliances at the dawn of the atomic age, even as its own intrinsic security became greater because of its possession of nuclear weapons. Evidence points in general to nuclear weapons contributing to the reduction of cross-border wars among countries after World War II.

The original national tradition advocated by George Washington of avoiding permanent alliances came from a legitimate fear of those alliances drawing Americans into needless wars—so germane today as the U.S. faces the prospect of being drawn into greater wars through its entanglements in Ukraine and support of Israel. Small's statement about countries not fighting wars for moral goals applies to the United States. The inventor of modern marketing and advertising techniques, the United States regularly fights wars for perceived national interests but then dresses them up as moral crusades to satisfy an idealistic American public.

University of Georgia historian Stephen Berry wrote that his generation, coming of age after the Cold War's end, has

> yet to fight a war that makes sense to a majority of us in our lifetime. The wars we've witnessed aren't even tragic; they just reek of farce and failed policy . . . to us, Clausewitz seems simply wrong; war is (with rare exceptions) politics not by *other* but by *less effective* means.[6]

Going further, one could conclude from a quick read of major American wars that most were optional, fought for lesser reasons than countering a direct strategic threat to the U.S. territory, citizens, or way of life.

During the first century of the American nation, most major U.S. wars were fought to pursue commerce or acquire new territory to enhance the domestic economy, first on the North American continent, then in the Caribbean and East Asia. After World War II, major American wars have been fought to maintain U.S. global hegemony, the need for which has not been driven by U.S. security but by domestic economic dependence on a new postwar permanent peacetime defense industry (military-industrial-congressional complex), which supplies an untraditionally large peacetime standing military at the disposal of the president.

The domestic causes of war are harder to uncover because politicians and policymakers, even in their memoirs or private papers, are wary to admit that these were a factor in their decisions. But a careful reading of the American past—albeit often between the lines—suggests that government officials and politicians regularly consider the domestic political ramifications of national security policy in their decision-making.[7]

Empirical research has shown that in democracies, domestic factors are the most important determinant of presidential foreign policymaking.[8] In few other countries have domestic politics influenced external relations as much as in the United States, because American foreign policy is derived from a combined effort of the executive and legislative branches, both of which are subjected to frequent elections by the public.[9]

When I give lectures critical of American wars, it is inevitable that a skeptic in the audience will ask, "Then which wars in American history do you support?" Such a question is intended to test the author's "patriotism." However, as I point out in this book, defending the U.S. Constitution is also patriotic—a document, which was designed to throw up many roadblocks to going to war and should be our guide.

Most analyses of American wars are done by experts in foreign policy. They often forget that the function of foreign policy is to first and foremost safeguard a country's territory, citizens, domestic political and economic systems, and cultural way of life. In other words, foreign policy is a means, not an end. Most American wars, often for lesser goals than these vital ones, in fact have harmed the republic and its institutions at home and thus should not have been undertaken. Even when wars were allegedly commenced to protect America's free political and economic systems and unique individual rights, it should have followed that the least intrusive domestic wartime measures should have been used. Instead, after the United States has entered wars of choice, draconian measures have often been adopted at home that undermined the Constitution and rule of law. Furthermore, the government fomented public emotions in support of its political and economic goals, thus in many cases fueling the march to war.

This book seeks to convincingly demonstrate that domestic factors— most importantly, domestic economic and political factors—have played a hitherto unheralded role in taking the country into wars of questionable strategic necessity, which in turn have had substantial deleterious effects on the republic's political and economic systems and cultural way of life

SECTION I.

MERCANTILIST WARS OVER OVERSEAS COMMERCE

>> CHAPTER 2 <<

THE QUASI- AND BARBARY WARS

The Quasi-War with France

While the Quasi-War with France happened on the seas, domestic factors were vital in causing it, with harmful effects on early republican institutions. When profitable trade with its former imperial master, Britain, became possible again after the American Revolution, the new United States violated the 1778 Treaties of Alliance with France, signing the Jay Treaty with the British in 1794, with the Senate ratifying it in 1795. This angered the French, who were again at war with Britain after the French Revolution, and who then began capturing American merchant ships sailing for the British Isles, causing a Quasi-War.

The most favorable precedent set during the Quasi-War with France was that the U.S. government abided by the founders' intent, engaging the approval of the three branches of government while certain founders were still in office.[1] Although President John Adams initially defended U.S. merchant shipping—emergency self-defense measures were part of the original constitutional framework—he received congressional approval for a limited war, which mostly followed stringent congressional rules. Congress only authorized defensive rather than offensive measures against France, fearing an escalation to total war with a more powerful enemy. Congress thus avoided a formal declaration of war, highlighting its constitutional power to authorize combat operations short of a general war.

A limited war with a former ally only fifteen years after the end of the American Revolution—in which the French monarchy had provided crucial aid but drove France toward bankruptcy—showed the alliance was one of self-interest despite the republican rhetoric in both countries.[2] In quick succession, revolutionary France had declared war against several major powers of Europe (1792–1797), including Britain. During George Washington's presidency, his pro-British, Federalist-leaning administration declared U.S. neutrality (1793) without consulting France or Congress and signed the commercial Jay Treaty favorable to Britain. France regarded this treaty as a violation of the 1778 accords of military alliance and commerce.[3] In response, during the subsequent pro-British Adams presidency, the French government began seizing American merchant ships, and French privateers (government-sanctioned pirates) began attacking and capturing commercial ships in U.S. waters, also violating the U.S.-French treaties.

Starting a rich American tradition of "not-so-neutral" neutrality in other nations' wars, the United States informally cooperated with the British Navy in military actions against the French Navy. American merchant ships would convoy under the protection of British warships, thus freeing up U.S. warships to clear its waters of belligerent French vessels.

Although Congress chose not to declare war for this limited martial dust-up, it eventually revoked the 1778 alliance treaties, authorized the use of U.S. forces to capture armed French ships, created a permanent U.S. Navy Department, commissioned twenty-four ships, resurrected the U.S. Marine Corps, enlarged the Army, and enhanced coastal fortifications.[4] Congress was reluctant at first to adopt these measures to enhance American defense capabilities for fear that they would transfer to the president its power to decide on war and peace[5]—exactly the problem the country still faces with powerful standing military forces at the chief executive's sole disposal.

At the beginning of the republic's history, Congress expected to dictate security and foreign policy while the president executed it, and it passed laws restricting executive actions during those wars.[6] Specifically, Congress stipulated strict rules of naval engagement to prevent the war's escalation.[7] As David J. Barron notes,

> When it came to the conduct of war, the final word, Adams insisted, must remain with Congress, and he did not back away from that position during the whole of his administration. In consequence, Adams accepted a stunning degree of congressional control over his conduct of what came to be known as the "Quasi-War" with France. . . .

In the forty years after General Washington first took command of the Continental Army, war had seemed to come to America in all its guises. . . . But these conflicts produced little precedent to suggest the president—by dint of his title, commander in chief—enjoyed an exclusive, uncontrollable power to determine the conduct of war. The Constitution did not by terms secure it. The delegates to the Constitutional Convention did not seem to endorse it. Congress had passed laws—most especially in restricting naval movements during the Quasi-War—that were predicated on the assumption that the Constitution was not intended to enshrine it. The Supreme Court issued rulings rejecting it. Presidents conducted them- selves as if they did not have it.

Justice Joseph Story, writing one of the first great con- stitutional treatises, summed up the standard view as it stood by the century's third decade: Congress's war powers were "unlimited in every matter essential to its efficacy," including the "formation, direction, and support of the national forces." Story thought the Quasi-War exemplary. It had been "regu- lated by the diverse acts of Congress, and of course [had been] confined to the limits prescribed by those acts."[8]

In the end, Congress passed more than twenty laws stipulating rules of engagement for the conflict.[9] And for good reason: George Washington had issued an executive order, which Adams rescinded, restricting mer- chant ships from arming in self-defense.[10] Washington had no unilateral power to restrict the arming of private merchant ships. Eventually, Congress acted and armed merchant vessels.

During the Quasi-War with France, America was divided domesti- cally over the pro-British tilt in American foreign policy. Despite its old alliance with France, the lure of lucrative American trade with its former imperial master was too enticing to pass up. The stronger British realized their advantages in Jay Treaty negotiations and demanded that the weaker United States sign a one-sided treaty that gave Britain most of the com- mercial advantages. When John Jay brought the treaty home, it caused a furor, especially from the pro-French Jeffersonian faction (called the Republicans, then the Democratic-Republicans, and later the Democrats). Not for the last time were domestic politics and factions a driving force in foreign conflicts: the Jeffersonians were less frightened of the French Revolution than were the more aristocratic Federalist Washington and Adams administrations.

American history books emphasize that the French began attacking American commercial ships. They soft-pedal the French perspective that U.S. merchant greed had caused the United States to renege on the U.S.-French commercial treaties. The French objected to the Jay Treaty because it allowed British ships to work out of U.S. ports to attack French commerce and made naval stores—armaments, naval supplies, and maybe foodstuffs—contraband that "neutrals," such as the United States, could not carry to France without British seizure. Because of the British naval blockade against France, the French were desperate to import food from neutrals until the development of European continental sources. American compliance with the Jay Treaty and violation of France's trade rules caused French rancor.[11]

Other domestic factors also tended to stoke tensions with France. Although Adams resisted pressure from his hawkish cabinet to declare war, he began to build ships, which poured government largesse into coastal cities that had lost private American exports during the economic downturn or Panic of 1797.[12] Yet, as in all conflicts, although such war spending helps certain regions or groups, the manufacture of military hardware creates "false war prosperity" by shunting money from the production of consumer goods to weapons—that is, the overall economic output statistics rise, but consumer satisfaction falls. In addition to French retaliation on the high seas for the Jay Treaty, the United States had been outraged by a French government attempt to bribe and otherwise influence the 1796 presidential election away from the pro-British John Adams in favor of the pro-French Thomas Jefferson.[13]

Although American history tends to focus on the U.S. furor over French Foreign Minister Talleyrand's attempt to solicit a bribe from U.S. representatives to negotiate peace in what became known as the XYZ Affair, the overall thrust of Talleyrand's policy was to avoid war by stretching out negotiations and trying to get the U.S. government to recognize its obligations to France under the 1778 treaties. Talleyrand was inclined to accommodate the United States but did not carry it out with alacrity because the French thought the possibility of war was more remote than did the Americans.[14] Fearing a general invasion by France, the United States also wanted to avoid all-out war.

President John Adams and his Federalist Party also used the limited war with France to increase their political power at home by raising a provisional standing army (with power-hungry Alexander Hamilton as its effective head), creating the Navy Department, and passing the Alien and Sedition Acts.

The last gambit tried to use a national security excuse in time of war to pass several laws that successfully intimidated immigrants and delayed the citizenship of French and Irish immigrants, who mostly supported the rival Jeffersonian Republican Party, and criminalized Republican dissent against the Federalist-run government.[15] Adams thought the acts were too severe but signed and used them against his opponents. Trying to preserve civil liberties from the Alien and Sedition Acts, Thomas Jefferson and James Madison drafted the Virginia and Kentucky resolutions, which claimed that states could nullify unconstitutional federal laws because the Constitution was a compact among the states. However, the doctrines of state nullification of federal law and secession—nullification of all federal laws—later would help cause the massive Civil War.

This war witnessed one of the worst violations of civil liberties in American history, with Federalist politicians prosecuting notable Republican newspapers for sedition. And like so many other restrictions on liberties in wartime, this one carried on after the war ended. The Alien and Sedition Acts expired at the end of the Adams administration, but the new Jefferson administration encouraged Republican governors to prosecute Federalist newspaper editors. The governors prosecuted more Federalist editors at the state level than the Adams administration did Republican editors at the national level.[16]

The U.S. Supreme Court later decided that a limited, undeclared war was constitutional. However, the court also ruled that even during a limited war, the president had to work within the strict guidance of Congress in carrying out military actions.[17] To avoid general war with France, Congress did not authorize offensive military action, allowing only defense of American merchant ships and authorizing resistance to an invasion of American soil, but stopping short of allowing attacks on unarmed French merchant ships or attacks on French territory.[18]

However, the irascible Adams did what few politicians in American history have done: he sacrificed his political career for peace. Unfortunately, history shows that war is often good politics (until the conflict goes bad). In 1800, Adams was confronted with either seeking peace, which the war-exhausted American public and opposing Republicans wanted, or escalating the naval war with France, which the hawks in his Federalist Party wanted.[19] With his intraparty rival, Alexander Hamilton, effectively in charge of the provisional standing army, Adams cooled on escalation.

Many were apprehensive that Hamilton would misuse the army because most officers appointed to the force were Federalists, and he had made statements that a standing army might root out treason among Republicans. (In fact, until the early 1950s, a majority of Americans were skeptical that a large peacetime standing army was compatible with democracy.)[20] When he found out about Hamilton's plot to cooperate with the British Navy to "liberate" possessions of Spain (allied with France) in the Americas, Adams fired almost half the Federalists in his cabinet who were involved in the plot while advocating a harsher public approach toward France.[21] The American public thought the war was too costly and lengthy, while many in Adams's party wanted to use force to grab Louisiana and liberate Latin America. Unbeknownst to his cabinet and his own party's more aggressive position, Adams had sent a peace mission to France. His negotiator achieved the Treaty of Mortefontaine, ending the "half war," but word of the good news did not reach American shores before the U.S. presidential election of 1800.

Adams had managed to defend against French attacks while avoiding a wider war.[22] Yet, because of a split in the Federalist Party and the unpopularity of the war and Alien and Sedition Acts, Adams lost to Republican Jefferson in possibly the most important presidential election in U.S. history. After twelve years of Federalist rule, the first peaceful transition of power took place in the young republic.

Wars Against the Barbary States

Domestic factors also drove conflict with some of the Barbary states (considered to be Tripoli, Algiers, Tunis, and Morocco) during the Adams and Jefferson administrations. The assumption today is that national navies will protect seaborne commerce, but at the turn of the nineteenth century, even countries with large fleets would pay privateers (state sponsored pirates) to stop capturing their merchant ships—and so the Europeans (and the United States for a time) paid off the Barbary states of North Africa. A libertarian argument against government's involvement is that business interests reap large rewards from international commerce, so their governments should not subsidize the added risks of trading overseas by supplying naval protection; the business interests should either provide their own protection or bribe the pirates to leave them alone.

John Adams treated the North African Barbary states haughtily, inconsistently, and cheaply after he and George Washington had decided to bribe them rather than fight them. Adams's envoys knew that the frugal president either had to pay them more or bring greater naval muscle to the Mediterranean to guard the lucrative U.S. trade there. He did neither. As it turned out, paying the North African privateers proved much cheaper than fighting them, as Thomas Jefferson later learned in his five-year war. However, the unpredictable and arrogant Adams treated Tripoli, which had become the most powerful Barbary state, as a vassal of Algiers and refused to pay its demands. Furthermore, an impatient Adams had insulted its leader, souring relations further.

Thomas Jefferson came into office ready to fight the Barbary privateers. Without asking or even notifying Congress or his cabinet, he sent U.S. naval forces to the Mediterranean. By accepting this congressionally unauthorized military deployment, Congress set a terrible precedent that would allow future presidents to deploy forces to places where hostilities were imminent without first getting congressional approval. Jefferson had claimed that U.S. forces would take only defensive actions and left it in Congress's lap to authorize offensive military operations in the theater.

Today it seems an easy decision that the U.S. Navy should protect American seaborne commerce. Although John Adams used limited violence to defend U.S. merchant ships from the French depredations during the Quasi-War, there was no consensus in the early republic on using armed force to protect U.S. trade.[23]

Before the American Revolution, the powerful British Navy protected American merchant ships. But after independence, the Barbary privateers realized that American vessels, no longer protected by the British Crown, were lucrative targets. Furthermore, after the revolution ended, the Confederation Congress had decided to dismantle the navy and rely on treaties and tribute to safeguard U.S. seaborne commerce in the Mediterranean.[24] Rather than fight the privateers, the Washington and Adams administrations had chosen to continue to pay them off.[25]

In 1796, the United States reached a treaty with Tripoli. From 1796 till the shooting started in 1801 (that is, mostly during the Adams administration), only one attack by Tripoli on an American ship had occurred, with the ship and its cargo quickly released while the officer, who captured the ship, faced discipline. Tripoli's ruler became incensed that the United States had not paid the money it promised him, nor supplied him any army and naval stores, nor given him a promised ship, and accordingly did not feel obliged to live up to a treaty that the Americans had not faithfully carried out.[26] More important, the United States continued to treat the more powerful Tripoli as a vassal of Algiers, unlike the U.S. relationship with Tunis. This ongoing slight triggered the breaking of diplomatic relations by Tripoli and its declaration of war against the United States.[27]

John Adams was responsible for the Barbary war, which conveniently did not occur until the beginning of Thomas Jefferson's administration.[28] Although Adams was then fighting the Quasi-War with France, the United States eventually got the French threat under control and could have spared a few ships for North Africa. Yet, as the Quasi-War wound down, Adams instead chose to cut the naval budget by two-thirds. That might have been a good move if he had also allocated more money to bribe the Barbary states, for at that time, the U.S. treasury was overflowing, and U.S. commerce in the Mediterranean had grown to 20 percent of America's overall trade. Instead, the war, lasting from 1801 to 1805, cost much more than the tribute.[29]

Even before becoming president, while serving as Washington's Secretary of State, Jefferson disagreed with Washington's policy of paying tribute to the pirates and advocated using military force. This belligerent policy was part of Jefferson's desire for what he termed an "empire of liberty"—a robust policy of westward expansion, pushing out the indigenous populations, and controlling overseas trade through embargoes and military action—all in the service of agricultural interests, which Jefferson regarded as a cornerstone of a virtuous republic.[30]

In early 1801, shortly after taking office from Adams and without notifying Congress or his cabinet, Jefferson deployed U.S. warships to the Barbary Coast of Africa with orders, through his secretary of the Navy, "to chastise" Algiers or Tripoli "in case of their declaring war or committing hostilities" on U.S. shipping.[31] This really stretched the founders' original allowance for unilateral action for self-defense in emergencies, especially when Congress was out of session, which in an agricultural nation was most of the time, given Congress's post-harvest December start date every year.

The founders never defined what self-defense entailed. However, John Adams, during the Quasi-War with France, had ordered unilateral defensive measures before Congress approved them, engaging with French warships and privateers in waters near U.S. territory. On the other hand, Jefferson sent U.S. warships halfway across the world into a potentially hostile environment and purposefully excluded Congress and his cabinet from his decision in what was not an emergency. Although the treaties with the Barbary states were deteriorating, he could have waited for congressional approval of the warship deployment or called in Congress to an early special session, as privateering by Barbary nations had been a problem for many years.

In the end, Congress acquiesced to Jefferson's stretching of the president's commander-in-chief role past the other founders' intent, which was that the executive be the top military official on the battlefield once fighting had already started. Jefferson's ordering of provocative military deployments before hostilities commenced opened a dangerous avenue of future unilateral executive action. As future conflicts have shown, presidents have repeatedly ordered deployments of U.S. forces into dangerous areas and then either ignored Congress or created a fait accompli, giving Congress no choice but to authorize the hostilities.

The Pasha of Tripoli, wanting equal treatment compared to what the United States had given Algiers, had threatened to declare war unless the United States supplied him a promised warship, paid tribute arrears, and inked a new treaty at three times the tribute level. To show the Pasha was serious, he had his soldiers overrun an American diplomatic compound, which was technically U.S. soil.[32] He then declared war on the United States.

However, following Jefferson's congressionally unauthorized and questionable orders, an aggressive U.S. ship captain started the shooting war against Tripoli's ships after it had declared war, but before any actual attack on an American ship. Alexander Hamilton, an outlying advocate of robust executive power at the Constitutional Convention, thought automatic war against an adversary who had declared war on the United States was acceptable. But the Convention clearly preferred a stricter scenario, thus giving Congress, not the adversary, control over U.S. war initiation.

This entire situation showed the danger of congressionally unapproved military deployments abroad. Jefferson's deployment and orders further stretched the executive self-defense exemption in the original constitutional framework. Jefferson had expanded self-defense from defending U.S. territory and waters to protecting faraway U.S. overseas commerce. Jefferson, never one of the most honest politicians, misstated the U.S. ship's actions as entirely defensive, and then finally turned it over to Congress to authorize offensive actions against Tripoli.[33]

Jefferson did get congressional approval for offensive actions against Tripoli's territory—although Congress decided there would be no declaration of war. Thus, Jefferson's unilateral, congressionally unauthorized ship deployment was constitutionally questionable, and stretched to the limit the "executive emergency self-defense/congressional approval for offensive action" dichotomy that the founders had envisioned at the Constitutional Convention.

Once the U.S. warships prevailed in the naval dustups, the U.S. began sending convoys to accompany American merchant ships and paid no further tribute to Tripoli. This aggressive military response to the Barbary privateers enabled Jefferson to deflect criticism from his cuts to the military budget.

Things were thus quiet along the Barbary Coast until 1803, when the U.S. warship *Philadelphia* and its three hundred crew members were captured by pirates. Jefferson got funds to build new ships by increasing tariff revenues and sent Stephen Decatur on an overland mission with marines to successfully scuttle the ship (1804). Even after this heroic exploit, Jefferson could not get Congress to appropriate money for more ships or to beef up the army.[34]

In a confusing domestic precedent, Congress authorized military action but did not declare war against the Barbary states four times: against Algiers in 1794, against Tripoli in 1802, against any Barbary state that committed aggression against the United States in 1806, and again with Algiers in 1815.[35]

SECTION II.
WARS OF TERRITORIAL ACQUISITION

>> CHAPTER 3 <<

THE WAR OF 1812

Declaring War on Britain Was Unnecessary, Unpopular, and Risky

In the Constitution, the framers assigned the decision to go to war to Congress and split the execution of war between Congress (which raises armies, maintains the navy, makes rules and provides money for the military services, and organizes, arms, and provides for calling up the militia), and the president (who, as commander in chief, controls troops or ships after any conflict has begun). In reaction to European monarchs, who quickly went to war, Jame Madison and other framers at the Constitutional Convention wanted to restrict the president's ability to unilaterally take the country into war, so their intent was to give greater war powers to the people through placing warmaking powers in the hands of Congress.

Ironically, several decades later, a reluctant President Madison led the country into a war that was unnecessary and lacked widespread support in either Congress or among the American public but was popular with important members of his own political party—the key to his getting renominated and reelected.[1] According to twentieth-century historian Samuel Eliot Morison, the War of 1812 was "the most unpopular war that this country has ever waged, not even excepting the Vietnam conflict."[2]

Before the war started, little threat of a British invasion to reconquer America existed. Madison never spoke of such a threat in his entreaty to Congress to consider declaring war against Britain. From 1812 through 1814, the threat from Napoleonic France and the island's ultimate survival preoccupied Britain. Spread quite thin by fighting the French globally for nineteen years (since 1793), the British had only a few thousand troops in North America to defend its huge Canadian colony. Even by 1814, when Britain had defeated Napoleon for the first time, the Duke of Wellington, Napoleon's nemesis, was not enthusiastic about launching an attack on the United States to break the stalemate in the concurrent war in North America. Although the British did finally send thousands of additional troops to America—easily burning and looting the White House, Congress, and other public buildings in Washington, DC—initially they had never sought the faraway dustup with the weakling new nation.

By declaring war on mighty Britain, the United States jeopardized its independence from the British Crown and helped an aggressive dictator, Napoleon. Both outcomes needlessly risked the young republic's survival.

Overall, the British were naturally inclined to be more benevolent toward the United States than toward the ruthless, two-faced, dictatorial, and empire-building Napoleon. Yet U.S. initiation of the War of 1812 against the British helped Napoleon by distracting Britain, the leader of the anti-Napoleon coalition, further eroding U.S. security. In fact, the War of 1812 between two of the freest countries on the planet goes against a modern political science nostrum that reveres what is a questionable democratic peace theory, which claims that democracies do not go to war with each other. Although Britain had a monarch, it had one of the world's most powerful and representative parliaments and a mixed constitution guaranteeing individual rights.[3]

Alleged and Real Reasons for the War

The United States fought the War of 1812 for several reasons, but national security was not one of them: first, the longstanding desire to take Canada away from the British promised tremendous economic benefits; and second, such a war would allow Madison and other Democratic-Republican politicians to use the dubious short-term "war prosperity" to try to alleviate the economic recession of 1811 and early 1812, a presidential election year. Further, failing the realization of either or both goals, they could make voters forget the recession by inducing a "rally 'round the flag" mood by starting a war.

While the gambit to grab Canada failed, the war did help Americans push westward. The Treaty of Ghent that ended the war finally removed British military outposts in the West, which allowed the white (European) American settlers and the U.S. military to move farther West—genocidally killing its indigenous populations and stealing their land in the process.

Most American accounts of the War of 1812 emphasize Britain's violation of U.S. neutrality rights at sea during the European wars with France and the impressment of American sailors to remedy personnel shortages in the British navy during wartime. Those depredations did hamper U.S. neutral trade, but the losses were more than made up for by the lucrative trade substitution the U.S. enjoyed with Europe during the larger European conflagration.

Once again, as in the Quasi-War, American neutrality rights and commercial interests during the European conflict became an issue for the young republic. This time both Britain and France targeted U.S. neutral trade on the seas.[4] Both countries thought their enemy's trade with neutral nations was detrimental to their war effort. More important, the Democratic-Republican administrations of Thomas Jefferson (1801–1809) and James Madison (1809–1817) had replaced the Federalist George Washington and John Adams administrations. Diametrically opposite to the pro-British Federalist Party, the Democratic-Republican Party was pro-France and anti-British. Unsurprisingly, the Jefferson and Madison administrations chose to focus on British violations of American neutrality at sea (British Orders in Council began as far back in 1807) rather than those of the French, despite that, from 1807 to 1811, French warships and privateers seized more American ships that did the British Navy.[5] And in 1809 and 1810, in certain respects, the French maritime depredations had also been worse; furthermore, Napoleon had double-crossed Madison about ending them. According to Melvin Small, the excessively idealistic Jefferson could have negotiated a workable settlement with the much more powerful British, but he was insistent that they should agree to a broad agreement repudiating their illegal maritime conduct toward America.[6]

Yet by 1812, British seaborne mischief toward Americans, which had been happening for a long time, was actually declining just before the U.S.-British war began.[7] The British Navy was the best in the world, and Britain, in a fight for its life, was serious about curtailing French trade with neutrals such as the United States, which were undermining its naval blockade of France. The British Orders in Council (issued in 1807 and 1809) focused on that goal, which entailed capturing U.S. ships hauling cargo between France and its colonies. Moreover, the British Navy had faced a shortage of sailors to fight Napoleon's navy, as some of them had decided to abandon the conflict and take advantage of lax U.S.

immigration and citizenship laws. Those wayward British seafarers had begun showing up in U.S. merchant ship crews when they made port calls in the United Kingdom—as many as half of these American ship crews were former or current British citizens. Thus, the British Navy began stopping such U.S. vessels and liberally "impressing" their erstwhile British sailors back into its service to remedy personnel shortages.

By 1812, however, these British seaborne depredations had been going on since the end of the American Revolution—notably, since 1803 in the Napoleonic Wars and since 1793 in the British wars with Revolutionary France before that. They would continue through World War I in the early 20th century.[8]

The most severe naval incident between Britain and the United States during the period leading up to the War of 1812 happened five years before the conflict (in June 1807), when the British warship *Leopard* fired on the ill-fated USS *Chesapeake*. The *Leopard* killed *Chesapeake* crew members and impressed three Americans and one Brit.[9] Then-President Thomas Jefferson tried to buy time and dissipate public anger toward the British; he knew the United States was woefully unprepared for war against Britain because he had halved the military budget, including that of the Navy. He sought a diplomatic solution, which he knew would take time, and resisted pressure to call an emergency session of Congress, fearing that the legislative body would come under pressure to declare war. However, Jefferson therefore had to bless hurried, unconstitutional federal government spending on military preparedness without congressional approval. Federal patronage in military contracts, pushing to expand domestic production of martial materiel, played a defining role in leading the nation into the War of 1812.[10]

Jefferson also nixed a belligerent draft of a proclamation, authored by then-Secretary of State James Madison, who was eager to foment public anger toward Britain in furtherance of his intention to run for president in 1808.[11] The draft was a harbinger of Madison's willingness to subsume republican principles by undertaking war for personal political gain. He would ultimately take the nation to war against Britain in 1812.

However, Jefferson tried to show he was nonetheless pushing back against British depredations at sea, which he did by imposing a disastrous self-flagellating embargo on all U.S. foreign trade in December 1807.[12] The harsh remedy was like a person shooting themselves in the head to get rid of a headache. France and Britain were likely to be less harmed by the embargo than would America, because they could easily replace lost trade, as even Jefferson's Secretary of the Treasury predicted.[13] In the end U.S. imports dropped by 60 percent and its exports plummeted by 80 percent.[14]

The embargo, as designed, did successfully quell the American war furor. However, in the long term, embargoes like Jefferson's typically fail to achieve their goals, are costly, and can lead to war when stringent trade restrictions do not change an adversary's behavior. Jefferson's embargo did not change French and British maritime depredations, and war with Britain erupted five years later. According to Melvin Small, Jefferson's refusal to compromise with the British and his embargo pushed the United States to war with Britain in 1812.[15]

Several other events also go against the standard U.S. narrative that British violations of American neutral rights at sea, impressment of U.S. sailors, and stoking of Indian attacks on the American frontier caused the War of 1812. The first two—longstanding irritants in U.S.-British relations from 1805 to 1812—certainly had some role in the leadup to the war, but unlike other U.S. wars, no casus belli had occurred in 1811 and 1812.[16] The American region most adversely affected by these maritime depredations was seafaring New England, which was so reluctant to fight Britain that it refused to provide troops to do so and came close to seceding from the Union over the war. New England was also the region of the country where U.S.-British trade was the most profitable, thus making New Englanders willing to endure British maritime depredations. By 1812, British impressment of sailors from American vessels—the U.S. secretary of the treasury had estimated that up to one third were legitimate British deserters—had attenuated and was no longer an underlying issue.[17]

British alleged stoking of and aiding Indian attacks on American western settlers south of the Canadian border had motivated some westerners to want war with Britain as an excuse to crush Shawnee Chief Tecumseh's powerful native confederation. However, in 1811 William Henry Harrison already had defeated the British-allied native confederacy at the Battle of Tippecanoe in what is now Indiana. In short, by the time the United States declared war in 1812, Britain had ordered its warships not to antagonize American commerce, had withdrawn much of the British Navy from the U.S. coast to prevent incidents, and had repealed the Orders in Council, the most important bilateral irritant—all in an attempt to head off war.[18]

Because of slow transportation and communication in the early nineteenth century, the word that Britain had terminated the Orders in Council of 1807 and 1809 did not reach American shores until mid-July 1812, about a month after the congressional declaration of war on June 18, 1812. Melvin Small has argued that historical evidence indicates that by early 1812, Madison should have realized that a repeal of the British orders was coming. So Small further asked why Madison did not wait to send a message to Congress asking it to consider declaring war.[19] Furthermore, on May 11, assassins killed British Prime Minister Spencer Perceval. When word of that killing reached the United States, some of Madison's friends urged him to delay the start of actual hostilities in the hope that the new prime minister would end the orders. Former Governor Henry Lee III of Virginia alerted Madison to a growing propensity in England for rescinding the orders and implored him to delay sending U.S. Navy ships and privateers on the attack.[20] Even after news of the rescinding of the British orders was received in America after Congress's war declaration, the British envoy in Washington, in another attempt to stop the march to war, unsuccessfully begged Madison to ask Congress for a repeal of the declaration of war. Madison declined all such pleas.

As a staunch republican, Madison correctly believed war under-mined a republic by threatening liberty at home. Therefore, it seems odd that he would do nothing to avoid conflict with a more powerful country that was only a limited threat to the republic. In fact, early on, Madison had been so reluctant to go to war that he had begged the British govern-ment to stop harassing U.S. ships temporarily or pretend to rescind the Orders in Council. Even in his message to Congress on June 1, 1812, Madison could not bring himself to ask for a declaration of war but merely suggested that Congress consider it, throwing responsibility to the legislative branch. Madison's desire for war ripened when he realized that he would not be renominated by his party for a second presidential term if he did not go along with it.

Madison's war message to Congress cataloged British impressment of U.S. sailors, blockade of U.S. ports and restriction of American com-merce, and alleged incitement of Indian attacks against U.S. settlers on what was then the northwest frontier. He misinformed Congress that the British were doing nothing about U.S. entreaties on the first two issues. As for the settlers, the British wanted an Indian buffer between British Canada and U.S. settlers. But Madison provided little evidence that the

British were colluding with the Indians to attack white settlers. In contrast, aggressive U.S. settler expansion was more of a threat to the Indian lands and the British. The removal of British military outposts after the war lifted any final obstacles to American westward expansion—a major goal of the "war hawks," a faction of the majority Democratic-Republican Party.[21] Native peoples were the biggest losers in the war because their autonomy east of the Mississippi River dissolved with a postwar rush of white settlers into their lands.

Furthermore, Bruce Bueno de Mesquita and Alastair Smith noted that international law on war, peace, and self-defense—embedded in the U.S. Constitution—did not require a declaration of war to deal with the self-defense issues that Madison had outlined to Congress. Executive action alone could have dealt with them, while offensive military operations would have needed a war declaration. They concluded that since Madison sent a message to Congress asking for consideration of such a declaration, he was implicitly recognizing the war hawks' offensive objective of conquering Canada but asking the legislative body to take responsibility for it.[22] Bueno de Mesquita and Smith are insightful because Congress did not declare war in the Quasi-War and Barbary Wars, which were mostly naval defenses of American merchant ships.

Digging Deeper into the Real Causes of the War

The mystery of Madison's actions can be solved by examining domestic politics during this time. First, one of the reasons New England, the region most adversely affected by brutish British behavior at sea, hated the prospect of war—so much so that it refused to supply any troops to fight it—was that it was a pro-British Federalist stronghold, while the war itself was an anti-British Democratic-Republican one.[23]

Second, and most important, despite the longstanding British depredations at sea, war fever in the United States strangely did not return till 1810, when elections in the nation's south and west produced the Democratic-Republican war hawks, including John Calhoun and Speaker of the House Henry Clay. Some historians have disputed that Congress had really turned hawkish,[24] but Madison foresaw that trend in the legislative body and public opinion, most likely because war hawks had gained control of key congressional committees.[25] Also, the hawkish Democratic-Republican "malcontents," who hated Madison, prowled the

Senate. Some authors go further, arguing that the Democratic-Republican majority in Congress increasingly advocated for war.[26]

According to Bueno de Mesquita and Smith,

> We believe the war had relatively little to do with its fre-
> quently attributed causes. It was, instead, largely about two
> matters. First was the quest for American territorial expansion,
> particularly, as others have also noted, expansion into what
> is today's Canada. Second and too infrequently noted, it was
> about the partisan interest of a segment of the majority party
> in Congress—the War hawks. The evidence will show that the
> War of 1812 was at least as much driven by Madison's desire
> to be nominated and reelected as it was by a desire to defend
> the United States against the threats of Great Britain and its
> allies....
>
> Like any group of self-interested politicians, they
> [Madison and the War hawks] unabashedly followed policies
> designed both to satisfy their quest for territorial gains and to
> secure, through the war effort and war propaganda, electoral
> advantage at the expense of their Federalist opponents. The
> war failed in its expansionist purpose, but it was a great suc-
> cess for those whose partisan interests were tied to the War
> Hawk faction in Congress, including President Madison. The
> Federalists' opposition to the declaration of war proved a
> short-lived boon followed by the collapse of their party and
> a realignment of American political competition along lines
> favored by the War hawks.[27]

As noted, Federalist New England was the region most hurt by British impressment and seaborne trade restrictions, yet ironically the one most unwilling to fight the war. It was unlikely that the majority Democratic-Republican Party, the most enthusiastic for war and having many members from the south and west, would be fighting to save New England from such British maritime depredations.[28]

Western expansionists made common cause with southern expansionists. Western expansionists wanted to invade Canada to get the agricultural lands there and smash the resistance of the Indians to American

westward expansion by removing their alleged British backers from that territory.[29]

Southern expansionist congressmen were pro-slavery and wanted to grab agricultural land in Florida from a weakened Spain then controlled by Napoleon.[30] In the early-to-mid-nineteenth century, there was a balance in the United States between adding slave states and free states to the Union.[31] To balance Florida, the war hawks clearly wanted to grab Canada from the faraway British Empire. In the months before the war, talk was afoot of taking Canada and Florida to enlarge the expanse of "freedom". The expansionists were in the end more successful in grabbing Florida than they were in grabbing Canada; in 1819, four years after the end of the war, the Spanish signed the Adams-Onís Treaty, handing over Florida to the United States.

The western war hawk faction's goals were the same as those of the American Revolution: to drive the British out of North America and the Indians from the American frontier. The problem was not just the British in Canada allegedly supporting Indians' harassing the frontier but the American leaders' belief in a larger British plot to block U.S. manifest destiny to rule the entire North American continent. For almost forty years, since the beginning of the Revolutionary War, Americans had written and talked about how desirable it would be to gain Canada. One of the first things the colonists did after the American Revolution broke out in 1775 was to invade Canada, and the colonies' military alliance with France in 1778 had allowed them to keep Canada if they gained their independence.[32] The colonies eventually won independence but failed to take Canada. Despite this failure, in 1781 the Articles of Confederation, America's first independent form of government that preceded the Constitution, claimed Canada as a future state in a growing union. Preceding the War of 1812, the rallying slogan was "Free Canada."[33]

In 1813, after the invasions of Canada in 1812, Daniel Sheffey, a southern Federalist, was skeptical that conquests of Canada and Florida were essential to American "security and happiness." He questioned the real goal of the congressional effort to augment the armed forces. Sheffey noted that Congress at certain times had been advised that Canada was only to be taken in exchange for U.S. maritime rights respect by Britain; at other times he was told that it would be taken to prevent future conflict and Indian mischief. Nevertheless, Sheffey had concluded, based on the behavior of American military commanders, that the War of 1812 was "a war for the conquest of Canada."[34]

The war hawks were not shy about their intentions toward Canada. Although noting British naval depredations, then-Senator Henry Clay of Kentucky, future leader of the war hawks in the House of Representatives, was blunt about his desire for war with Britain to conquer Canada, arguing to the Senate that "The conquest of Canada is in your power." He said unequivocally he wanted to conquer "the last of the immense North American possessions" held by England, and thereby "acquire the entire fur trade connected with that country." Clay was not alone; others wanted to invade Canada to gain virgin lands, additional free states to balance slave states in the South and West, or new markets to combat the ongoing economic recession. In 1810 Clay, having been elected to the House of Representatives, became Speaker, using his position to pressure Madison to be more truculent against Britain and promoting in the House three new war hawks.[35]

War hawk Congressman Felix Grundy of Tennessee was very blunt about his faction's territorial goals: "This war, if carried successfully, will have its advantages. We shall drive the British from our Continent . . . I therefore feel anxious not only to add the Floridas to the South, but Canadas to the North of this empire."

Another war hawk, Richard Mentor Johnson of Kentucky, proclaimed:

> I shall never die contented until I see her [Britain's] expulsion
> from North America and her territories incorporated with
> the United States. . . . In point of territorial limit the map will
> prove [conquering Canada's] importance. The waters of the St.
> Lawrence and the Mississippi interlock in a number of places
> and the Great Disposer of Human Events intended those two
> rivers should belong to the same people.[36]

Arrogantly, the war hawks predicted that if war came, the United States could conquer Canada easily.[37] They also wanted to remove the British from their military outposts on the frontier so that westward expansion could go ahead. John Randolph, an antiwar hawk Democratic-Republican, criticized "this war of conquest, a war for the acquisition of territory and subjects."[38]

Inexplicably, given the failed earlier invasion attempt during the American Revolution, shortly after the United States declared war on Britain on June 18, 1812, a multipronged U.S. invasion was launched to conquer Canada—on the presumption that such a conquest would be a simple matter because Canadians were now ready for independence from the British Empire.

If a more reality-based assessment of Canadian sentiment had taken hold, the War of 1812 would have been unnecessary. But even if conquest had succeeded, the conquered population, many of whom were displaced loyalists from the American Revolution, was likely to be hostile; a better outcome might have been achieved (if it could have been at all) at much lower cost by trying to entice Canadians voluntarily into the United States with financial and other incentives.

Madison's Second Term Political Ambitions Depended on Taking the Nation to War

As a loyal republican, Madison was staunchly against war in principle. Yet his own political interests trumped ideology. During the 1812 presidential election, fulfilling his desire to serve a second term first depended on being renominated by his anti-British party's congressional caucus. Historian Sydney Howard Gay noted that Madison had long been against a war with Britain because the U.S. military was in no condition to go to war with world's greatest naval power, and because he thought the war aims could be achieved more cheaply using peaceful means.

However, in 1808 Madison had not been the unanimous choice for the Democratic-Republican nominee for president, and in 1812 he had two rivals to be the party's presidential nominee (at the time, a surefire bet to win the presidency), both of whom advocated war.[39] Thus, some argue that war hawks Henry Clay, John Calhoun, and others successfully pressured Madison into lukewarm support for war. Although some authors dispute that war hawks drove the war decision,[40] others conclude that politics within the dominant Democratic-Republican Party pushed Madison into a war that much of Congress and the country did not want to fight.[41] Madison had lost some key support within his fractious party—one important issue being his foreign policy—and was not in a strong position for the 1812 nomination. According to historian J.C.A. Stagg, "The coming of the War of 1812 can be understood not merely as the termination of a long crisis in Anglo-American relations but also as the outcome of the politics of the first American party system.... Ultimately, the exigencies of domestic politics were to provide a sufficient cause for the president's decision to prepare for war."[42]

Ronald Hatzenbuehler and Robert L. Ivie acknowledge that "Madison's personal and political problems came to a head in 1811–1812," leading them to argue that he, Secretary of State James Monroe, and the congressional leadership shaped the war movement, with the Democratic-Republicans developing the key argument that the British system of maritime depredations would end in a British attack and attempt to recolonize America. Thus, the conflict would be for national existence, really a "Second War for Independence."[43] This rhetorical justification was so far-fetched, given the British actions to try to avoid war, that it resembles one of George W. Bush's justifications for invading Iraq in 2003—that Osama bin Laden and Saddam Hussein were in cahoots for the 9/11 attacks on New York, Washington, and Pennsylvania. Historically, grandiose concocted justifications for war usually have camouflaged more unseemly ulterior motives for conflict.

Garnering his renomination at least required Madison to make an unenthusiastic appeal to Congress, asking them to merely consider war with Britain. Illustrating the misreading of early U.S. history by modern-day hawks—who assert the president's questionable power, using his commander-in-chief authority, to unilaterally take the nation to war—was Madison's entreaty to Congress to consider war. In the nation's first presidential appeal for a congressional declaration of war during a major conflict, Madison wrote, "Whether the United States shall continue passive under these progressive [British] usurpations ... is a solemn question which the Constitution wisely confides to the Legislative Department of the Government."[44]

Madison had released to Congress documents that stoked the war fever domestically and were unfavorable to the opposing party, including documents showing Britain trying to buy Federalist Party support.[45] Thus, politics explains Madison's dismissal of the British envoy's plea for him to ask Congress to revisit its war declaration after it became known that Britain had repealed an alleged major reason for the coming war: the British blockade of American shipping and the Orders in Council that interfered with U.S. neutral rights at sea.[46] He told the envoy that Congress had spoken, and he was required to execute its will unless it reversed course[47]—technically true but, given his role in spurring Congress to consider war in the first place, disappointing. Thus, Madison chose personal political gain over republican principles by allowing the United States to stumble into the first major war in its young life.

Actions Reveal the True Economic Drivers

Yet the comparatively weak United States, which was miserably unprepared militarily for conflict with the British superpower, could very well have lost the war. Because of Democratic-Republican suspicion of standing militaries and consequent Jefferson and Madison administrations' budget cutting, the United States had a very weak navy but was fighting the world's foremost naval colossus. Its small army was of low quality, and state militias were even worse. The navy had sixteen ships (excluding Jefferson's useless gunboats) while the British had the most powerful navy in the world, with six hundred ships. On the ground, the United States had about 6,700 regular troops compared to Britain's half million highly trained regulars. The only saving grace was that, when the War of 1812 started, Britain was fighting a large conflict in Europe against Napoleon, so all this power could not be used against the United States. Also, in the spring of 1812, little support among the American public existed for war, and the country had little spare cash because of an economic recession. None of this was a good hand to play in the game of war, especially when the opening stratagem for the war was to invade British Canada. That invasion began less than a month after the U.S. declaration of war.[48] In the end the United States mostly fought the war on Canadian territory.

Congress had declared war on one of the greatest powers on earth from a weak position and knew it. Despite the war declaration driven by the war hawk faction, Congress was oddly and dangerously reluctant to provide money for the forces or the supplies needed to fight such a formidable enemy.[49] A convincing "tell" that the War of 1812 was not fought primarily over the stated maritime issues was that Congress had a modest willingness to increase funding for the army, which would be used to conquer territory, fulfilling the goals of the war hawks in the ruling Democratic-Republican Party, but no inclination to supply new ships for the navy.[50] Actions talk and rhetoric walks. Ironically, however, the land war against the British went badly and, despite the war-hawk Congress's refusal to fund a naval build up, American privateers had some success capturing British merchant ships.[51]

Another telling fact that the United States did not primarily fight the war because of British maritime depredations was the congressional vote for war. The 79-49 vote for war in the House had no Federalists (dominant in the seafaring Northeast) voting in the affirmative, and around half the approving votes were from the region from Maryland to Georgia, which did not feel as strongly about Britain's maritime depredations. Also, Congress could have limited the war to reprisals against Britain by the U.S. Navy and privateers, as it had in the exclusively maritime Quasi-War against France fourteen years before, but that restriction would have stopped the attempt to invade Canada and also to clear the way for American westward expansion.

Historian Michael Beschloss best sums up Madison's high-risk strategy for war, despite the United States's glaring military, political, and financial problems: "Inexperienced in military affairs, Madison deluded himself into thinking that this war would be predictable and brief, with a few quick battles against a British force distracted by the struggle against Napoleon, after which Canada would tumble into American hands and London would plead for peace."[52]

Madison's logic was strangely obtuse, for as a founder he knew well that less than thirty years earlier in the American Revolution, it had taken eight years to beat the British even with the decisive help of France and Spain, which would not be assisting this time.

The Deleterious Domestic Effects of a Risky War

The stakes in the conflict were high. If the United States had lost the war, it could have lost territory or even its independence—thus posing a significant risk of Americans again becoming supplicants to the British Empire. Moreover, opposition to the war in New England was so strong, it almost seceded. Luckily for Americans these outcomes did not happen, despite a measurably lackluster U.S. military performance in the conflict—the war itself ended in a standoff, with a return to the military and territorial situation before the war. Fortunately, because of the Napoleonic Wars, North America remained ancillary to Britain, which was reluctant to fight in North America again, wanting only to secure Canada from U.S. conquest, which they did with clear success.

Some American elites had long dreamed of a North American continent controlled by the United States and devoid of British presence—an outcome not achieved.[53] And nothing in the postwar settlement of 1814 addressed the original alleged causes of impressment of sailors and British respect of neutral rights at sea. However, the British had removed trade restrictions by rescinding the Orders in Council and had attenuated naval impressment before the War of 1812 had started. Furthermore, as the Napoleonic Wars ended in 1815, Britain no longer had a need to interfere with U.S. neutral trade with France nor an incentive to impress American sailors to deal with war-induced naval personnel shortages. In addition, after 1815, Britain no longer needed to supply limited support for Indian resistance against American settlers to safeguard Canada from a U.S. invasion. Thus, historians—who disagree on causes of the war— have mostly agreed that the war ended in military stalemate and did not achieve U.S. goals on land or sea.[54]

Other Americans were in fact the losers. Next to Native Americans, the biggest losers in the war were Federalist New Englanders, who bore most of the war's costs, with political enemies calling them traitors for opposing the conflict and for having contemplated secession at the 1814 Hartford Convention. Because of such public opprobrium for its "traitorous" conduct, the Federalist Party eventually became extinct.[55] The *New York Evening Post* had best summed up the war for America: the conflict had been "adopted without cause, declared without being prepared, and carried on for more than two years amidst every disaster and disgrace."[56]

This unimpressive outcome was achieved at a cost of 15,000 American and 8,600 British and Canadian lives and increases in U.S. public debt to the point of default, which then led to an unconstitutional national bank revival. This, the only foreign invasion of the United States in its history, included the burning of all public buildings in the nation's new capital in retaliation for the American burning and pillaging of York (Toronto). British Rear Admiral George Cockburn, who invaded and burned Washington, noted that if George Washington had been president instead of James Madison, he would not have "left his capital defenseless, for the purpose of making conquest abroad," meaning the U.S. invasion of British Canada. The burning of the city of Washington occurred because of the incompetence of Madison, and because his selection to defend the capital, General William H. Winder, was picked only for his political connections.[57]

The most important result of the war, however, may have been that the British finally removed their military outposts from the American West. They were supposed to have done so after the American Revolution but had not. The Americans also violated the peace treaty ending the revolution by not paying debts to Britain and by not restoring confiscated property to loyalists. Those British frontier outposts had been forestalling American settlers and soldiers from committing ethnic cleansing and genocide in wars against indigenous nations in their push westward across the North American continent. In short, the War of 1812 simply led to more conflict, as wars in general tend to do.

With Madison's sporadic commitment to republican government, his past opposition to the Alien and Sedition Acts during the Quasi-War, and the prevailing public view in favor of executive restraint, he did not substantially restrict civil liberties during the larger War of 1812.

Although U.S. initiation of this conflict was dangerous and foolish, to Madison's credit, this war became one of only a few in American history where political liberties were not undermined. The one exception was Madison's weak response to General Andrew Jackson's unconstitutional declaration of martial law in New Orleans and jailing of a resistant judge there. These actions occurred after Jackson's famous victory against a British invasion of the city, when neither he nor the British knew the war was over. Madison was reluctant to criticize a "war hero" who had made an otherwise abysmal war seem like a smashing victory for the United States, even if after the fact.[58] However, history shows Madison and his advisers were quite aware that they had barely avoided disaster in the war.

Unlike Jefferson, Madison did not take actions that would erode Congress's ability to declare war.[59] Furthermore, the Supreme Court ruled, during the War of 1812, that in war, Congress supplied direction for the executive, who could not act without it. Madison accepted the court's ruling, deferred to Congress, and overruled his military—which wanted, despite the congressionally passed Articles of War, to try a U.S. citizen for espionage in a military tribunal rather than in a civilian court.[60]

To pay for most wars throughout American history, nervous government officials would prefer to take out loans or print money rather than take the politically risky route of raising taxes. The War of 1812 was no exception; electorally vulnerable politicians chose not to raise taxes but instead to take out loans. What taxes the Democratic-Republican Congress did use to fund the war were not internal taxes but instead were tariffs that most heavily affected trade-dependent, Federalist New England, the region most opposed to the war in the first place.[61]

The massive debt incurred by the war—virtually bankrupting the United States—and attendant currency disorder would resurrect the (unconstitutional) National Bank. The old bank had expired in 1811.[62] This centralization of banking had come at the expense of the state banks. Andrew Jackson would later end this Second National Bank. However, the first and second iterations of central banking would lay the seeds for the modern-day Federal Reserve System, enacted just before World War I, which really took hold of the economy during and after the war, laying the seeds for 1930's Great Depression.

Also, the war pointed out the need for new transportation facilities, thus leading to government-funded "internal improvements," such as roads, canals, and ports. In total, support for tariffs, a national bank, and internal improvements generated by the push westward resembled the old Federalist Party program. Ironically, as the Federalist Party died, the Jeffersonian Republicans, previously the party of minimal government, easily adopted such big-government programs.

This program of tariffs, central banking, and internal improvements eventually became Henry Clay's American System program of the Whig Party (the old anti-Jackson wing of the Democratic-Republicans). However, the program for an enhanced central government role in these areas was not completed until an even bigger war—the Civil War—allowed the new Republican Party, a successor to the Whigs, to implement it fully during and after the worst war in American history.[63]

>> CHAPTER 4 <<

THE MEXICAN WAR

A War to Steal a Weaker Nation's Land

According to Melvin Small, the U.S.-Mexican War was the most "distasteful" war, the least justifiable, and one that involved "territorial aggrandizement." He noted that despite Mexican soldiers "attacking" U.S. soldiers, who were provocatively deployed in disputed territory along the Texas-Mexican border, Mexico was no threat to U.S. national security because its military did not have the offensive power to invade the United States or any disputed territory.[1] Similarly, Norman A. Graebner noted that until the Vietnam War, the Mexican War was the most pilloried war in American history. President James Polk, Secretary of War William Marcy, the last President of the Republic of Texas Anson Jones, British observers, and the nation of Mexico all knew Mexico was no threat to invade the United States and would be on the losing side of any war.[2] These facts have been lost on too many historians.

Unlike the War of 1812 and later wars, the causes of the Mexican War are less difficult to debate or mask. Even at the time, the war and President Polk's conduct of it brought domestic opposition, notably from then–Illinois Congressman Abraham Lincoln. Suspiciously, Lincoln never received an answer from Polk when he asked publicly whether the first deaths of U.S. soldiers, which started the war, occurred on U.S. soil.

Polk practiced the self-serving doctrine of *manifest destiny*—the belief that God wanted white Protestant American settlers to expand across the North American continent with their unique virtues and institutions. This was little more than a cover for stealing California and its ports and the American Southwest from Mexico. The president took advantage of a minor border skirmish in Texas to launch a wider war of territorial expansion—a war condoned, soft-pedaled, or celebrated by certain historians and portions of the American public ever since. Polk further set a precedent for future U.S. wars by doing what the American founders feared most: like European kings, Polk developed a false pretext for war with a sinister ulterior motive. He claimed the U.S. was fighting Mexico to avenge the border skirmish and collect debts owed by its southern neighbor but really intended a massive territorial grab. Nowadays, few Americans are in favor of giving back to Mexico the land essentially stolen at gunpoint. Therefore, Polk's naked aggression needs rationalizing by subsequent generations, who posit a modern version of manifest destiny, claiming it was inevitable anyway that the United States would expand across the North American continent to the Pacific Coast.

Even today, to justify the Mexican War, Americans will say that Polk paid Mexico $15 million for more than half of Mexico. However, Polk had used force after Mexico turned down an opening American offer to buy the territory. This "paying for the victim's land" would become a recurrent theme in American history—in the Indian Wars, the Spanish-American War, and later. Democrat Polk paid the Mexicans for the land only to placate anti-expansionists in the Whig Party. It turned out to be a deal tantamount to theft because Polk announced in December 1848, ten months after concluding the Treaty of Guadalupe Hidalgo and ending hostilities with Mexico, that miners had found gold in California, which had a notable share of the world's richest mines. This caused a massive westward migration that would have dire consequences for the indigenous peoples in the region.

Mostly forgotten today is the unacceptable military risk taken by the aggressive Polk. He had risked two wars at the same time, one with Mexico and another with Britain. The British, like the United States, held territorial claims in the Pacific Northwest, which extended down from what is now Canada. Thus, Britain was ready to block the excessively ambitious U.S. territorial claims in the Pacific Northwest and Oregon territory.

The Seeds of War

After Mexico's independence from Spain in 1821, the new Mexican government—struggling to control its frontier from raids by the powerful Comanche nation in the sparsely populated northern part of its country—made the mistake of inviting American settlers into the region of Texas to act as a buffer against the Indians, providing them with huge plots of native land for less than what they could get in the United States.

The immense potential bonanza of growing cotton with slave labor in the fertile soil of coastal East Texas beckoned. However, the Mexican government required the incoming settlers to declare loyalty to Mexico and convert to Catholicism. The incoming Americans, mainly Protestants, took the free land but never intended to fulfill the other requirements. Soon American settlers, both legal and illegal, were overrunning Texas.[3]

As in Florida and California, American settlers in Texas agitated for those regions to break with their homelands and join the United States. Contributing heavily to the Texans' revolt, which began in 1835, was Mexico's scrapping of its existing federalist constitution in favor of one that made the government increasingly centralized, thus eroding settlers' ability to immigrate from the United States and still own slaves in Texas. In 1829 the Mexican government had outlawed slavery, including in Texas. Although Mexican enforcement of the ban had been lax, the potential for settlers to lose the right to own slaves became a major cause of the Texas rebellion. Tariffs and land taxes were also grievances in the revolt, but the Mexican government felt Texans did not appreciate Mexico's original generosity in handing out cheap land.

By 1835, white American immigrants in Texas (only a few of whom were legally there) outnumbered Mexicans ten to one. In that year, Antonio López de Santa Anna, an autocratic populist, had seized power in Mexico City and wanted to enforce Mexican laws on the unruly white Americans in Texas—especially those banning slavery and requiring conversion to Catholicism. The autonomy-loving Anglo Texans revolted. Despite its portrayal in American history as a scrappy band of Texans winning their independence from an authoritarian central government in Mexico, the Texas War of Independence (1835–1836) was actually a proxy war for land, waged by the United States against Mexico with American volunteers, guns, and money. According to historian Daniel Sjursen, it was a racial, religious, and political conflict involving white-supremacist Protestant Texans against a would-be despot who was trying to exert central control over Mexico.

While according to Sjursen, slavery was not the leading cause of the Texas revolt but was a contributing factor,[4] other historians and analysts consider the prohibition against slavery to be the overweening cause of the rebellion.[5] Regardless of its cause, the most important outcome of the Texas War of Independence and the subsequent U.S.-Mexican War was the expansion and empowerment of slavery as an American institution.

Mexico's leader personally commanded forces that rode north to, in Santa Anna's words, "combat with that mob of ungrateful adventurers."[6] However, Sam Houston's Texan army eventually vanquished Santa Anna at the Battle of San Jacinto, took him prisoner, and Texas declared independence from Mexico in 1836. Yet the Texas question went undecided until the U.S.-Mexican War of 1846–1848.[7]

The Panic of 1837, a severe economic downturn in the United States, created unemployment in the East, which triggered a large migration westward of people wanting a fresh start. More whites, along with their enslaved Africans, flooded into the newly independent nation of Texas. The United States needed new land for an influx of European immigrants in the 1840s. Yet for westward bound settlers, while Texas had few Mexicans residing there, numerous Indians lived there.[8]

In exchange for his life and liberty, Santa Anna had agreed that Mexican troops would withdraw south of the Rio Grande River. Santa Anna also promised to recognize Texas's independence, but this never happened, and sporadic outbreaks of violence with the new Republic of Texas recurred. In 1841 Santa Anna returned to power in Mexico and wanted Texas back, periodically skirmishing with Texan forces in the early 1840s, finally ceasing to do so because he did not want to antagonize the United States. Exploiting Santa Anna's weakness, the United States then annexed Texas in 1845, which led to the U.S.-Mexican War in the following year. In short, the United States inherited Texas's war with Mexico.

From the beginning, Texans had wanted the United States to annex it, but that did not happen until nine years after independence in 1836. Mexico would not accept the loss of Texas to the United States without war, and since 1820 the United States had kept an uneasy balance between admitting slave and free states. Between 1837 and 1845, after Texas's independence, the slave population in the area—now unencumbered from Mexican central government restraints—ballooned by a factor of almost seven. Admitting Texas to the Union would mean disruption of the delicate free-slave state balance—there was talk that up to *five new slave states* could enter the country from the large territory of Texas.[9]

Therefore, U.S. domestic political considerations delayed Texas's annexation plans until the election year of 1844. President John Tyler, thrown out of the big-government Whig Party for standing on small-government principles, was desperate for a popular policy to garner votes as an independent in the election. Unfortunately, elections sometimes make politicians like Tyler deviate from their principles. He signed an annexation treaty between the United States and the Republic of Texas in April 1844 but lacked the two-thirds Senate majority for ratification because a Northern anti-slavery minority opposed it. He then brought Texas into the Union via an unconstitutional majority vote in each house of Congress,[10] thus setting a bad precedent for future presidents to skirt the Senate's supermajority requirement for treaty approval.

This U.S. intention to annex Texas (as a single state) then angered Mexico, which threatened war because it had never recognized the loss of its former province. Moreover, the United States had been a military threat to Mexico since that nation's independence from Spain in the 1820s. By the 1840s the Mexican elite feared a showdown soon with their northern neighbor. They saw that the balance of power was deteriorating against them.[11] In May 1845, Mexico finally recognized Texas's independence, but that was too little and too late to avoid its annexation by the United States.[12] By 1846 there was an uneasy situation at the border. While war fervor in Mexico had cooled, James Polk, Tyler's provocative successor, decided to start a war with a Mexico to grab even more of the weaker nation's land.

Polk had cared little about Texas or Mexico before the 1844 presidential campaign. However, his aggressive rhetoric about annexing Texas and western expansion helped him win the presidency over Henry Clay, a Whig who merely wanted to improve the interior of the existing United States instead of adding territory. If Clay had become president, the U.S.-Mexico War probably would not have occurred. So too the Civil War, which ignited because the free state/slave state balance in the United States was ruined by the question of whether slavery would expand into the vast territory that Polk conquered in the war with Mexico.[13]

However, Polk's belligerent behavior, much like Lincoln's later during the Civil War, might be explained by the presidential candidate winning a hefty Electoral College majority despite winning more narrowly in the popular vote. Unwarranted, they likely believed that they and their campaigns were far more popular with the public than they truly were, causing them to act more aggressively. Polk's agenda became expansion westward in fulfillment of manifest destiny based on a razor-thin win in the popular vote. This outcome may have translated into a decisive Electoral College win of 170 electoral votes to Henry Clay's 105, but not a mandate to go to war.[14]

Polk Starts a War of Expansion

As with the Quasi-War, the Barbary Wars, and the War of 1812 (and wars to follow), the economic causes of the Mexican War are key. In earlier wars, threats to U.S. international commerce at sea played a central role in, or excuse for, causing the war. However, in the War of 1812, the economic advantages of attempted territorial expansion into Canada and Florida were huge. In the Mexican War the motive of territorial expansion was even more blatant than in the War of 1812. Valuable land and Pacific Ocean ports were in Northwest Mexico—what would become the Southwest United States after the war. Zealously expansionist, Polk believed in the religion-infused doctrine of manifest destiny. Kept from the American people and Congress, however, were manifest destiny's less "spiritual" objectives, which included getting ports on the California coast (San Francisco and San Diego) for Pacific trade. Under the doctrine, most Americans had been told taking land, resources, and sovereignty from "inferior" peoples helped spread freedom and Christianity.[15] Although made more palatable over time, the United States to this day still believes in certain underlying principles of this nineteenth-century doctrine—that exporting freedom, democracy, and civilization using military force abroad was a righteous endeavor. Yet, then as now, such rhetoric often has been a fig leaf for ulterior motives of hegemony over other peoples and economic gains.

Many historians reject the thesis that a conspiracy of Southern-state slaveholders (including Polk himself) pushed to conquer the desert Southwest from Mexico and admit a plethora of new Southern states, increasing that region's political power, especially in the U.S. Senate. Although many southerners might have had this objective and many northerners might have feared it, there was nonetheless initially wide support—North and South and across political parties—for the war, based on the economic benefits it would bring.[16] Although in his diary, Polk implied that the climate and topography of California and New Mexico would not be conducive to the institution of slavery,[17] that does not mean the Civil War was not inadvertently caused by the internal conflict caused by the Mexican War—that is, whether states created from the recently won territorial war booty would enter the Union as slave or free.

Whig President John Tyler had decided to annex Texas in early 1845, in the waning days of his administration. Earlier, Mexico had threatened that U.S. annexation would make the United States legally at war with its Mexican neighbor. The reason was that under international law, Texas was still legally part of Mexico, and Tyler's action was tantamount to a declaration of war against Mexico. In response to Mexico's earlier threat, President Tyler had sent troops to western Louisiana near the Texas border in the summer and fall of 1844. Upon annexation, Mexico broke diplomatic relations with the United States and rushed troops to the new U.S.-Mexico border.[18] But no war ensued because Mexico's military power did not match its rhetoric. Mexico had glumly accepted reality.

In 1845, after Tyler had left office but before Texas annexation was made official, according to the memoirs of Anson Jones (the last president of independent Texas), U.S. Commodore Robert Stockton, with either a blessing or wink from newly inaugurated James Polk, tried to get Jones to put Texas "in an attitude of active hostility toward Mexico, so that, when Texas was finally brought into the Union, she might bring war with her." Jones said that an aide to Stockton told him that Polk was behind Stockton's covert activities, which included getting the U.S. Secretary of the Navy to provide the Texas Navy with gunpowder and supplies.[19]

Polk sent General Zachary Taylor and U.S. troops to Texas allegedly to protect the "new state" from an incensed Mexico. Polk also had a list made of all Mexican transgressions against the United States, further developing excuses for war. Despite Mexico's heated rhetoric, it had not attacked Texas after its annexation into the United States in July 1845. Polk did not think Mexico would strike Texas, so the troop deployment and U.S. naval presence in Mexican waters were less to defend Texas than to engage in coercive diplomacy to obtain territorial concessions. Polk and his advisers assumed Mexico would peacefully give up half its territory and its honor for a paltry amount of cash rather than go to war with the United States, though few Americans, when faced with the same choice, would have chosen capitulation.[20]

Like Texas, California had valuable ports and natural resources. On failing to convince Mexico to agree to his demands to sell California and its ports and recognize Texas's independence—through the likely pro forma and even counterproductive Slidell diplomatic mission in early

1846[21]—Polk intentionally and provocatively moved Taylor's forces into disputed territory between the Nueces River and the Rio Grande River in Texas. In past negotiations with France and Spain before Mexico's independence from the latter, the United States had concluded the Texas-Mexican border was at the Rio Grande, which was south of Mexico's claim of it being at the Nueces River.[22] Yet the Adams-Onís Treaty between the U.S. and Spain in 1819 and Mexican ratification of the Treaty of Limits in 1831 both put the Texas-Mexican border well north of the Rio Grande.[23] Simply because captured Mexican leader Santa Anna—in exchange for his life and freedom during the Texas War for Independence in 1836—had agreed to cede Texas to the Texans, and move his troops south of the Rio Grande, did not mean that Mexico agreed to that waterway being the border between Texas and Mexico (now the United States and Mexico). In fact, under international law (or under any law for that matter), any agreement reached under coercion is invalid, as Santa Anna's would have been as a Texan prisoner. Thus, Mexico had dismissed Santa Anna's treaty and continued to press its justifiable legal claim to possession of Texas with the border between Texas and the rest of Mexico being at the Nueces River.

Although the Mexican government had kept its troops south of the Rio Grande, it had unapologetically said that it would defend the Nueces River border. For the United States, the border dispute over the unpopulated wilderness between the rivers was relatively minor; the country had lived with undefined borders before without war, this particular dispute was new, and it had not particularly troubled Texans before Polk emphasized it to provoke the war.[24] Because by 1846 Mexico did not really want war with the United States and knew it was not going to get Texas back, Polk could have diplomatically settled this border dispute, but he wanted more—California.[25]

Abolitionists, the Whig Party, and even much of Polk's Democratic Party did not think Mexico was much of a threat to the United States and warned the president that the U.S. troop presence on the Rio Grande would provoke a war, yet Polk's zealous expansionism prevailed.[26]

Polk sent Taylor's forces already in Texas into the disputed area between the two rivers and near the Rio Grande as a provocation and hoped the Mexicans would either acquiesce to his territorial demands or take the bait and start a war. Polk, as Abraham Lincoln would do in the Civil War, used a military deployment to goad the enemy into taking the first shot, which appears to be important for justifying wars to the often ill-informed and naive American public throughout the country's history. In fact, Polk had already made plans to converge the U.S. Army and Navy on California and New Mexico before the war with Mexico started.

After Taylor moved into the disputed area, the Mexican government declared that it was in a "defensive war" with the United States.[27] Taylor's forces paraded, taunted, and eventually provoked the Mexicans. At a cabinet meeting on May 9, 1846, Polk predicted an "imminent" attack on Taylor's forces by the Mexicans and wrote in his diary, "All agreed that if the Mexican forces at Matamoros committed any act of hostility on Gen'l Taylor's forces I should immediately send a message to Congress recommending an immediate declaration of war."[28]

Most historians agree that Polk provoked the war with his risky deployment of American forces on disputed territory between the two rivers, but they gloss over that Taylor's four thousand troops (almost half of the U.S. Army) had blockaded the port of Matamoros on the Rio Grande to try to starve out six thousand Mexican troops there.[29] Traditionally, blockades have been regarded as an act of war. Neither the provocative troop deployment nor the blockade had Congress's approval. Thus, one could argue that Polk started a "presidential war" with Mexico, that is, an unconstitutional one.

Angry that the United States had annexed Texas (which the Mexicans had only a dim hope of getting back), Mexico believed U.S. forces had violated their territory by crossing into the disputed territory between the two rivers and were deeply perturbed by the blockade of Matamoros on the Rio Grande. The blockade, which brought a battery of U.S. cannons within three hundred yards of the town, caused the Mexicans to cross the Rio Grande and fire on American forces, killing eleven soldiers.[30] Border skirmishes between countries often kill a small number of people but do not start major wars, as cooler heads prevail, but Polk had in his hand a request to Congress for a declaration that war existed with Mexico, even if the Mexicans had not taken the bait.[31] Polk sent the war bill to Congress soon after receiving word of the Mexican attack, questionably claiming that the Mexicans had invaded American territory and attacked U.S. soldiers on American soil. Many in Congress, especially opposition Whigs, were skeptical of Polk's claims, but because American troops were already in harm's way, and Congress did not want to vote against supporting the troops, the legislative body obliged by taking the country from peace to war and funding the troops and the conflict.[32]

Polk's provocative troop deployment in disputed territory, his blockade of Matamoros, the wording in his suggested declaration that a state of war already existed, his hiding of the real war aims of grabbing California and New Mexico, and Congress's fear that voters would oppose their refusal to support troops already under fire undermined Congress's ability to assert its constitutional power to initiate hostilities. Thus, Polk had boxed Congress in, preventing any serious deliberation about whether the nation should go to war. Also, Polk had his congressional whips encourage instead the belief among congressmen that the skirmish that killed eleven troops between the two rivers would be the last blood spilled, because the Mexicans would capitulate quickly.[33]

Moreover, in 1845 John C. Fremont, a U.S. Army officer, went to Oregon and California under orders to survey and scout them. He arrived in California during a local rebellion of white settlers against their Mexican rulers and Indian allies. Fremont tried to take control of the revolt, thus undertaking a bald U.S. intervention into Mexican affairs. According to Melvin Small, Polk's provocative actions in Texas and California justified a Mexican declaration of war against the United States.[34]

In any case, the major lesson of the Mexican War was that the president, by such unilateral force deployments, could undermine Congress's constitutional power to declare war. In May 1846, Whig Senator Tom Clayton responded to Polk's war message by questioning the constitutionality of his troop deployment. This showed that the expectation was that Congress would approve force deployments that could push America into war. Clayton said, "I do not see on what principle it can be shown that the President, without consulting Congress and obtaining sanction for the procedure, has a right to send an army to take up a position, where, as it must have been foreseen, the inevitable consequences would occur."[35]

Senator John C. Calhoun complained presciently that Polk's actions toward Mexico "sets the example, which will enable all future Presidents to bring about a state of things in which Congress shall be forced, without deliberation, or reflection, to declare war."[36] Also, he objected that Polk had "stripped Congress of the power of making war, and what is more and worse, it gave that power to every officer, nay to every subaltern commanding a corporal's guard." John Quincy Adams noted that the war resolution "established as an irreversible precedent that the President of the

United States has but to declare that War exists, with any nation, and the War is essentially declared."[37] In August 1845, a full nine months before the United States declared war on Mexico, the *National Intelligencer*, a leading Whig newspaper, already was accusing Polk of a constitutional infraction in his bellicose response to the border dispute with Mexico by burdening the American public with an "*offensive war*, and *not* the necessary defense of Texas." The newspaper predicted that soon "the President will be MAKING WAR, in the full sense of the word, on his own authority, and beyond all plea of need, and even without any thought of asking legislative leave."[38]

The Quasi-War in 1798—occurring shortly after the new U.S. Constitution was the law of the land—showed the framers' original intent that Congress was to make the decision for war and the rules governing it, and that the president would simply execute Congress's will. The stiff resistance that Polk received for his run around Congress showed that, as late as the mid-nineteenth century, that expectation still carried weight. Senator Tom Corwin in February 1847, in the middle of the war, gave the best summary statement showing what the framers had in mind: "How is it that a peaceful and peace-loving people ... have been forced to ... plunge into ... the scourge of war? The answer can only be, it was by act and will of the President *alone*, and not by the act or will of Congress, the war-making department of the Government."[39]

Internal Politics Affect Even the Fighting of Wars

The United States had a much larger population, a much bigger economy, and a greater combat-experienced military than the relatively new nation of Mexico. The United States had fought the British twice and had an ongoing war with the indigenous peoples. Mexico did not stand a chance, and any military fighting would have been over quickly if contained between the Rio Grande and Nueces River. By mid-1846, however, Polk had ordered General Zachary Taylor to invade Mexico to as far south as Monterrey; later, he ordered General Winfield Scott on an amphibious mission to take the port of Veracruz and march overland to Mexico City. Polk had sent the U.S. Navy and Generals Stephen Kearny and John C. Fremont to take California, the real prize of the Mexican War.

Ideally, wars are supposed to be rare, critical events undertaken only for the security of nations, but it is surprising how often petty domestic politics enter into them. During the war, Democrat Polk's actions heavily politicized the American military.[40] In Polk's winning election campaign of 1844, he pledged to serve only one four-year term to quiet fears of a potential dynasty of Tennessee Democrats (Andrew Jackson was the first). Thus, with the Mexican War beginning in 1846, the door was open for a war hero to win the election of 1848. Winfield Scott, the ranking general of the army, developed the daring plan to land U.S. forces amphibiously at the port of Veracruz and march to the Mexican capital. However, Polk stalled the plan; with his top generals—Scott and (lower-ranking) Taylor, both Whigs—Polk felt Scott had the greatest ambition to be president. Thus, after Taylor had won a couple of battles in northern Mexico, Polk quickly promoted him to major general, a rank equal to that of Scott. Then Taylor won the battle of Monterrey, becoming a national hero and a bigger threat to run for president than Scott. Polk then began undermining Taylor and approved Scott's plan to land at Veracruz, even stripping forces from Taylor's army to give to Scott. Ironically, while Scott successfully executed what would be his boldly decisive campaign to take Veracruz and Mexico City, Taylor eventually ran for president in 1848, won, and handed the presidency to the Whigs.[41]

However, by 1847 public opinion was beginning to turn against the war, as U.S. casualties mounted and reports of American atrocities against Mexican civilians surfaced. For example, Scott's bombarding of Veracruz's elderly, women, and children in the town siege; Taylor's bombarding of the city of Matamoros with artillery; the pillaging of villages; and the murdering of civilians all were condemned in the United States. Like many wars in democracies that last too long or begin costing too much in lives or money without a national security imperative, the Mexican War was becoming unpopular at home.

Anti-war sentiments before the Mexican War were initially drowned out by the overwhelming votes for war in both chambers of Congress and for its funding[42] because of the lingering memory of the Federalist Party's collapse after opposing the War of 1812.[43] As the war lingered and became less popular, Congress began to find the courage to criticize it. (This initial support of the president in war and later buyer's remorse when the war dragged on or difficulties ensued would be repeated throughout American history.) A one-term congressman from Illinois, Abraham Lincoln, correctly encapsulated the conflict by saying it was "a war of conquest to catch votes." Even more prescient was Ralph Waldo

Emerson's prediction: "The United States will conquer Mexico, but it will be as a man who swallowed the arsenic which brings him down in turn. Mexico will poison us." Little more than decade later, the monstrous and calamitous Civil War was caused by a caustic sectional argument over whether slavery would expand to the lands conquered from Mexico. War often leads to more war.

In January 1848, as the conflict dragged on, it became clear that Polk wanted much more Mexican land than that between the Nueces River and the Rio Grande River in Texas. Less than two years after the House of Representatives voted overwhelmingly for a declaration of war, the House reversed course, passing an opposition Whig Party resolution asserting that the war had been "unnecessarily and unconstitutionally begun by the President of the United States."[44] Henry David Thoreau, in a lecture that would eventually be published as part of his famous essay "Civil Disobedience," argued that Polk's Mexican War was the worst form of governance, "the working of comparatively a few individuals using the standing government as their tool."[45]

Only after the war had ended did Congress demonstrate that it could—and would—control troop deployments by overruling Polk's postwar redeployment of troops. During the debate over this redeployment, one member of Congress best summarized the Constitution's original concept of executive-congressional powers over the military: control of the army "is altogether in the executive" but only "when legislation is done with it."[46]

But as subsequent history has revealed, when the executive, via unilateral action, has deployed U.S. troops into harm's way, Congress has been consistently leery of being thought "unpatriotic" for not supporting them, thus having little choice but to approve and finance a conflict already imminent or underway. John Calhoun doubted that a popular majority would have supported a war for territorial expansion; he concluded that, had Congress had the opportunity beforehand to thoughtfully debate the "question of war deliberately, the vote would have been two to one against it."[47]

Polk's furtive ambitions proved too great.[48] He wanted California's mineral, manufacturing, and agricultural resources, as well as California's good harbors for military bases and for trading with China and other nations in East Asia—so that the United States would have "ascendancy on the Pacific."[49] Eventually, Polk had to ask Congress for money to buy

California, thus necessitating that he finally come clean about his grand war aims—but too late for Congress to do much about it with U.S. troops already under fire.

In addition, long forgotten was the expansionist Polk's simultaneous risk-taking in the Pacific Northwest by making expansive territorial claims in Oregon, which had been jointly governed by Britain and the United States under an agreement signed in 1818.[50] Driven by pressure from American settlers and a desire for more ports on the Pacific for enhanced trade, Polk claimed the entire Oregon Territory for the United States and asked Congress for a unilateral abrogation of the joint agreement in December 1845.[51] Polk first believed that the British would be unwilling to fight for the territory but then, in February 1846, got wind of British naval preparations that seemed to go beyond just the defense of the Canadas and might permit offensive operations. Because of his own provocative actions that led Congress to declare war on Mexico in May 1846, Polk might have faced two wars at the same time against enemies to the North and South. In early 1846 the much more powerful British, with a superior bargaining position, proposed a new treaty to divide the territory and Polk, eager to avoid two conflagrations at the same time, signed the pact that same month on June 15, 1846.[52]

Consequences of the Mexican War

Not only does war often lead to more war, but sometimes war leads to revolution; sometimes revolution leads to war. The Texas Revolution or War for Independence led to the U.S.-Mexican War; the U.S.-Mexican War led to the most catastrophic war in American history, the Civil War.

Robert W. Johannsen best sums up the Mexican War's role in laying the basis for the Civil War:

> To be sure, wars often create more problems than they settle, and the Mexican War was no exception. A bitter and divisive sectional struggle over the issue of slavery's expansion into the territories gained from Mexico was an unintended consequence of the conflict. Many Americans were later convinced, as was Ulysses S. Grant (himself a participant in the war), that "the Southern rebellion was largely an outgrowth of the Mexican War." Writing 40 years after the fact, failing in health,

the old general influenced much subsequent thinking about the war when he charged that it was "one of the most unjust ever waged by a stronger against a weaker nation."[53]

But there were certain ambitious Americans more audacious than Polk, who wanted to take the spoils of war even further. There was some support for keeping all of Mexico, instead of the 51 percent Polk grabbed. Yet there were limits to manifest destiny. Polk and his allies only wanted the sparsely populated north of Mexico, largely because the United States did not want to absorb large populations of dark-skinned "inferior" peoples in southern Mexico, such as Indians and mestizos (mixed-race people), most of whom were Catholic.[54] The thinly populated California and what is now the American Southwest could be settled with white Protestants and molded and developed as the U.S. government wished.

Thus, the war had its most dire effects on Hispanic, mestizo, and Indian populations in territory conquered from Mexico. Under Mexican rule, these groups were full citizens. Hispanics and mestizos had been around for 250 years before this Anglo-American conquest, and the Indians had been around for more than 10,000 years. Despite provisions of the Treaty of Guadalupe Hidalgo, the new Hispanic inhabitants of the United States were lynched, intimidated, and swindled out of their land in California and the Southwest; the Indians there were enslaved and slaughtered, with their population plummeting from 150,000 to 30,000 in California in little more than a decade of American rule, because the U.S. governor of California had called for the Indians' extermination.[55]

Although Polk's war did ultimately ravage indigenous populations, undermine the republic, and even the Union itself, he did not restrict the freedoms of white citizens at home during the war. Unlike John Adams during the Quasi-War with France in 1798, he did not try to lock up people for speaking out against him. He did not try to censor journalists reporting from the battlefronts in Mexico. Unlike James Madison during the War of 1812, he did not try to ask Congress or the states to compel people to fight in the war. However, Polk had the luxury of many battlefield victories to mute most criticism of the war, and the flood of volunteers to fight obviated the need for conscription.

The United States could have tried harder to add California, its valuable Pacific ports, and the Southwest without initiating a full-blown U.S.-Mexican War. After all, the United States had gotten the Floridas and Texas by American settlers first filibustering there, and a rebellion by American settlers in California had happened just before the larger war broke out.[56] However, these slightly more subtle forms of conquest would still have been morally questionable.

Finally, the Mexican War would set a pattern for future American wars. The stronger United States, with no direct vital security interest at risk, would try to impose, by threats, stringent demands on a weaker party; the frantic weaker party would then be blamed by the United States for starting what was a war of desperation.[57] The U.S. resupply of Fort Sumter lit the match for the Civil War; the intimidation mission of the battleship *Maine* to Havana harbor led to the Spanish-American War; Woodrow Wilson's demand that Americans should have the right to travel on belligerent ships carrying war matériel through conflict zones led to American involvement in World War I; attempted U.S. strangulation of the Japanese imperial economy with an embargo on oil and certain metals triggered the Japanese response that led to U.S. entry into World War II; and covert U.S. raids on the North Vietnamese coast in 1964 led to an alleged North Vietnamese attack on a U.S. destroyer to kick off U.S. war escalation in Southeast Asia. All these provocative American actions ultimately triggered wars. Polk's insertion of U.S. forces into disputed territory between Texas and Mexico would become the prototype that American democracy would employ to start its wars—by using a casus belli to win popular support for aggressive wars.

In his memoirs, President and Civil War hero Ulysses S. Grant, who fought in the Mexican War under both Generals Taylor and Scott, best summed up U.S. provocation of war against the weaker Mexico to steal its land at gunpoint: "I was bitterly opposed to the measure [America's policy toward Mexico from the annexation of Texas forward] and to this day regard the war which resulted as one of the most unjust ever waged by a stronger against a weaker nation. It was an instance of a republic following the bad example of European monarchies in not considering justice in their desire to acquire additional territory."[58]

>> CHAPTER 5 <<

THE CIVIL WAR

Far Less Glorious than Believed

In 1820, Congress passed the Missouri Compromise, which chose a latitude line south of which federal territories would enter the Union as slave states and north of which they would enter as free states. The booty of added prime territory gained in the Mexican War disrupted this free/slave balance. After the Mexican War ended in 1848, Congress then passed the Compromise of 1850 and the Kansas-Nebraska Act of 1854, both of which eroded the Compromise of 1820. Contrary to the 1820 statute, the latter law, which allowed territories to choose whether they wanted to enter the Union as slave or free, led to a mini civil war in the Kansas territory over whether it would become a free or slave state and to the creation of the new Republican Party, an anti-slave regional party in the Northeast and Midwest.

The Supreme Court's horrendous Dred Scott decision (1857) saying Congress could not make laws restricting people from bringing slaves into any territory was also a major factor leading to the Civil War. It completely upended the underpinnings of the original Missouri Compromise of 1820. The court ruling overlooked a glaring constitutional provision saying that Congress had responsibility for making laws for the territories, not the court.

The slavery issue split the dominant Democratic Party into Northern and Southern wings. Although this split allowed Republican presidential candidate Abraham Lincoln to win the popular vote with less than 40 percent in a four-candidate field, he garnered a substantial majority of more than 59 percent of the electoral vote. Not long after his portentous election win, Southern states began seceding from the Union, eventually leading to the Civil War. President-elect Lincoln's uncompromising behavior to those states—likely due to the inflated "mandate" he received from his electoral vote performance—provoked their attack on a federal fort, which triggered his invasion of the South.

The South's major transgression leading to the Civil War is well known—perpetuating the heinous institution of slavery long after most major countries had abolished it through peaceful gradual or compensated emancipation. On March 23, 1861, shortly after Southern states had seceded and the Confederate States of America (CSA) was formed, Alexander Stephens, the vice president of that incipient nation, bluntly rejected even the Declaration of Independence's theoretical premise that "all men are created equal": "Our new government is founded upon exactly the opposite idea . . . its foundations are laid, its cornerstone rests, upon the great truth that the negro is not equal to the white man; that slavery subordination to the superior race is his natural and normal condition."[1]

White supremacy, and slavery based on it, should forever condemn the CSA to infamy in American history. Yet seceding Southerners probably exaggerated the acute threat that the newly elected Republican Abraham Lincoln posed to slavery.

More important, Lincoln's militaristic dealing with Southern secession was much less helpful to African American rights in the long term than is commonly believed. In reality, the "glorious war for slaves' freedom" delayed real black emancipation for a century. Both sides' actions in sparking a full-blown war should attract blame for bringing net long-term harm to African Americans.

War often leads to revolution or more war. The Civil War was ultimately caused by the question of slavery's expansion into the western lands conquered during the Mexican War and the concomitant potential alteration of the balance of political power internally between North and South.

History evaluates American presidents quite favorably if they were victorious wartime leaders, even if they provoked the conflict, ruled like a dictator, or were ineffective leaders during the tug—like Abraham Lincoln. Lincoln is deified as the greatest American president for winning the titanic Civil War and freeing the slaves. This downplays, if not ignores, Lincoln's role in provoking the conflict for other reasons; choosing war over more effective and less costly peaceful means of ending slavery; effectively not freeing many slaves during the war; mismanaging and prolonging the massive slaughter that lead to the cataclysmic loss of 750,000 Americans; and helping to set up the failed Reconstruction in the South—which ultimately relegated African Americans to almost a century of neo-slavery. Southern whites' bitterness resulting from the war eventually led to the neo-slavery that subjected African Americans to oppressive black codes, discriminatory Jim Crow laws, terrorism by the Ku Klux Klan, and lynching until the civil rights movement of the 1950s and 1960s about a century later.

For most Americans the Civil War, like World War II, is an unassailably righteous war, logical and consequential in effect[2]—two wars respectively fought to end human bondage and to defeat Nazism, fascism, and militarism. What may seem logical and consequential, however, is often more complex on a second look.

Most Major Countries Ended Slavery Peacefully

If there were ever an American cause to fight and die for, it was ending slavery. Pro-slavery Southern states seceded from the Union to protect their "peculiar institution" because of a perceived threat that the newly elected Republican President Abraham Lincoln posed to slavery's continuation in America. But Southerners likely exaggerated Lincoln's threat to slavery where it already existed, had there been no secession. Furthermore, an aristocratic South that had a one-party state—which featured human bondage, censorship, and little manufacturing other than a socialized armaments industry—hardly strikes a sympathetic pose. Yet an erroneous direct link between Lincoln's winning the 1860 presidential election, Northern victory in the Civil War, and an enhancement of African American rights in America remains fixed in the American popular mind.

History shows, however, that Americans may not have needed to fight a monstrous war to end slavery. The United States was the only major country plagued by slavery that resorted to a massive war to end it. In retrospect, it would have been far less costly, in terms of human misery and money, to have used gradual or compensated emancipation—as most major countries did—to end slavery, rather than going to war. During the American Revolution and afterward, the Northern states had ended slavery using gradual emancipation. Alternatively, for the exorbitant price of the Civil War—$750 billion dollars (in today's dollars)—all slaves in the South could have been peacefully emancipated by compensating their owners and then some.[3] Lincoln advocated such a policy in the late 1840s but had abandoned the option by the time he won political power in the 1860 election. Perhaps this alternative to war in late 1860 or early 1861 would not have been successful in avoiding war, but it was never tried before the war was already raging. Once shots had been fired and the bitter internecine war began, attitudes hardened dramatically on both sides, making any compromise involving graduated or compensated emancipation impossible.

In the face of this broader international comparison, Lincoln's record on ending slavery does not look so stellar. Although it may now seem questionable, in the wake of a victorious war, to pay aristocratic Southern slaveholders to end this wicked human bondage, the massive destruction of the South and a cavernous sectional schism caused by the greatest war in American history caused Southern bitterness to institute a new system of discrimination and violence against African Americans that made them second-class citizens in a potent kind of neo-slavery for another hundred years.

Boston abolitionist Wendell Phillips presciently foresaw more clearly than anyone that restoring the Union after a long miserable war, with at least 100,000 killed (even he grossly underestimated the eventual 750,000 dead), would not restore national unity. The continuing bitter sectional division would ensure that "we know not where it [the war] will end." Phillips was implying that the effects of any war might not be good for African Americans; unfortunately, he was spot on. Three days before the Confederate attack on Fort Sumter, which commenced the war, he made a desperate and unsuccessful call to remain at peace.[4]

A major reason Lincoln did not attempt this tried-and-true compensated emancipation method before going to war was that his overriding goal after Southern secession, which he later admitted, was to restore the Union[5]—not to end slavery. Yet the preservation of slavery was the major underlying cause of Southern secession and the ensuing conflict. Famously, in August 1862, Lincoln told abolitionist Horace Greeley, the most prominent U.S. newspaper editor at the time, that preserving the Union was his goal, whether he freed any slaves or not.

> My paramount object in this struggle is to save the Union, and is not either to save or to destroy slavery. If I could save the Union without freeing any slave I would do it, and if I could save it by freeing all the slaves I would do it; and if I could save it by freeing some and leaving others alone I would also

do that. What I do about slavery, and the colored race, I do because I believe it helps to save the Union.[6]

But Lincoln had been too eager to go to war to reunite the country rather than negotiate with the Southern states, after his election and then after his inauguration, to try to lure Southern states back into the Union with compensated emancipation. A few years before secession, Lincoln had arrived at the conclusion that the Union could only be preserved by force. He only unsuccessfully offered compensated emancipation to the slave-holding border states after the shooting had been going on for some time.

And Lincoln ordered the emancipation of slaves only in areas held by Southern armies—essentially freeing no slaves unless they traversed a dangerous route to Union lines—after the war had started and was not going well for the North. The Emancipation Proclamation was merely a propaganda effort to keep Britain and France from recognizing Southern independence; to encourage slave revolts and runaways, thus weakening the South economically and militarily; and to strengthen the Union by adding the critical fighting manpower of freed African Americans to the depleting Union armies.

When pressured as president-elect to seek a compromise with seceding states before the fighting began, Lincoln repeatedly refused and wrote in a letter to a senator, "There is, in my judgment, but one compromise which would really settle the slavery question, and that would be a prohibition against acquiring any more [slave] territory." William Herndon, Lincoln's law partner, best summarized Lincoln's view on any compromise: "Away—off—be gone! If the nation wants to back down, let it—not I."[7] Lincoln, a moderate in the Republican Party on slavery, held a legally radical position; banning slavery in all western territories would have nullified forty years of American history—the Missouri Compromise of 1820, the popular sovereignty of the Kansas-Nebraska Act of 1854, and the Supreme Courts' Dred Scott decision of 1857. Along with Lincoln, the Republican platform of 1860 would have allowed entry to the Union of only free states in the West.

Lincoln and the Republicans had in fact sent mixed messages on slavery to Southerners beginning in the summer of 1860. The Republican Party's platform had guaranteed as "inviolate" states' rights—exclusive control over their domestic institutions, such as slavery. In his first inaugural address, Lincoln reiterated his support for a constitutional amendment guaranteeing existing slave states' power to maintain slavery in perpetuity (after his election, Lincoln was reported to have secretly proposed the amendment to his congressional allies before his address):

> I understand a proposed amendment to the Constitution, which amendment, however, I have not seen, has passed Congress, to the effect that the federal government shall never interfere with the domestic institutions of the States, including that of persons held to service. . . . Holding such a provision to now be implied constitutional law, I have no objection to its being made express and irrevocable.[8]

Of course, certain fans of Lincoln have argued that regardless of his alleged purposes, winning the Civil War and ending slavery were huge accomplishments. However, killing 750,000 Americans, including 40,000 African American soldiers, to ultimately free the slaves in name only and with residual bitterness in the South seems an inferior option to peacefully compensating slaveowners for genuinely freeing them at a much lower cost in lives and money. Any efforts by Lincoln to negotiate compensated emancipation before the fighting began might have failed— despite that it had been successful in peacefully ending slavery in other major slave holding countries—because compensation to slaveholders would soon run out but their entire economic system would have been radically altered. Yet Lincoln did not try such an offer before the shooting started; free labor, even then was known to be a more productive and profitable economic system than was slavery, as was demonstrated by the differential in economic development between North and South; and compensation would have been more profitable than the threatened costly war.

Slavery's Privileged Political Power Led to Conflict

Since the beginning of the republic, the South had held a privileged place in American political life. Consequently, the federal government had always supported slavery—an implicit condition of its founding at the Constitutional Convention.

The disproportionate political power given to the South was a leading reason the United States was comparatively late among countries to free its slaves and why no other major nation had a massive bloody war to end slavery. Instead, most countries—including British, French, Spanish, Danish, and Dutch colonies—used peaceful compensated emancipation. Most of the Northern U.S. states had peacefully freed their slaves with gradual emancipation as they industrialized. Slavery provided terrible incentives for increasing worker productivity and should have slowly died out as industrialization and wage labor spread from the North to the agrarian South, thus upending the vile institution.[9] However, Eli Whitney's invention of the cotton gin at the turn of the 19th century revolutionized the cotton industry, increasing demand for land to grow cotton and slaves to pick it.[10]

In 1860, slaves' market value was estimated to be $2.7 billion.[11] Slavery supplied brutal, low-cost labor for aristocratic slaveowners, which they did not want to give up—despite the moral depravity of human bondage. However, paying the slave owners $2.7 billion would have been much cheaper than conducting a grueling war that slaughtered hundreds of thousands of Americans, destroyed large parts of the South, and cost $4.2 billion even at the time.[12] An alternative to compensation would have been letting the South secede peacefully, and one addition might have been amending the U.S. Constitution to prohibit, instead of require, the return of runaway Southern slaves, thus likely causing an increased outflow of escaping slaves to the North. The latter addition might have gotten push back from a racist North but its absence wouldn't have prevented an amicable separation. Even the basic option would have acknowledged the South's desire for self-determination (albeit with odious slavery intact), as such separation was defended in the Declaration of Independence, and would have also allowed the remaining Northern states the muscle to easily pass and ratify a moral constitutional amendment genuinely banning slavery forever.

Politically, the South had fewer people than the North—one-fourth of the nation's population—but enjoyed certain political advantages from the U.S. Constitution to make up for their smaller population. Every state, for example, had two Senate members, regardless of their population; most of the Southern states had smaller populations, thus enjoying a disproportionate number of votes in that legislative body. Even in the House of Representatives, which had representation based on population, the Constitution gave the slaveholding South an advantage by allowing whites to count their nonvoting slaves as three-fifths of a person for added apportionment of representation. Slavery enabled Southern whites to control a disproportionate share of representatives in the House and thus gain raw political power in Congress in addition to enslaved labor.

Southern leverage also found its way into the Electoral College. The Constitution gave each state a total number of electors equal to its two senators plus the number of representatives in the House, thus allowing whites in the South to launder extra apportionment from the three-fifths rule that a national popular vote would not have permitted (which allowed only one vote per white person).

Even in the nomination for president in the Democratic Party, then the dominant party in the country and more so in the South, a candidate had to have a two-thirds majority, thus ensuring Southern dominance until 1860.[13] Thus, of the fifteen presidents from George Washington to the inauguration of Abraham Lincoln in 1861, nine, or 60 percent, were born in the less-populous, slaveholding region of the country. Ten of the first sixteen presidents owned slaves. And even this figure understates slaveholding states' influence in the White House; of the six other non-Southern-born presidents, the three just before Lincoln's term were "doughfaces"—Northerners who supported Southern positions, especially on slavery. Thus, the Constitution's fugitive slave clause, which required escaped African slaves to be returned, and the three-fifths rule for House apportionment put slavery squarely in the document, although euphemistically avoiding the term. In turn, Southern political advantages in the House, Senate, and Electoral College helped support and strengthen the "peculiar institution" up until 1860.[14]

Both Parties Would Have Kept Slavery Legal

While Lincoln and the Republican Party, outside a thin sliver of abolitionists, opposed the expansion of slavery into the western territories, they accepted its continuation in the South.[15] Their opposition to its expansion was the principal reason Democrats viewed Lincoln and the Republicans as a threat to slavery. The Republican Party had their economic reasons to oppose slavery's expansion in the West. At that time, it was the party of white workers. The lower marginal cost of employing slave labor or even the cheaper wage labor of freed blacks still would lower the wages of white workers. Ironically, the climate and soil in most of the West were not ideal for growing large-scale cash crops—such as cotton, tobacco, or rice—with the use of slave labor. Yet Southern planters aggressively sought new lands in the West to substitute for depleted soil farther East, to bring in more Democratic votes, and to admit new slave states to the Congress to bolster the political power of that "peculiar institution."[16] Both Northern Republicans and Southern Democrats agreed that slavery had to "expand or die" eventually, whether from being locked up in existing Southern states, or getting outvoted by an increasing ratio of free to slave states in the Senate if there were enough Western territories added only as free states.[17]

It was the question, then, of whether the federal government could either prohibit or permit slavery in the western territories that pushed the country over the edge, not the practice of slavery per se in the Old South. Although in his first inaugural address Lincoln noted that the Constitution did not determine one way or the other with regard to slavery in the West, it did in fact say that Congress had the authority to make "needed rules and regulations" for territories before they became states. Before and after the Constitution's ratification, most constitutional observers believed this provision allowed Congress to prohibit slavery in the territories. (Similarly, the Constitution's stipulation that Congress had the exclusive power to legislate for the District of Columbia allowed it to ban slavery within this area, too.)[18] Furthermore, Congress had banned slavery before in the territories: the Northwest Ordinance prohibited the practice in the Northwest Territory (now the upper Midwest) before the Constitution was ratified, and the Missouri Compromise in 1820 banned it north of a certain latitude but allowed it south of that latitude in territories gained from the Louisiana Purchase.

Southerners had concluded Lincoln's provocative statements during the political hustings in the 1850s were warlike. In 1858, for example, he had said, "'A house divided against itself cannot stand.' I believe this government cannot endure, permanently half slave and half free."[19] Until 1857, no one would have made this statement while running for national office—and Lincoln was advised not to say it, for the country had lived peacefully in a state of "half slave, half free" throughout its history.

All this had changed for the worse in 1857 when the Supreme Court's Dred Scott decision declared unconstitutional the longstanding Missouri Compromise of 1820 (the "half slave, half free" arrangement), which had held the country together up until then, and ruled that Congress could not regulate or exclude slavery in the territories. Regarded as the worst Supreme Court decision in American history, it contributed hugely to escalating tensions before the Civil War.[20] After the ruling, some in the North—including Lincoln—feared that creeping slavery would eventually contaminate states that were free. With the Dred Scott decision, the South—hypocritically, given its "states' rights" doctrine—was making progress toward the nationalization of slavery throughout the country, while also causing slave and free white labor to come into greater competition, thus fueling the rise of a sectional Republican Party in the North that was the party of white workers.[21] The Dred Scott decision not only overturned the Missouri Compromise and the idea that Congress could regulate slavery in the territories, it also nixed the idea of territories deciding the slavery issue for themselves, enshrined in the Kansas-Nebraska Act of 1854, which had split the dominant Democrat Party into Northern and Southern wings, giving a national opening to the then-sectional Republican Party.[22]

The Republicans had a "radical" abolitionist wing, but Lincoln was not a member of it. Lincoln would have accepted a permanent guarantee of slavery where it already existed in the South.[23] Also, he stated his support for the fugitive slave clause of the Constitution and the Fugitive Slave law, both requiring that escaping enslaved Africans be returned. These positions showed that Lincoln's Republican anti-slavery orientation was more tempered and less threatening than the abolitionist stance, but the South viewed him as just as dangerous. In the 1860 election, the Republicans had billed themselves as the "white man's party" because they wanted to ban slave labor—and generally blacks—from their states and territories, instead consigning them to the South.[24]

Fearing a Lincoln presidency, Southern states began to secede.[25] While it might have appeared to be an overreaction, since Lincoln was not an abolitionist, the election of a Northern anti-slavery Republican president, whose party was against the expansion of slavery in the West, was a huge threat to Southern political power.[26] The Civil War was not just about slavery in the Western territories but also the declining power of the Southern slave states in the national government. The more populous North already had a majority in the House and had just won the presidency for the first time; if slavery was banned in all Western territories poised to become new states, free states might eventually outvote the slave states in the Senate—including perhaps eventually passing and ratifying a new constitutional amendment banning slavery everywhere.

Southerners were certainly aware that Lincoln had thought war was inevitable after the Dred Scott decision,[27] when he made his famous 1858 Senate campaign "house divided" speech. By using such inflammatory rhetoric, Lincoln intended to divide his opposition in the dominant Democratic Party, as the only way he thought the smaller sectional Republican Party could win a national presidential election. But the tactic also increased the chances of a civil war, which Lincoln knew. After Lincoln's election as president, Southern states remembered Lincoln's earlier veiled threats of war and bolted from the Union. In addition, the South feared that Lincoln's election would lead to a race war, heightened by abolitionist John Brown's raid on the Harpers Ferry federal arsenal in 1859 to capture weapons for a slave revolt.

After South Carolina became the first state to secede following Lincoln's election, Lincoln refused to compromise on the Republican platform provision banning the extension of slavery into the American West, saying, "The tug has to come and better now, than any time hereafter."[28]

By 1860 the South simply had become too accustomed to a weak, friendly president in the White House. Southern loss of political power resulted from divisions in the Democratic Party and the shifting balance of power against the South in the political branches of government, which Lincoln's election heralded, even as the South's wealth and economic power had risen on the profitability of cotton in the 1850s. Historian Michael E. Woods best sums it up: "Slaveholders' conflict with northern voters, the collision that triggered secession and war, grew not out of clashing racial views but out of competition for political power."[29]

Some historians have argued that also contributing to the war were high tariffs, which disproportionately cost the South. Instituted with a view to protecting Northern industries and raising money for internal improvement projects—roads, canals, port improvements, etc.—that disproportionately benefitted the North. As a result, the less developed South had to import manufactured goods at greater cost and faced retaliatory tariffs by other countries on their agricultural exports. Furthermore, if the Southern states were allowed to secede and then reduced tariffs, as the new Confederate Congress quickly did, trade would naturally migrate from Northern to Southern ports.[30] Although this may have been a factor in longstanding tensions between North and South, tariff rates did not more than double until months after many Southern states had already seceded (the Morrill Tariff had passed the Senate and was signed by then-President James Buchanan only two days before Lincoln took office). Until then, the South had won most of the political battles over the economy; tariffs had been low in the 1840s and were the lowest of the nineteenth century in the 1850s. Instead, the war and the need for massive amounts of revenue to fight it allowed the Republicans to do what they had wanted to do for several years—institute a steep hike in tariff rates that remained permanent after the war because the protected industries lobbied for their retention.[31]

Lincoln's Electoral College Victory Discouraged Compromise with the South

Lincoln believed that if he compromised with the South, it would nullify the 1860 Republican election victory. Even before taking office, Lincoln complained about compromising with the South to avoid war: "We have just carried an election on principles fairly stated to the people.... Now we are told in advance, the government shall be broken up, unless we surrender to those we have beaten, before we take the offices ... Either way, if we surrender, it is the end of us, and of the government."[32]

As many presidents behaved before and after Lincoln, the sixteenth president was exaggerating the electoral mandate for his party's program. Because Lincoln's own inflammatory political rhetoric in 1858 after the Supreme Court's Dred Scott decision[33] aggravated the dominant Democratic Party's split into Northern and Southern wings over slavery, the new regional Republican Party won the popular vote with less than 40 percent of all the ballots cast in a four-candidate field. Because the Electoral College system can magnify a minority, plurality, or majority of popular votes into a greater majority, the lowest popular vote total in American history became a substantial Electoral College majority of 59 percent. If no Electoral College system had existed, it would have been hard for Lincoln to have claimed a mandate for the Republican program by earning less than 40 percent of the popular vote. Lincoln gained no electoral votes in the South or border states; his victory was due to a substantial Electoral College majority deriving from his vote tallies being concentrated in the more populous states of the Northeast and Midwest.

The uniquely American Electoral College victory seemingly contributed to Lincoln's intransigence.

Lincoln Provoked the Civil War

In December 1860 the outgoing president, James Buchanan, ordered the *Star of the West*, a commercial steamer loaded with troop reinforcements and military supplies, to restock Fort Sumter in Charleston Harbor, South Carolina—one of only two federal forts left in the South not taken over post-secession by the new Southern Confederacy. The federal government had abandoned fourteen other military installations in South Carolina alone.[34] A hotbed of secessionists, South Carolina was the first state to leave the Union after Lincoln's election. Buchanan and his incompetent and Southern-sympathizing Secretary of War, John B. Floyd of Virginia, had been reluctant to reinforce Union forts in the South up until then. When the *Star of the West* arrived in Charleston Harbor in January 1861, South Carolinians fired on it. The ship turned around without replenishing the federal installation. To avoid a war, Buchanan, the last of the Southern-sympathizing doughface presidents, ignored the incident.

In Lincoln's 1861 inaugural address, he warned the South that any violence against the federal government would be "insurrectionary or revolutionary." And after his inauguration, Lincoln knew what would happen if he sent another resupply ship to the fort; more so, after Secretary of State William Seward had assured the South that a second relief mission would not occur. Since the late 1850s, Lincoln believed war between the sections was unavoidable. Overriding Seward, Lincoln told the governor of South Carolina that another supply ship was on its way, knowing that South Carolinian artillery surrounded the fort on all but the ocean side.[35] Historian Michael Beschloss concluded that Lincoln knew very well the South Carolinians would retaliate against any resupply mission:

> By late March 1861, Lincoln had concluded that the days for Anderson's garrison to stay at Fort Sumter were ending. If there had to be a civil war, it would be easier for the President to unite Americans of the North and get them to fight should it be clear that the Confederacy was the aggressor. The Union side would enjoy a moral and emotional advantage if this

conflict began with an assault by the South, and Lincoln was not above tinkering with the lights and scenery to make sure that this military drama had maximum impact.[36]

The same day Lincoln notified the South Carolina governor he would be sending a resupply ship to Fort Sumter, he had written to six Northern governors that war might be imminent and received pledges from three of them to supply militiamen if conflict arose. The president also told a White House visitor that they would soon learn "whether the revolutionists dare to fire upon an unarmed vessel sent to the rescue of our starving soldiers." Intercepting Fort Sumter's mail earlier, the Confederate government had known about the relief mission even before Lincoln had told the governor. Confederate President Jefferson Davis foolishly ordered General P.G.T. Beauregard to demand the surrender of the fort, and if it refused, to fire away. Robert Toombs, Davis's secretary of state, presciently warned Davis that attacking the fort would unleash a hornet's nest from the North. Lincoln later confided to his friend Orville Browning, "The plan succeeded. They attacked Sumter—it fell, and thus, did more service than it otherwise would."[37] Lincoln's provocative actions had worked according to design.

A question few ask about the now-deified Lincoln is whether he could have prevented the bloody conflict by evacuating instead of resupplying Fort Sumter. Lincoln's military advisers and most of his cabinet (at least initially, until those politicians discerned what the boss really wanted) recommended that he withdraw from the fort because it was militarily indefensible. A withdrawal would have allowed more time to negotiate with the South over secession.[38] In the North, most people did not want war with the South and expected that Union forces would abandon the fort, as they had most other federal installations in the South.

On November 17, 1860, before any state had seceded, the *Davenport Democrat and News*, a Northern newspaper, noted that, "The leading and most influential papers of the union believe that any State of the Union has a right to secede." Similarly, on March 21, 1861, less than a month before South Carolina's attack on Fort Sumter, the *New York Times* editorial board noted, "There is a growing sentiment throughout the North in favor of letting the Gulf States go."[39] Thus, the public pressure on Lincoln to go to war over secession was not great—as it would later become after Lincoln succeeded in provoking the Confederacy to attack Fort Sumter.

Lincoln had provoked what would become a massive war, yet secessions can end peacefully, as had the 1989 Velvet Revolution in Czechoslovakia. Americans can honestly debate whether Southern secession was constitutional. Under the founders' original conception of the republic, the seceding states that formed the Confederate States of America had certainly violated the spirit of the Constitution's compacts clause, which prohibits states from banding together in compacts. Furthermore, President Buchanan had believed, with some justification, that a strict reading of the Constitution did not allow the president to use military force against an illegal secession—which he believed it was—unless it turned violent. Buchanan's attorney general, Jeremiah Black, told him that even then his authority to enforce the laws of the Union allowed him to use force only against those persons impeding the collection of customs duties at Southern ports or against those threatening a federal facility (under the Militia Act of 1795 and the Insurrection Act of 1807, which allowed the president to call up militia and regular forces, respectively). In addition, the founders at the Constitutional Convention had clearly rejected a provision allowing the federal government to undertake an exertion of force against a delinquent state.[40]

In the spirit of the Declaration of Independence, Lincoln, unlike George III, could have respected Southern wishes; he had not thought secession so crazy in 1848, when he said in the House of Representatives about Texas seceding from Mexico:

> Any people anywhere, being inclined and having the power, have the right to rise up and shake off the existing government, and form a new one that suits them better. This is a most valuable, a most sacred right.... Nor is this right confined to cases in which the whole people of an existing government may choose to exercise it. Any portion of such people that can may revolutionize and make their own of so much of the territory as they inhabit.[41]

And in yet another twist, Lincoln was later more than happy to welcome the secessionist northwest part of Virginia back into the Union to become a key border state, West Virginia.

Even though Lincoln also agreed with Buchanan's attorney general's conclusions that the Constitution permitted only a limited response to the South Carolina's firing on a federal fort, after he took office, he clearly went well beyond this limited legal interpretation by calling up a large militia force, expanding the army and navy, blockading the Southern coasts, and invading the South (not just South Carolina). He took all those actions without congressional approval even after Congress previously had denied Buchanan the increased authority to call up militia and regular troops, take in volunteers, and allow the navy to collect customs duties just outside Southern controlled ports.[42] Law professor Noah Feldman summarized the legality of Lincoln's actions: "When he took office, Lincoln had no clear legal or constitutional ground to go to war to preserve the union."[43] As would become apparent, Lincoln did not believe in a strict reading of the Constitution; he also knew from American history that idealistic Americans reacted best to war when the other side fired first.

Despite knowing beforehand of Lincoln's intentions to start a war at Fort Sumter, the South Carolinians foolishly took the bait. After the relief ships arrived but before they could land supplies, the South Carolinians began attacking the fort with artillery barrages. As predicted by Lincoln's military advisers, the vulnerable and virtually surrounded fort did not last long. As Lincoln had hoped, as soon as the South "fired on bread" and the fort surrendered, "rally-'round-the flag" emotions took hold and gripped the North.

During secession, the new Confederate government had offered to pay for any property the national government owned in the South and to assume its share of the national debt, but Lincoln had refused to meet with the Southern delegation sent to Washington to negotiate a settlement. He had promised in his inaugural address in early March 1861 that he would only "hold, occupy, and possess the property and places belonging to the [federal] government, and to collect the duties and imposts; but beyond what may be necessary for these objects, there will be no invasion—no using of force against or among the people anywhere."[44] He also claimed there would be no bloodshed or violence unless it was forced on the national government. Yet after South Carolina's attack on Fort Sumter and its surrender—instead of a constitutional, limited military response to enforce federal laws in South Carolina, Lincoln escalated to a full-blown invasion of the South and an offensive blockade of its coastline (regarded internationally as an act of war).

The South clearly blundered by responding to Lincoln's provocation, initiating open hostilities. Yet the slaveowners had also remembered
Lincoln's provocative statements in the 1850s, which he continued to
make after winning the White House. On his long journey to Washington,
DC for his inauguration, Lincoln had asked in a February 11, 1861,
Indianapolis speech whether it was coercion if the federal government
kept its forts in the South and retook others occupied by Southerners?
The *Baltimore Sun* noted that many Americans found those remarks
to be "a declaration of war against the South." Later on that same trip,
in Harrisburg, Pennsylvania, Lincoln doubled down, saying a military
parade he had just watched made him optimistic about "what may be
done when war is inevitable."[45]

Did Lincoln Free the Slaves?

As noted, the protection of slavery was the Southern states' main
reason for secession, but Lincoln's reason for provoking the war was
to rescind the fissure and save the Union—not to free enslaved blacks.
Despite his issuance of the famous Emancipation Proclamation and
grudging support for the Thirteenth Amendment, which has gained him
the reputation as being the "great liberator," Lincoln was not the driver in
freeing slaves.

While Lincoln did begin to talk about freeing Southern slaves as the
North's war fortunes sank in 1861 and 1862, he remained a white suprem-
acist who had said that blacks were an inferior race compared to whites.
He opposed blacks' political and social equality—in other words, their
right to vote, serve on juries, hold public office, and marry interracially.[46]
Most embarrassingly, he believed that the presence of blacks in the United
States was the reason for the Civil War; that the real victims of slavery
were whites, not blacks.[47] He also thought that whites and freed blacks
could not live together, thus necessitating that freed blacks should leave
the country and be "colonized" in black-populated nations such as Liberia
or Haiti—thus ensuring that the two races would not amalgamate.[48]

Despite the North's huge advantages in economic, industrial, material, and military power compared to the South, the Union had not fared
well in the earlier stages of the war, mostly because of Lincoln's poor
leadership. Because of this failing record on the battlefield, Lincoln's
famous Emancipation Proclamation "freed" the slaves mostly for military

reasons, with Union generals and Congress leading the way—not the sixteenth president.

The United States had long recognized the internationally accepted practice that belligerents during conflicts could confiscate enemy property used in war.[49] However, given that the U.S. Constitution gave Congress most of the war powers, the executive branch, prior to the Civil War, usually deferred to the legislature on such issues. After all, the original scheme that the Constitutional framers had envisioned empowered Congress to "make Rules for the Government and Regulation of the land and naval Forces" and "make Rules concerning Captures on Land and Water," while the president, as chief general on the battlefield, was merely to carry out Congress's orders during the war.[50] Nevertheless, Benjamin Butler, a Union general and lawyer, cleverly argued that because the seceded Southern states were claiming to be a foreign nation and were using slave labor directly in the war effort, the Northern armies could seize slaves fleeing to Union lines as war contraband rather than returning them to their Southern owners under the Fugitive Slave Act of 1850. For military reasons, Lincoln approved of Butler's idea, and Union forces initially put fleeing slaves to work in menial jobs. But before and after Butler's policy, the enslaved Africans flocked to Union armies. Conveniently left unsaid at the time was whether or not they would be permanently free.

Congress liked Butler's idea and thought that emancipating the fleeing slaves might lead to slave revolts behind Southern lines. Congress passed the First (August 1861) and Second (July 1862) Confiscation Acts, which allowed Union armies to confiscate slaves as war contraband. The first act closely tracked Butler's existing policy and left the permanent emancipation of the confiscated slaves undetermined, yet on the road to freedom. Only after Congress approved the forfeiture of contraband slaves used in the rebellion—by passing the First Confiscation Act in August 1861—did Lincoln's secretary of war then emancipate them (likely unconstitutionally). Therefore, slaves should get much more credit from history for self-emancipation. Before and after Lincoln's mostly symbolic Emancipation Proclamation, they were courageously fleeing across hazardous battle zones to the Union Army.

As the North's war effort bogged down in early 1862, support for damaging the Confederate war effort by striking at slavery was burgeoning. In between the First and Second Confiscation Acts, in April 1862, Congress, which ruled the District of Columbia directly and clearly had the power to end slavery there, legislated freedom for those slaves and agreed to compensate those claiming their ownership, as well as in states that voluntarily freed their slaves. However, Lincoln should have at least proposed compensated emancipation nationwide before the shooting started to try to avoid war in the first place.

The monumental Second Confiscation Act of July 1862, a virtual emancipation proclamation that avoided saying so and came before Lincoln's later preliminary one in September 1862, permanently liberated blacks termed as "confiscated slaves"—those who were owned by rebellious Southern civilians or military personnel and were fleeing to Northern armies or to Union-occupied areas of the South—and made them "forever free."[51] This law also opened the way for the president to recruit black soldiers into the Union ranks to help meet the manpower requirements that a long war required. Lincoln was ambivalent, but he signed the act.[52]

Only after this congressional action did Lincoln realize that Congress wanted to add freeing slaves to saving the Union as a major war aim. He then decided that he would use the Second Confiscation Act to justify his famous preliminary proclamation of emancipation.

Since Northern white resistance to the draft created manpower shortages, the 170,000 to 200,000 black troops were vital to the Union war effort. About 40,000 of them died in action—a 20 percent death rate that was much higher than that of white soldiers. Although only one percent of the North's prewar population, black soldiers eventually represented 10 percent of the Union volunteers, with 85 percent of the North's eligible black population enlisting.[53] By December of 1863, black soldiers' admirable combat record in the Union Army and the Confederate atrocities against black troops had changed public opinion in the North regarding unconditional emancipation—with some Northern Democrats accepting it and one anti-black New York newspaper noting that slavery would have been eliminated even without Lincoln's Emancipation Proclamation.[54] Similarly, the *Indianapolis Star* pointed out that Lincoln's Emancipation Proclamation was unneeded because "the freeing of the slaves of the rebels can be attained when our forces occupy rebel territory" (under Congress's Second Confiscation Act). In fact, Lincoln was heavily criticized at home and overseas for exempting Union-held regions of the South from the proclamation, because if it had applied there, slaves would have been unambiguously freed in all those areas.[55] However, Lincoln's exemption allowed Delaware and the three border states, all still in the Union, to maintain slavery.

Although most histories of the war have concluded that the Emancipation Proclamation made Lincoln the great liberator, it was really a wartime propaganda ploy that effectively freed no slaves. In a sleight-of-hand, the proclamation only theoretically freed slaves in areas of the South still in rebellion—that is, in control of the Confederate rather than the Union armies. The Second Confiscation Act had already more meaningfully freed slaves that were in areas of the South controlled by Northern armies or who had courageously made the risky journey through war zones to Union lines. Although Lincoln hoped the faux freeing of slaves would prevent Britain and France—somewhat dependent on Southern cotton exports for their textile factories—from recognizing Confederate independence, the empty Emancipation Proclamation may have had more downsides than upsides.

Because Lincoln had issued the final Emancipation Proclamation by claiming wider commander-in-chief powers than the Constitution gave him, it was likely unconstitutional and, as a war measure, would have ended when the war stopped. Also, because much of the Northern population did not want the freeing of slaves to be a war objective, the proclamation also led to draft riots in New York City and spiked desertion rates in the Union armies to more than one-third. Furthermore, the proclamation increased the numbers of anti-war Democratic "Copperheads" in the North and drove some pro-slavery Unionists in the border states to withdraw support from the Lincoln administration. Moreover, the Democrats used the proclamation against the Republicans in the 1862 congressional elections; as a result, although the Republicans gained a seat in the Senate, they lost 20 percent of their seats in the House of Representatives and some state houses. Lincoln even admitted that although he had hoped announcing the preliminary proclamation before the midterm elections would be an electoral plus, it instead had been a "great mistake."[56] Finally, because of the desperate need for more bodies to be thrown into the military quagmire, Lincoln relented at last and agreed in the proclamation to admitting blacks into Union forces, which Congress already had made possible in the Second Confiscation Act. Therefore, although American history has depicted Lincoln's Emancipation Proclamation as a brilliant political ploy done for moral motives, the preponderance of evidence questions the former and flatly rejects the latter.

In the end, all four million slaves finally were freed countrywide by the Thirteenth Amendment to the Constitution, which abolished slavery. But this was Congress's idea and effort, not Lincoln's. In fact, Lincoln, in early December 1863, had raised Congressional Radical Republicans' doubt about his commitment to the permanence of postwar emancipation. Lincoln had issued his Proclamation of Amnesty and Reconstruction, which had lenient criteria for establishing postwar Southern state governments and gave rebels a way to rapidly re-acquire power in those governments, thus creating the possibility that many blacks would remain enslaved.[57] This vision comported well with Lincoln's original war aim of reuniting the country, but not necessarily permanently freeing all slaves. Congress, fresh off major Union victories at the battles of Gettysburg and Vicksburg, wanted an ironclad way to ensure that all blacks would be freed after a long and tumultuous war, which resulted that same month in the Thirteenth Amendment being introduced in Congress. Further demonstrating that the Radical Republicans' suspicions about Lincoln were likely correct, in late August 1864, nine months after the amendment was introduced, when Lincoln believed he would lose the election, he drafted an ultimately unsent message to Confederate President Jefferson Davis proposing "peace upon restoration of the Union," thus abandoning the demand for emancipation.[58]

Congress passed the Thirteenth Amendment permanently freeing the slaves at the end of January 1865, and the states ratified it by December of the same year—finally taking effect long after Lincoln was dead, and the war had ended. The constitutional amendment process is one of the few things in the American system of government that does not require the president's participation. Waiting till after he was safely reelected in November 1864, Lincoln was slow to support the amendment but eventually helped behind the scenes to get congressional approval (although to what extent is in dispute). What is known is that favors, federal appointments, and alleged bribes bought votes in Congress for the amendment. Thaddeus Stevens, one of the most ardent proponents of the measure, admitted that "the greatest measure of the nineteenth century was passed by corruption, aided and abetted by the purest man in America [Lincoln]."[59] Another Radical Republican, George S. Boutwell, years later admitted, "Such was the exigency for the passage of the resolution that the means were not subjected to any rigid rules of ethics." Democrats alleged that Secretary of State William Seward bribed defectors from the bill to change from no to yes or to stay away during the vote.

Yet when Lincoln met with Confederate commissioners in early February 1865, with the war still raging and just after the Congress had passed the Thirteenth Amendment, it is rumored that the president had hinted to the Southerners that once they rejoined the Union, they could vote down the amendment. He told them that three-fourths of all thirty-six states [27 states] in the Union had to ratify it, including eight Southern states that had not yet rejoined the Union, instead of three-fourths of the twenty-five Union states plus three Southern states that had rejoined the Union by then [21 states].[60] Thus, at least two former Confederate states would need to ratify the amendment before it would be law.

In any case, the only formal constitutional role that Lincoln ever had in freeing any significant numbers of slaves was his signing of the congressionally driven confiscation acts during wartime, which laid the basis for his wartime-only, unconstitutional, empty, and rather charlatanic Emancipation Proclamation.

The War Did Not Go as Planned

Even if we were to concede that the only way for Lincoln to save the Union was to fight a civil war, his management of the war itself, contrary to Lincoln's popular and historical aura, was a disaster. Most important, his meager military resume and lack of executive experience at the national level led him to naively believe in a non-existent latent pro-Union spirit among most white Southerners that would bubble to the surface when the federal army quickly defeated the South's forces and radical fire-breathing elite. After all, on paper, the North had the upper hand. Northerners had 70 percent of the non-slave population, built 90 percent of the manufactured goods and 70 percent of the railroad tracks, had 80 percent of the banking, and grew 70 percent of the grain.[61] Many a leader has underestimated the length, costs in lives and money, and destruction of going to war; Lincoln was foolishly no exception. And as in the North, when the shooting started, most Southerners rallied around the flag. The result was the worst war in American history, with 750,000 dead on both sides, including 100,000 civilians.

After the attack on Fort Sumter, instead of disciplining the South Carolinians or launching a limited attack on a comparable Confederate military facility and negotiating with the rebels, Lincoln launched an invasion of the South at Bull Run, Virginia near Washington, DC. Lincoln's dramatic escalation is evidence that he wanted to intimidate the seceding states, through the direct use of force, to rejoin the Union rather than to negotiate a solution to the crisis. However, he lost at Bull Run, and his troops chaotically retreated to the nation's capital, which was thus endangered.

Instead of a costly frontal invasion so early, the old veteran General in Chief Winfield Scott had advocated encircling the South instead, imposing a naval blockade along Southern coastlines and conducting a flanking operation on the Mississippi River. After having provoked the war, Lincoln believed that the Northern public was eager for a fight and would not have the patience for such a long-term strategy. Instead, Lincoln chose the eastern theater to fight, hoping to get quick, victorious headlines, when he could have gone on the attack in the western theater, which was more strategic to controlling the strategic Mississippi and Ohio Rivers. He had made a bad decision.

Alost everything about Abraham Lincoln has been reflexively posthumously deified, including his wartime leadership. However, his peers in government during the Civil War believed he was timid, indecisive, and inept—a bumbler in chief, whom they regarded as too disorganized, timid, and passive.[62] In fact, the congressional Committee on the Conduct of the War found Lincoln was incompetent.[63]

As James Madison had done during the War of 1812, Lincoln started a war that the Union was not prepared to fight. At the beginning of the conflict, the geographically expansive United States only had an army of about sixteen thousand men, mostly stationed in Southern states. The nation's capital was vulnerable because it was sandwiched between secessionist Virginia and Maryland, which was on the fence but had many secessionist elements. Washington, DC had several ineffective militias but most had Southern sympathies.

Furthermore, his poor choice and management of generals, indecisiveness in war management (even as his quick book learning of military strategy led to the right approach in theory), and excessively authoritarian rule of the North led to the prolongation and cost of the war.

Lincoln's paltry military and national executive experience made him reluctant to fire timid or incompetent generals, even though he realized, which most of them seemingly did not, that to snuff out an insurgency,

government troops needed to kill or wear down the rebel force, not capture cities, hold favorable terrain or other geographical points, or even
win every battle. Lincoln above all else was a politician, and he often
chose incompetent generals for political reasons (for example, Joseph
Hooker, so he would not run against him for president) or was reluctant to
fire them for the same reason (George McClellan had enormous political
support and eventually ran against him in 1864).

Finally, after years of many battlefield losses, Lincoln promoted
Ulysses S. Grant to general in chief, who wore down the Confederate
armies by crushing them with greater numbers and by attacking all the
armies at the same time so they could not transfer forces within the
Confederacy to meet any one attack. Confederate generals exacerbated
their own disadvantage in numbers by engaging in swashbuckling
offensive warfare, which tended to burn more men and equipment than
assuming a defensive posture would have. In short, Lincoln's meekness
was at the root of his war mismanagement, which his contemporaries
roundly criticized. Secretary of War Edwin Stanton and former General
in Chief General Henry Halleck believed Lincoln was gullible in trusting
those who claimed to be conversant in military affairs.

One late 20th century military model—based on relative military and
economic strength, military strategies, governments, and terrain—concluded that with all the advantages the Union had, Lincoln should have
liquidated the Confederacy in six months rather than the four years it
took.[64]

In order to win the war, Lincoln and his key generals—Grant,
William Sherman, and Phil Sheridan—violated accepted moral codes
(including Lincoln's own Lieber Code on military conduct) and international laws of war by their scorched-earth policies in the South.[65] As in
other wars, such as the bombing of German and Japanese cities at the end
of World War II, such war crimes tend to happen late in a long conflict,
when leaders and armies become fed up with enemy intransigence, rather
than because they are strategically necessary to win the war.

This practice made Lincoln and his generals war criminals. They
had used scorched-earth policies on Southern civilians and their property,
euphemistically calling same a "hard war" or "total war." At the time,
Lincoln knew the South had already lost the war. His policy was not a
response to battlefield situations but a willful policy.[66] As a result of the
military victories of Sherman at Atlanta and Sheridan in the Shenandoah

Valley, Lincoln's 1864 electoral fortunes changed dramatically for the better[67] because a Union victory in the war finally looked assured. Thus, Sherman's later torching of Georgia and the Carolinas on his March to the Sea was unnecessary. Grant had ordered Sherman to damage the Confederacy's war resources in the countryside. A vengeful Sherman did so vigorously.

It was not the first time that Union generals had used such harsh measures on Southern civilians. In mid-1862, in Union-occupied West Tennessee and northern Mississippi, Grant had demanded that civilian families of Confederate-sympathizing officials take a loyalty oath or face expulsion further South, outside Union lines. Also, he had directed the confiscation of Southern sympathizers' property near guerrilla attacks on Union forces. Lincoln and his administration had approved of Grant's harsh policies.[68] At the key siege of Vicksburg (1863), Grant had shelled and starved out the town's civilians, including children and hospitals, and he had ordered his generals to savage the country around Vicksburg.

In 1864 before the election, General Philip Sheridan had used the same scorched-earth tactics late in the war to burn the Shenandoah River Valley in Virginia, the breadbasket of the Confederacy. Lincoln and Grant had approved of these unnecessary and inhumane policies, with Grant even ordering Sheridan to take the families of Confederate guerrilla raiders hostage to ensure the fighters' good behavior. These policies violated norms of war widely accepted for hundreds of years, including Lincoln's own Lieber Code of proper military conduct and the international law of war, codified in the nineteenth century and taught at West Point. The norms were straightforward: do not attack civilians intentionally and do as little harm to them as possible, pay for any food or other staples taken from civilians, refrain from looting private property, and avoid burning or bombarding towns of civilians.

Union soldiers regularly bombarded Southern civilians, looted their homes, and burned the structures down—with the fires often allowed to spread to livestock and crops, leaving the innocents starved for food. Lincoln even intervened in the court martial of a colonel convicted of atrocities and promoted him to brigadier general. Sherman wrote his wife that his primary aim in the conflict was "extermination, not of soldiers alone, that is the least part of the trouble, but the [South's] people." Grant had ordered Sheridan to make the Shenandoah River Valley in Virginia a "barren waste."[69]

Although the Confederacy also committed war crimes—for example, the horrendous conditions at the Andersonville prison camp and Confederate massacre of black Union troops after they had surrendered, including at Fort Pillow in Tennessee—the Lincoln-led atrocities were on a larger scale.

Domestic Ill-Effects of the War

The Civil War set terrible precedents. It led to a concentration of power in Washington and the presidency at the expense of the states and people and allowed Lincoln to rule virtually as an unconstitutional dictator. Although Lincoln was skittish about keeping his generals focused on the grand prize of destroying the Confederate Army, he was bold in usurping constitutional powers from other branches of government, engaging in lawlessness, and ruling like a dictator to silence his opponents. One might defend Lincoln by arguing that any excesses were understandable because a massive war was happening on American soil. Yet even under these circumstances, Lincoln engaged in excessive and grossly unconstitutional behavior.

The nation's founders had reached an arrangement at the Constitutional Convention in 1787 that Congress would declare war, especially for offensive military actions; however, the executive could take any emergency actions needed in self-defense when Congress was not in session. Lincoln, like Jefferson, abused this latter provision, only on a much grander scale. South Carolina had attacked a federal fort off its coast, not the Northern states or Washington, DC. Thus, the key question Congress should have decided, had it been called into early session, was whether and how South Carolina's attack on the fort should have been answered, with a tit-for-tat non-escalatory response or escalation to a full-blown invasion and blockade of the Southern states—that is, general war. Lincoln's escalation to an invasion of Virginia in May and June of 1861 and naval blockade just after Fort Sumter surrendered went much farther than a law enforcement function or a smarter and more legally surgical military response against South Carolina alone, which would have preserved the possibility of negotiation that might have averted full-scale war. As things transpired, Lincoln usurped Congress's constitutional power to take the country to general war and to determine the scope of military action.

In the late 1840s, when asked about his antiwar stridency as a Whig congressman in reaction to Democrat James Polk's actions leading to the Mexican War, Lincoln had replied that if Americans would "allow the president to invade a neighboring nation whenever he shall deem it necessary to repel an invasion ... you allow him to make war at pleasure." Lincoln then correctly concluded the Constitutional Convention in 1787 had assigned the war power to Congress because "kings had always been involving and impoverishing their people in wars, pretending generally, if not always, that the good of the people was the object." Eloquently, he wrote that the nation's founders had concluded "that no one man should hold the power of bringing this oppression upon us."[70] Yet after he became president, in responding to a seceding state's attack on a federal fort off its coast, which fell far short of an invasion of the North, he threw aside the founders' restraints on executive war-making and unilaterally took the country into what became the most consequential war in American history while Congress was out of session.[71] After the attack on Fort Sumter in April 1861, Lincoln had deliberately avoided calling Congress back to session until early July of that year so that he could act unilaterally without any congressional resistance.

Thomas DiLorenzo, one of the few Lincoln critics around, accurately summarizes Lincoln's questionable constitutional transgressions to retain the geographical territory of the entire Union:

Lincoln eviscerated the U.S. Constitution. He illegally suspended the writ of habeas corpus; started the war without the consent of Congress; made mass arrests of tens of thousands of political dissenters (not spies) across the North without proper due process; declared martial law; confiscated private firearms; shut down hundreds of opposition newspapers; imprisoned their editors and owners; censored all telegraph communications; nationalized the railroads; unconstitutionally invoked universally unpopular military conscription, yet another form of slavery; orchestrated the secession of West Virginia from Virginia without the consent of the latter, as required by the Constitution; denied the Southern states representative government while they were under federal occupation; ordered federal troops to interfere in elections in the Northern states; deported Democrat Clement L. Vallandigham, a congressional critic from Ohio, to the Confederacy; effectively nullified the Ninth and Tenth Amendments to the Constitution; and more. All of this was supposedly justified by Lincoln's novel theory that the Constitution had to be suspended, if not destroyed, in order to save it....[72]

One of Lincoln's worst unconstitutional acts was illegally suspending the sacred writ of habeas corpus, a fundamental constitutional right Americans enjoy in challenging their detention in court, even in areas of the North not near combat where the courts were still functioning. At the beginning of the Civil War, when Roger Taney, Chief Justice of the Supreme Court, ruled that the Constitution gave only Congress—and not the president—the authority to suspend it, Lincoln simply defied the Court and then expanded the area of suspension.

Lincoln calculated that Congress would validate most of his extreme, and admittedly unconstitutional, measures when it met in special session on July 4, but he still had reason to worry because it previously had blocked Buchanan from implementing three of five of Lincoln's later usurpations—the calling up of additional militias, the recruitment of volunteers, and a naval blockade of Southern ports. Only the unilateral executive suspension of habeas corpus and the private funding of military supplies, both clearly unconstitutional, had not been previously rejected by Congress. However, Lincoln knew that after the shooting had started at Fort Sumter, Congress would have little real choice. The Republican-controlled rump Congress, which after secession had removed Southern Democrats, would not want to be seen as impeding the war effort after federal troops had been under fire—the ultimate weapon executives would use in the future to conduct similar unilateral military actions and get some form of congressional approval only later. Lincoln had demonstrated his full understanding of how war usually allows the executive to escape some of Congress's normal oversight, criticism, and pushback when he declared, "Bring on a war . . . and . . . escape scrutiny by fixing the public gaze upon the exceeding brightness of military glory."[73] Unfortunately, in the first years of the war, glory for the Union was rare.

The Lincoln dictatorship was a tipping point in American history because it heralded the dangerous, Constitution-destroying precedent that the chief executive could throw away Americans' constitutional rights and protections in times of emergency.[74]

More generally, wars lead to bigger government, even in areas seemingly unrelated to the war. The Civil War ushered in the first tranche of big government in American history. Republican-dominated congressional actions during the war set a precedent for a huge public debt; an income tax and a federal revenue collection agency to commandeer resources (the forerunner of the IRS); even higher tariffs to protect industries leading to big trusts and monopolies in the late 1800s; corrupt transcontinental railroad subsidies and other questionable government promotions of business justified by defense of the west; land grant colleges; a Homestead Act that was designed to give federal western land to white settlers rather than selling it to them; a new Department of Agriculture; a resuscitated unconstitutional national banking system of federally chartered, regulated, and advantaged banks; and the first national currency, the inflationary paper money called greenbacks, which were not tied to gold or silver.

For the first time in American history, the federal government would try (and fail) to take control of the country's money supply. Yet as burdensome as new taxes to fund the war were, the government financed less than 20 percent of the conflict's costs that way. Even more pernicious, government borrowing and printing of greenbacks filled the huge remaining funding gap. Price inflation—too much money chasing too few goods—drove up the costs of living for people in the North and South and the cost of the war. The war brought about the first welfare state in American history, as Civil War pensions ballooned to such an extent that a public backlash followed.

Post-War Reconstruction Failed

During the postwar Reconstruction period, after a few years of improvement with the end of slavery and some black governments taking power in Southern states, African Americans faced a concocted system of neo-slavery that included black codes, discriminatory Jim Crow laws, coercive voter suppression, Ku Klux Klan terrorism, and lynching until the civil rights movement of the 1950s and 1960s permanently improved their lives.

In 1969, John S. Rosenberg boldly questioned whether the Civil War was worth fighting because the war freed the slaves mostly in name only, since "what little progress Negroes have been allowed to achieve has occurred almost exclusively in the past fifteen years." He provocatively concluded that the most important question was not "whether Negroes are better off today than they would have been" without the war but "whether the quantity and quality of freedom our society has been willing to grant is valuable enough to justify the death of one man for every six slaves who were freed." Rosenberg also questioned the value of saving the Union: "Arguments that nearly any amount of death and suffering one hundred years ago were justified to preserve the United States because of its moral attributes can no longer be maintained, if, indeed, they ever could. It has become clear that we are a nation like all nations, that as a Great Power we are behaving no more morally than have other Great Powers." Undoubtedly, the civil rights movement and the Vietnam War influenced Rosenberg's observations (both were happening at the time he was writing), but he was at least questioning the standard heroic narrative surrounding Lincoln and the Civil War.

In 1913 W. E. B. Du Bois, the famous African American professor and civil rights activist, in one sentence best summed the results of the Civil War and Reconstruction: "The slave went free; stood a brief moment in the sun; then moved back again toward slavery."[75]

Given the South's virulent intransigent stance toward the individual rights of African Americans, there was always an inherent contradiction during Reconstruction between justice for blacks and reconciliation between North and South. Unfortunately, during Reconstruction, neither one was well achieved. And Lincoln's actions before his assassination did not really help all that much.

Lincoln was a politician first and made many of his key decisions with politics in mind. One decision had notably bad consequences for African Americans in the Reconstruction era. During his first term, Lincoln's vice president had been Hannibal Hamlin, an abolitionist from Maine. The joke was that Vice President Hamlin was Lincoln's best security against assassination—for if that stark event happened, the South then would face a zealous abolitionist as president. However, in 1864 Lincoln was up for reelection, and in the middle of that year, his prospects did not appear promising. After three and a half years of tumultuous and exhausting war, the Union's financial situation was in dire straits and war-induced inflation was roiling commerce and threatening social unrest. Thus, Lincoln was desperate to win as many Democrats and pro-slavery border-state votes as possible. So, pushed by the crafty Lincoln, the Republican Convention dumped Hamlin and chose Democrat Andrew Johnson, the only Unionist senator from a Southern state, to win votes by signaling that Lincoln would be conciliatory to a defeated South. (If Hamlin was an assassination shield, Johnson would have been the opposite, and ultimately Lincoln's assassins apparently did not fear the Southern sympathizing Johnson from taking over the presidency.)

During the war, Lincoln favored lenient policies toward the Southern states brought under Union control. In his second inaugural address in March 1865, he spoke of charity, not revenge toward the South. However, charity to Southern whites would come only at the expense of Southern blacks. Lincoln had pocket vetoed congressional Republicans' more stringent Reconstruction requirements for Southern reentry into the Union. Benjamin Wade, one of the most powerful of those congressional radicals, thought Lincoln's Reconstruction plan left too much potential for the readmitted Southern states to reinstitute slavery.

Although Johnson, like Lincoln, favored lenient postwar conditions for the readmission of Southern states, he was a virulent racist and rejected black suffrage, which Lincoln had only belatedly favored late in his presidency to recruit black soldiers and other "very intelligent" African Americans. Lincoln knew that the only dependable Republican voting bloc in the postwar South would be freed slaves. This fact led the Republican Congress to pass the Fifteenth Amendment, which assured African Americans the right to vote. In contrast, Democrat Johnson had no incentive to help Republicans ensure that freed slaves in the South could vote.

When Johnson became president after Lincoln's assassination, his continuation of Lincoln's tolerant plan for the postwar reconstruction of the South ran into the buzz saw of a newly resurgent Radical Republican rump Congress. These radicals had taken control of Congress after the 1866 congressional elections because of Johnson's lenient Reconstruction policies and opposition to freed-black voting rights. Thus, a conflict arose between conciliatory policies toward the South favored by Johnson—and previously Lincoln—and the expansion of basic rights for ex-slaves favored by Radical Republicans. But the military occupation and regulation of the of the South by the victorious North could only last so long.

With an exhausted North, Reconstruction was effectively dead after the 1873 recession, but there were still Union troops in certain Southern states until 1877. They were then withdrawn because of a settlement of the disputed 1876 presidential election, whereby Republican Rutherford B.

Hayes was awarded the presidency in exchange for withdrawal of federal troops from the South—the mission of which had been to enforce federal law and safeguard black voting and other rights. Once troops were out, Democrats regained control of the Southern states, taking away newly won African American rights, which resulted in suppression of black votes and violation of many other important African American civil rights for the better part of one hundred years until the Civil Rights Movement of the late 1950s and early 1960s.

Thus, the cataclysmic war's ultimate outcome was the worst of all worlds: a costly Northern military occupation of the South followed by evaporating African American rights—even those guaranteed in the Fourteenth (blacks supposedly got equal protection under the law) and Fifteenth (black voting rights) Amendments. No matter how noble the cause, Reconstruction is a cautionary tale of trying to use offensive military power to change an ingrained and resistant local culture—as the U.S. government repeatedly rediscovered in Vietnam, Afghanistan, Iraq, and other places.

The war ended white Southern plantation owners' political dominance nationally but not in the South. After the war, for congressional apportionment, each slave freed by the Thirteenth Amendment counted as a person rather than only three-fifths of one. Thus, the overall apportioned House seats went up for formerly slaveholding states in the South. Under military occupation this was beneficial to blacks, but after 1876, Southern whites started to suppress African American voters. Thus, ironically, even though they lost the war, the Southern whites were given more House seats in Congress to control, and thus more Electoral College votes than they had before the war. Among other things, the Fourteenth Amendment was supposed to penalize the suppression of black votes by reducing the number of representatives a state had in proportion to the percentage of total voters improperly denied the right to vote; but this provision went unenforced—yet another way in which the North won the war and lost the peace. Unfortunately, African Americans, who were supposed to be the principal beneficiaries of the war-driven Thirteenth, Fourteenth, and Fifteenth Amendments had to wait another century before real attempts toward racial equality occurred, though black voting rights would continue to be plagued by numerous vote suppression techniques down to the present.

In sum, this chapter argues that avoiding war by freeing slaves peacefully, as most major countries of the world did in the nineteenth century, would have made their freedom more permanent instead of short-lived, because there would have been much less Southern white bitterness arising from the destructive effects of a cataclysmic war that ravaged the South and the forced forfeiture of their "property" without compensation. Instead, the Southern elite cleverly constructed a form of neo-slavery via Jim Crow laws that endured for almost a century, and has led to lingering political, economic, and social discrimination against African Americans even today.

>> CHAPTER 6 <<

THE WAR AGAINST NATIVE PEOPLES

White Settlers Abused the Indigenous Peoples Right from the Start

Which American war lasted the longest? The media tells Americans that the war in Afghanistan (2001–2021) was the longest in U.S. history. This perspective is possible only because the wars against Native Americans are continually relegated to the margins of U.S. history. The media consistently fails to take account of the fact that Americans fought with North American Indian nations for more than a hundred years from the start of the republic until the turn of the twentieth century.

Of course, violence against Native Americans goes back much further than American independence. It began with European colonization of indigenous peoples' lands, which various indigenous nations had long inhabited. At first, the various peoples—mistakenly and generically termed "Indians" by the Europeans rather than by the names they called themselves—tolerated small numbers of white fur trappers and traders, but when settlers started arriving in an area in sufficiently large numbers to endanger their way of life, many fought back, sometimes brutally. Over time, the white man would break every treaty signed with Indian tribes guaranteeing their sovereignty over their lands, leading tragically to today's small Native American reservations.

Christopher Columbus and other Spanish conquerors led the way. They treated those whom they mistook for Indians brutally in the late 1400s and early 1500s. The Spanish under Columbus committed the first genocide of the modern era by murdering up to eight million natives in the Caribbean in the first decade of settlement alone, leading to the advent of African slavery in the new world to replace dead Indian slave laborers.

Due to Spanish success in finding precious metals in the New World, their English rivals also wanted a piece of any action north of Spanish holdings. The settlers at Jamestown were seeking gold when they landed on future colonial Virginia's shores. Predictably, English violence against the native peoples began soon after the colony's founding in 1607, with an attempt to convert Indians to Christianity and oust them from their land. And further north of Virginia, despite rosy Thanksgiving stories commemorating Indian–colonial English settler cooperation, in less than two decades after the English landing in 1620 at Plymouth Rock, Massachusetts, whites seized Algonquian lands along Long Island during the Pequot War (1636–1637).[1]

Throughout European settlement of the Americas, the desire for Indian land and the resources both under it (for example, gold and silver) and in it (animals for fur trapping and rich soil for farming) motivated the violence. The imported feudal nature of European society made it easier for white settlers to use interventionist military power to conquer and occupy Indian lands, where the native peoples' greater libertarian culture had prevailed. Unlike the more enlightened French colonial policy of not seizing native peoples' lands and instead trading with them for its resources, the English colonial policy—adopted by the American government and settlers after independence—required supremacy over the land and Indian submission.[2]

With North American settlement by Europeans increasing, it was inevitable that their superior military technology would overcome the native resistance. Added to this technological advantage was the huge population disparity between a growing white population and a shrinking Indian population—to less than five hundred thousand by 1900. This white population explosion and migration westward was due to a combination of high birth rates and a flood of immigrants. But it was the white men's diseases for which the Indians had no immunity—for example, measles, cholera, and smallpox—that were the primary cause of dwindling native numbers, along with violent white ethnic cleansing to steal Indian lands.

The Indian Wars were not the only wars to bring America great shame. Yet allegations of racial inferiority as a rationale to cover its theft of a weaker people's land and destruction of its way of life at gunpoint should top any list. Early on, the government could have negotiated native autonomously governed territories on desirable, non-arid, historic tribal lands and used the army to keep white settlers, miners, and railroads off it. However, whites could vote, and Indians could not, giving the federal government little political will to protect the lands of those now termed Native Americans.

As with Slavery, the Founders Set the Precedent

While the American Revolution gained independence and freedom for European Americans, the revolt worsened the plight of the native peoples. After almost three centuries of war with European colonists, their population had already declined precipitously, thus facilitating further white ethnic cleansing, land theft, and usurpation of their rights using armed force.

In addition to American colonial resistance to Crown taxation policies and fears among slaveowners that the British Parliament would free the empire's slaves, the settler population also revolted because of the so-called British Proclamation Line. When the losing French transferred their North American territory to the victorious British at the end of the Seven Years' War (French and Indian War), the British drew a line in 1763 running down along the Appalachian Mountains. This line was needed after Chief Pontiac's rebellion against the new British rulers to prevent conflict between migrating American settlers and the Indian confederation. The line prohibited private (non-Crown) purchase and settlement of land west of the Appalachians, making this area an Indian reserve. Those prohibitions on American colonists' buying and settling land in that area enraged elite colonial land speculators—such as George Washington, Benjamin Franklin, Thomas Jefferson, and Patrick Henry—who wanted to profit from selling it to settlers. Thus, later, during the American Revolution, many Indian tribes aligned with the British. They feared correctly that if American colonists achieved their independence from Britain, they would erase the line and unlimited numbers of white settlers would pour into the region.

Because most of the Iroquois Confederacy (consisting of five Indian nations: the Mohawk, Oneida, Onondaga, Cayuga, and Seneca) sided with the British during the American Revolution, George Washington authorized General John Sullivan to conduct the most severe scorched-earth war policy in American history. Washington's formal orders to Sullivan in 1779 were as follows: "Lay waste all the [native] settlements around ... that the country may not be merely overrun but destroyed. ...

Rush on with the war whoop and fixed bayonet." Sullivan was accorded one-third of Washington's Continental Army to raze all Iroquois towns save one, destroying food stores, killing children and older women, and raping and then killing the younger women.[3] Washington, like most of his white contemporaries, was especially ruthless with the indigenous peoples because he regarded them as subhuman "savages." Washington's scorched-earth tactics during the Revolution served as an inhumane but effective blueprint for Kit Carson and other later U.S. Army Indian fighters to combat mobile and elusive tribal guerrilla bands.[4] As president, Washington improved his treatment of the Indians, but only in comparison to other American presidents.

In the Treaty of Paris of 1783, which ended the American Revolution, the British—to keep profitable economic relations with their former colonies—gave the new United States generous land concessions westward to the Mississippi River, including the "Old Northwest" (current upper Midwest). However, neither party to the treaty—because both regarded the Indians as an inferior race—ever thought to give the native nations any of the land or a say in its disposition. At first, after American independence, the excuse for stealing ancestral native land was that most of the Indians had sided with the Crown in the war. This rationalization was questionable because even tribes that supported the colonists' cause had their land taken by force and their tribal members pushed onto reservations.

The Northwest Ordinance of 1787, issued the same year the founders wrote the U.S. Constitution, set up the Old Northwest area for future U.S. territories and then states. The ordinance stipulated that Indian land could not be taken from tribes except through "just" wars—leaving a mile-wide loophole for white mischief.[5] The lack of inclusion of native nations' interests in the Treaty of Paris would lead to an Indian War in the Old Northwest from 1785 to 1795 and set a bad precedent for the future disposition of huge amounts of North American land (for example, U.S.-French negotiations over the Louisiana Purchase took place without the participation of the existing Indian inhabitants).

After American independence, continued Indian confederation resistance north of the Ohio River also helped inform the U.S. Constitution. Many prominent land speculators became delegates at the Constitutional Convention in 1787 because the Indian resistance had inhibited sales of their land to white settlers. The speculators favored centralizing authority in a more powerful federal government, which could secure better the lands they had seized. They were right—the new Constitution spiked land sales in that area.[6]

Although the first two American presidents, George Washington (1789–1797) and John Adams (1797–1801), adopted a more enlightened strategy for their time, they still viewed Native nations as primitive peoples whom the white man could civilize. Later presidents, however, influenced by political pressure from self-interested racists on the frontier, regarded Indians as inferior aliens that needed to be removed from their lands. Washington and Adams thought Native Americans could learn farming techniques, convert to Christianity, and stay on their lands. Farming took up less land than hunting, thereby likely reducing Indian resistance to the white man getting more of their land. Of all the presidents up until the American frontier closed in 1890, George Washington had the mildest Indian policy. One cause of the more benevolent policy was that the new nation was close to bankruptcy, did not have the money to remove Indians, and hoped to buy Indian land cheaply. Washington best summarized the policy himself, asserting "that policy and economy point very strongly to the expediency of being upon good terms with the Indians, and the propriety of purchasing their lands in preference to attempting to drive them by force of arms out of their country. There is nothing to be obtained by an Indian war but the soil they live on and this can be had by purchase at less expense."[7]

The government solemnly promised never to take native land without Indian agreement or go to war with them without congressional approval. In 1790 Congress passed six laws to prevent states or white settlers from violating Indian rights, which banned state governments or private settlers from buying indigenous lands without federal approval; imposed harsh punishment for crimes against Indians; and authorized the federal government to provide them with agricultural implements. President Washington even tried to assert Native American rights, but land-grabbing white settlers on the frontier—outside of effective government control—paid no attention, thus making Indian rights a joke. Henry Knox, Washington's secretary of war, blamed recurring hostilities with indigenous peoples on the "desires of too many frontier white people, to seize, by force or fraud upon the neighboring Indian lands." Further, he deplored whites' treatment of Indians, complaining, "Our modes of population have been more destructive to the Indian natives than the conduct of the conquerors of Mexico and Peru."[8] And that was saying something!

To prevent war between the settlers and Indians, Washington sent military forces to the frontier. Hypocritically, the soldiers ended up spending twenty years in undeclared wars that pushed the Indians out of the Old Northwest Territory (now the Upper Midwest). This episode set an ignominious precedent in which legal protections for the Indians would only cloak land-stealing by whites, which Congress tried to legitimize by annual cash payments and gifts of manufactured goods to the Indians.[9]

After the Founding, U.S. Indian Policy Gets Worse

After Washington and Adams, American presidents cared little about Indian freedoms, property, or welfare, and the executive branch led the way in stealing Indian lands. Although fascinated with Native culture, Thomas Jefferson—the founder of American westward expansion with dreams of a continental "empire of liberty"—nonetheless began to orient the country's Indian policy toward ethnic cleansing. Westward white expansion would swamp the much-smaller population of Indians and doom their way of life. Jefferson's unconstitutional Louisiana Purchase from France in 1803 opened vast territory for Indians east of the Mississippi River to "exchange" their homeland for lands west of the river, as an alternative to assimilation east of it. However, different Indian nations already lived in Louisiana, forcing them farther west. For example, in a letter to William Henry Harrison, governor of Indiana Territory, Jefferson noted:

> To promote this disposition to exchange lands ... we shall push our trading houses, and be glad to see the good and influential individuals among them run in debt, because we observe that when these debts get beyond what the individuals can pay, they become willing to lop them off by a cession of lands. ...
> In this way, our settlements will gradually circumscribe and approach the Indians, and they will in time either incorporate with us as citizens of the United States or remove beyond the Mississippi.[10]

For Indian tribes who did not choose to assimilate, their removal to west of the Mississippi River was a backup plan for Jefferson. A year after the Louisiana Purchase, in the Louisiana Territorial Act of 1804, Jefferson was given the power "to stipulate with any Indian tribes owning land on the east side of the Mississippi, and residing thereon, for an exchange of lands, the property of the United States, on the west side of the Mississippi, in case the said tribes shall remove and settle thereon."[11] Jefferson is on record desiring such power. At first the United States pursued voluntary removal, but most Indians declined. The State of Georgia wanted all Indians out, and Jefferson managed to persuade a thousand of thirteen thousand Cherokee Indians to move west of the Mississippi to Arkansas.

But Jefferson was clearly prepared to use more aggressive means to confiscate Native American lands: "Should any tribe be foolish enough to take up the hatchet" to defend their lands, it could be used as justification "to seize the whole country of the tribe, driving them across the Mississippi as an example to others, and a furtherance of our final consolidation"—that is, white dominance east of the Mississippi.[12]

This policy of ethnic cleansing, adopted by future presidents despite often-benevolent rhetoric to the contrary, was to push Indians westward into less desirable land because whites wanted the more proximate Indian lands, resources in them, or minerals under them. For example, in 1817 President James Monroe, who introduced the first official policy of Indian removal, said to Indian-hating and fighting General Andrew Jackson: "The savage requires a greater extent of territory to sustain it than is compatible with the progress and just claims of civilized life, and must yield to it." When Jackson became president, he used the congressionally passed Indian Removal Act of 1830 to push, sometimes forcibly, the Indians of the South and Old Northwest to west of the Mississippi River.[13] Under Presidents Jackson and Martin Van Buren, the "Trail of Tears" forced march of Cherokees and other tribes over vast distances to what was then termed Indian Territory (now Oklahoma), under adverse conditions, resulted in mass deaths of Native Americans.

As settlers, miners, and bison hunters moved westward, those groups coveted native lands, illegally encroached on them, and demanded government protection against unwanted Indian attacks. As shown by Abraham Lincoln's blasé attitude toward white violations of treaties with Native Americans and eradication of their way of life—expressed to

Cheyenne chiefs wanting peace and visiting the White House in 1863—
the government's excuse was often that it could not control these white
intruders:

> You have asked for my advice . . . I can only say that I can
> see no way in which your race is to become as numerous and
> prosperous as the white race excepting living as they do, by the
> cultivation of the earth. It is the object of this government to
> be on terms of peace with you and with all our red brethren . . .
> and if our children should sometimes behave badly and vio-
> late treaties, it is against our wish. You know it is not always
> possible for any father to have his children do precisely as he
> wishes them to do.[14]

Vividly showing the frequent difference between government Indian
policy and practice on the ground far west of Washington, DC, the very
next year, Lean Bear, the leader of the Cheyenne chiefs, was murdered
in eastern Colorado with Lincoln's peace medal around his neck and the
president's peace papers in his hand.

Distant eastern peoples, with less to gain or lose from the Indians,
tended to favor a more benevolent policy toward the natives than people on the frontier. Indians of the east had been either annihilated or
"cleansed" westward within a generation of the nation's independence;
pacification of the Native Americans in the west took much more time—
about a hundred years longer, finishing around the turn of the nineteenth
century—because the territory needing subjugation was so much greater.
Yet even in the East, when Indians killed a substantial number of Western
whites—for example, during General George Armstrong Custer's disaster at the Little Big Horn in 1876—public opinion quickly turned surly
toward Native Americans, and pressure built to avenge the deaths.

Although America is known worldwide for its culture of individualism, in practice white businesses and settlers successfully used their
political power to get the state and federal governments to use collectivist
policies to develop the country according to their interests. East of the
Mississippi River, individuals and state governments drove development
on land claimed by states since colonial times. However, during and after
President Thomas Jefferson's purchase in 1803 of the Louisiana Territory
from France, this small government proponent deviated dramatically

from his philosophy west of the Mississippi River by starting top-down development by the federal government on what was federally claimed land. The federal government would organize, fund, and forcefully protect white settlement of the west. The less-populated west was overrepresented in Congress, with its minimum of one representative and two senators per state, no matter the population. Thus, Western settlers and new states were the largest recipients of federal aid. In contrast, Native Americans, who for millennia had lived on land now state and federally claimed, disagreed with all these governments' claims but had no voice at any level of government.

Jefferson began his federal development of the American west by getting Congress to authorize missions of "scientific research and exploration" into the region—for example, the Lewis and Clark expedition (1803–1806). Collectivist state and federal development policies had a dire impact on the native nations, bringing settlers, state militia, U.S. Army aggression and strange foreign diseases—for example, smallpox—that likely killed more Indians than the violence. Also, unlike the east, the dry west needed irrigation, which required aggregated capital and labor to build dams, canals, and pipelines, which drove yet more federal intervention.

Especially during and just after the Civil War, the exit of the Southern states had allowed centralizing Republicans in Congress to pass the Pacific Railway Act and the Homestead Act, which subsidized large railroad companies and white settlers by giving them free land instead of selling it to them. This state-subsidized economic development might have been good for the railroads and settlers—whether it was good for the country is highly doubtful—but certainly the flood of activity going westward was devastating for native peoples. The railroads and white settlers could bring much more political pressure on Congress than the Indians, who could not vote. Diseased, ousted from their land, slaughtered by the U.S. Army and white settlers, and their way of life destroyed, the indigenous populations fell precipitously. This ethnic cleansing went on for more than a hundred years after American independence until the U.S. Census Bureau declared the American frontier "closed" in 1890.

The U.S. government broke every treaty signed with the many Indian tribes, and in the end, these tribes ended up on the worst land and even then, had their reservations drastically reduced or eliminated. Great nations—for example, the Cherokee, Creek, and Seminoles in the

East; the Sioux and Comanche on the prairie and the Great Plains; the Nez Perce in the Pacific Northwest; and the Apache and Navajo in the Southwest were slaughtered and ethnically cleansed onto the pathetic reservations where they remain to this day.

Teddy Roosevelt, criticized for getting the federal government even more deeply involved in the American west, justified U.S.-Indian policy thusly: Washington had obtained Western lands by purchase (from France), by diplomacy (with Britain), by war and purchase (from Mexico), and by war and treaty (from the Indians). He therefore believed those lands belonged to the people of the United States, which of course excluded the Indians.

In the west, initially, the U.S. Army's role was to guard the trails going through "pass-through" country on the way to the west coast, but after the Civil War, the army's mission changed to pushing the Indian tribes onto squalid reservations and stopping them from escaping. In the beginning, the soldiers did this ineffectively with large unit sweeps. Eventually, they began using smaller, faster units that could keep up with the agile Indians. The troops also purposefully attacked Indian villages to wage economic warfare on Native American supplies.[15] They intentionally destroyed infrastructure, food stores, crops, bison, horses, and other supplies so that cold and starving Indians would need to surrender. The army found that Indians, encumbered with women and children, were most vulnerable in the winter. Soldiers burned sedentary camps, which were no longer mobile in the weather, and food, which was usually in short supply in the winter. Cavalry and Indians typically fought on horses, but a surprise attack on an Indian village would catch the Native Americans dismounted, putting them at tremendous disadvantage.

Moreover, there is a misconception that white settlement gradually, not suddenly, swept westward from the East Coast. Just after the American republic was born, however, it didn't take long to remove the remaining Indian populations to west of the Mississippi River. Then came the onslaught. Polk started the Mexican War to conquer California and the Southwest and grab west coast ports from Mexico. And quickly on the Mexican War's heels, prospectors discovered gold in California, and they and hangers-on settled the state. In the Pacific Northwest, the rich agricultural lands of the Willamette Valley in Oregon drew people westward on the Oregon Trail. When settlers in substantial numbers arrived, conflict with Indians arose in western areas. "Pacified" first were the Indian tribes on the west coast. Then settlement of "pass-through" areas of the north and south Great Plains and the southwest cleansed of Native Americans at last.

Even many of the army's generals—who regularly killed native peoples, burned their villages, destroyed their food supplies to starve them in the winter and pushed them onto or kept them on reservations—were sympathetic to the plight of the Indians. Surprisingly, in a public statement to a reporter, George Crook, the general that had the most military success conducting operations against Indians by using rapid guerrilla hit-and-run tactics, summed up best the U.S. government's horrendous policies toward the Indians:

> I do not wonder, and you will not either, that when Indians see their wives and children starving and their last source of supplies cut off, they go to war. And then we are sent out there to kill them. It is an outrage. All tribes tell the same story. They are surrounded on all sides, the game is destroyed or driven away, they are left to starve, and there remains but one thing for them to do—fight while they can. Our treatment of the Indian is an outrage. [16]

Only in a few instances in American history did various Indian tribes try to form alliances against the settler intrusion onto their lands, which rapidly depleted their game, grass, and timber. In fact, the tribes continued to fight amongst each other. Some tribes allied with the whites to protect themselves from attack by stronger or more vicious tribes. Competition among tribes for the same lands led to fighting, often after a tribe had to move into another tribe's traditional area because white settlers had displaced it from its own land. Also, in most tribes there was a split between those Indians willing to move onto reservations, adopt the whites' agricultural way of life, and live in peace with them, and those who wanted to keep their traditional ways and were willing to fight whites' attempts to move them out. This enabled whites to use a divide and conquer strategy within a tribe or between tribes to prevail in most conflicts—much like the British Empire did with native populations the world over.

Although the indigenous peoples had been living on what became U.S. territory long before European settlers ever set foot there, they were the last group to get U.S. citizenship—only in 1924. And even then, they did not get the unsuppressed right to vote until the 1960s. Not being able to vote without hindrance until long after their land had been taken by force or other shady means, they could mount little pressure on the U.S. government to treat them fairly, except by making life difficult for white settlers or the railroads.

The End of the Wild West

During the many episodes of white encroachment on Indian land, gold, silver, or other valuable minerals were found on it. As part of the gold rush of 1849, about 100,000 native people in California died. Similarly, George Armstrong Custer led an exploratory mission to Lakota Sioux lands and found gold. When he publicized this discovery, miners and hangers-on flooded the area. The army was then called in to "protect" the Indians from white encroachment. In reality this troop deployment pushed the native peoples away from the gold to protect the miners. Unsurprisingly, this led to conflict with the Sioux, the Cheyenne, and allied nations.

Yet the smashing victory of Crazy Horse over George Armstrong Custer at the Little Bighorn in 1876 was short-lived. In fact, so short-lived that it led to the demise of the Northern Plains Indians. Because Custer was such a self-made celebrity, news of his death and that of his 210 soldiers flashed back east via telegraph. As in earlier instances of numerous whites being killed by Indians, President Ulysses S. Grant, who felt Custer's own arrogance led to his spectacular demise, felt over-whelming political pressure to avenge the military debacle. (The same level of public outrage, however, had not been felt when nearly 500 Cheyenne, mostly women and children, were massacred at Sand Creek, Colorado in 1864 or when Custer massacred the Cheyenne at Washita River, Oklahoma in 1868.) The Indian Bureau and army even settled their bureaucratic dispute over how best to pacify the Indians—through positive means (payments) versus negative methods (inflicting death and destruction). Death and destruction won out. Congress, also under public pressure, approved money for more troops to be sent west.

Victory in the northern plains followed the usual pattern: a scorched-earth policy in which the army torched tribal villages and winter food supplies. Nelson Miles, for example, the future general in chief of the

U.S. Army, chased Sitting Bull, who was not much of a military commander, and attacked his Hunkpapa Sioux force, which had to abandon their supplies and horses. In November 1876, Ranald Mackenzie attacked the Cheyenne, then used the same tactic of burning villages so that the Indians would starve during the winter. Crazy Horse's Oglala Sioux band then attacked Miles, but Miles used his artillery to parry the attack at Wolf Mountain. Historians believe this minor battle convinced Crazy Horse and Sitting Bull they could not defeat Miles. First, the starved Sioux and allies came to the reservation in the spring of 1877. Then Crazy Horse and his band came to the reservation on the promise of a new reservation in the Powder River country instead of the Dakota Territory. All Crazy Horse got instead was arrest and death, killed while allegedly "trying to escape"—an unlikely event given that his wife was sick. The Great Sioux War had ended.

Sitting Bull went into exile in Canada, though he and his band returned to the Dakota Territory in the United States in 1881. But once again, the white man had deliberately starved them; the mass hunting of bison for non-dietary purposes had drastically reduced the number of bison on the plains.[17]

After the demise of the Nez Perce under Chief Joseph and the Apache under Geronimo, it was only a matter of time before "the West was Won."

Desperate Indians spread out over the west, nostalgic for the old days when game was plentiful and white settlers were scarce, began a Ghost Dance to bring about a Christian-like second coming and liberation from the white man. Allegedly, the Great Spirit had revealed to Wovoka—a Paiute shaman in the Sierra Nevada mountains in Nevada—that the dance would save the Indians, create a new world, resurrect the Indian dead, return their lands, restore the decimated bison, and make the white man and his ways disappear. In 1889 and 1890 many hopeless tribes in the west were doing the dance. This dance worried the U.S. military in the Dakota Territory, because they were afraid that it could lead to violence against whites, even though the shaman had originally taught that Indians could achieve a state resembling nirvana only by living a peaceful, clean life in cooperation with other Indian tribes. The military ordered the Lakota Sioux to end the dancing, showing once again that the First Amendment did not apply to native peoples. However, the members of the tribe would not stop and declared that they would fight for their religion, if necessary.

Predictably, the military's effort to halt the dancing made it spread farther and wider.

Lakota Sioux chiefs learned that troops were coming to the Pine Ridge reservation in Dakota Territory to prevent the dancing. They went to a Sioux camp on Wounded Knee Creek. There they learned that the Indian police had shot dead Sitting Bull, who had been at his cabin after returning from Canadian exile, because white authorities suspected him of being behind the Ghost Dancing and wanted him arrested. In fact, as in the Battle of the Little Bighorn, Sitting Bull was more of an observer than an active leader of any Ghost Dance. The movement, however, was far less threatening to the white man than the Indian Bureau and the army feared. In fact, belief that doing the dance would inevitably lead to a nirvana devoid of white interlopers probably prevented an uprising in reaction to the murder of Sitting Bull. After all, it did not seem sensible to Native Americans to fight the white man when the dance was supposed to cause him to disappear anyway.

A band of Miniconjou Lakota Sioux followers, led by Spotted Elk, left their reservation for the Pine Ridge reservation, where the Oglala Sioux had invited them to a council. When troops of the seventh cavalry, Custer's old unit, caught up with Spotted Elk's band, the chief explained that they were traveling to the council at Pine Ridge and agreed to let the army escort them to that reservation. The band camped at Wounded Knee Creek and their army "escort" surrounded them, including with artillery positioned on a hill above the Indian camp. The colonel commanding the army units then ordered the Indians to disarm and most of them complied by stacking their guns.

As in many cases in the Indian Wars, one stray shot led to tragedy. One Indian did not want to give up his weapon, causing a scuffle, and a shot was fired. All hell then broke loose. Spotted Elk and at least 152 Indians, including 62 women and children, were killed. The seventh cavalry suffered its biggest losses since the Civil War, except at Little Bighorn, with 25 killed and 35 wounded. The army then intimidated the rest of the Lakota Sioux to return to the reservations. Historians regard the needless carnage at Wounded Knee in 1890 as the last major battle in the brutal Indian wars, occurring ironically shortly after the Bureau of the Census officially "closed" the American frontier.[18]

With all their obvious disadvantages, it was amazing that native nations proved to be such a worthy adversary to the army and state and volunteer militias. Their mounted hit-and-run guerrilla tactics used to raid small army and militia units, isolated settlements, farms, wagon trains, and even railroad personnel were highly effective. Military analysts ranked them among the best cavalry in the world. Indians usually did not attack heavily fortified forts or large military units, instead retreating to fight another day. They had the advantage of fighting on their lands, thus knowing the geography, topography, and terrain much better than did the army.

According to historian Bill Yenne, the Indians could have been even more formidable if they had formed intertribal alliances as Tecumseh tried to organize around the time of the War of 1812. Some temporary confederations did occur, but they were often seasonal and then broke up—for example, the huge Lakota Sioux and Cheyenne confederation that defeated both Crook and Custer in 1876 and the Kiowa-Comanche coalition on the Southern Plains. However, eventually the vast numbers of whites moving westward inevitably crushed the Native American way of life, and Indian sanctuaries dwindled.[19]

As historian Daniel A. Sjursen says, Native Americans mostly followed the treaties the white man broke and ended up far worse off than secessionist white Confederates, who got a relative light reprimand as punishment. Instead, Indians were victims of genocidal slaughter, had their legally promised lands stolen, and ended up on undesirable barren reservations. Unquestionably, America's longest war against Native Americans is one of the most shameful episodes in U.S. history.

>> CHAPTER 7 <<

THE SPANISH-AMERICAN WAR

America's Coming Out Party as a World Power

In 1898 Americans believed they were going to war to liberate Cuba from Spanish colonial brutality. That said, the United States, as it had since the early 1800s, wanted to relieve the weak Spanish Empire of its possessions in North America and now the Caribbean. Under political pressure, a reluctant President William McKinley was reacting to avenge the alleged Spanish sinking of the USS *Maine* in Havana harbor. The fighting, however, quickly concluded with the United States replacing the former colonizers. The U.S. forced the Spanish out of Cuba and then grabbed Spanish territories in the Caribbean, the Pacific, and East Asia (Puerto Rico, Guam, and the Philippines), and it also annexed Hawaii. The imperial outcome resulted from overt mission creep. Both Congress and the American public called for the United States to show that it was finally a global power. With U.S. motives so blatantly on display, the Spanish-American War stands in striking contrast to James Polk's covert planning during the Mexican War to grab the Southwest from Mexico. As with all imperialism, territorial conquest was only part of the story. U.S. imperialism in the Caribbean, the Pacific, and East Asia supplied economic opportunities for U.S. businesses.

The short war with Spain had big long-term implications for U.S. foreign policy. The nation, now with the biggest economy in the world, had become a great power, flexing its muscles globally and acting as the Western Hemisphere's policeman. Before the war, the United States had used the Monroe Doctrine to try to thwart European ambitions in the Americas. In the future, the United States would add the (Teddy) Roosevelt Corollary to the Monroe Doctrine. Instead of only blocking European imperialism in Latin America, the United States would now reserve the right to intervene if any country in the region was experiencing "instability," which often simply meant adversely affecting U.S. interests.

With or without fully understanding it, McKinley also pioneered the much-abused modern day "responsibility to protect" doctrine. This doctrine justifies U.S. military intervention into weaker nations' affairs to further American interests under the guise of stopping alleged human rights abuses. In 1897, a newly sworn in President McKinley sent the U.S. Minister to Spain a blunt message: "the rights of humanity exceeded the rights of states."[1] Even if humanitarian motives had originally initiated the Spanish-American War, the United States did not continue such "noble" interventions in Latin America. Instead, the U.S. has often set up or strengthened undemocratic or despotic regimes in the region—including in the new U.S. protectorate of Cuba after the 1898 war.

Rhetoric aside, domestic pressures, not security considerations, pushed McKinley into the Spanish American War more than humanitarian ideals. Businesspeople saw the possibility of the military prying open new markets. Imperialist politicians—such as Theodore Roosevelt, Henry Cabot Lodge, and Elihu Root—wanted to flex U.S. muscles abroad. Naval enthusiasts desired bases and coaling stations for power projection. Newspaper chains wanted to sell papers by exaggerating Spanish brutality and beating the war drums. Missionaries wanted to "Christianize" and "civilize" foreigners, even though oddly neither McKinley nor the missionaries seemed to realize that Filipinos were already Christians.[2]

These political facts and the 1898 congressional elections pushed McKinley toward war. Indeed, politicians in both parties supported the war. The American business community had flipped from opposition to support for the war, backed by the jingoistic yellow press, which stoked public support for underdog Cuban rebels against imperial Spain. Eventually, public support for manifest destiny overseas pushed the American public's support for war with Spain. In early 1898, as public pressure built in the United States for war, McKinley remained silent, offering no public pushback to dissipate the snowballing sentiment for U.S. military intervention in the Cuban civil war. People pay attention when their leaders stick their necks out in opposition to a trajectory, but McKinley did not speak out. He allowed the biggest U.S. overtly colonial war to simply just happen. It was a war which would result in, among other things, a brutal American counterinsurgency in the Philippines that killed two hundred thousand Filipinos.

In 1898, going to war became so popular with the American people that both parties in Congress began pushing for it to get an electoral advantage. McKinley himself admitted such political motives led to his war decision. Public warmongering pressures also overcame the business community's initial skittishness about possible negative effects of the war on the domestic economy. Finally, in a fierce competition to sell publications, the two new national newspaper chains of Randolph Hearst and Joseph Pulitzer irresponsibly invented or embellished stories about Spanish misbehavior in Cuba that inflamed public bellicosity. After the USS *Maine* sunk, public pressure to fight reached such a crescendo that McKinley could no longer ignore it.

However, once war began, McKinley was not weak in pursuing it. After he had made his decision to fight, he wanted a blank check for conducting the war—something even Abraham Lincoln did not get from Congress during the Civil War. McKinley also grew comfortable with imperial adventurism. With ease, he grabbed Spanish colonies, "liberated" Cuba, and annexed Hawaii, for like the American business community, the older colonial powers, and even Vladimir Lenin, McKinley believed capitalist economies needed new markets overseas to soak up overproduction at home, making foreign expansion not just a matter of greed, but one of necessity. McKinley became the first in a continuing line of "modern" (strong) presidents during the twentieth and twenty-first centuries, after a period of congressional dominance in the post–Civil War nineteenth century.

On the other hand, several historians and military analysts believed the war was needless, irrational, and devoid of national purpose or for securing vital interests.[3] They might have added immoral, too, in denying Cubans, Puerto Ricans, Filipinos, Guamanians, and even Hawaiians true sovereignty, independence, and self-determination. Furthermore, two hundred thousand dead Filipinos signaled a humanitarian disaster. President McKinley might have averted the whole thing by speaking out forcefully against war in early 1898—or failing that, waiting for Congress to declare war and then vetoing the declaration. Instead, he succumbed to congressional, press, and public pressure and let the shameful war mongering go ahead. As Woodrow Wilson would later do during World War I, McKinley claimed he wanted peace but put forward unreasonable and unrealistic terms to secure it.

In the Spanish-American War, history was even repeated, but far worse. The same scorched-earth tactics the U.S. Army used to kill hundreds of thousands of American Indians in the nineteenth century were repeated during the long counterinsurgency to execute the new U.S. occupation in the Philippines. The perceived racial inferiority of the Filipino enemy motivated extreme brutality, making the vicious U.S. counterinsurgency (COIN) conflict in the Philippines (1899–1903), and the disease that came along with it, another sordid episode in American history. This horrendous death toll had accumulated in only five years, compared to the more than one-hundred-year destruction of the American Indian wars.

The smashing, one-sided victory over the creaking Spanish Empire in Cuba and the Philippines was like a coming-out party for the United States as a world power. Historian Melvin Small best summarized the new reality in the international system caused by a rising republic:

> The 1890s were a watershed in the history of America's foreign relations. Until that point, its unusual system, in which domestic politics not only influenced but often determined foreign policy, little affected major international developments. Now the assertive young nation was an emerging great power, and an expansionist one at that. Thus, partisan wrangling over external affairs on Capitol Hill and parochial interests of ethnic and economic lobbies began to concern observers in world capitals.[4]

The far more charismatic Theodore Roosevelt, McKinley's successor after his assassination in 1901, usually gets the credit for pioneering the activist chief executive role of the twentieth century. He made use of the famed and aptly named presidential "bully pulpit" to build public pressure on Congress to enact his policy priorities. However, it was the Spanish-American War that had allowed McKinley, before Roosevelt, to first use the new national media to bypass Congress. It allowed him to pitch his policies directly to the people over the heads of members of Congress.

Traditionally, a taboo had existed on presidential public pronouncements and speeches. McKinley, Roosevelt, and later Woodrow Wilson abandoned this tradition. McKinley first made speeches around the country and took advantage of new national networks of newspapers for policy promotion countrywide, making McKinley the genuine bully pulpit inventor. Though later, Roosevelt and Wilson were superb orators who improved the art, McKinley's practice of going straight to the people over the heads of their elected representatives to sell his policies was the most important development in presidential power after the turn of the twentieth century. It laid the cornerstone for the ultimate rise of the "imperial presidency." Also under McKinley, the presidential staff began to grow to meet the administrative demands of a more powerful presidency.

Domestic Causes of the War

From the 1820s to 1878, there had already been schemes to buy or steal Cuba in certain circles of American society, including influential diplomatic circles. Four American presidents before William McKinley had tried to buy the island because of its geographical location in the Caribbean, its proximity to the United States, and its agricultural potential. However, Spain regarded Cuba as an important part of its empire, having originally been claimed by no less than Christopher Columbus during his first voyage in 1492. Thus, repeatedly, Spain refused American attempts to buy the island, even when threatened with war.[5]

Although the Spanish faced revolts in their Cuban colony for decades, Presidents Ulysses S. Grant and Grover Cleveland had avoided military intervention on the island. Grant had realized something McKinley later missed—both the Cuban rebels and Spanish were committing atrocities.[6] Republican Grant and Democrat Cleveland even offered to mediate between Spain and the insurgents. Cleveland declared a neutrality proclamation to keep Americans from aiding the Cuban rebels and used diplomacy rather than intervention to solve crises on the island. But William McKinley went to war with Spain, albeit reluctantly, over yet another rebellion in Cuba, which posed little threat to U.S. security. The American Monroe Doctrine had in fact exempted European colonies already in place before its 1823 proclamation (so technically, U.S. intervention in Spanish Cuba violated its terms). Here are the main domestic factors that led to war:

The 1893 Depression Incentivizes Overseas Expansion

The domestic economic depression of 1893 had been the greatest in American history up until then and played a crucial role in leading to war.

People and countries can be bellicose when coming out of a depression, which best describes the American mood in 1897. In addition, many American elites falsely believed overproduction had caused the domestic economic downturn. They believed the cure was overseas expansion and new markets. (Ironically, this view was close to Lenin's theory of imperialism, a thought that would have been abhorrent to American leaders.) The overproduction thesis carried the day and generated war along with U.S. retention of the Philippines, Guam, Puerto Rico, and Cuba (as a protectorate) after the conflict ended.[7]

Tariffs on Cuban Exports Provide a Revolutionary Animus

By 1894, Cuba depended on the United States for 90 percent of its exports—mostly sugar, the island's dominant crop. In that year, Congress enacted the Wilson-Gorman Tariff, which placed a huge tariff on Cuban sugar imports. When matched by Spanish retaliation and plummeting worldwide sugar prices, the new U.S. tariff crashed the Cuban economy. Sugar production dropped more than 75 percent in two years, and many plantation workers lost their jobs. The unemployed workers were ripe recruits to be revolutionary cannon fodder. Leaders recruited by José Martí during Cuba's last rebellion against Spain (the Ten Years' War from 1868 to 1878) saw another opportunity to fight against Spain's colonial rule starting in 1895.[8]

Media Competition Drives Warmongering

Another major difference with earlier Cuban revolts was that the new U.S. national newspaper chains, which McKinley later took advantage of to promote his policies, had fanned the flames of war, thereby boxing in the president. The competing William Randolph Hearst and Joseph Pulitzer newspaper chains outdid themselves in peddling exaggerated and sensationalized Spanish atrocities and promoting Cuban liberation, yellow journalism, and American jingoism and imperialism. The yellow press focused on cruel Spanish concentration camps for insurgents and the depredations of the brutal Spanish general, Valeriano Weyler, who ran them. The term "concentration camps", evocative of the later extermination camps of Nazi Germany, arose because Spanish forces were trying to concentrate the civilian population in areas of insurgency so that the Cuban guerrillas could not get cover, intelligence, and supplies from

the people. The Spanish reasoned that, once civilians were so seques-
tered, they could then impose a free-fire zone to shoot at anything that
moved. The American strategic hamlet program operationalized during
the Vietnam War would pursue a similar tack. However, many Cubans
voluntarily went to the concentration camps for reasons of relative safety.
Most of those who died in the camps did not perish because of Spanish
mistreatment or torture, but instead because of communicable diseases
and the squalid conditions at the camps. These conditions were inex-
cusable, but through the lens of the U.S. yellow press, many Americans
believed the Spanish were purposefully trying to commit genocide against
the Cuban people.[9]

Moreover, Weyler's draconian actions—burning towns and crops
and killing livestock—responded to the rebels' own scorched-earth policy. The insurrectionists purposefully desired to make Cuba an economic
wasteland, thus making the costs to the Spanish of keeping the island
prohibitive. The rebels destroyed crops, factories, and machinery to get
unemployed workers to join the insurrection, according to President
Grover Cleveland's Secretary of State, Richard Olney. The rebels' harsh
policy sought to push American investors to pressure the U.S. government to do something to end the Spanish counterinsurgency war against
them. This played well in the United States, which itself had undertaken
an underdog rebellion, fighting for independence from an oppressive
colonial power.

All in all, the Cuban civil war killed about two hundred thousand
Cubans, mostly from malnutrition and disease.[10]

Rebel Lobbying

The Cuban rebels' sophisticated lobbying and public relations teams
knew how to manipulate such important American newspapers to promote their cause. The insurgents pointed out the Spanish transgressions
but not their own. Many of the rebels' stories were exaggerated or even
false, but the jingoistic chains were competing to sell newspapers. The
Cuban insurgents even secretly paid some American journalists to plant
fake stories about Spanish depredations. The efforts of Cuban rebels and
the American yellow press fell on the very receptive ears of the then-ex-
pansionist-minded American public.

Domestic Proponents of Imperialism

There was an imperialist faction in the United States. It was led by General Leonard Wood, McKinley's doctor and an army surgeon who had won the Congressional Medal of Honor in the fight against the Apache in the American Southwest; Theodore Roosevelt, then assistant secretary of the Navy; and Senator Henry Cabot Lodge, the chairman of the Senate foreign relations committee. They cared less about the welfare of the Spanish rebels and were more concerned about making war on Spain to flex U.S. muscles.[11] Lodge had written that when the United States built a canal across the Central American isthmus, a naval station in Cuba would be needed to guard the waters near its entrance. In 1895, Roosevelt opined that he "[s]hould welcome almost any war, for I think the country needs one."[12] These Republicans further advocated military intervention in Cuba as a cudgel against the incumbent Democrats in the 1896 presidential election.

Once Republican William McKinley won that election and took office in 1897, the parties changed places, with the new president being less inclined for military intervention than the Democrats.[13] But the Republicans pressured McKinley for war. Lodge pushed for hostilities because he was afraid of a Democratic election victory in 1898 using the issue of weakness when it came to Cuba. Given the public mood in favor of continued expansion of the American frontier, manifest destiny, overseas, both parties sought to benefit politically from jingoism and warmongering.[14]

The United States never had any critical economic need for colonies. Unlike the European countries that had them, the huge American landmass and plentiful national resources made its economy much more self-sufficient and less dependent on foreign trade. However, joining the quickening European quest to snap up overseas colonial possessions during the last two decades of the nineteenth century, Lodge's "Large Policy" sought to achieve and keep great power status, an idea that enchanted the American foreign policy elite, notably Roosevelt, Wood, Hearst, Pulitzer, and others. To get and protect such colonies, many of these aggressive men believed the United States should invest in even greater sea power. The push for that would be enhanced by a successful colonial war against Spain—a circular logic of sorts.[15] Of course, the imperialists' goal of becoming a great power had more to do with national prestige than with safeguarding U.S. security. For decades the United States had benefited from being oceans away from the world's centers of conflict. Americans already enjoyed a natural security.

"To Hell with Spain, Remember the Maine"

In September 1897 McKinley vaguely threatened Spain with "action" if the Spanish did not reach a "righteous peace" with their Cuban subjects. The U.S. Navy's cancellation of sailors' leave, orders for them to remain ready, and an increase in defense spending reinforced McKinley's oblique threat. To try to avoid war, Spain made significant concessions, including firing the aggressive General Weyler, ending the concentration camps, allowing in U.S. aid, and offering Cubans limited home rule under looser Spanish military and commercial authority. McKinley, in his first annual message in December 1897, had originally supported Spain's reform efforts and urged patience with the Spanish government. Then in January and March 1898 he tried unsuccessfully to buy Cuba from Spain. However, when in February 1898, a jingoistic Hearst newspaper published a letter received from the Cuban rebels. The letter had been written by the Spanish minister to Washington to a friend, calling McKinley "weak" and asserting that Spanish reforms merely were an attempt to buy time;[16] upon its exposure, the Spanish minister resigned. Even if the Spanish reforms were done to delay, McKinley could have used the pledged reforms to stay out of the conflict with the Spanish. The longstanding Spanish possession of Cuba had not threatened U.S. security, so there was no need to initiate a conflict.

However, the triggering event for the war came in the same month when the "visiting" American battleship, the USS *Maine*, exploded and sank in Havana harbor, killing 266 of 354 U.S. crewmembers. If the explosion had not happened, McKinley and Congress might well have avoided engaging Spain in a two-theater imperial war over exaggerated Spanish atrocities in Cuba. The ship's sinking only emboldened the American press and public opinion against Spain. Thus, the demise of the *Maine* converted the decision for war from a foreign policy issue to a domestic one, with the public actively pressuring McKinley and Congress for war.

The Spanish had realized that the battleship was in Havana to intimidate Spain but did not officially protest the visit. If the Spanish had sabotaged the ship, they never admitted it; instead, they quickly proposed to arbitrate claims arising from the explosion. A Spanish study at the time said the explosion happened within a coal bunker next to the munition storage area on the ship.[17] Similarly, at the time, other independent naval experts said a fire caused the explosion.[18]

Even Charles Dwight Sigsbee, the captain of the *Maine* and top U.S. Navy officer on the scene, had some doubts about whether the Spanish had sabotaged the ship. His suspicions were finally proved correct when much later multiple investigations showed that the explosion was most likely an accident from combustible dust in the coal bunker that set off explosions in the ship's magazines. Sigsbee had every incentive, however, to blame the Spanish, for the alternative was an accident that would reflect poorly on his command. Nonetheless, he initially wrote in a cable to the secretary of the navy, which he knew would be well publicized, that "public opinion should be suspended until further report." Sigsbee had the power to ignite instant American popular support for war but chose restraint because he believed elected civilian leadership should decide on war and wanted to give them time for an investigation into the explosion. The secretary of the navy himself concluded that the explosion was "probably the result of an accident." Also, a professor at the U.S. Naval Academy and the country's foremost authority on explosions at sea, wrote "no torpedo [mine] such as is known in modern warfare can of itself cause an explosion as powerful as that which destroyed the *Maine*."[19]

Yet allowing the U.S. Navy to investigate the incident instead of Congress doing so was a mistake. Rear Admiral William Sampson headed up the navy's court of inquiry. He had been Sigsbee's teacher at the Naval Academy. He was also close to pro-war Assistant Secretary of the Navy Theodore Roosevelt. Roosevelt had pressured him into supporting the imperialists' accusation that an external mine caused the explosion. Sampson knew his future career depended on finding that the explosion was not an accident, absolving the navy of any fault. Sigsbee, too, had come to conclude that such a finding would save his career too, and asserted in testimony, as chief witness before Sampson's panel, that his conduct and that of his crew had been impeccable. He noted that Spanish officials were hostile toward Americans and hinted at ways that Spain could have sabotaged his vessel.

Thus, there was little doubt beforehand that Sampson's inquiry would absolve Sigsbee and his crew of negligence, thus implying that Spain was the bad guy; yet Spain still went unmentioned as the culprit.

Sampson's report said that an unnamed external source destroyed the ship; it had caused the partial explosion of two or more ammunition magazines. Yet, even if true, what went oddly uninvestigated, and could have also saved Sampson's and Sigsbee's careers, was whether Cuban rebels had used a mine to start a war between Spain and the United States or whether certain radical Spanish loyalists, not connected to Spanish government in Cuba, had committed an anti-U.S. attack.

However, the last thing the Spanish government needed was war with the stronger United States. In fact, Spain's goal had been to keep the United States out of Cuba. McKinley may have seen the lack of motive when he argued that the Spanish government was responsible in general for what happened in Havana harbor and that the sinking of the American ship showed the disarray of Spanish rule.[20]

Most redeeming for the Spanish was that Sampson's report did not mention that, in the past three years, a whopping thirteen other American warships had had fires caused by spontaneous combustion of dust in their coal bunkers. Indeed, calamities were common worldwide with battleships, which were experiencing rapid technological change.[21] Yet for absolving the Navy, Sampson was promoted to head the North Atlantic squadron during the ensuing war.

Two later Navy studies and one *National Geographic* analysis in 1911, 1974, and 1998, respectively, concluded that it was unlikely a Spanish mine was responsible for the explosion. The studies all pointed to either a coal bunker fire or the magazines blowing up, or both.[22] But even in 1898, there was enough doubt about the explosion's cause for McKinley to have avoided war with Spain. But politics intervened.

Of course, conventional American histories often ignore this question: What was a U.S. warship doing in Havana harbor? Historians say McKinley had sent the *Maine* to Havana to protect "American life and property" from the insurrection. Yet this excuse for "showing the flag," which would be employed many times by U.S. policymakers in the future, was used too easily to justify American meddling in Cuba. The truth is that sovereign Spain, which ruled Cuba, had sole responsibility for protecting American life and property on the island.

The true reason the *Maine* had been sent to Havana was coercive diplomacy. Wild rumors were circulating in Washington that four German warships sailing in the Caribbean were there to secretly transfer Cuban rule from Spain to Germany.[23] The American battleship's visit had been to show the flag and put pressure on Spain to grant self-government to the Cubans. The Spanish seemed to see it that way too, complaining that "Yankee pigs who meddle in our affairs" had deployed the *Maine*, "a man-of-war of their rotten squadron … Spaniards! The moment of action has arrived. … Death to the Americans!"[24] McKinley had been culpable therefore for putting the *Maine* in a vulnerable position in a hostile adversary's harbor during a civil war in Cuba in which the United States had few security interests.

After the *Maine*'s explosion, McKinley might be viewed as slow to ask for a declaration of war. According to then-Secretary of the Navy John D. Long's memoirs, when McKinley first heard about the ship's sinking, "it was manifest that the loss of the *Maine* would inevitably lead to war," but "hasty action was inadvisable" because "the President desired to give the civilized world no ground for criticizing the American Republic."[25] In his war message to Congress McKinley did not mention the ship once and instead pushed for war to stop Cuban carnage.

After the ship sank, McKinley even tried secretly to buy Cuba from Spain. When that failed, on March 27, 1898, McKinley issued an ultimatum to Spain that he thought Spain would refuse, which would enable him to start a war. Ignoring the salient fact that Cuba was a Spanish internal matter, even under the Monroe Doctrine, McKinley demanded that the Spanish close the concentration camps in Cuba, allow in humanitarian aid, treat Cuban civilians better, establish a six-month armistice, and negotiate with the Cuban rebels for peace. If the parties did not reach an accord, the Spanish would then have to accept U.S. arbitration. McKinley first said he wanted Cuban self-government with reasonable indemnity but then the next day changed it to Cuban independence, which the Spanish were highly unlikely to accept. Of course, the rebels had no incentive to negotiate in good faith, since independence was their primary goal.

The Spanish government, fearing collapse of the monarchy if it yielded to Washington's demands, nevertheless made concessions to Washington short of independence and won the diplomatic support of European powers. Spain knew it would most likely lose any war with the United States. It accepted, in waves, most of McKinley's demands. On April 1 the Spanish accepted the end of concentration camps, allowance of humanitarian relief, and more Cuban autonomy. On April 4 McKinley told them these concessions were not enough. On April 6, without waiting long for more Spanish responses, McKinley composed his war message to Congress. On April 9, Spain made a substantial concession, accepting the six-month armistice. McKinley now had received most of what he wanted, and Spain had not rejected outright U.S. arbitration. Although McKinley had managed to stall a war after the *Maine* disaster, he did not publicize these Spanish concessions. By this time McKinley even seemed impatient for war and was therefore not moved by Spain's significant concessions. He further rejected mediation by the pope. On April 11, believing that Spain would never accept Cuban independence, McKinley sent his war message to Congress.

As Woodrow Wilson would later during World War I, McKinley constantly said he wanted peace, but then put forward conditions that were extensive, inflexible, and unachievable. Ever since taking office in early 1897, he had used the threat of force to try to motivate Spain to accede to these unrealistic demands.[26]

As analyst Nick Kapur pointed out, war could have been avoided if the Spanish had accepted U.S. arbitration of its dispute with Cuban rebels or if the United States had accepted the considerable Spanish concessions. Yet the Spanish knew, with public opinion surging against them in America, that the United States would not be a neutral arbitrator, despite McKinley's purported interest in using the process to avoid war. It foresaw that the likely outcome would be Cuban independence, which McKinley later added as an explicit requirement for Cuba to avoid a U.S. attack. McKinley's ultimatum put Spain's national honor and sovereignty at stake if it were to capitulate under duress in what was an internal dispute. The United States might well have understood this sentiment: in 1897, just the year before, Congress had used national sovereignty as a rationale for refusing to ratify an Anglo-American Arbitration Treaty. Even more hypocritically, McKinley refused Spain's proposition to take the explosion of the *Maine* to neutral outside arbitration. He demanded to be the arbitrator, not the arbitrated.[27]

McKinley later noted, and administration officials backed him, that pressure for war in the United States had been so great that if he had not requested a war declaration, Congress would have passed one anyway.[28] Maybe so, but nothing in the Constitution seems to indicate that declarations of war are exempt from a presidential veto and a two-thirds congressional vote to override it. If McKinley had wanted to avoid war, he could have easily vetoed a congressional declaration.[29] However, McKinley never took this route, instead asking Congress for the declaration.

In his first inaugural address McKinley had stated, "We have cherished the policy of non-interference with affairs of foreign governments wisely inaugurated by [George] Washington, keeping ourselves free from entanglement, either as allies or foes, content to leave undisturbed with them the settlement of their own domestic concerns."[30] So why did he violate Washington's wise dictum and intervene in a rebellion in another country's colonial territory?

The Decision for War Is Often Affected by Elections

The best explanation for McKinley's turn to war among leading historians is that midterm elections were coming up in 1898, and McKinley and the Republicans in Congress did not want Democrats to capitalize on public war fever. Incumbent presidents usually lose congressional seats in midterm elections. As one historian noted, "Republican legislators made war on Spain not to obtain control of Cuba but to retain control in Washington."[31] Many other historians would agree with this statement, arguing that the Republicans, in the elections of 1898 and 1900, needed war to keep the party unified and successful.[32] Even McKinley later admitted to a friend: "If peace negotiations had been prolonged, the Republican Party would have been divided, the Democrats would have been united [for war], nothing would have been done, and our party would have been overwhelmed in November [1898]."[33]

Some historians have pointed to a "Republican revolt" in Congress in early April 1898, which ultimately triggered McKinley's decision to request on April 11 a congressional declaration of war.[34] On the release of the Sampson report in late March identifying an unnamed external cause for the explosion of the *Maine*, public and press enthusiasm for war spiked. More than one hundred House Republicans, worried about the upcoming congressional elections, caucused to discuss joining the Democrats' call for war. This had prompted McKinley's ultimatum to Spain. Vice President Garret Hobart, Secretary of War Elihu Root, Senator Henry Cabot Lodge, and fifty Republicans of the House Republican caucus had told the president that if no military action took place, the party would face their worst defeat ever in the upcoming November 1898 elections. Speaker of the House Thomas Reed told McKinley he could no longer hold the House and that it would, together with the Senate, declare war on Spain.[35]

The Spanish had mostly observed McKinley's ultimatum, though stating that an armistice was acceptable only if the Cubans first asked for one, which the rebels would not. On April 10, Spain then agreed to a declaration to suspend hostilities with the insurgents, but the Cubans still demanded independence. Because of pressure from the American press, public opinion, and Congress, McKinley now asked for war in support of the Cuban rebels, even though they were more intransigent than the Spanish.[36]

For Republicans, electoral victory by the William Jennings Bryan wing of the Democratic Party represented free silver, easy money, and financial ruin—something far worse than the unpredictable costs of war. By asking for war, McKinley stanched erosion of Republican support for him in the face of a Democratic Party unified for war, thus reestablishing his control over the party and retaining both houses of Congress on election day.[37]

In October 1898, as further evidence of his support for war, McKinley did what no president had done since Andrew Johnson in the 1866 midterm elections: he used the presidential bully pulpit to go on a multistate speaking tour, taking a victory lap to help his party's chances in the upcoming November poll. And in 1900, his reelection year and after the Spanish-American War was long over, he outright embraced the imperialist mantle, reveling in U.S. conquests and military superiority. Notably, however, before the war he had conspicuously avoided doing a similar tour to *dampen* public zeal for war by publicly trying to sell a diplomatic solution with Spain. Thus, sentiments for war had brewed without presidential riposte in 1898. Even though the war made him the first strong, modern president of the twentieth century, McKinley had not spoken beforehand, believing then that a president should follow public opinion and Congress, rather than leading them.[38]

Business Interests

McKinley had faced pressure from American lenders and business investors in Cuba, many of whom had invested in the Cuban sugar industry, who wanted McKinley to stop the destruction of sugarcane fields caused by the insurrection. Some also envisioned greater dollar signs resulting from Cuban independence. Cuban expatriate cigar makers in the United States, who were suffering from a Spanish embargo on the

Cuban tobacco crop, also wanted U.S. intervention in Cuba to see it lifted. Merchants, manufacturers, steamship owners, and agents in American cities involved in U.S. import and export trade with Cuba wanted McKinley to end the conflict between Spain and the Cuban rebels.[39] Finally, U.S. heavy industry—for example, those producing electrical equipment and machine tools—would obviously benefit from a war.[40]

In contrast, the Republican-friendly general business community not invested in Cuba came out at first against a war because of the potential Spanish threat to U.S. merchant ships on the seas, fearing it would stall the U.S. economic recovery from the recession of 1893–1896 and might balloon federal spending, resulting in an increase in the money supply by the coining of silver, thus leading to higher inflation. Some of the mainstream and business press warned that many advocates of war really had little sympathy for the Cuban people and more for replacing the gold standard with the free silver standard. They believed increasing the national debt due to the war would undermine the currency, bring the country nearer to free silver coinage, and the consequent repudiation of public debt. In the last half of 1897 the budget deficit had already ballooned, dampening business's desire for even more federal spending. Therefore, much of the business press was solidly in the anti-war camp.[41]

However, due to spiking public pressure and media jingoism driven by the sinking of the *Maine*, even the broader U.S. business sector eventually transferred into the war camp. McKinley, elected by eastern business money, paid close attention to what the business community said. Though unratified by the Senate, the Anglo-American Arbitration Treaty of 1897 meant, in effect, that the British Navy was likely to protect U.S. merchant ships in case of war with Spain. The discovery of gold in Alaska meant the war could be financed with gold instead of silver, and military patriotism assuaged many war doubts. After the *Maine* explosion but two days before sending his ultimatum to Spain, McKinley received polling results that the general business community had turned toward war. Thus, the chronology shows that in addition to political midterm-election considerations, the changing opinion of big business influenced the president's decision to go to war.[42]

In the end, McKinley asked for approval for the use of force, and Congress granted it. However, his request was not based on the desire to liberate Cuba or to avenge the sinking of the *Maine*. McKinley instead asked for humanitarian protection of Cuba, so near the United States.

He added the revolution was a constant threat to U.S. peace. Also, he mentioned the Cuban civil war's threat to U.S. commerce with the island. Nevertheless, in the background, the sinking of the *Maine* was a major catalyst in public fervor for action.

Henry Moore Teller (R-CO) successfully added an amendment to the war resolution stating that any U.S. military intervention in Cuba would "leave the government and higher control of the island to its people."[43] Although seemingly putting forward a noble demand, Teller in actuality wanted to ensure Cuba became a separate country instead of being annexed into the United States, for if Cubans had their own country, then higher tariffs could be applied to Cuban sugar entering the United States, thus protecting sugar beet growers in his state of Colorado.

According to analyst Richard W. Maass, the U.S. government also did not annex Cuba into the United States because of anxiety about incorporating 1.6 million Catholic, darker-skinned inhabitants of an alien culture. Even McKinley himself alluded to such racist and sectarian xenophobia by saying his administration "did not wish to annex the island because it did not want two Cubans voting in the Senate."

Another roadblock to annexation was Cuba's massive debt, which the United States did not want to assume. However, Senator Redfield Proctor (R-VT) advocated something which many of his Senate colleagues also supported: a lesser "commercial annexation" of the island. He wanted America to supply Cuba's land and water transportation, rebuild its sugar mills, and sell it food and other exports.[44]

The American protectorate that was set up on the island after the U.S. won the war avoided the costs and day-to-day responsibility for governing. The United States government did not recognize Cuba as an independent nation until 1902, and only after the U.S. Congress forced the Platt Amendment down its throat. The Platt Amendment formalized Cuba's status as a U.S.-dominated protectorate, especially because Cuba guarded the sea route to the envisioned canal across the Central American isthmus.[45] This restrictive postwar protectorate status for Cuba, the U.S. Navy's shelling of the city of Santiago during the war, and the two hundred thousand Filipinos killed in the Philippines counter the American rhetoric that the war was fought for humanitarian reasons or to liberate Cubans from evil Spain.

When McKinley signed the war resolution that Congress then passed, Spain broke diplomatic relations with the United States. McKinley then committed a clear international act of war by blockading Cuba's northern coast and its southern port. After the Spanish then declared war, McKinley asked Congress for, and received, a declaration that a state of war existed with Spain.[46] However, as in the War of 1812 and the Mexican War, the United States had essentially initiated the Spanish-American war.

Conduct of the War

Although the United States had become the nation with the largest economy in the world earlier in the nineteenth century and had begun to build a modern navy, the Spanish-American War was its coming-out party as a great power. The Spanish Empire, conversely, had been declining for many decades. It was economically backward and financially bankrupt. Yet neither nation had a first-rate navy, and the entire U.S. Army was smaller than the Spanish Army exhausted by fighting the insurgency in Cuba. Before the war started, it was often surmised by both sides that America would win the war, but no one could have predicted how easily.

Insofar as the Spanish-American War was fought over Spanish Cuba, there was no real reason to fight in the Spanish Philippines. However, before he had left his post to volunteer to fight on the ground in Cuba, and even before war began, Assistant Secretary of the Navy Theodore Roosevelt, without checking with the secretary of the navy or the president, issued preemptive orders to Admiral George Dewey's Pacific fleet if war in Cuba were to start. Dewey, stationed in Hong Kong, was to sail to Manila Bay in the Philippines and sink the Spanish ships docked there.

After the war started, Dewey rapidly disposed of the Spanish Navy in Manila Bay in one of the most lopsided naval contests ever fought. Before American reinforcements arrived, Dewey thought he could get help to take Spain's garrison in Manila from Filipino rebels, who were already fighting the Spanish for Philippine independence. Dewey transported rebel leader Emilio Aguinaldo by sea from Hong Kong to Manila. Aguinaldo believed he had a deal with Dewey that once the joint American-Filipino force liberated the islands from Spain, the United States would recognize Philippine independence.

When the Spanish Manila garrison capitulated, Aguinaldo was not invited to the ceremony. McKinley, under pressure from other Republicans, at the beginning of 1899 annexed the Philippines and instituted military rule there instead of granting the country independence.

Before redirecting their guerilla war against Spain toward the new U.S. rulers, Filipinos elected a legislature and drafted their constitution on Western models.[47] The ensuing brutal U.S. counterinsurgency against the Filipino insurgents was one of the worst episodes in American military history and, in tragic irony, resembled the alleged worst excesses of the Spanish counterinsurgency in Cuba that supposedly caused the United States to go to war.

The U.S. Navy and Army both had a role in quickly conquering Cuba over the weak opposition of Spanish forces. McKinley ordered the navy, which had bottled up the Spanish Caribbean fleet in the harbor of Santiago, to shell the Cuban city and civilians. As in the Vietnam War, apparently "liberating" ordinary Cubans entailed killing many of them. Overall, while at both Manila Bay and Santiago the U.S. Navy did not perform well, the Spanish Navy performed pathetically worse. The U.S. Navy was able to defeat the Spanish Navy at Santiago and throw up a strangling blockade around Cuba, assuring the United States victory in the war and making land combat on the island of secondary importance. Despite George Dewey's and Theodore Roosevelt's "heroics" in Manila in the Philippines and San Juan Heights in Cuba, respectively, the key battle of the war was the unsung naval victory in Santiago.

Despite the barely acceptable performance of U.S. armed forces during the war, McKinley, as had Madison in the War of 1812, started a war with a great power while having only a small Army, down to nineteen thousand men after the Civil War. McKinley had to beg for two hundred thousand shoddily disciplined and equipped volunteers that were received after the war had started.[48] The Navy, however, had begun building up in the 1880s and was thus in better shape when the conflict started—thus accounting for the lopsided results against the poor-performing Spanish Navy.

One of the reasons the Army was in such poor shape at the start of the war was that McKinley had nominated the unqualified Russell A. Alger as secretary of war, mostly for political reasons. Alger knew nothing about war planning and floundered at the War Department. Early in the war, McKinley lost confidence in Alger but did not fire him. Instead, he went around him to deal with the Army.[49]

Pernicious Effects of the War

The Spanish-American War led to the United States becoming a world power, the deaths of two hundred thousand Filipinos from a brutal U.S. counterinsurgency, and the creation of a modern strong presidency. After the 1898 acquisition of Cuba, Puerto Rico, Guam, the Philippines, and Hawaii, the U.S. government designated territories as either incorporated into it or unincorporated, a scheme still used today. This policy was a transparent concoction to justify imperial rule over "inferior" populations, who were deemed racially unqualified to be equal citizens or to govern themselves.[50] In 1901 the Supreme Court, in one of the Insular Cases, ruled that the Constitution did not apply to territories because the islands were "inhabited by alien races." As historian Daniel A. Sjursen points out, Americans, who once complained about "taxation without representation" vis-à-vis the British Empire, have held Guam, Puerto Rico, and Samoa in a similar status for decades—their residents are citizens but have no voting representation in Congress or a vote in presidential elections.[51] (Micronesia, the U.S. Virgin Islands, and even the imperial capital Washington, DC, do not have full political participation in the American system either.)

In the end, Cuba won its independence in name only. In 1898 Congress passed the Teller Amendment, which declared that the United States would not invoke sovereignty or control over Cuba—but with an ominous exception if the island needing future pacification. This amendment enabled the U.S. to avoid recognition of the island's independence. After the war was over, U.S. military and governmental personnel discovered that a substantial percentage of the Cuban population and the rebels they were supporting were black. These officials' racist thinking was similar to that applied to the Philippines—that the indigenous population, this time a large Catholic Afro-Cuban population, was incapable of self-government, would be restive, and should not be annexed into the United States. Instead, the U.S. government of occupation, from 1898 to 1902, instituted Jim Crow–style property and literacy requirements for voting that disenfranchised two-thirds of the Cuban population, causing protests on the island. When the United States withdrew its occupation forces in 1902, then-President Theodore Roosevelt secured the colonial outpost of Guantanamo Bay as a U.S. military base in perpetuity, while the United States was able to dominate Cuba economically.[52]

In 1901 Congress passed the Platt Amendment, which Secretary of War Elihu Root had authorized. It governed conditions for the withdrawal of U.S. occupation forces from Cuba. The amendment required the newly "independent" Cuba to write provisions into its constitution allowing U.S. military intervention on the island if needed, to permit the United States to have military bases there (the U.S. base at Guantanamo Bay remains to this day, despite the modern-day communist government on the island), and to ban Cuba from adopting a treaty with a foreign power that compromised its independence (in essence, the Platt Amendment violated itself).[53] However, General Leonard Wood, an expansionist friend of Theodore Roosevelt and the new U.S. military governor, gleefully concluded, "There is, of course, little or no independence left Cuba under [the amendment]."[54] Protests in Cuba erupted after Congress passed the amendment, but Cuban leaders accepted the humiliating conditions for fear of otherwise never getting rid of the U.S. occupation. The U.S. government granted a restricted form of "independence" to Cuba in 1902.

By 1920 North American sugar companies produced 63 percent of this vital crop for the Cuban economy. The U.S. government used the Platt Amendment on a few occasions to send troops to safeguard U.S. investments or shore up friendly Cuban governments. Thus, undertaken allegedly to liberate Cubans from Spanish rule, a victorious U.S. war against the Spanish ironically turned Cuba into a protectorate forced to heel close to the U.S. line for many years. And there is still debate among historians whether the U.S. intervention in 1898 interrupted the Cuban rebellion for independence just as it was about to send the Spanish packing.

As a result of the war, the United States also invaded and took Puerto Rico, making it effectively a U.S. colony. The island sat astride the entrance to the Caribbean and guarded access to a future canal across the Central American isthmus. It also presented business and investment opportunities. In short, the war transferred the island from one colonial master to the other.

Unlike the peoples of the other islands conquered in the Spanish-American War, many in Congress regarded Puerto Ricans as mostly white and capable of self-government. Yet Puerto Rico is still a U.S. colony today. The simple definition of a colony is a territory controlled by another country, without the inhabitants having equal standing with the citizens of the mother country. Puerto Rico lagged in assimilation into the United States more than California, New Mexico, Florida, and even Texas because Congress did not want to set a precedent for an ensuing incorporation of the large dark-skinned population of the Philippines.

U.S. rule in Puerto Rico was worse than that of the Spanish Empire. The Spanish had given Puerto Ricans the power to create a legislature and currency and control tariff rates. After its invasion, the United States rolled back those reforms with the Foraker Act of 1900, which allowed the U.S. president to appoint a governor and council to run the island, with Puerto Ricans only allowed to elect representatives to a legislature and a nonvoting member of the U.S. Congress. The United States then sent a progression of incompetent and hated governors to the island, one of whom used his time in office to buy up land that would become Domino Sugar. Other U.S. corporations also poured money into Puerto Rican sugar interests, resulting in five American companies dominating the sugar market on the island.

Over time, Puerto Ricans have gained U.S. citizenship and more local autonomy but still have not fared well under continued U.S. colonialism.[55] Because Puerto Rico still does not have equal voting representation in Congress compared to the fifty states, it remains a colony.

In the 1910s and 1920s, success in the Spanish-American War emboldened the United States to undertake a spate of mercantilist military interventions in Central America and the Caribbean. To justify such interventions, President Theodore Roosevelt developed a corollary to the original Monroe Doctrine, whereby the United States did not have to wait for European interventions in the western hemisphere to act. Instead, U.S. military interventions could happen if countries in the western hemisphere became embroiled in financial trouble, excessive debt, or political instability that made them ripe for European intervention. In reality, this corollary allowed U.S. military intervention in Central America and the Caribbean for any reason, but usually when U.S. interests were perceived to be in danger.

In the Pacific, war aims quickly expanded once the fighting started. McKinley decided to keep the Philippines not to "civilize and Christianize" Filipinos, as he claimed, but to use the islands for a naval base and coaling station to control trade with a weakened China—a goal similar to that of other imperial great powers. The Philippines was only four hundred miles from China. As with the American Indians, even the veneer of civilizing and Christianizing the predominantly Christian

Philippines showed that the principles of self-government in the U.S. Declaration of Independence were hollow if applied to "inferior" darker-skinned peoples. The American president appointed a governor and executive council, which could veto any legislation passed by the elected Filipino legislature.

Also, the United States feared that Germany or Japan—both, like the United States, coming late to the imperialist scene—would grab the Philippines if the United States failed to establish a colony there. As in the Mexican War, the United States paid the vanquished former colonizer so that its aggression would not look as bad. Although Spain received $20 million for the Philippines, Filipinos got nothing, which angered them enough to start an insurgency against the new U.S. colonial power in an ongoing effort to gain their independence.

The United States had entered its first imperial war against Spain, which had resulted in a quagmire in the Philippines. Senator Carl Schurz, a Union general during the Civil War and a former friend of McKinley, best summed up the contradictions of the war by saying that the United States had let Filipinos "believe that in fighting on the same side with us, they were fighting for their own independence. We deliberately turned our loudly-vaunted war of liberation and humanity into a shameless war of conquest.... We killed many, many thousands of them, and still go on killing them at the rate of 1,000 to 1,500 a month."[56]

A blockbuster report written by Major Cornelius Gardener, the civil governor of a Philippine province, concluded that brutal U.S. behavior had turned initially friendly Filipinos into a virulent anti-U.S. insurgency. The U.S. miliary had come to regard all Filipinos as insurgents and did not distinguish between friend and foe. And here it was that the army perfected the "water cure" by torturing Filipinos (still used in the post-9/11 U.S. war on terror under the name of waterboarding).

Close to the same time that the Gardener report was released, Major C.W. Waller testified to Congress that General Jacob Smith, "Hell-Roaring Jake Smith," a veteran of the scorched-earth Indian Wars, had given the following orders in the Philippines: "I want no prisoners. I wish you to kill and burn. The more you kill and the more you burn, the better you will please me." Waller then asserted General Smith had said that he "wanted all persons killed who were capable of bearing arms," down to ten-year-old boys. Smith confessed to issuing those horrendous orders and was court-martialed, then only reprimanded. Other military men confessed to brutal U.S. tactics: General Arthur MacArthur, the top American commander in the Philippines, acknowledged his forces had been ordered to employ "very drastic tactics." A reporter from the Philadelphia *Public Ledger* confirmed the horrible killing of questionable classes of people by concluding, "Our men have been relentless, have killed to exterminate men, women, children, prisoners and captives . . . lads of ten and up, the idea prevailing that the Filipino, as such, was little better than a dog." One reporter from *Outlook* magazine noted, "In some of our dealings with the Filipinos we seem to be following more or less . . . the example of Spain [in Cuba]. We have established a penal colony; we have burned native villages . . . we resort to torture as a means of obtaining information." In short, the hundreds of thousands of Filipinos killed by the United States over a period of four years was much greater than those who had died during the three and a half centuries of the allegedly horrible Spanish rule.[57]

American critics argued that American scorched-earth tactics and resulting atrocities in the Philippines were as bad as Spanish General Weyler's had been in Cuba—the alleged original impetus for the United States starting the war with Spain. To stop such criticism affecting the troops, the U.S. postmaster seized the mailings of the American Anti-Imperialist League to U.S. soldiers in the Philippines.

The Philippines would not finally gain its independence until after World War II—and even then, would continue to house huge U.S. military installations.

As the Philippine horrors became public, Americans grew weary of direct imperialism.[58] Instead of pursuing further overt colonialism, American imperial impulses were later channeled into building an informal U.S. global empire of military bases, foreign assistance, alliances, and temporary (at least theoretically) military interventions in the twentieth century. More immediately, the U.S. victory in the Spanish-American War emboldened the United States to annex Hawaii and undertake a rash of smaller military interventions in Mexico, the Caribbean, and Central America in the 1910s and 1920s.

The loss of the war also had made Spain give up the Pacific island of Guam, which McKinley kept as a naval base and coaling station, ruled by the U.S. Navy from 1898 to 1950. The combination of U.S. bases in the Philippines, Hawaii, and Guam made the United States a formidable

Pacific power, able to compete with other Western powers for a share of coerced trade with China.

Success in the Spanish-American War spurred McKinley's joining, without congressional approval, the Western powers' suppression of the Boxer Rebellion in China in 1900.[59] American business interests, using the "overproduction" thesis, strenuously demanded that the U.S. government do something to protect America's share of trade and investment in a potentially gigantic Chinese market.

According to members of McKinley's cabinet, the president did not seek congressional approval for military action during the Boxer Rebellion, despite China's declaration of war against the United States. McKinley feared Congress would pass other related legislation that would harm his reelection effort that year. Also, Congress, without a fight, earlier had given him free rein to conduct the Spanish-American War; obviously, McKinley had become comfortable expanding his powers in violation of the Constitution.[60] That is one more reason that McKinley should be called the first "modern president."

Finally, the Spanish-American war set a precedent for more rigorous enforcement of the Monroe Doctrine in Latin America. Using the Roosevelt Corollary of the doctrine, numerous U.S. military interventions occurred in Central America and the Caribbean to further U.S. political, economic, and business interests. This spate of profligate interventionism did not quiet until Herbert Hoover and Franklin D. Roosevelt instituted the "Good Neighbor" policy in the late 1920s and 1930s.

SECTION III.
MERCANTILISM OF COMPETING EMPIRES

>> CHAPTER 8 <<

WORLD WAR I

The U.S. Joined the War for Economic and Political Reasons

It's little wonder that many historians see World War I as the most important event of the twentieth century. As if the vast slaughter were not bad enough, it planted the seeds of later turmoil: the Bolshevik Revolution, the Great Depression, the rise of Adolf Hitler, World War II, and the Cold War. Nor did the redrawn boundary lines in Europe and the Middle East bring any lasting peace. According to historian Jim Powell, the purportedly idealistic President Woodrow Wilson, before he took the United States into the war, knew that the Allied Powers had already negotiated secret agreements to carve up Europe and the Middle East, merely to grab their enemies' colonial possessions.[1]

Nothing forced either Britain or the United States to enter the European conflict that began in 1914. For Britain, Kaiser Wilhelm II's Germany did not threaten the European state system or balance of power. For the United States, with the Atlantic Ocean protecting it from the European conflict, Germany did not threaten its national security, either. Woodrow Wilson understood the U.S. benefits from its geography and accordingly should have kept America truly neutral in World War I. Under his orders, American ships and people should have stayed away from the waters of belligerent countries or traveled at their own risk. However, Wilson and American businesses could not resist the bonanza of trading with desperate warring nations in Europe.

But that trading was one-sided. Wilson was never a neutral observer, concerned solely with protecting American lives or interests. He led a nation that traded extensively with Allied countries but had little commerce with Germany, a situation that eventually dragged America into the war. Countries at war need food, weapons, ammunition, other war supplies, and money to buy them. The fragile U.S. economy began to depend on such wartime exports to the Allies. Once the Allied nations, most notably Britain, were accorded significant wartime loans and credit to buy American goods, the United States, to ensure its repayment, thus developed a significant financial stake in Allied victory. Rather than trading with or loaning money to the Kaiser as well, Wilson took sides and tacitly acquiesced to the Royal Navy's Hunger Blockade of Germany. To counter the blockade, the German U-boats tried to intercept and sink ships transporting war weapons and goods to Britain and France. Wilson demanded the Germans restrict U-boat attacks on U.S. "neutral" maritime commerce in warzones near Allied countries but never demanded that the British let U.S. vessels through the British Hunger Blockade to trade with Germany.

Many historians point to the cause of U.S. belated entry into World War I as the resumption of German unrestricted submarine warfare on February 1, 1917. But Wilson's response to the threat was unhurried; he didn't ask Congress for a declaration of war until two months later, on April 2. Thus, for Wilson, the underlying cause of U.S. entry into the war was not German submarine activity.

As noted, Wilson had compromised U.S. neutrality, leading to the United States developing a strong economic interest rather than a national security interest in Allied victory over Germany. For more personal reasons, Wilson had long itched to enter the war so he could help decide the fate of Europe and the world and felt he needed a justification to sell intervention in the war to the American public. Wilson held naïve, idealistic ideas about spreading democracy, national self-determination, and collective security. Up until his reelection in late 1916, he believed the appearance of neutrality would better preserve the roaring U.S. economy by selling war provisions to the Allies and thus boost his reelection chances. Eventually, in early 1917, after he won the election, the British convinced him to give up on neutrality and join the fight or otherwise lose his seat at the postwar peace table to redesign Europe and the world.[2]

In 1914, Wilson could have been wiser and protected American lives better if he had banned Americans or their ships from entering overseas warzones and denied them government help if they foolishly did so. In that way, he could have kept the U.S. out of the European bloodbath. By 1918 the United States would have had unparalleled power globally by avoiding war. But as the European war went on, the U.S. dependence on war exports to Allied nations made such restraint politically impossible. Thus, the misguided American "success" during World War I led to the tragic belief that U.S. military adventurism made the United States the indispensable nation in "making the world safe for democracy."

But World War I and U.S. participation solved few pre-1914 problems and added several severe ones: the Russian Revolution in 1917, the Great Depression beginning in 1929, and World War II starting in 1939. Indeed, it is not an exaggeration to call World War II instead World War: *Part II*. The blustering Kaiser Wilhelm II, the German leader in World War I, unlike the truly hyper-aggressive Adolf Hitler in World War II, retreated from conflict most of the time. In fact, other nations bear equal or greater responsibility than Germany for the start of the Great War—a tragic war few wanted, including the Kaiser.

Blame also lies with Woodrow Wilson for unnecessarily entering a European war that had been going on for almost three bloody years without the U.S. Many historians looking back on the period do so through the dark glasses of Nazism in Germany and conclude that the Americans had not done enough to secure post–World War I peace. Yet Europe may well have been a much better place after World War I had Germany either won or lost the war without American entry—insofar as in either case, all parties likely would have been exhausted, thus providing incentives for a more balanced negotiated settlement that avoided the humiliating, one-sided Versailles Treaty that boded ill for the future. However, like President William McKinley before the Spanish-American War, Wilson kept saying he wanted peace yet made unreasonable and unrealistic demands on Germany, whose refusal predictably enabled the United States to enter the war.

Origins of World War I in Europe

Since 1914, the world has routinely blamed Kaiser Wilhelm II for starting World War I. In 1890 the bumbling Kaiser fired Otto von Bismarck, his chancellor (prime minister) who had been the master statesman of Europe for two decades. In that same year, the Kaiser then made a fateful decision that led to realignment of powers in Europe, and in turn to World War I. He did not renew Bismarck's secret so-called Reinsurance Treaty with Russia, signed in 1887. The treaty pledged that either Russia or Germany would remain neutral if one of them warred with a third great power. After the treaty lapsed, a fateful alliance between France and Russia formed. This led to a realignment of powers in Europe that confronted a rising Germany with the potential for a simultaneous two-front war from east and west. This much-anticipated debacle for Germany finally occurred when World War I broke out in August of 1914. Moreover, in the war, the weak and declining Austro-Hungarian Empire would be Germany's only European ally.

In the years before 1914, Germany was rising economically and militarily. So too was Russia. The despotic, nontransparent, and unpredictable Russian tsar, aided by loans from France, began a rapid military buildup after 1910, which gave Germany every incentive to go to war against it sooner rather than later. However, the German Reichstag, controlled by Social Democratic opponents of Bismarck's conservative constitution, was initially reluctant to supply money for competitive German armaments.[3] Adding to the volatile mix was tsarist Russia's guilt over its lukewarm support for its Slavic brothers in the Balkans during the small wars there in the years just before 1914. Slavic Serbia was opposed to the Austro-Hungarian Empire annexing the region of Bosnia-Herzegovina and the Serbs living there. What was worse, the heir to the empire's throne, Archduke Franz Ferdinand, was talking about internal reforms in the empire that would give such minorities more power. These reforms would wreck Serbia's plans for an independent greater Serbia.

The Serbian government hatched a plan to assassinate Archduke Ferdinand when he visited Sarajevo, Bosnia, on June 28, 1914. The assassins successfully carried out the attack, which led to war between Serbia and Austria-Hungary, and through a system of rigid alliances, dragged the entire continent of Europe, and later the world, into the fighting. After the killing, the general sentiment internationally was that Austria-Hungary had a right to take the aggressive Serbs to task for assassinating its number two man. Austria-Hungary went to its more powerful ally, the Kaiser's Germany, and asked for its backing in case Serbia's Slavic big brother, Russia, entered the fray. Germany foolishly gave Austria-Hungary a blank check of support against Serbia. However, in Germany's defense, it thought Austria-Hungary's military intervention would be quick and limited.

The problem was that Austria-Hungary had given many members of its military leave for agricultural work at home. So, after a month's delay, Austria-Hungary finally declared war on Serbia on July 28, 1914. By then, for the rest of Europe, the urgency of retaliation had passed. Russia decided it had better supply more help this time to its Serbian brothers, or its prestige would be damaged. Thus, Russia took the provocative step of mobilizing all its huge military forces, instead of just those arrayed opposite Austria-Hungary. In those days, mobilizing forces was an offensive action that meant war was a certainty.

Germany at once became alarmed that Russia had mobilized its forces and then strengthened its eastern border. France then mobilized forces on Germany's western border. The French had been in a nationalist and revanchist mood toward Alsace-Lorraine, a region sandwiched between France and Germany and acquired by Germany during the Franco-Prussian war (1870–1871). Confronted with the likelihood of a two-front war, Germany had to move quickly. Its war plan called for holding the line against Russia while rapidly defeating France. Yet Germany at first resisted taking the provocative step of responding with its own mobilization, as the Kaiser tried to avoid a European conflagration. Finally, Germany not only mobilized its forces in response to its adversaries' mobilizations but foolishly declared war first, then moved troops across the borders of neutral Belgium and preemptively against France.

The Kaiser's diplomacy had proven dreadful, leading up to and during the war. Being the first among the great powers to declare war and move troops across national borders has long hung the label of "aggressor" around the Kaiser's and Germany's neck. While few historians now place the sole blame for the war on any one nation, most Americans have viewed Germany as the culprit since 1914. The German U-boat campaign attacking ships in the Atlantic Ocean from 1915 to 1917 did nothing to dispel this American view, then or now.

The rise of Germany had caught the Americans off guard. They had come to accept the seemingly permanent U.S. rivalry with Britain in the Atlantic and Latin America after the American Revolution (1775–1783), the War of 1812, the kerfuffle over Oregon (1846–1848), naval issues during the Civil War (1861–1865), and the dustup over Venezuela in 1895. But unknown to Americans, a similar British rivalry was brewing with Germany.[4]

Britain should have stayed out of the war. Being on an offshore island, it had better intrinsic security than the continental countries. Without Britain entering the fray on the side of France and Russia, the Kaiser's Germany, blustery and rising, likely would have won the war without dragging the world into it. In fact, a German victory would have left the Kaiser in power and made it unlikely that this scenario would have eventually given rise to Hitler and World War II. Vital for an island nation is its navy and, by 1914, Britain had already won the naval arms race with Germany. The Royal Navy ruled the seas, including the Atlantic, thus ensuring Britain's safety.

However, in the years before the war, British Foreign Secretary Edward Grey—unbeknownst to the British public, parliament, and full cabinet—had entered a secret entente with France, giving assurances of support in time of war albeit not necessarily direct military intervention.[5] The two countries even had made secret joint military plans in the event of war with Germany. Even so, an entente is less than a formal alliance, and the British government could have opted out of a massive and costly European war.

U.S. Enters the War Despite a Manageable German Threat

If Britain had stayed out of World War I, it is equally likely Woodrow Wilson would have kept the U.S. out too. Instead, a vindictive peace against the vanquished Germany was arranged with the help of American diplomats and lawyers under Wilson's instructions. Moreover, Wilson's insistence that the Kaiser abdicate power cleared Hitler's future pathway to power in Germany.

Some have argued that the United States needed to enter the war because German control of the Atlantic was a threat to the European balance of power and therefore to U.S. security. However, before the war took off in Europe, Germany had obviously already lost the naval arms race to Britain. During the European war, the Royal Navy had kept the German (surface) Navy bottled up in the Baltic Sea. German submarine warfare was essentially guerrilla warfare at sea by an inferior navy. Until February 1917, the Germans were only attacking U.S. shipping in European war zones by mistake. On the other hand, in retaliation for the illegal British naval blockade against Germany, the Germans purpose-fully attacked British merchant vessels in those areas with submarines, including British ships carrying U.S.-produced war supplies for the Allied nations' land forces. If the Allied nations had lost the war, it would have done so on land; the Royal Navy would still have ruled the Atlantic. Even in the worst case, if the German Navy had come to dominate that ocean—improbable because, unlike Adolf Hitler, the Kaiser had failed to take France and obtain ports on the Atlantic—the United States had lived through the late 1700s and 1800s with another hostile power in control of that body of water: Britain. However, the United States, with by far the largest economy on the planet at the time of World War I, could have built up its navy to challenge any German attempt to dominate the Atlantic.

Finally, the balance of power on the European continent had changed many times during American history without significantly adversely affecting U.S. security. That is why the United States had developed a long tradition of staying out of distant European wars. So by 1917, without U.S. entry, even if one side or the other had won the long-stalemated land war, it would have been a Pyrrhic victory for there was no threat of any nation achieving complete domination over Europe nor, accordingly, of threatening the United States.

Many Americans have since viewed U.S. entry into World War I through the lens of World War II. This leads them to the erroneous conclusion that the United States had had to get involved in both conflicts to save Europe from an aggressive Germany. This thesis, which might reasonably be applied to Adolf Hitler's Germany, is fallacious for Kaiser Wilhelm II's Germany in World War I.

At the turn of the twentieth century, Germany was regarded as an enlightened and modernizing nation, with a wider voting franchise than Britain. Its most powerful party was the progressive Social Democratic Party. Although historian Walter Laqueur claims that Wilhelmine Germany was not a Western liberal democracy, it was a "permissive country" in which legal due process and rule of law applied to both leaders and common citizens. The press critiqued the Kaiser, and censorship was for extreme cases only.[6] As for Britain and France, their liberal practices at home were discarded when it came to the "inferior peoples" of their vast empires, which Germany could not match.

However, through British government propaganda during its successful naval competition with Germany before the war and after the war began, the Kaiser's Germany had been successfully painted as a militarized and aggressive monster, bent on Europe-wide conquest. This British propaganda machine, unanswered by Germany, had been secretly brought to America's shores to try to lure the United States into war against the "evil" Kaiser too.

Yet while the Kaiser, blustering and bumbling, did not want a continental war either, he feared an attack from mobilized forces from two directions. In addition, the Kaiser was not in complete control of the incompetent German diplomacy before or during the war. It was obvious early in the European war that—unlike Hitler' blitzkrieg across Poland, France, other northern European countries, and Russia during the early years of World War II—Germany's plan to knock out France quickly and then defeat Russia had failed. France and Britain had stopped the German advance in northern France, locking the Germans into a three-year war of attrition in the trenches on a front that barely moved. On the western front, the British and French together had more men than Germany but inferior generals and numbers of weapons.[7] Even after Germany facilitated the Bolsheviks' taking the Russians out of the war in 1917, enabling Germany to transfer troops west to fight the Allies, the stalemate continued.

U.S. Partisan "Neutrality"

President Woodrow Wilson took the United States into a war that the country could and should have avoided. As in the War of 1812 with Britain, the ostensible reason the United States got into the war was violations of U.S. neutrality rights at sea by belligerent parties in an already ongoing war. Also, in both wars, both belligerents were committing naval depredations against the United States, but America chose to focus its ire on only one belligerent; in World War I, it was Germany. Having authored academic books on episodes in American history, Wilson recognized the parallels between his situation and that in the War of 1812. He had correctly concluded that President James Madison had been too weak to keep the war hawks from driving the United States into that earlier conflict; yet he also was too weak to keep the United States out of the war with Germany.

Belligerents in large-scale, high-stakes wars—such as the Napoleonic Wars and World War I—are motivated to be ruthless even with neutral countries if the combatants think these nations are helping their enemy's war effort via trade. The United States under the Wilson administration was even guilty of faux neutrality. Wilson and Colonel Edward House, his principal advisor, were both strong Anglophiles; as early as 1915, Colonel House had assured the Allied nations of Britain and France that the Wilson administration would not let them lose the war.[8]

The British Navy, having won the naval arms race with Germany, used its naval advantage to set up the Hunger Blockade around Germany to starve Germans into submission. The Triple Entente of Britain, France, and Russia had a larger GDP and greater military material than the Central Powers of Germany and Austria-Hungary before the war started, and were further advantaged by superior British shipping, financial markets, and credit underlying the entente. This enabled Britain and its allies to mobilize their economies and wage economic warfare against the weaker Central Powers.[9] As for the United States, the Allied Powers had taken some 63 percent of its prewar exports, while only 15 percent had gone to Germany.[10]

Although Wilson periodically protested British violation of U.S. maritime neutrality rights, he tacitly accepted Britain's Hunger Blockade of Germany, a violation of international law, and never condemned this inhumane naval action. William Jennings Bryan, Wilson's secretary of state, even wrote an unanswered note to the president asking, "Why be shocked at the drowning of a few people [by German submarine attacks] if there is to be no objection to starving a nation [by Britain's naval blockade]?"[11]

The Germans were the first to use mines by scattering a few off the British coast. However, the British used this permissible German action to take the unprecedented step of indiscriminately mining the entire North Sea and then tightening up their naval blockade's "contraband" rules to include food. The British required neutral ships to stop in Britain for inspection before indicating the safe routes through the minefields. In short, the British were trying to starve out the German nation, including civilians, which Wilson did not condemn and which by 1918 made Germany desperate for food. The British mines had the potential to kill more indiscriminately than the German counter to the British blockade—a submarine campaign against shipping—and were unpopular with other neutral countries near the North Sea. However, because the British minefields had the potential to be so lethal, neutral ships usually stopped in London first; in contrast, the lower effectiveness of German submarines invited neutral and merchant ships to try to make it past them into Britain. Therefore, British mines killed almost no Americans, while German submarines killed foolish American risk-takers in the low hundreds.

Rather than criticizing the British blockade and other violations of American neutral maritime rights, Wilson chose to focus on condemning the German establishment of war zones around Allied countries. German submarines would attack Britain-, France-, and Italy-bound commerce without warning ships of their submarine's presence—attacking mostly ships of belligerent nations but occasionally those of neutral nations by mistake. No international law existed on the use of submarines when the Germans began deploying them in 1914; thus Britain, the United States, and other neutrals preposterously applied "cruiser rules" for surface vessels to the U-boats. Those rules required a submarine to surface to give a merchant vessel a warning before shooting an undersea torpedo at it, and these under-armed and thin-skinned boats were quite vulnerable to attack by merchant ship cannons or ramming when not submerged.

Overall, Germany's submarine campaign wanted to build pressure on Allied shipborne commerce to obtain relaxation of the Britain's Hunger Blockade against it. Had Wilson demanded that the British end the Hunger Blockade while threatening to end all economic relations with Britain, he could have hurt this maritime power much more than he could have the German land power. However, right from the start of the European war in 1914, increased trade with Britain and France had brought the United States out of a severe recession, giving it faux wartime prosperity as well as giving Wilson and the minority Democratic Party a shot at doing well in the 1916 presidential election.[12] If the United States had been truly neutral—instead of selling great quantities of arms, other war supplies, and food to the Allies (but almost none to Germany) and giving those financially strapped nations credit with which to buy them—German submarines might have scrupulously avoided any risk of attacking Americans and their ships traveling through war zones. Indeed, Germany was suffering under the British blockade, needing all the friends it could muster.[13]

In early February 1915, when Germany declared a war zone around Allied nations, warning its submarines would attack adversary merchant ships, their intent was to force neutral nations to keep their people and cargoes off those vessels. However, contrary to international law, British ships regularly flew neutral flags to confuse the Germans, putting genuinely neutral ships at risk. German mistakes were bound to happen.[14] Furthermore, Woodrow Wilson asserted the right of Americans to travel on ships of belligerent nations, some armed or carrying war munitions, through the dangerous war zones.

On May 7, 1915, a German submarine sank the British ship *Lusitania* in St. George's Channel between Ireland and Wales in the war zone, killing almost 1,200 people, including 128 Americans. The *Lusitania* was carrying weapons and supplies from the United States to Britain. Before the *Lusitania* sailed, the German embassy in Washington, DC had placed advertisements in major American newspapers warning that travelers should avoid sailing on ships of Britain or her wartime allies because they were susceptible to attack and destruction. Despite the German warning and that Americans were traveling on a belligerent ship sailing through a war zone carrying British munitions, many Americans were outraged at the *Lusitania*'s sinking.

Wilson (like McKinley) initially kept his indignation to himself, possibly remembering how the sinking of the battleship USS *Maine* in Havana harbor in 1898 had caused pressure to mount for the United States to go to war with Spain, However, the *Lusitania* incident would begin a cascade of events that would lead to America's entry into the war almost two years later. The incident inflamed American public opinion and destroyed German-American diplomatic relations during that period.

The idealistic Wilson believed that if the United States were to have a voice in the postwar peace—one of his major goals—it would need to defend international law and neutral maritime rights to keep its global prestige. Wilson wanted to be tough when the Germans refused to make an apology or give reparations for those killed on the *Lusitania*, but Secretary of State William Jennings Bryan recommended the simple solution of stopping Americans from boarding belligerent ships; alternatively, Wilson could have announced that if Americans traveled on belligerent vessels, the U.S. government would not take responsibility for their safety. If Wilson had adopted Bryan's simple solution and kept Americans off belligerent vessels, the United States would likely never have taken the disastrous path of entry into World War I against the Germans.

Wilson did not want a dispute with Bryan, the head of the powerful "isolationist" wing of the Democratic Party, since it could hurt his chances of getting reelected in 1916. Bryan quit anyway; he felt Wilson was not neutral, would continue with his warlike rhetoric toward Germany, and was ignoring his counsel.

Bryan was not the only one who thought Wilson's aggressiveness in holding the Germans responsible for American deaths in the war zones was unnecessarily provocative; many in Congress did so too. In February 1916 Congress tried to pass the Gore-McLemore Resolution, which would have kept U.S. citizens and their trade from entering warzones. Wilson would have none of it.[15] He erroneously believed Congress was unconstitutionally intruding on his power to conduct foreign policy. He also insisted on the breathtakingly dubious right of Americans to ride on belligerent British merchant ships—some of them armed, making them actual combatants—carrying munitions through the war zones.

Kaiser Wilhelm II best summarized the hypocrisy of Wilson's neutrality rights assertions:

> Humanity in Wilson's head means unlimited possibilities for real or hypothetical citizens of the USA to cruise about on hostile and armed merchantmen whenever they like in a war zone. Should these partially paid protections to British ships by chance be killed or wounded by us is inhuman. But sending millions of shells and cartridges to England and her allies to kill and maim thousands of German soldiers is not inhuman but quite proper because very lucrative. . . . [That] the British threaten the hunger war against all noncombatants women and children in Central Europe is absolutely not inhuman in Wilson's eyes and quite right. But that Germany should by all means possible parry this diabolical plan and the practices of England to put it into execution even at the expense of some American passengers who have no right to get in its way—that is inadmissible and very wrong in the eyes of Wilson and most inhuman. Either starve at England's bidding or war with America. This is in name of Wilson's humanity.[16]

Alternatively, Wilson could have banned all armed ships from U.S. ports. Under neutrality rules, neutral countries could allow defensively armed foreign merchant ships into their harbors but not offensive warships. If the United States had also banned defensively armed merchant vessels from American ports—that is, armed British ships hauling U.S.-made munitions and other war supplies to Britain—the vulnerable German submarines might have been more willing to surface safely, warn the contraband carrier, and allow the crew and passengers to get into lifeboats before sinking the merchant ship.[17] Because this possible U.S. policy change made the submarine's hunting easier, Wilson rejected it as being unfair to Britain. (He did not regard the original British transgression, the illegal Hunger Blockade against Germany that drove all else, as being unfair to the German civilians.) However, it might have saved more neutral and even British lives.

Germany did not want the United States, with the world's largest economy, to join Britain, France, and Russia as an adversary. In March 1916 a reckless U-boat commander sank the *Sussex*, a French cross-English Channel passenger ferry. Despite the "unrestricted" moniker for German submarine warfare policy, it allowed the sinking of armed merchant marine ships without warning but not passenger ships. The *Sussex* attack had violated even the stated German policy and caused eighty casualties, including four injured Americans. Wilson warned the Germans that if such indiscriminate attacks against cargo or passenger vessels continued, the United States would break diplomatic relations with Germany. This threat, based on Wilson's unrealistic demands concerning U.S. neutrality rights, would later drag the United States into the war when Wilson had to make good on it.

In March 1916, fearing U.S. entry into the conflict, the civilian German government rescinded unrestricted submarine warfare against the Allies, which they had begun in early 1915. Germany issued the Sussex Pledge, which restricted its submarine warfare to not targeting passenger ships and American merchant ships unless they carried weapons—and even then, only after arranging for the safety of the merchant crew and passengers (reestablishment of "cruiser rules"). Of course, private Americans and companies were benefitting or making money off such shipping through a war zone, so they should have borne the personal or commercial risk of doing so. Wilson could have simply declared, "If American citizens choose to assume the considerable risk of traveling or shipping to a belligerent country through a war zone, the U.S. government will not be responsible for the safety of their efforts." He did not do that but instead accepted the Sussex Pledge, which ensured the Germans would abide by international rules of not attacking merchant ships without warning them first.

Wilson was now free from worry in an election year about Germans sinking and killing Americans, no matter how irresponsible his fellow U.S. citizens had been. He knew that the Germans might prefer his election, because the alternative Republicans were more hawkish about the United States joining the war on the Allied side.[18] In fact, the timing of the Sussex Pledge in March 1916, and its recission at the end of January 1917 after the American election was over, indicates that Wilson's surmise was correct. Wilson leaned into the peace theme during the 1916 election campaign, using the slogan "He kept us out of war" to nail down the support of the Bryan wing of the Democratic Party and women voters, who could then vote in twelve states. Wilson's slogan may have provided the margin for his narrow reelection victory in November 1916 because he won ten of those twelve states.[19] However, Republicans managed to gain seats in both houses of Congress, eroding the large Democratic majorities of his first term and leaving only razor-thin control in the House.[20] These lackluster election results were a slim reed on which to bolster his ultimate postelection decision for war, especially after his apparently winning anti-war slogan.

In December 1916, after Wilson had been reelected, Germany made a peace overture to the Allied nations through the still ostensibly neutral United States. However, Britain and France rejected Germany's offer because the Germans wanted to keep the portions of France and Belgium that they had already gained and occupied. The Allied nations refused because they expected the United States to enter the war, allowing them to win it instead of compromising with Germany. Thus, if the United States would have remained on the sidelines, a negotiated settlement would have most likely occurred, moving Europe's boundaries only slightly.[21]

The German Sussex Pledge to restrict submarine warfare, however, came with the stipulation that it was only good if the British ended their illegal violation of neutral maritime rights, including their Hunger Blockade against Germany. The Germans expected Wilson to pressure Britain to end the blockade. However, when the British asked Colonel House, Wilson's principal adviser, if they should remove the blockade, the Anglophile said no. It was not in the British interest to remove their blockade—for its own sake of putting immense economic pressure on Germany and because German submarine retaliation for it might eventually bring the United States into the war on Britain's side. And because no pressure existed from the Americans to do so, why abandon such an effective tool—one which would contribute heavily to Allied victory in the war.

After his reelection, on January 22, 1917, Wilson went to the Senate to declare that only a "peace without victory" among equals in Europe, guaranteed by the United States, would be sustainable. Wilson's desire for a key role in negotiating any postwar settlement in Europe and elsewhere was a motivating force for his eventual entry into the war—because, the

British told him, such entry would be necessary for that outcome to happen. Yet Wilson's role in such a refashioning of the world was not needed and was thus merely a vanity project.

Triggers for U.S. Late Entry into the War

The triggering events for U.S. entry into the almost three-year-old war were the resumption, on February 1, 1917, of unrestricted German submarine against all sea traffic in the European war zones (near Britain, France, Italy, and the eastern Mediterranean) and the Zimmermann Telegram. A good chance existed that the United States would enter the conflict if Germany reinstituted unrestricted submarine warfare, and some in the German government may have believed U.S. entry was inevitable with or without it, given the faux U.S. neutrality that existed.[22] The swashbuckling German military, whom the war had made the effective rulers of Germany, had overoptimistically concluded that its submarines could defeat Allied forces by cutting off their munitions, food, and other imports from abroad before the United States could effectively get military forces into the war (the German submarine effort nearly worked, before the British adoption of an effective convoy system, which grouped merchant ships and protected them with surface warships). However, Erich Ludendorff, the general that was really in charge of the German state and war effort at the time, told a fellow military officer, "The Americans are just bluffing. They have no intention of declaring war against us."[23] After the U.S. military's failure to capture bandit Pancho Villa in its failed invasion of Mexico in 1916, the Germans had only derision for the martial capabilities of America's ill-prepared and inexperienced forces.

Nevertheless, the Germans understandably felt that U.S. neutrality had been compromised by supplying munitions, food, and loans to the Allies and not protesting Britain's Hunger Blockade against Germany, while loudly complaining about Germany's submarine activities. The British had even blacklisted eighty U.S. companies that legally traded with Germany. In fact, as the European war progressed and American exports to the Allies increased, U.S. policy had become more favorable to the Allies and more aggressive against the German submarine campaign, which threatened those exports and thus the American economy.

In early 1917, when the Germans overoptimistically resumed the unrestricted submarine policy, if Wilson had earlier stopped U.S.

commercial ships from being in war zones and banned American citizens from riding on belligerent ships, even this German reescalation would not have necessitated U.S. entry into the war. The Germans did not even resume a completely unrestricted policy and would have allowed some well-identified U.S. ships to travel over specific routes through the war zones.

Because the tacitly unneutral United States' economic prosperity had come to depend on exports and loans to the Allies, Wilson, later in the European war, found it harder to ban American people and ships from war zones. Britain and France were now almost broke; only by openly siding with the Allies could the U.S. government safeguard the credit given by American banks to those nations.[24] And even more U.S. credit was only provided to the financially desperate Allied nations when the United States entered the war.[25] Had the Germans known Britain and France were very near financial collapse, they would have been smarter to keep submarine warfare restricted to keep the United States out of the war.

That U.S. politicians were acutely aware of their need to preserve the American war-induced trade, and the prosperity derived from it, was shown quantitatively by Benjamin Fordham. In a probit regression analysis of key congressional war votes, he discovered a relationship between pro-war votes and regions of the country increasing their exports to the Allied side in the conflict. Wilson was also aware of the need for "war prosperity" for his electoral health and that of his party. Historical sources have demonstrated that Wilson had repeated concerns about the 11 percent of the U.S. economy that exports represented, 80 percent of which went to Allied powers in 1917. Fordham concluded that from the spring of 1915 until the U.S. declaration of war in April 1917, the aggressiveness of Wilson's policy toward the German submarine campaign tracked closely with the increasing export boom to Allied nations and German success in sinking shipping.[26]

In the wake of German resumption of an unrestricted submarine policy, Wilson broke diplomatic relations with Germany but still hoped to avoid entry into the war. He did not believe the Germans would attack U.S. (and other neutral) merchant ships in the war zones without warning or passenger rescue. Wilson was wrong again and not for the last time.

As for the Zimmerman telegram, German Foreign Minister Arthur Zimmermann had issued a secret diplomatic cable that ordered his minister in Mexico to propose an alliance with Mexico if the United States entered the war against Germany. The cable said if Mexico were to join to fight, it could get back Texas, Arizona, and New Mexico, taken by the United States in the Mexican War (1846–1848). Wilson had enabled this hypothetical possibility by two needless and reckless invasions of Mexico in the years just before U.S. entry into the European war. The British had intercepted the Zimmermann Cable and eagerly gave it to Wilson, who then made it public instead of issuing a stern private missive and waiting for a German explanation.

In the wake of the Zimmermann Telegram, Wilson bowed to his cabinet's demand that the United States arm its merchant ships, making them legal combatants in contravention of Congress's refusal to approve doing so. Originally, Wilson had dubiously claimed his implied "constitutional duties and powers," not a congressionally passed statute, allowed him to arm the ships but that he preferred that Congress back his effort[27] (similar unconstitutional reasoning was used by both George Bushes in the two Iraq wars). When Congress did not do so, Wilson took unconstitutional unilateral action anyway under the equally dubious anti-piracy law of 1797[28]; this move was a clear instance of the executive encroachment on the legislative branch's constitutional power to initiate war by presenting it with a fait accompli and putting U.S. ships in imminent danger of being attacked.

Americans should not have expected their government to guarantee their travel to or trade with countries in conflict through war zones while travelling on belligerent ships or to obstruct Germany from entering into an alliance with Mexico, which Mexico said it was not even considering. Furthermore, such a German proposal for alliance was only conditional on the United States going to war with Germany. Still, Americans were outraged by both Germany's restoration of "unrestricted" submarine warfare and the Zimmermann Telegram. When President Wilson asked that Congress recognize a state of war with Germany on April 2, 1917, it complied. By earlier threatening to break diplomatic relations with the Germans if they did not stop unrestricted submarine warfare and having obliged himself to follow through on his severe threat when they resumed the practice, Wilson had put the United States on the road to war.[29] Wilson believed American honor and prestige was at stake.

U.S. Entry in the War Was Avoidable

U.S. Politics

At the start of the European war in the last part of 1914, most Americans were mildly pro-British, but 20 percent of the U.S. populace were of ethnic populations who strongly favored Germany—German Americans, the second-largest nationality in America; Irish Americans who hated Britain; and Jewish and Scandinavian Americans who disliked Russia. These ethnic populations—"hyphenated Americans" as Woodrow Wilson derisively called them—perhaps had kept the strongly Anglophile U.S. government and Woodrow Wilson out of the war longer than either of them had desired. The American nongovernmental elite—the media fueled by a British propaganda effort in America, U.S. business interests, and the educational community—were also pro-British. Benjamin O. Fordham's probit analysis of congressional votes on war-related matters showed that political jurisdictions with larger percentages of the population born in Ireland or the Central Powers correlated with anti-war votes of their members of Congress.

The choices were not between which side of the war to join but whether to join the Triple Entente or to stay truly neutral. While clearly having favorites in the European war, most Americans wanted to stay neutral because U.S. security was not at stake in the conflict. Nevertheless, in late 1915, as the United States was pursuing a policy of faux neutrality, Wilson accused these ethnic Americans of disloyalty for supporting the very policy that he claimed he was following.

More generally, an anti-imperialism attitude arising from the long and brutal American counterinsurgency in the Philippines was driving the preference for neutrality among the U.S. electorate with regard to the European war. For this primary reason Wilson ran for reelection in 1916 on the slogan, "He kept us out of war." In particular, he was courting the vote of women, whose vote had led to wins in some western states. Their votes more than likely put him over the top in his uphill battle for reelection, because many women feared a Republican president would send their boys to the European war. Instead, they voted for a man who promised to continue neutrality. However, after Wilson safely, but narrowly, won reelection, war soon followed in 1917.[30]

U.S. Economics

Although Wilson protested ever-increasing British maritime neutrality rights violations, for economic and political reasons, he could not realistically threaten Britain in that regard. Britain, with the most powerful navy on the planet, controlled Atlantic shipping and had begun rapidly buying American explosives, farm products, and iron and steel for its war efforts. The United States had been in a severe two-year recession beginning in January 1913 and, by early 1914, the country was on the cusp of an economic depression, with its industrial capacity, the largest in the world, running at only 60 percent. Allied war orders from August through October 1914 turned the economy around quickly and enhanced the minority Democratic Party chances in future elections. Wilson had won the presidency in 1912 only because the then-dominant Republican Party had split in two between supporters of former presidents William Howard Taft and Theodore Roosevelt.[31]

After the Germans met Wilson's demands in early 1916 by restricting submarine activity, U.S. trade in weapons, food, and other war supplies to Britain and France became less risky, allowing Americans to prosper even more than in the early years of the European war. Originally, Wilson had outlawed loans to belligerents as unneutral, but when the Allied nations could no longer afford to pay cash for U.S. exports, he rescinded the ban on credits and then on loans. U.S. bankers believed the more self-sufficient Germany was more likely to lose the war and were thus more reluctant to lend money there. Thus, although claiming to be neutral, the United States was hardly so in practice. Early in the European War, and long before U.S. official entry in April 1917, the United States was an economic ally of Britain and France.

The longer the war remained in a stalemate, the more the financially desperate Allies became dependent on U.S. credit to purchase war supplies. On the other hand, because of the continuing British naval blockade, the United States did not conduct much commerce with or lending to Germany. Because the United States had made many more loans to the Allies than to the Central Powers, it developed an interest in an Allied victory in the war so that the loans could be paid back more readily to overextended American banks—although some loans to Britain had collateral from the British Empire backing them that would not have been much affected by a German victory in the war (provided that a triumphant and colony-hungry Germany did not demand Britain surrender some of its colonies).

When the Germans reinstituted unrestricted submarine warfare in the war zones around Britain, France, Italy, and the eastern Mediterranean in January 1917 and began intentionally sinking American ships transiting those zones, U.S. commerce with the Allies again became riskier, threatening "neutral" American war prosperity. Thus, although even then Wilson was not thirsting for war with Germany,[32] he had allowed the health of the U.S. economy to become artificially dependent on the export to European allies of munitions and other war supplies.

Geopolitics

If Britain had not entered the conflict and blockaded Germany by sea, the United States could have easily stayed out of the conflict. Niall Ferguson, a prominent British historian, believes that Kaiser's Germany was not an existential threat to Britain. Two prominent analysts agreed, disputing German historian Fritz Fischer's claim that Germany's desire to be a world power was driving German behavior during the European crisis of 1914. They noted that such German ambitions were trending at the turn of the twentieth century but had since dissipated. Instead, Germany wanted to set up a subcontinental power base in Eastern Europe that would enable it to carry out expected future global competition. Revival of German ambitions to be a global power only happened after the war started. However, even then, Britain and France, with their worldwide empires and unconstrained access to the Atlantic Ocean, were better bets than Germany to decide the future of the world. Germany was even less of a threat to a United States across that big ocean. Nevertheless, despite the limited German threat to the United States per se, one of the Wilson administration's reasons for entering the war was also an exaggerated fear that Germany might become the leader of a Eurasian power bloc.[33]

However, a German victory over France and Russia would only have made Germany the leading power on the European continent. It would not have destroyed the European security system. Ferguson believes that British's entry into World War I eventually led to World War II and that these two expensive victorious wars led to the eventual financial exhaustion and collapse of the British Empire, which he thinks was a needless turn of events. The British government felt obligated to enter the war because of the entente (informal alliance) its foreign minister had arranged with France and kept secret from its own cabinet, parliament, and public in the years leading up to the war. Unlike the more formal alliances that had dragged reluctant continental nations into what would become a Europe-wide conflagration—Russia by Serbia, France by Russia, and Germany by Austria-Hungary—the more informal nature of the entente, despite secret British military planning with France against Germany, could have more easily allowed Britain to stay out of the war on the continent. (The lesson here is that both formal and informal alliances are supposed to be a means to achieve security, not an end in themselves, and should be entered with caution because they can actually undermine security by dragging countries into unwanted war.)

Another rationale the British government had used for entry into the conflict was the need to guarantee the neutrality of Belgium, which Germany had moved through to conduct its preemptive attack on France. Yet Germany had offered to let Belgium surrender in advance, and Belgium's neutrality was guaranteed by multiple nations, not just Britain. The huge international outrage about overstated German atrocities in its transit of small, innocent, and neutral Belgium contrasted sharply with its indifference to the fact that not long before, Belgian King Leopold II had used torture and forced labor to loot the Congo, his personal colonial possession, of resources and had committed genocide, killing ten million Congolese.

The German Threat to the U.S. Was Limited

If the Kaiser's Germany posed little existential danger to the offshore island of Britain, it was an even more remote threat to the United States, half a huge ocean away. Unlike in World War II, after Adolf Hitler declared war on the United States following the Japanese attack on Pearl Harbor, German submarines before U.S. entry into World War I were not attacking American commerce just off the U.S. coast but instead had set up their war zones only around Allied nations in Europe. The United States could have just kept its ships and commerce out of those faraway combat areas, but the opportunities to trade with Allied belligerents were just too lucrative to pass up.

By the time Wilson asked Congress to recognize a state of war against Germany on April 2, 1917, this action was more than two months after Germany had resumed unrestricted submarine warfare on February 1 and more than a month after Britain had showed the Zimmerman telegram to Wilson on February 22. By then the telegram had diminished in importance in triggering Wilson's action; as he noted in his message to Congress, the sinking of U.S. merchant ships in the European war zones and loss of American life was the primary cause of his request for a declaration of war.[34] Yet from 1914 up until the April 6, 1917, U.S. war declaration, 222 of the 236 Americans killed by German submarines had been riding on ships of belligerent nations.[35] Similarly, from 1914 to the resumption of unrestricted submarine warfare at the beginning of February 1917, the Germans had only, and mistakenly, put ten American merchant ships below the waves. After the declaration, however, in March 1917 alone, nine were purposefully sunk, an immediate acceleration in American loss of life.

Studies of American public opinion show that even after the Zimmermann Telegram and the increasing U.S. ship sinkings by German submarines in February and March 1917, few Americans favored U.S. entry into the war. Most members of Congress in both houses were undecided; Wilson's war message of April 2 had persuaded a large majority to vote for war, but his restraint could have pushed them the other way.[36] Thus, Wilson led the United States needlessly into its first war on the European continent—and a cataclysmic one at that—purportedly to avenge only 236 American deaths at sea, with little inkling how his decision would dramatically change Europe and the world in the 20th century.

American Idealism

America tends to be an idealistic country, especially when *rationalizing* war. Wilson supposedly had entered the war to "make the world safe for democracy." As has been the case with many wars in the history of the American republic, President Wilson—whose purported idealism was at odds with his actions—felt he had to demonize the German enemy and glorify his allies, including Russia which, after the initial revolution overthrowing autocratic czarist government, now seemed to fit more neatly into the "liberal democracy" category. Yet Britain and France still had extensive empires. The German government, which before the war had been a liberal state with a powerful parliament and, ironically, a wider voting franchise than Britain, did not become so militaristic until the war started. Wilson—though elected—had more power than the hereditary German Kaiser and would go on to ruthlessly stamp out domestic dissent on U.S. entry into the war, though he understood quite well that the European war was not solely Germany's fault. Instead of explaining to Americans that the European-wide war was the fault of several countries (including Britain), nationalism, imperialism, and European alliance systems, Wilson made Germany out to be the lone villain.[37] Otherwise, how could the president justify the threat to the United States after waiting almost three years to act? The American public became disillusioned by the gap between Wilson's rhetoric and reality. A new international order did not arise after the war—as U.S. "democratic" allies (the brutal British and French empires) either feasted on new imperial possessions or, farther east, fell further into a despotic totalitarian revolution (Russia).

Late U.S. Entry Ensures Allied Victory

Unlike Germany's successful eastern theater against Russia, its western theater in France was locked into a static war of attrition within the trenches early in the European war. By the spring of 1917, when the United States entered the war, the military fortunes of Britain and France were particularly abysmal and did not improve as Russia left the war after its revolution later that year, allowing Germany to transfer troops from the eastern front to the western sector.[38] The carnage was staggering for Germany, Britain, and France, and the front in the west had hardly moved in four years. U.S. entry into the war eventually helped break this gridlock in favor of Britain and France.[39]

The American declaration of war in April 1917 had a profound impact on the outcome of the war, less by its battlefield participation than by opening new lending to financially collapsing Britain and France. An Entente financial meltdown in 1917, when combined with battlefield reversals that year, would most likely have ended the war in Germany's favor. To prevent that, from the summer of 1917 to the spring of 1919, the U.S. government lent the Entente countries $11 billion.[40]

The Bolshevik Revolution in Russia in late 1917 allowed the Germans to transfer more divisions to the western front and launch offensives to try to win the war in 1918, which they came close to doing. However, the American declaration of war in April 1917 had allowed Britain and France, expecting eventual American reinforcements, to commit reserves to battle in 1917 they were saving for 1918. Also, U.S. entry caused the Germans to launch the costly (in men and money) offensives on sea and land to try to win the war before masses of fresh U.S. troops arrived in France (in all, two million). If Americans had not declared war and eventually made their way to the front, the Germans could have fallen back to a defense line and inflicted heavy casualties on Britain and France. At that point in history, due to the invention of the machine gun, defensive warfare was dominant over offensive attacks.

In the spring of 1918, the prospect of U.S. reinforcements to Europe boosted British and French morale, allowing them to beat back the last of several German offensives. Later in 1918, after the failure of the German spring offensives, German morale collapsed during an Allied summer counteroffensive that included 850,000 fresh American forces. The likely reason for German losses was the failure of the earlier offensives and because of the bleak outlook for Germany, given the anticipated infusion of even larger numbers of fresh U.S. troops.[41] Also, the British naval blockade was causing German starvation and malnutrition. To end the suffering, Germany signed an armistice, and the guns fell silent on November 11, 1918.

U.S. Contributes to German Revenge and Communism's Rise

Wilson and the Punitive Peace

If the United States came out of the Spanish-American War as a world power, it emerged from World War I as the premier nation in the world.[42] Although faraway America had sustained a high casualty rate (116,000 deaths in only about a half a year of fighting), it experienced no domestic physical destruction and far fewer total casualties than the nations in the thick of the four-year European fight. World War I led to the collapse of the German Hohenzollern, Austro-Hungarian Hapsburg, Russian Romanov, and Turkish Ottoman Empires. Even the victorious French and British empires suffered immense physical or psychological damage. Everywhere, the smashing of social fabrics brought on by the war's unbridled carnage gave rise to violent extremism at both ends of the political spectrum.[43] U.S. entry into the war made violent anticolonialism, fascism, and communism possible.

Woodrow Wilson hoodwinked the Germans. They reached an armistice thinking they were going to get a generous peace settlement based on Wilson's idealistic Fourteen Points. The president announced his war aims publicly on January 8, 1918, more than nine months after entering the conflict. No matter: during the ensuing post-war peace negotiations at Versailles, which excluded the Germans, the Allies forced a harsh and humiliating peace deal on them. Rather than the late enunciation of war aims, Wilson should have used the presidential bully pulpit, as he had on many other occasions, to tell Americans before the U.S. entered the conflict in early April 1917 why he believed they needed to join the fight. He could have then used his tremendous leverage with Britain and France, before U.S. entry, to establish the peace terms for Germany. After the United States had entered the war those allies, hard-nosed realists, paid little attention to what they regarded as Wilson's annoying and naïve idealism.

The Versailles peace agreement levied heavy reparations against the Germans to be paid to the now heavily indebted Britain and France; allowed France to occupy a portion of Germany and confiscate its resources; transferred German military equipment to Allied nations; established limits on the capabilities of the future German military; and made Germany sign a humiliating war guilt clause, even though it had been no more culpable in causing the conflict than had any other belligerent. With little negotiating leverage at the peace negotiations at this late date, even after having tipped the balance in the war, Wilson had pleaded with Britain and France to go lighter on the reparations, which they quickly rebuffed. He and Secretary of State Robert Lansing, who was Bryan's successor and a pro-British hawk, acknowledged privately that the final peace agreement at Versailles was draconian and humiliating for Germany. Instead, Wilson disingenuously declared publicly that the peace was "severe only because great wrongs done by Germany are to be righted and repaired." A young Wilson adviser, William Bullitt, understandably felt that the awful terms of the treaty were much more painful than Wilson had promised or admitted. Bullitt organized a mass resignation to protest them. Bullitt presciently predicted that the new suppressions would bring "a new century of war."[44] Even an important war ally—Japan—walked out of the Versailles talks when the Allies rejected its proposed "racial equality" section in the treaty. Japanese anger over this significant slight would cause adverse repercussions, contributing to the causes of World War II in the Pacific.

Unlike the enlightened peace reached by the Congress of Vienna in 1815 after the Napoleonic Wars, which had wisely welcomed a defeated France back into the European system, the peace of Versailles was foolish, punitive, and bound to cause a revanchist backlash in a nationalistic German nation. At Versailles, a vindictive Britain and (especially) France wanted to punish Germany and keep it down. Instead, they caused the rise of National Socialism (Nazism) not long after. The reparations they demanded may have contributed to Germany's hyperinflation in the 1920s by giving the country an incentive to inflate its currency to pay Britain and France in devalued German Rentenmarks. The hyperinflation disrupted the German economy, contributing to Hitler's demonic rise, along with a German nationalist backlash against the reparations and the war guilt clause of the peace treaty.

Republicans in control of Congress correctly feared that Wilson would give away too much to Britain and France at Versailles to get their agreement for the creation of a League of Nations, a world association of nations that was the crown jewel of Wilson's idealistic Fourteen Points.[45] Although the United States had tipped the stagnated war toward Allied victory, Wilson let Britain and France outmaneuver him to rub Germany's nose in defeat. Wilson made concessions to get his two wartime allies to agree to his League, which the U.S. Senate rejected joining because of the legitimate fears that American sovereignty would be compromised and Congress's power to declare war would be eroded by transferring it to other members of the League.

The war helped cause the 1930s Great Depression by pushing a far more open prewar world economy back toward economic autarky. The pain of Germany's war reparations eventually had to be lessened, and the French occupation of the German Ruhr region was finally ended. Yet economic depression, hyperinflation induced by the war, reparations, and the humiliation of the war guilt clause of the Versailles Treaty damaged the postwar Weimar Republic. Adolf Hitler's later mesmerizing attack speeches focused on German humiliation at the Versailles peace negotiations.

In addition to Wilson allowing his wartime allies to impose such humiliation on Germany, he also paved the way for Hitler's ascent by demanding the abdication of the Kaiser. He then insisted that democratically elected German representatives sign the armistice ending the war. These horrendous Wilsonian missteps allowed the Kaiser and the German

Army to transfer the blame for Germany's defeat onto the new democratic Weimar government, from which it never recovered.[46]

Bolshevism

Wilson also contributed to the Bolshevik Revolution in Russia. In contrast to Britain and France in the western theater, the Russians lost decisively in the eastern theater in a much more mobile war. The horrible carnage of the war led to the first revolution in Russia in early 1917, overthrowing the autocratic tsar and putting a Provisional Government, dominated by Alexander Kerensky, in power.

In February 1917, even before the United States declared war, Wilson offered the broke Russian Provisional Government the equivalent of about $4 billion in today's dollars if it would stay in the war; the Provisional Government took the deal. In general, Wilson and the leaders of Britain and France made Western aid conditional on Kerensky's shaky and desperate government staying in the war and keeping open a second front against Germany. Yet staying in a very unpopular war undermined Russia's nascent democratic experiment and turned out to be the Provisional Government's undoing. The Germans also helped by sending Bolshevik leader Vladimir Lenin back to Russia secretly on a special train. The Bolshevik Party was the only party in Russia that advocated an immediate peace with the Germans, which was popular with a war-weary Russian population (1.7 million Russians were killed in the war). Also, Russian offensives against the Germans had badly decimated and exhausted the Russian economy and army, leaving it too weak to defend the Provisional Government. In late 1917, Lenin ruthlessly seized power. He famously said, "Our revolution was born of the war." To concentrate on consolidating power in Russia, Lenin then quickly capitulated to a one-sided peace with Germany, thus blowing up the Western strategy to keep Russia, at any cost, in the war as a second front against the Germans.

Now the Allies had the worst of all worlds—no second front against Germany and a brutal and radical communist regime in Russia. George Kennan, diplomat, historian, and a great authority on Russia, concluded:

> It may be questioned whether the United States government, in company with other western Allies, did not actually hasten and facilitate the failure of the Provisional Government by insisting

that Russia should continue the war effort, and by making this demand the criterion for its support. In asking the leaders of the Provisional Government simultaneously to consolidate their political power and to revive and continue participation in the war, the Allies were asking the impossible.[47]

According to historian Jim Powell, Lenin would have been at best only a minor footnote in history if Wilson had not bribed and browbeaten Kerensky's Provisional Government into staying in a horrendous war. That said, the prospect of U.S. entry into the war gave the Provisional Government some hope of being on the winning side.

Wilson and his British and French allies then compounded their earlier blunder by invading Russia as the war ended. They fecklessly intervened to help White (anti-Bolshevik) forces against Lenin and Trotsky's Red (Bolshevik) forces in the Russian civil war, which had followed soon after the Bolshevik Revolution. After the Bolsheviks won the civil war, this Western intervention led to many years of bad blood between the capitalist West and the Soviet Union. The roots of Russian suspicions of the West began at the end of World War I, not at the Potsdam Conference toward the end of World War II.

Conservative historian Richard Pipes best summarizes the war-induced Russian Revolution's effect on Germany and the world: "Had it not been for the Russian Revolution, there very likely would have been no National Socialism; probably no Second World War and no decolonization; and certainly no Cold War."[48]

Adolf Hitler used the Bolshevik threat as a foil in his rise to power in Germany and in his justification for invading the Soviet Union in 1941. At the end of World War I, the ideological clash between Bolshevists and Western powers planted Cold War seeds, as did the postwar invasion of Russia by the western Allies to try and fail to help non-Bolsheviks defeat Lenin and Trotsky.

Domestic Ramifications of the War

Unconstitutional Suppression of Civil Liberties

The "neutral" years, from the start of the European war in August 1914 to the U.S. declaration of war in April 1917, saw U.S. law enforcement pursue German foreign agents on American soil much more ardently than their British counterparts. The British operated freely on U.S. soil, even running a huge propaganda campaign for their side in the war.

As noted, the war led directly to the Bolshevik Revolution in Russia and Wilson's military intervention against the new government in the subsequent Russian civil war, which brought the overseas battle against the "reds" home. Actions against the "reds" in Russia led to irrational fears of a communist takeover in the United States, a country that was not prone or conducive to communism. As in the Cold War later in the century, U.S. fighting with communists overseas led to so-called red scares at home and the violation of domestic civil liberties. War-induced xenophobia and nationalism fueled the first Red Scare. After a bomb went off at Wilson Attorney General A. Mitchell Palmer's house, the president threw civil liberties to the wind. Wilson ordered the Palmer Raids (1919–1920) against alleged subversive leftists and anarchists, especially those of Italian and Eastern European Jewish descent.

The postwar raids were a hangover from the massive civil liberties violations perpetrated by the Wilson administration against war dissenters, draft protestors, and others who did not support the president's war. In general, Wilson's encroachment on civil liberties ranks as one of the worst in American history—more severe than even the civil liberty infringements by George W. Bush after the 9/11 attacks. With tragic irony, Wilson's request for a declaration of war on April 2, 1917, claimed to be fighting for foreigners' right to have a voice in their governments even as he violated Americans' rights to dissent against U.S. involvement in the conflict:

> The right is more precious than peace, and we shall fight for the things which we have always carried nearest our hearts— for democracy, for the right of those who submit to authority to have a voice in their own Governments, for the rights and liberties of small nations.[49]

Throughout American history, war has been the likeliest way to lose liberties at home. World War I was no exception. While Wilson claimed that the United States entered the war to "make the world safe for democracy," as in almost every other American war, the opposite happened. Vanquishing an alleged foreign aggressor was purported to guarantee American democracy's survival. However, the process of defeating an aggressor builds an undemocratic security state apparatus, which tends to become permanent.

Congress passed the Espionage Act of 1917 to squelch draft protesters and the Sedition Act of 1918 to intimidate and prosecute war dissenters. The Sedition Act banned "uttering, printing, writing, or publishing any disloyal, profane, scurrilous, or abusive language about the United States government or the military." Under the two acts, the Justice Department convicted almost one thousand people; Wilson's attorney general used the two laws to go after the anti-war union, Industrial Workers of the World ("Wobblies"). After the passage of the 1917 and 1918 acts, the FBI created the General Intelligence Division headed by J. Edgar Hoover, who violated Americans' civil liberties not just during the first Red Scare (1919–1920) but for more than fifty years afterward until his death during the Nixon administration.

During the first Red Scare, four thousand suspected radicals were arrested, and hundreds had their U.S. citizenship stripped from them and were deported to the USSR. One prominent dissenter jailed for ten years was Eugene Debs, the Socialist Party presidential candidate. When conservative Warren Harding assumed the presidency in 1921, he wisely freed Debs. The Espionage Act is still in force today, being used to prosecute journalists.

Demonstrating how war warps the rule of law, the Supreme Court ruled unanimously that the Espionage Act did not violate First Amendment free speech rights. The Postmaster General's revocation of inexpensive second-class mailing rates for socialist publications or those soft on the war was a more subtle approach to limiting free speech.[50] Ironically, Wilson resorted to military conscription, a form of state-commandeered hazardous labor to allegedly fight for American liberties and democracy abroad. Wilson demanded and Congress approved censorship, strict export controls, regulation of food production and consumption, and the nationalization of railroads. Congress even delegated its power to appropriate funds to the executive (likely unconstitutionally) by passing the Overman Act in May 1918, which allowed Wilson, in conducting the war, to redirect duties among executive branch agencies and transfer all funding as needed.[51]

The Committee for Public Information, a U.S. government propaganda arm set up to further war efforts, lied about or exaggerated German misdeeds. The propaganda stirred up uber-patriot vigilantes, with government encouragement, to open mail illegally and spy on suspected turncoats. Violent actions against such suspects followed. Nativist and xenophobic sentiments from the war spilled into hatred against immigrants, Jews, Catholics, and African Americans. Race riots happened in twenty-seven cities and a rise in lynching in the south occurred, especially directed toward returning black war veterans who were often proudly wearing their uniforms. The Ku Klux Klan, which first appeared during the post–Civil War Reconstruction, made an even bigger reappearance and this time organized openly, with its members holding political offices. War nativism and xenophobia also led to strict postwar immigration legislation in 1917, 1918, 1921, and 1924 that almost shut down a century of mostly open immigration. Based on race and ethnicity, the new laws drastically reduced immigration from Southern and Eastern Europe and almost ended immigration from Africa and Asia.[52]

Removing Checks and Balances

War usually increases executive power, sometimes enormously. Wilson had dubiously decried the founders' congressionally dominant government as being out of date in a globalized world economy; expanded on McKinley's creation of the bully pulpit to build public pressure on Congress to pass the executive's desired agenda; resumed early presidents' tradition of directly addressing Congress (which Thomas Jefferson had suspended for being too monarchical); and believed that the president should be as big a man as he wanted to be. From his academic career in governmental studies, Wilson knew that foreign policy, and particularly war, would allow presidential power to expand and took advantage of the war to be all he could be.

Wilson took Lincoln's almost-tyrannical rule during the Civil War as a model. Like McKinley, he was able to squelch the creation of a powerful special congressional committee to conduct oversight of executive actions during the war, avoiding how one such panel had at least needled Lincoln at the margins. This exemplifies how executive power in the United States during the Spanish-American War and during World War I had grown even past Civil War levels. In fact, World War I began a series of wars, a severe depression, and a Cold War in the twentieth century that would send U.S. presidential power to unconstitutional and then stratospheric levels.

Wilson had increased his power vis-à-vis Congress since the European crisis began in 1914. After the war ended, he displayed it again by dispatching U.S. troops—with his British and French war allies and without congressional authorization (following McKinley's unilateral precedent in China in 1900)—to fight in the Russian civil war.

This questionable augmentation of presidential power led members of Congress from both parties to fear that the League of Nations would further weaken Congress's power, especially to declare war.[53] The war-induced imbalance of power among the branches was a major reason Congress voted down the Versailles Treaty and its attendant membership in the League of Nations. Ironically, Wilson had more power in the United States than the allegedly authoritarian Kaiser had had in Germany, especially in control over foreign policy. The Soviet Union and now Putin's post–Cold War Russia have never forgotten Western intervention in Russia's civil war. This episode may have been a start, or at least an important precursor, to the U.S.-Soviet Cold War.

Wilson was trying to use his oratorical bully pulpit to sell the public on the treaty and the League through a national speaking tour when he had a series of strokes that incapacitated him. In the ultimate demonstration of how powerful the presidency had become, his second wife, Edith Wilson, secretly ran the country nepotically for around a year and a half until Wilson's second term ended.

Perpetual Big Government

World War I led to the beginning of permanent big government in the United States. War usually leads to government intrusion into the private sector not only in undermining civil liberties but by burrowing its tentacles deeper into the domestic economy. Usually, the bigger the war, the greater the government expansion. Although the growth of government during the Civil War was large, it retracted somewhat after the war was over. During World War I, the effect was even more pronounced, with nearly all economic sectors permanently affected by the government. This government-directed economy elevated levels of government spending and taxation, which lasted into peacetime.

Before World War I, the U.S. federal government expenditure was less than 5 percent of GDP but it ballooned from the "war socialism" of that conflict and never returned to prewar levels. During the war, the federal government, dominated by the military and industry, managed the economy for the first time in American history. The War Industries Board (WIB), controlled by businessmen, regulated industry. The board reduced commercial production, converted industries to war production, and controlled prices, wages, and priorities for production and resource allocation. Yet the board's decisions were stalemated by the War Department's huge requirements for munitions orders. The government was often inefficient or incompetent in producing war matériel for the troops; for example, the crash government effort to produce combat aircraft was a failure, spending much money with limited success.[54]

The U.S. wartime economy became so dysfunctional that President Wilson had to put the board under his direct supervision. An augmented WIB, with Bernard M. Baruch as chairman beginning in March 1918, then integrated military representatives and regulated the economy.[55] According to one of its leaders, the WIB "was an industrial dictatorship without parallel." Wilson's National Labor Relations Board (NLRB) was supposed to mediate industrial disputes between management and labor but that did not prevent wartime strikes. Backed by police, militia, and active troops, the NLRB crushed worker aspirations.[56]

The government nationalized some industries thought to be vital to the war effort, such as the railroads. More important, certain industries used the war to profit from government protection and largesse—for example, government price supports for agriculture—and did not want this to end during peacetime.

This war-induced model of government intervention in the economy during World War I made a reappearance during a later crisis during peacetime: the Great Depression. According to William E. Leuchtenburg, "World War I stimulated a variety of experiments in liberal collectivism and offered analogues for crisis management of the depression years."[57] The government brought back familiar-sounding agencies and some of the same people to run them during the great 1930s economic slowdown. Also during the interwar period, planning for economic mobilization to fight future wars continued, modeled after World War I planning—that is, planning by federal agencies run by military and industrial personnel.[58] Then World War II, arising from the wreckage of World War I and the Depression, brought much more government intervention into the American economy—outright state management of defense that would go on to become the military-industrial-congressional complex.[59] Thus, since World War I, the federal government has never returned to any-where near its small historical level before the First World War.

Globally, most economic historians believe that the war disrupted the first era of economic globalization of the nineteenth century, which had reached its pinnacle after 1870. The great conflict's dislocations of world trade were not fully restored, thus contributing to the later Great Depression, which in turned gave political ammunition to a revanchist Nazi Germany and fascist Italy and helped cause World War II. In the United States, there was plummeting post-World War I demand (espe-cially for U.S. farm exports to Europe), soaring unemployment, deflation, and the claim that the chemical and metal industries needed protection for reasons of defense, which led to greater economic inefficiency. Also, the war bolstered inefficient economic state management of the economy and enhanced the role of central banks in many countries after the war.[60]

To finance the expensive war, Wilson relied heavily on loans. However, he also taxed at levels unseen since the Civil War and Reconstruction days. Unlike Lincoln, Wilson enjoyed constitutional protection after ratification of the Sixteenth Amendment (1913), which gave Congress the power to create an income tax, displacing the tariff as the major source of government revenue, which it had been since the beginning of the republic. To keep a majority supporting the war, the rich faced exorbitant taxation—the income tax rate for the highest income bracket went from 7 percent in 1913 to 77 percent in 1918.[61] Budgetary problems arising from the war led to the creation of the first centralized executive budget in U.S. history through the Budget and Accounting Act of 1921. Centralization of congressional budgeting eventually followed.

Even the disastrous Prohibition movement to ban the production and distribution of alcohol accelerated after U.S. entered the fighting. Led by pietistic Protestants who were hoping to remove the social ills caused by drinking, the movement resorted to flimsy justifications that the gov-ernment had to save grain for wartime use, that well-trained troops should not be allowed to drink in their spare time, and that beer and schnapps were German drinks.

Partisan Politics over Peace

In the end, the war, as most do, came home to partisan shores. Wilson had refused to take important Republicans to the Versailles negotiations and stubbornly refused to court nine Republicans with minor reservations about the League of Nations treaty. Instead, he resorted to the bully pulpit to conduct a speaking tour in the American countryside to pressure senators into voting his way. During this tour, Wilson grandiosely admitted that he had taken the nation into the massive war for reasons other than U.S. national security: "Thousands of our gallant youth lie buried in France, and buried for what? For the redemption of America? America was not directly attacked. For the salvation of America? America was not immediately in danger. No, for the salvation of mankind."[62]

This approach failed. Congress voted down the League of Nations treaty in 1919 because it required signatory nations to help other members defend their territories from aggression, a provision that undermined Congress's power to declare war.

Wilson also ignored Americans disillusionment with the war's carnage. Because of its late entry, America's dead were far smaller than those of the Europeans or Russians, but the intensity of the conflict killed 116,000 Americans from both combat and disease in their mere seven months of engagement on the front (it took a year to get the mostly unprepared American ground forces to Europe). The European meat grinder killed Americans at a faster rate than had the cataclysmic American Civil War.

Wilson had thought that no large-scale U.S. forces would be needed to tip the balance of the war to the allies, only material, financial, and political support after American entry. Wilson thought the belligerents would be so exhausted after almost three years of war that U.S. entry would compel them to reach a negotiated settlement of the conflict. The United States would then be in a dominant position to shape the peace. Yet U.S. formal entry predictably made Britain and France fight harder. At the same time, Germany assumed that the unprepared United States, despite its entry, would not be able to get significant numbers of troops to Europe until two years hence. Once the United States did enter the war, it lost its bargaining power with its allies and thus did not dominate the postwar peace negotiations.[63]

"And the carnage was for what?" Americans asked. After the Bolshevik Revolution in Russia, Vladimir Lenin released Russian documents showing agreements between the governments allied with the United States to carve up the world after the war. So much for Wilson's new world order based on his Fourteen Points. Americans justifiably felt swindled, just as did the Germans.

In the November 1918 midterm election, American public dissatisfaction with the mindless carnage, sacrifice, and economic and social turmoil from the war caused voters to transfer control of both houses of Congress to Wilson's Republican opposition. Voters rejected Wilson's war leadership and his usurpation of government powers. The debacle was one of the worst midterm election defeats in American history and unprecedented during wartime.[64] It kneecapped Wilson's ability to join the League of Nations and shape the postwar world at the Versailles peace conference. In fact, the war led to the eclipse of the Democratic Party for over a decade. Wilson's poor and later vacant leadership; public frustration with the war; and its aftermath of strikes, the first Red Scare, a rocky postwar economy, and the League of Nations fiasco led to Democratic defeats in the presidential elections of 1920, 1924, and 1928.

Furthermore, the unprecedented and massive Democratically-controlled government intervention into the American economy during the war—called *war socialism*—led to a massive transformation of the Republican Party. Since its start in 1854, the Republican Party had been a big-government party, favoring high tariffs, national banking, giving free federal land to settlers, and using federal money to build roads, canals, and ports. The Democratic Party had been the party of small government throughout most of the nineteenth century until it had adopted anti-capitalist populism and even some Republican progressive ideas. War socialism scared the business community, as did progressive war financing and the Bolshevik Revolution in Russia.[65] Although it still had a progressive wing, the Republican Party was predominantly a small government party only during the brief window of the post–World War I Warren Harding and Calvin Coolidge administrations. The expansion of government during the war was the progressives' dream, yet the backlash from its wartime excesses put progressivism into the closet for most of the 1920s.

Post-War Reinterpretation of History

A saying goes that history is often captive of the present (or at least later events). Its subsequent moniker "World War I" illustrates that this is true in spades about the Great War—for the war was, in reality, "World War Part I." The rise of totalitarian fascist Adolf Hitler so tarnished Germany in the twentieth century that the Kaiser has been lumped in with him as an aggressive autocrat.

Despite his rhetoric about self-determination and democracy, Wilson acquiesced to America's imperialist allies' desire to impose a harsh peace on Germany and to their plan to grab more colonial territory, which was known to him but kept from the American people. Wilson allowed himself to become a useful idiot in the allied effort to achieve these questionable goals. Also, Wilson's added demand that the Kaiser abdicate helped clear the political way for Adolf Hitler's later dictatorship. These historical facts are often buried in American textbooks today. In fact, over the years, it would become quite unpopular to criticize Wilson's war record. "Wilsonianism" became an ostensible guiding principle of most American foreign policy elites.

But not at first, only later. By 1919 public horror had grown over the high American casualty rates along with its dismay over the peace settlement. Justly disillusioned, many Americans saw Wilson and other politicians' actions influenced by crude economics. The U.S. boom of general exports to the Allied side—exports as a percent of the U.S. economy doubled from 1914 to 1916—had motivated Wilson to be aggressive in his claims against the German submarine warfare's economic threat. By 1917, that pugnaciousness had led to outright U.S. involvement in the war.

Benjamin O. Fordham's probit analysis correlating the large American export boom to war-related votes in Congress have lent credence to the claim that economic factors were motivating politicians' thinking in the run-up to U.S. entry. Fordham also noted that the historical record shows Wilson's repeated concerns with the effect of the European war on U.S. trade. This overseas commerce had a big impact on his quest for reelection in 1916, helping him win the key exporting state of Ohio.[66]

Alternatively, if Wilson had maintained strict neutrality in the European war by stopping American exports, ships, or people transiting the war zones, or at least declared that the U.S. government was not responsible for their safety, it could have meant a substantial American economic downturn and consequent personal election peril.

The pyrrhic economic advantages derived from U.S. entry into World War I would influence congressional debates and lead to restrictive neutrality legislation in the 1930s to stop it from happening again. Blaming Wilson's economic motives, however, became unfashionable after Pearl Harbor and the horrors of fighting Nazi Germany, fascist Italy, and Imperial Japan and is now considered an odd, "revisionist," and "isolationist" view.

That the larger issues facing the U.S. economy in general served as the impetus to U.S. entry into the war explains more than the crude theories of the interwar period about the excessive influence of "merchants of death"—the narrow interests of munitions makers and the bankers who funded them—who allegedly drove the nation to war. Although the entire American economy gained from war trade with the Allied nations, munitions and food were especially important exports. Thus, if a general export boom led Wilson to make aggressive claims against German submarines to protect it, munitions were nonetheless a sizable part of that boom. By November 1916, a whopping 40 percent of British military spending was happening in the United States. The manufacturers of those munitions were in certain congressional districts and states and had lobbyists and members of Congress advocating for their export, which influenced the decision to go to war. Also, to pressure the British to end their Hunger Blockade, which was starving Germany, the implicit threat always existed of a U.S. weapons embargo against Britain. Strangely, that potential arms embargo, ardently advocated by certain members of Congress, was never voted on by either house of Congress; this absence of action could have reflected the strength of the nascent military-industrial-congressional complex of the day.

The word *nascent* is important. Although the roots grew in American society for such a complex, the armistice happened only about a year and a half after the United States entered the war. The peace cut short the experiment in industrialized warfare.[67] A full military-industrial-congressional complex would not start to develop until World War II and thereafter.

Finally, the liberal idea of international trade inhibiting war among nations—by causing business interests in potentially belligerent countries to lobby for peace and prosperity—seemingly was decimated by World

War I. But Benjamin O. Fordham thinks the notion still applies but is limited. The case of World War I confirms that trading partners are less likely to fight with each other. But Fordham notes that this may not be the case for third parties left out in the cold without substantial trade to increase interstate cooperation—in this case, Germany. Not having an extensive pre-war trading relationship with Germany allowed Wilson to issue threats and go to war against Germany to protect lucrative U.S. trade with Britain and France.[68]

>> CHAPTER 9 <<

WORLD WAR II

Myths about the War

The Civil War and World War II are the holy grails of American conflicts. Rarely are their morality or necessity questioned. In the popular mind, the wars are associated with freeing black slaves from Southern plantations and ending the oppression (including the Holocaust) of Jews in Nazi Germany, respectively, neither of which were war objectives. Chapter 5 on the Civil War showed that Abraham Lincoln's invasion of the South in 1861, after South Carolina had attacked Fort Sumter, had the goal of forcibly reuniting the country but not freeing any slaves.

Likewise, the United States did not enter World War II at any time to save Jews from Adolf Hitler.[1] Hitler was elected in Germany in 1933. Yet by 1940, long after Hitler had been horribly mistreating Jews and romping militarily over much of Western Europe, the American public—disillusioned by the outcome and high casualty rates of World War I that had ended just 22 years earlier—overwhelmingly wanted to stay out of another European war. In fact, before U.S. entry into the war, in May 1939, President Franklin D. Roosevelt (FDR) had turned away a large ship of fleeing German Jews from American shores. The Holocaust Encyclopedia notes that FDR refused to admit them because of the general national hostility to immigrants, "isolationist" Republican gains in the 1938 congressional elections, and the possible sullying of his own reelection chances in 1940 in support of an unpopular cause.[2] The Great Depression had cooled public acceptance of immigrants in general. Despite persecution of German Jews, the restrictive U.S. immigration quota for them was not increased. The Nazis first offered to deport all Jews, but even after the worst Nazi pogrom against Jews, FDR and Congress refused to relax the quota.[3]

After American entry into the war, Rabbi Stephen Wise asked FDR to try to stop the Holocaust, which began in 1942. FDR told him punishment for war crimes would need to wait till after the war and that his main goal was first to win it. This, despite the massive number of Jewish murders between then and the end of the war. Also, in June 1944, FDR refused the entreaties of American Jewish leaders to bomb the train tracks from Hungary to Poland's Auschwitz, the most notorious of Nazi extermination camps, because he believed there were higher priority targets. So, as with the freeing of the slaves after the Civil War ended, stopping the persecution of Jews and liberating Jews from Nazi concentration camps were more the result of a cataclysmic conflict, not the original goal of U.S. entry into the war. In fact, it was the victorious Soviet Union, coming from the east, that would liberate Auschwitz. Ironically, the United States was fighting German Nazis, Italian fascists, and the Imperial Japanese militarists—all of which were oppressive to other religions, races, and ethnicities—even as the United States was oppressive to Black people, Japanese Americans, and other minorities at home.

Of all American wars, World War II is certainly the most justifiable because it prevented two aggressive powers—Nazi Germany and Imperial Japan—from overrunning much of what was valuable on the Eurasian landmass. However, even this conclusion can be challenged.

If the United States had not entered the war to stop them, neither power had the capabilities to significantly threaten the United States directly in the near or intermediate term. Japan's expansion might have been contained without war by negotiating a sphere of influence for that nation in East Asia,[4] and as subsequent events showed, Germany likely would have been defeated by the USSR alone or by merely giving the Soviets U.S. Lend-Lease aid. The large number of anti-interventionists in the United States plausibly argued: (1) that the Axis nations posed neither a direct military nor economic threat to the United States, (2) that the Soviet Union would emerge as the conflict's primary winner if the United States helped it crush its German enemy, (3) that Great Britain would again use victory in a world war to expand its empire, (4) that support for the Allies would come at the detriment of national defense, (5) that the United States should continue its traditional strategy of hemispheric defense, (6) and most important, that the American founders' lasting principle was still valid: overseas wars cause a significant distortion of the republic at home.

The myth that the U.S. government entered the war only reluctantly is also fallacious. Historian John M. Schuessler provides the correction:

> In the realm of national mythology, Americans remember World War II as "the good war." According to the standard narrative, the United States desired only to be left alone but was forced to fight in the face of German and Japanese aggression. When one takes a closer look at the historical record, though, it becomes clear that World War II was hardly forced on the United States. Well before the Japanese attack on Pearl Harbor on December 7, 1941, President Roosevelt came to the conclusion that the United States would have to act as a balancer of last resort in Europe, but he understood that public support for a declaration of war was unlikely to be forthcoming in the absence of a major provocation. In this light, both the "undeclared war" in the Atlantic and the oil embargo on Japan should be understood as designed, at least in part to invite an "incident" that could be used to justify hostilities. While controversial, a plausible case can be made that Roosevelt welcomed U.S. entry into the war by the fall of 1941 and manufactured events accordingly. . . . There is compelling evidence that Roosevelt settled on a war policy well before Pearl Harbor and that in the interim he engaged in a significant amount or deception, maneuvering the country in the direction of open hostilities while assuring a wary public that the United States would remain at peace.[5]

In fact, the United States entered World War II against aggressive Nazi Germany through the back door—through Japan, Germany's ally. The U.S. attempt to strangle the economy of Japan provoked its desperate attack on Pearl Harbor. Like the start of the Civil War, a direct attack on a U.S. military installation changed American public opinion quickly in favor of war. In an "honor among thieves" moment, Hitler—who had been trying to avoid all-out war with the United States in the Atlantic despite U.S. harassment and attacks on German U-boats—foolishly honored his loose Axis alliance with Japan after its attack on Pearl Harbor by declaring war against the United States. Hitler likely did so because he concluded the U.S. leviathan would put most of its war effort against an attacking Japan rather than against Germany.[6] If Hitler had waited to declare war, it would have complicated FDR's options on how to handle the global conflict.

In 1941, the total value of the four major Axis nations' economies— Germany, Japan, Italy, and Austria—amounted to about 71 percent of the value of the U.S. economy.[7] Before the United States joined the war, the economies of the major Allies—the Soviet Union, Britain, and France— only slightly exceeded the four major Axis nations. The belated addition of the U.S. to the Allied camp gave a huge edge to the Allies, raising their economic ratio to almost 2.5 to 1 over the Axis nations. Since the advent of modern conventional warfare, it has been the case that the side with the greatest economic power usually triumphs, so it is unsurprising that the Allies eventually won the war. But what may be surprising to the typical reader of American history is that Germany was already close to defeat before the United States and its Allies ever landed troops in the hallowed invasion of Normandy, France, three years later in June 1944.

Origins of the War

World War, Part II

Conflict in the European theater of World War II, which began about twenty years after World War I ended, should have been called "World War, Part II." Both World Wars had been preceded by economic down- turns. The second war's origins arose from Germany's hyperinflation, the Great Depression, and its nationalistic outrage at the huge war reparations and humiliating peace imposed after its defeat in the first world war, which the unnecessary U.S. entry into that conflict ensured. As even FDR admitted in a speech on January 6, 1941, the first European conflict that began in 1914 posed "only a small threat of danger to our own American future."[8]

World War I disrupted globalized trading patterns and replaced them with economic nationalism, reducing world trade by two-thirds and deepening the subsequent worldwide Great Depression. When the American banking system collapsed after the Wall Street crash of 1929, the international repayment system went down with it.[9]

Waldo Heinrichs, author of *Threshold of War: Franklin D. Roosevelt and American Entry into World War II*, best summed up how the first war led to the financial exhaustion of Britain, global economic collapse, and the nationalism that led to the rise of Hitler:

> The world economic crisis of the 1930s shriveled international-ism. A chain of failures and errors occurred in systems already weakened by war: declining commodity prices, exchange difficulties, foreign trade shrinkage, debt default, collapse of investment values, bank closings, factory shutdowns, and devastating unemployment. Britain was unable to continue as sta-bilizer of the international system and no successor appeared. Economic disorder led to political instability. Governments were less concerned with harmonizing relations with other nations than with staying in power. Nations turned inward and autarky prevailed.[10]

Adolph Hitler

American President Woodrow Wilson played a role in ultimately bringing Hitler to power by demanding Kaiser Wilhelm II's abdication from the German throne at the end of WWI. Hitler—an Austrian—cap-italized on German shame and indignation over the Versailles Treaty, arousing Germans by scapegoating Jews for the country's economic and other problems. He openly flouted the Versailles Treaty; conducted a mil-itary buildup; reoccupied the demilitarized Rhineland area of Germany near France and the low countries in 1936; and annexed German-speaking Austria into Germany in March 1938 as well as the German-speaking part of Czechoslovakia, the Sudetenland, later in 1938, under an agree-ment with British Prime Minister Neville Chamberlain in Munich. In the summer of 1940, a young John F. Kennedy published his senior thesis at Harvard on *Why England Slept*, which correctly argued that Chamberlain had "appeased" Hitler at Munich only to buy valuable time to augment insufficient Allied military capabilities for war. Notably, it is more than likely that Chamberlain saved Britain during the later Battle of Britain in 1940 by transferring money from the offense-oriented Bomber Command to enhance British air defenses. In reality, the Allies were not ready to fight in 1938 and besides, before that infamous year, appeasement had been an acceptable diplomatic maneuver to avoid conflict.

Yet the narrative of Chamberlain's appeasement of Hitler is told differently in America's version of world history. Chamberlain's "failed" agreement with Hitler is used instead to arrive at a bedrock principle of post–World War II U.S. foreign policy of vilifying democracies for negotiating with autocrats. The Munich 1938 narrative is used to justify discarding the American founders' vision of a restrained foreign policy in favor of U.S. triumphalism, military empire, and incessant foreign interventionism.

However, World War II was a unique situation which posed two serious challenges at once: from Germany and from the USSR.

At first, Hitler sought lebensraum ("living space") for German-speaking peoples. Famously breaking his promise to Chamberlain in Munich, he now invaded non-German-speaking Czech lands in March 1939 then Poland in September 1939. After the Czech invasion, FDR concluded Hitler was a madman and secretly, without telling Congress or the American people, changed U.S. policy from neutrality to "unneutral rearmament," supplying furtive help to the Allies. After Hitler invaded Poland, France and Britain declared war on Germany, distracting Hitler from his real goal of conquering the Soviet Union and provoking him to invade Denmark and Norway in April and May 1940. Then in May and June 1940, Hitler's forces tore through Luxembourg, Belgium, and the Netherlands to conquer France. By June 1940, all continental Western Europe, except neutral Sweden and Switzerland, was in his hands.

Unlike the western theater of WWI—in which the dominance of the machine gun, a defensive weapon, created the trench warfare stalemate—technological improvements in mobile armored vehicles and air power between the wars allowed the Germans to combine them in World War II in a rapid, offensive attack called the blitzkrieg ("lightning warfare"). The Germans had swiftly overrun France and pushed the British troops helping French forces back to Britain. The swashbuckling German dictator then began to plan an invasion of the British Isles. However, he first had to achieve air superiority to cover the amphibious operation. Here, using newly developed radar, British air forces stymied him in the Battle of Britain, which lasted from mid-July through to the end of October 1940. Chamberlain's investment in air defense had paid off. Once Germany lost the air battle, Hitler shelved plans for an amphibious invasion across the English Channel and fatefully decided to ignore Napoleon's catastrophic precedent by returning in June 1941 to his original lebensraum project of conquering the vast lands of the western Soviet Union to repopulate them with Germans. To do this, Hitler had to break his nonaggression pact with Joseph Stalin signed less than two years earlier, which had led to the division of Poland between them. In June 1941 Hitler plunged into an invasion of the USSR.

President Franklin Roosevelt could have taken this respite for Britain as a chance to attenuate his support for helping to protect British maritime sea lanes in the Atlantic. FDR instead chose to redouble his efforts to support Britain and risk war with Germany.

In addition to ideologically despising the communist regime, Hitler's main goal had always been to conquer the resources of the Soviet Union—the grain of Ukraine and the oil of the Caucuses—to perpetuate Nazi control of Europe. Thus, 75 percent of Hitler's formidable army was directed toward what became a three-pronged invasion of the USSR that ultimately failed.[11] The combat on this Eastern front would be the most titanic in human history and would turn the European war decisively against the Nazis at Stalingrad by the beginning of 1943—long before the United States, Britain, and Canada launched the famous June 1944 amphibious assault on the Normandy beaches in France, already depleted of German defenders who had been siphoned off to the Eastern front.

Japan

Although Hitler's aggressive actions in Europe in the late 1930s get most of the public attention, World War II really started in 1931, with the Japanese invasion of Manchuria. But imperial great power competition over the China market had begun in the 1800s, well before the Japan's Manchurian incursion in 1931 and Hitler election as chancellor of Germany in 1933.

Mesmerized by the potential of the populous Chinese market, the United States at the turn of the twentieth century had adopted the Open Door Policy to protect open access to get a share of China's economic pie in competition against ambitious European powers. In 1900 President William McKinley sent thousands of U.S. troops to China to help the European militaries put down the Boxer Rebellion, an indigenous Chinese revolt against coerced trade with the West.

In the 1930s, however, the United States and Europeans began to complain about Japan using military power to gain advantage in China.

The American Open Door Policy clashed with Japan's Greater East Asia Co-Prosperity Sphere.

After the Japan launched an incursion into Manchuria in 1931, it then brutally invaded a part of China proper in 1937. These actions disturbed U.S. and European colonial powers. But the Japanese did not want to conquer the entire country, so the United States might have been able to negotiate a deal. Instead, after the Japanese invasion in 1937, the United States began funneling economic and technical aid to Chinese Nationalists under Chiang Kai-shek, who opposed the Japanese presence. Already, by 1940, the Japanese were bogged down in an intractable quagmire in China, a weakness the United States could have exploited short of war.

Moreover, by the 1930s, the China market had proved disappointing and not worth fighting over. U.S. trade with Japan was greater than that with China in the 1930s,

Was U.S. Entry into the War Necessary?

Lost to today's American audiences—fed on movies and television shows exhibiting nationalistic visions of glorious U.S. triumph over the dark enemies of Nazi Germany and Imperial Japan—is the reality that Nazi Germany and Imperial Japan posed little direct threat to the mainland United States, only to far-flung U.S. outposts and their neighbors. Most Americans understood the United States' advantageous geography far away from the world's centers of conflict; they were reluctant for the U.S. to enter the war even after Hitler's takeover of much of Western Europe in 1940, and as late as early 1941, 83 percent still wanted to avoid war. The Atlantic and Pacific Oceans had always been wide moats. By the fall of 1940, after the British had defeated the German Luftwaffe in the air battle over Britain, little danger existed that the Nazis could amphibiously invade even that defensible offshore island and commandeer the powerful British Navy, which patrolled the Atlantic. Moreover, British Prime Minister Winston Churchill had guaranteed to FDR that if Britain looked ready to fall to the Nazis—unlikely with British naval superiority against Hitler's comparatively weak fleet—the British Navy would scuttle vessels or disperse ships around the world to the British Empire so that they did not fall into Hitler's hands. British warships could even have found safe bases and launch points in the United States to continue the struggle.

With centuries of failed invasions of Russia preceding his, it was clear that Hitler would have his hands full. Even if Hitler had succeeded, his depleted armies would have been exhausted and stretched too thin with the task of occupying the western USSR and most of Europe to take the conflict to America. Even without U.S. entry into the war, if, as Churchill warned, both the Germans and Japanese had succeeded in their expansions in continental Europe and East Asia, their alliance was one of convenience; they could not have controlled the entire Eurasian landmass. Thus, even the worst case—the indirect "America alone in the world against a colossus" threat—was exaggerated. The beefed-up U.S. Navy and the formidable British fleet still could have protected the United States and Britain. Although FDR dubiously claimed that Hitler wanted to conquer the entire world, he surely knew that Germany must "break through to command of the ocean" to do so. Viewing Germany as contained to a land war in Europe and bearing the albatross of ever-expansive land occupation, FDR correctly concluded that Hitler would finally lose. But he notably avoided mentioning that the inferior German surface fleet (compared to the British Navy) and its U-boats, which could only deny the use of parts of the Atlantic Ocean to others, would never be capable of affirmatively commanding the sea.[12]

The Japanese threat could have been confined to the coastal rim of East Asia had FDR not tried to strangle the Japanese military with economic embargoes, including on petroleum products and key metals.[13] Furthermore, during the 1930s, FDR had built up the U.S. Navy beyond Washington Treaty (1921) ceilings, and after Chamberlain's agreement with Hitler in Munich in 1938, FDR had begun increasing U.S. airplane production. After Hitler invaded France and the low countries in 1940, FDR accelerated the earlier naval and aircraft buildup and dramatically expanded the U.S. Army using conscription.

Nevertheless, FDR's military buildup was still slow considering the threat as portrayed. He did not want to raise voter fears of U.S. entry into the war during an election year. After the election in 1941, however, a bigger buildup began.[14] Even then, America was not ready for war when it happened; for that reason, civilian leaders were more enthusiastic about entering the conflict than were the U.S. Army and Navy. At the end of 1940 the U.S.-British "Europe-first" military plan, which FDR quietly supported, recognized that the United States did not yet have naval forces of a scale sufficient to fight both the Nazis and the Japanese at the same time—requiring the United States to avoid war with Japan at all costs while prioritizing defense of the Atlantic supply lines to Britain. And yet, FDR's aggressive denial of petroleum and metals to Japan pushed that nation to a logical, but desperate, acceleration of its military expansion to take Dutch East Indian (now Indonesian) oil and thus the militarily necessary attacks on Pearl Harbor and the U.S. colony in the Philippines.

Finally, in 1934, FDR's recognition of the Soviet Union, which had been an East Asian rival of the Japanese and had strong forces to the north of Japan, showed the potential of a future U.S.-Soviet alignment opposing Japanese expansion. Such developments, managed well, could have slowed Japan—only a second-order power at best—and checked its East Asian expansion.

FDR's Deceptive Entry into WWII

Roosevelt Pushed Japan into War

The global Great Depression affected the island nation of Japan more than others because of its heavy reliance on foreign trade. Between 1929 and 1931, Japan's exports fell by 50 percent, cratering its economy and faith in Western liberalism. As a result, the Japanese military became dominant in governance, leading the nation down the costly and danger-ous road to imperial autarky[15] and hence its eyeing of much of East Asia for expansion.

Japan was the only industrialized nation in East Asia. Noting the British, French, Dutch, and U.S. empires in East Asia, it wanted one too. As with most empires, Japan wanted preferential trade with less developed countries in its region—processing imports of raw materials from those nations into manufactured goods, which were then sold back to them. And as with most imperial powers, the Japanese believed it was improving living standards, diffusing their technology, and "civilizing" those poor countries in their region—much as does the U.S. Monroe Doctrine in the Western Hemisphere. That said, the Japanese proved more brutal in their imperial efforts than had the United States been in Latin America (but not in the U.S.-occupied Philippines). Because they are constantly involved in coercion and war, it has since been shown that empires are not cost-effective.[16] Imperialism is in fact more costly in lives, money, and moral standing. Stealing raw materials at gunpoint and coercing trade with weaker countries are inefficient and ruinous ways to do business. It is far better to pay the market price in a free exchange of goods and services. Japan was later to prove this fact—after it had been devastated in the costly war. After the war ended, the newly pacifist, resource-poor island began buying raw materials from abroad, turning them into manufactured items, and became a world economic power by exporting excellent products that other countries wanted to buy.

With racism always in the background, the United States and the European powers became alarmed at pre-WWII Japan's rise and expansionist ambitions that would threaten their economic interests in that part of the world. Specifically, Japan's Greater East Asia Co-Prosperity Sphere threatened the traditional U.S. Open Door Policy, which demanded the United States not get cut of the great powers' exploitative trade with China. The Open Door Policy arose from the longstanding contention that overproduction in capitalist economies required their acquiring overseas markets to absorb their manufacturing output—or economic and political instability at home would result. Thus, the U.S. government did not want Japan to preclude America from the enticing Chinese market (because of its large population), but which proved disappointing in the 19th century and for most of the 20th century.

Yet the Japanese regarded their empire like America's Monroe Doctrine in the western hemisphere. Japan noted it had stayed out of western hemisphere and therefore believed the United States should honor its sphere of influence in China, which was more than six thousand miles from the U.S. coastline. The so-called Lodge Corollary to the Monroe Doctrine had warned Japan to stay out of Latin America, even in the quest for peaceful trade. However, the United States, with imperial possessions in the Philippines, Hawaii, Guam, and Wake Island did not intend to give up on Chinese and East Asian trade. Today, few Americans know that the road to Pearl Harbor ran through an imperial great power competition for the then-exaggerated potential of the Chinese market.[17]

The more Japan expanded, the more it felt threatened by encirclement by Western powers—Britain, the Netherlands, the Soviet Union, and the United States. Not unreasonably so, insofar as the United States sent heavy bombers that could bomb Tokyo to the Chinese nationalists opposing the Japanese, along with almost nine hundred aviators and technical experts The U.S. also was building air bases in southwest China, conducting a military buildup in the colonial Philippines and gradually increasing trade restrictions against Japan. The Japanese Navy had vehemently wanted to break what it feared was a tightening U.S.-British-Dutch encirclement in East Asia before it was too late. The Imperial Navy had known that any southward advance in that region might precipitate a U.S. oil embargo, forcing Japan to seize the Dutch East Indies' (now Indonesia's) oil, thus in turn triggering a war with the United States, Britain, and the Netherlands.

Yet Japan believed that the Americans would back off and first focus on the greater threat to Europe from Nazi Germany. After all, the United States had committed to Britain and was planning to run a Germany-first strategy. High-level U.S. military and diplomatic officials were recommending that FDR avoid opening a second front, which going to war with Japan would entail. Containment and deterrence of Japan was supposed to be the U.S. strategy. The United States was just beginning its rearmament program and did not have sufficient forces to simultaneously fight Germany and Japan. In short, war with Japan should not have happened. Nonetheless, FDR bumbled into a simultaneous two-front war on a grand scale by running an excessively hardline policy toward Japan, resulting in a desperate Japanese attack on Pearl Harbor.

FDR's strangling oil embargo on Japan came about because the president misapprehended the lessons from Neville Chamberlain's "appeasement" of Adolf Hitler at Munich in 1938. As noted, Chamberlain's settlement with Hitler in 1938 most likely saved Britain because it was not yet ready to fight Germany. Insofar as FDR had no need to appease Japan, he should have at least avoided unnecessarily provoking it into an attack on the U.S.—at least till the primary enemy, Germany, had been defeated.

While the Japanese military began to drive Japanese foreign policy, and invaded Manchuria in 1931 and then part of China in 1937, the United States did not try to penalize the Japanese heavily until 1940 after war broke out in Europe. The National Defense Act of 1940 allowed the president to regulate the export of materials vital to U.S. defense, which FDR used against Japan. To put further pressure on Japan, FDR cancelled a commercial treaty, extended the economic embargo to cover aviation gasoline and high-grade scrap metal, and moved the U.S. Pacific Fleet from the West Coast to Pearl Harbor, Hawaii. In September 1940 Japan then retaliated by forming the Axis alliance of convenience with Germany and Italy. The alliance was aimed squarely at the United States, which had not yet joined the conflict. The members agreed to help each other if any of them were "attacked by a power at present not involved in the European War." Both Japan and Germany wanted to keep the U.S.

colossus out of the war by threatening a two-front conflict it chose to jump in.

Beginning in mid-1941, after the Japanese created a protectorate over Indochina, in a clear effort to strangle the Japanese economy and military, America, then the world's largest oil producer, effectively instituted an embargo on oil going to Japan by freezing Japanese assets in the United States able to buy it and imposed a general trade embargo including on scrap iron. While the United States used Indochina as an excuse for a hardline policy toward Japan, FDR had not intended to embargo all oil to Japan but only to tighten oil shipments. He thought that "to cut off oil altogether at this time would probably precipitate an outbreak of war in the Pacific."[18] Disregarding his boss, an insubordinate and arrogant Assistant Secretary of State Dean Acheson nonetheless aggressively halted all oil to Japan. FDR did nothing, either afraid to countermand Acheson's policy for fear of the label "appeaser,"[19] or worse, he too wanted to provoke war, but insofar as possible, shift the blame. The Japanese, with only one year's petroleum supply left, would then either need to withdraw from China or invade the Dutch East Indies to conquer its oil, which would bring about certain conflict with the United States.

The Japanese were surprised by this American reaction to their expansion in Indochina and, from August to late November 1941, unsuccessfully tried to reach an agreement with the United States to get the embargo lifted while keeping certain territorial gains. There are two plausible reasons why an agreement did not happen. The preternaturally confident FDR either bungled the United States into a two-front war with Japan and Germany or was duplicitous, another well-known FDR character trait, actually wanting war. His aggressive attempt in the Atlantic to provoke Hitler to start a general war had failed. So, the argument goes, provoking the Japanese to attack somewhere in the Pacific was his only way to "back door" into war with Germany, Japan's ally.[20]

Japan imported about 90 percent of its gasoline, 80 percent of its oil products, 74 percent of its scrap iron, and 60 percent of its machine tools from the United States.[21] In addition, U.S. companies owned much of the oil in Latin America, and American, British, and Dutch firms owned all the oil in Southeast and Southwest Asia. Japan initially proposed not extending its military presence beyond Indochina and withdrawing its forces from Indochina upon settlement of the war in China, if the United States would cease its military buildup in the region (in China and the Philippines), end the economic embargoes against Japan, and pressure Chinese Nationalist leader Chiang Kai-shek to negotiate with the Japanese to end its China bog. None of these Japanese proposals would have lessened U.S. national security. FDR should have taken almost any deal because he supposedly wanted to direct U.S. resources against the more menacing Nazis, and could have done so, given Japan's desperation to get out of the U.S.-assisted military quagmire in China and attendant American embargoes, especially oil restrictions.

Japan and the United States had negotiated before to prevent conflict. This time, however, the United States threatened Japan with apocalypse if it went after the Dutch East Indies—even as it looked like the Americans had forced the Japanese into it by cutting off their oil. To have negotiated the doable withdrawal of Japanese forces from Indochina and no invasion further south would have kept the peace.

FDR strung out negotiations and was uncompromising with Japan to allow time for a U.S. air and ground force buildup in the Philippines. With Japan's oil supplies plummeting, its population growing hungry,[22] and its government fearing the U.S. military buildup in the Pacific region, Prince Fumimaro Konoye, the civilian Japanese prime minister, made a final effort to meet with FDR in Hawaii to head off war.

FDR's hawkish Washington advisers pressured him to stiff-arm Konoye, which he was inclined to do anyway. And especially damning for FDR, U.S. intercepts of secret Japanese communications revealed that the Japanese government put a high priority on such a meeting to avoid war. According to the intercepts, the Konoye cabinet believed the only way to address the "critically tense" situation with the United States was for the heads of government to meet, "lay their cards on the table, express their true feelings, and attempt to determine a way out."[23] In addition, Kichisaburō Nomura, Japanese Ambassador to the United States, told Secretary of State Cordell Hull that his government "would make concessions in order to avoid war."[24] Not only that, the Japanese emperor admonished his military by saying that he preferred peace over war, and the Japanese government dumped its anti-American foreign minister.

The U.S. ambassador to Japan advised FDR to meet with the Japanese prime minister, since the Japanese had told him that their prime minister would make far-reaching concessions to avoid any conflict and would effectively end Japan's alliance with Germany. The harm of meeting with the Japanese prime minister to avoid war was minimal since the

U.S. already knew that the Japanese concessions would be sincere, unlike those of Hitler at Munich. But FDR continued the military buildup in China and the Philippines and demanded that Japan abandon expansion and adopt the American Open-Door program for trade and resources in the Pacific before any meeting.

The American side was simply playing for time, ensuring the talks went nowhere—even after the Japanese indicated their membership in the Tripartite Pact (Axis) would not prevent better relations with the United States. This posture could only mean the Japanese were signaling they would stay out of an American war against Germany. Yet FDR wanted to believe Japan would remain loyal to Germany.[25]

The Japanese did not regard the Axis alliance as an offensive alliance but only a pro forma one that would allow them to do what they did during World War I—expand their empire at the expense of distracted European colonial nations at war. And even if it wasn't only pro forma, Japan miscalculated that the United States would take care of the greater German threat first, allowing them to expand in East Asia with minimal U.S. interference.

The Japanese were nonetheless eager to make significant concessions to avoid a disastrous war with the United States—a country with an economy much larger than those of all the Axis countries combined and already massively outproducing Japan in war matériel. But the United States rejected the Japanese proposal and did not offer a counterproposal. FDR stalled for a month or two, buying more time until the U.S. military buildup in the Philippines was far enough along to deter a Japanese attack. Given the U.S. rearmament schedule, the Japanese estimated that they had only two years of naval superiority left in the Pacific and so needed to reach an agreement soon.

Civilian Prime Minister Konoe's failure to succeed in negotiations with FDR led to the fall of his government in mid-October 1941 and to the grabbing of power by the aggressive Japanese military. However, even the hawkish Hideki Tojo, the general who then became prime minister, obeyed the emperor's wishes for peace. He created a new peace plan and pushed back the drop-dead date for a settlement with the United States from October to December 1941. The United States did not respond to Tojo's peace plan but instead sent back further hardline demands.

FDR said no to withdrawing the embargoes and asset freezes and to a peace settlement unless Japan withdrew forces from Indochina and

China—the latter, the United States considered the real war prize. FDR also demanded that Japan recognize Chiang Kai-shek's government in China; renounce all imperial claims on China, as would the U.S. and the western powers; negotiate with Chiang over Manchuria; and shred the Axis alliance with Germany and Italy.[26] Japan was willing to lessen its role in the Axis alliance and slow down in Indochina. But it was unwilling to leave China totally, as FDR knew. Back in April 1941, the Japanese had offered a withdrawal from China if Chiang Kai-shek would accept Japanese control of Manchuria and enter a coalition government with pro-Japanese Chinese. The United States cared little about Japan's mostly pro forma Axis agreement. FDR was unflinching in his demand for Japan's acceptance of the U.S. Open Door Policy and an unconditional Japanese withdraw from China.[27]

In demanding a Japanese withdrawal from China, analyst Jeffrey Record concluded, "the United States was, in effect, demanding that Japan renounce its status as an aspiring great power and consign itself to permanent strategic dependency on a hostile Washington. Such a choice would have been unacceptable to any great power."[28] Certainly, no Japanese government could have agreed to FDR's terms. Even U.S. diplomats who presented this final hardline position to the Japanese knew diplomacy had failed. The Japanese did not want war with the United States, but they also wanted to control China. The American public was never told it was going to war with Japan over China.

FDR's military advisers continued to be opposed to his oil embargo and demand for Japan to withdraw from China. To them, it contradicted U.S. overall strategy of deterring the Japanese until the higher priority war against Germany had been won. They believed he was too eager for a second war against Japan at the same time he was engaged in hostile actions against the Germans in the Atlantic.[29]

FDR was clearly heading in the direction that he and his advisors had wanted to avoid—fighting a two-front war. Even the aggressive James Polk eventually had avoided simultaneous wars with Britain and Mexico in 1846 by settling the U.S. boundary in the Pacific Northwest with the British. FDR instead chose an aggressive policy on both fronts simultaneously: vigorously pursuing and attacking German U-boats in the Atlantic while strangling the Japanese military with embargoes on oil and key metals as he maintained his demand that Japan withdraw from China. Even British diplomats saw clearly that the U.S. embargo was "slowly strangling" Japan, thus forcing the island nation to "break out or give way."[30]

The Japanese generals now running General Hideki Tojo's more aggressive government realized that if the U.S. oil embargo were not lifted, the Japanese military would desperately need oil from the Dutch colonial East Indies. That supply, some in the Japanese military asserted, would give Japan the ability to fight a protracted war; others in the Japanese government were skeptical. The problem was that the maritime supply line for the long Japanese amphibious invasion route to the East Indies and other points south passed near the Philippines, then a U.S. colony hosting U.S. military bases and forces. Japan could not allow such a vulnerability; but that meant war with the United States.

In 1941, the deployed Japanese Navy outnumbered the Anglo, American, and Dutch naval forces in aircraft carriers by ten to three, and eleven to nine in battleships, but a massive U.S. building program was underway (the United States had about three times the naval tonnage under construction as did Japan), giving the desperate Japanese military government an incentive to attack to the south before the balance of forces changed dramatically in U.S. favor.[31] They hoped that a devastating surprise attack on the U.S. Pacific fleet, recently re-headquartered at Pearl Harbor, would impair U.S. reaction to Japan's southward advance, giving the Japanese breathing space to fortify their defense perimeter in the Pacific and finish their war in China. It might also make America negotiate for peace. However, Japanese Admiral Isoroku Yamamoto— who planned the attack on Pearl Harbor and knew the Americans, having earlier studied and been a naval attaché in the United States—thought the last outcome was improbable. The moderate Yamamoto respected immense U.S. industrial power, was against a surprise attack, and feared the outcome of a long war with the United States. Even the hawkish Japanese military knew that a protracted war against the American industrial colossus would end in defeat, but with the strangling U.S. oil embargo already in place, they had to take their chances.

During November 1941, Allied intelligence picked up clear indications of Japanese forces moving into positions of attack. The Japanese government's news agency Domei even warned that Japan was finishing its "war structure" for an "armed clash in the Pacific." The anti-American diatribe noted that the U.S. oil embargo was forcing Japan to "drastic action" to defend itself.[32] Joseph C. Grew, U.S. Ambassador to Japan, warned the State Department in early November that the grinding American economic coercion could produce a violent Japanese reaction rather than a retraction. Cogently, he wondered if war with Japan was in American interests. Also, in early November, a full month before the attack on Pearl Harbor and with still plenty of time to avoid war, intercepted and decoded Japanese secret diplomatic communications indicated that the lower-level negotiations still ongoing were a "last effort" to address a "very grave" situation in U.S.-Japanese relations—diplomatic lingo for war. FDR had to know an attack was coming. Frantic intercepted Japanese communications said the "absolutely immovable" date for an agreement was November 25. Indicating his knowledge that war with Japan was imminent, FDR ordered the withdrawal of the remaining U.S. Marines in China on November 14.[33]

The Japanese preferred to launch surprise attacks against their foes, as they had in the 1905 Russo-Japanese war. However, what is also unrecognized in American history books is that at the same time Japan was planning such an attack on the United States, FDR was planning one on Japan. On July 23, 1941, FDR had approved a plan for American civilian pilots in U.S. planes with Chinese markings to bomb mainland Japan. The attack never happened because Japan beat the United States to the punch.[34]

A Japanese attack on the United States was never a total surprise. Eventually, FDR and the U.S. military knew that war was near and that the Japanese would attack somewhere. On November 25, two weeks before the attack on Pearl Harbor, Secretary of War Henry Stimson recorded in his diary that FDR anticipated a Japanese surprise attack shortly and wanted ideas about how the U.S. government could maneuver Japan to fire the first shot without incurring too much risk.[35] On November 27, ten days before the Japanese attack on Pearl Harbor, General George Marshall, Army Chief of Staff, sent a message to Lieutenant General Walter Short in Honolulu informing him that "negotiations with Japanese appear to be terminated," "hostile action is possible at any moment," and "the United States desires that Japan commit the first overt act."[36] On December 6, FDR made an appeal for peace directly to the Japanese emperor but proposed no concrete plan to get it done. Given FDR's duplicitous effort to maneuver Japan into taking the first shot, like Lincoln before him, this last-minute entreaty was made only to enable the U.S. to play the victim.

Japan: The Back Door to War?

A small minority of historians believe that FDR was willing to sacrifice the augmented U.S. Pacific Fleet. They believe that he had moved
it into harm's way from San Diego to Pearl Harbor to be sunk by the
Japanese to win U.S. public support for entering a war against Hitler in
Europe—a war that had little support in the United States during 1941.
They conclude, however, that FDR, knowing the Japanese were likely to
attack Pearl Harbor, sent the valuable aircraft carriers away on a mission
to save them from the imminent attack.

We know FDR wanted to drag a so-called "isolationist" public into
another European war. Yet a few issues remain problematic with this
minority narrative. First, it had yet to be understood that the capital (premier) ships of world navies were now aircraft carriers. Up to that point,
the most valued had been battleships, and these remained in Pearl Harbor
and suffered badly from the Japanese attack. Only after the successful
Japanese surprise attack using aircraft carriers, and the U.S.-Japanese epic
carrier battles during the rest of the war, was it obvious that the capital
ships in navies had changed from vulnerable battleships to carriers that
could operate at longer range. A second problem with the hypothesis is
that instead of letting the Japanese ruin much of the Pacific Fleet and kill
about 2,500 military personnel, the U.S. Navy—had it been adequately
warned by intercepted communications of the impending attack—could
have set an ambush for the attacking Japanese Navy, thrashed it, and still
had the same excuse to go to war. A third issue is that although FDR
wanted to get into the war against Hitler, he had no way to be completely
sure that an attack by German-allied Japan would trigger a foolish Nazi
declaration of war against the United States. The Axis alliance had been
written sufficiently flexibly that either Japan or Germany could opt out of
any war that the other country undertook, and Hitler already was trying
to avoid war with the aggressive U.S. Navy in the Atlantic. Finally, FDR
had been assistant secretary of the navy for Woodrow Wilson and loved
the navy, making it doubtful he would knowingly sacrifice the battleships,
then thought to be the jewels of the fleet.[37]

One fact supporting the cynical thesis of FDR letting such an attack
take place is that Admiral Husband Kimmel and Lieutenant General
Short were not privy to closely held intercepts of Japanese diplomatic
communications gathered under the Magic program. While these offered

clues that Japan was planning a large and dramatic surprise attack on U.S. military forces and installations in Hawaii, they passed the desks of several U.S. decoders and were allegedly ignored. Nor were these field commanders going to be in the loop in any event. Any reaction by them would have tipped off the Japanese that the United States was reading its coded diplomatic messages. However, FDR and the top military brass in Washington *were* in the loop. Yet, General George Marshall claimed that the Magic intercept pointing to the attack on Hawaii had not been processed until after the attack.

FDR's efforts to provoke Hitler in the Atlantic thus far had fallen short; there is a strong possibility that he decided instead to accept a war with Japan as a Hail Mary attempt to open a back door for war with Germany. As a strategy, it worked. Former President Herbert Hoover, FDR's predecessor and an expert on Asia, had privately and presciently warned that FDR and his people were "doing everything they can to get us into war through the Japanese back door."[38] Even the Honolulu newspapers printed rumors of an imminent Japanese attack there—one accurately warning that the Japanese might strike on the weekend of December 6–7. However, Kimmel and Short continued to believe any Japanese attack on Hawaii would be only on a small scale.[39]

However, a conspiracy to make almost the entire Pacific Fleet an enticing target for Japan would have required many people to be involved to carry it out. Yet despite congressional investigations, including examining documents and interrogating witnesses, no demonstrated evidence of FDR's prior knowledge of the specifics of a Japanese attack on Pearl Harbor exists. In FDR's defense, one hour before the Pearl Harbor attack, he told the Chinese ambassador that he expected a Japanese attack momentarily on another country's possession in the Pacific and that he hoped he could then bring the United States into the war without a direct attack on a U.S. possession. Others close to FDR said similar things just before the attack.

Notably, even before the extensive damage to the fleet in Pearl Harbor, the U.S. Navy in the Pacific was inferior to the Japanese Navy. Therefore, endangering most of the U.S. Pacific Fleet was extremely risky. Furthermore, losing much of it was unnecessary to supply a back door to war since an attempted Japanese attack alone would have done it. FDR had no incentive to withhold warning from the fleet at Pearl Harbor.[40]

However, the narrative does not need to assume grand cynicism and trickery by FDR to still fault him for allowing the back door to war to happen. Most historians have concluded that FDR and the U.S. military expected that the Japanese attack would come but did not know where—the Philippines, Thailand, Malaya, or the Dutch East Indies? They assumed that if the Japanese fleet did have the ability to attack Hawaii, it could be detected in the open Pacific before it got within range to attack Pearl Harbor. However, U.S. intelligence had lost track of the Japanese aircraft carriers because they took an unusual route to get near Pearl Harbor.

When Japanese movement was finally detected, Washington should have warned Pearl Harbor to be ready. A message was sent via a private telegraph system rather than a standard military communication system. It arrived a few hours after the attack. Historian David Reynolds reflects the consensus of historians that, "the evidence points to confusion and complacency, not conspiracy, in Washington."[41] This quote generally squares with the author's sixteen-year experience with how the U.S. government usually works.

On December 7, 1941, radars at Pearl Harbor picked up the unthinkable: incoming Japanese planes. The military ignored it as impossible. Shortly thereafter, the Japanese attacked Pearl Harbor and the Philippines. U.S. planes at military installations on Oahu had been bunched together to guard against locally based saboteurs or sabotage originating from Japanese mini submarines. They had not been spread out to protect against attack from the air. Kimmel did not order long-range patrol planes in the air to look for incoming Japanese aircraft; he was concerned about smaller-scale attacks from the mini-submarines. Although the carriers were distant from Pearl Harbor, the battleships were sitting ducks.

Despite the greater likelihood that the Japanese attack could come in the Philippines, General Douglas MacArthur remained grossly unprepared for one and could have been court-martialed for his negligence. Despite forewarning of an attack, he waited hours to get his bombers and modern fighters into the air; the Japanese destroyed half of each type on the ground.

By late November 1941, FDR and his cabinet had known that war with Japan was highly likely and highly undesirable. Secretary of War Henry Stimson noted in his diary, "The question was how we should maneuver [Japan] into the position of firing the first shot without allowing too much danger to ourselves."[42] Losing five battleships and about 2,500 military personnel at Pearl Harbor surely fell into the "allowing too much danger" category.

Yet Harry Hopkins, a top adviser to FDR, described an environment at the White House after Pearl Harbor that may also support the historians' consensus that FDR did not intentionally sacrifice the Pacific Fleet at Pearl Harbor but was thankful that the Japanese provided him a back door to war with Germany: "The conference met in not too tense an atmosphere because I think that all of us believed in the last analysis the enemy was Hitler and that he could never be defeated without force of arms; that sooner or later we were bound to be in the war and that Japan had given us an opportunity."

Hopkins also reported that the president was aghast at the unexpected significant strike on U.S. possessions. But he also noted that FDR was relieved Japan had not restricted its attack to British and Dutch possessions, which would have stymied his desire to build U.S. support for declaring war:

> It always disturbed him [FDR] because he really thought that the tactics of the Japanese would be to avoid a conflict with us; that they would not attack either the Philippines or Hawaii but would move on Thailand, French Indo-China, make further inroads on China itself and possibly attack the Malay Straits. This would have left the President with the very difficult problem of protecting our interests. Hence his great relief at the method that Japan used. In spite of the disaster at Pearl Harbor and the blitz-warfare with the Japanese during the first few weeks, it completely solidified the American people and made the war upon Japan inevitable.[43]

FDR's stonewalling of the Japanese government, desperate to negotiate to avoid war, and what Stimson and Hopkins divulged is at least some evidence of intent by FDR and his advisers to use any Japanese attack to justify getting into the European war. Yet by the time the Japanese attacked Pearl Harbor in early December 1941, Hitler's attempt to invade Britain had failed, and he had suffered his first reversal in his invasion of the Soviet Union, thus making the necessity of FDR's risky two-front war questionable. In the Pacific, even without the damage inflicted at Pearl

Harbor, the U.S. Navy at the start of hostilities would have been inferior to the Japanese fleet. Furthermore, U.S. merchant ships, which had been hauling war supplies to Britain and the Soviet Union under Lend-Lease, now needed to be transferred to the Pacific after the Pearl Harbor attack, thus severely compromising the then-raging undeclared Battle of the Atlantic against the German Navy to protect such shipments to Europe—a reported higher U.S. priority. Also, the Japanese attack brought intense public pressure for revenge against Japan, but FDR wanted to send U.S. forces as soon as possible into the fight against the Nazis.

These cross-pressures may have contributed to FDR's later questionable military decision to send U.S. forces in 1942 to help the British keep their empire in North Africa and around the Mediterranean, which delayed the more important opening of a cross-channel invasion in Northern France to ultimately invade Germany to knock out Hitler.[44] FDR was forever the politician, and albeit he likely saw no harm in letting Germany and the USSR further bleed each other, politics can also be a significant explanation for the North African excursion. Because the cross-channel invasion of Normandy was not yet ready in 1942, FDR begged General George Marshall, Army Chief of Staff, to strike Germany somewhere and "please, make it before [midterm] election day." Even General Dwight D. Eisenhower, commander of the North African invasion, believed it was "strategically unsound," and that it would not help relieve German pressure on the Soviets on the Eastern front. Then, to further assist the British secure their empire via military activity around the Mediterranean, the U.S. helped Britain fecklessly invade Sicily and Italy, which further delayed a cross-channel invasion into France. Stalin was apoplectic. Such Allied diversions would contribute to the tensions underlying the future Cold War.

The War Against Germany

To rally the democracies against Hitler in April 1939, FDR had implied in a press conference that U.S. involvement was inevitable in any major European war. In June 1939, even before the European war started with Hitler's invasion of Poland that September, FDR—a Wilsonian (that is, anglophile, idealist, and interventionist)—met with Britain's King George VI in Hyde Park, New York. FDR told the American public about this meeting with an important head of state but neglected to mention that he guaranteed the monarch full American support in any military conflict with Germany.[45] He told the king that the United States would take over British bases and have its navy range a thousand miles into the Atlantic in search of German submarines to sink. This pledge became reality in mid-1941, long before the attack on Pearl Harbor.[46]

However, this promise to the king flagrantly violated the U.S. Constitution's provisions that the initiation of war was the responsibility of Congress. FDR's secret pledge also went against the current of the times, when "isolationism" was surging among the American public right up to the Japanese attack on Pearl Harbor because of disillusionment over the after effects of U.S. entry into World War I. FDR had to take the slow and secretive road to war so that the "isolationists" would not have fodder to use against him in the 1936 and 1940 presidential elections. For example, in 1935, he told the chairman of the Democratic National Committee, "I am walking a tightrope. I realize the seriousness of this from an international as well as domestic point of view,"[47] the implication being that he had to tread carefully when it came to giving any public indication of pro-war views.

While an overwhelming majority of the American population was firm in not wanting war, a majority of that majority still approved of indirectly aiding the democracies against the Nazis. That segment of America believed, implausibly, that if Hitler defeated Britain, he would next attack the United States. A minority faction (the America First Committee) opposed any U.S. deviation from the Neutrality Acts of 1935, 1936, and 1937, correctly believing such a course would drag the country into the war.[48]

By the spring and summer of 1941, months before the Japanese attacks in the Pacific, FDR was directing a hands-on, undeclared war against German U-boats and surface warships in the Atlantic. In short, FDR was at war with the Germans informally before he was at war with the Japanese formally. America's entry into World War II was different than that of World War I. U.S. ships were not in danger of being sunk by German U-boats; in fact, Hitler was scrupulously trying to avoid war with the United States. The U.S. Neutrality Acts made it illegal for American vessels to transit war zones; Woodrow Wilson had foolishly insisted on the right to do so during World War I, and Congress had intended to prevent FDR from replicating that way into a European war. So, unlike the Quasi-War, the War of 1812, or World War I, the United States before entry in World War II had no grounds to claim violation of its rights as a neutral (although the Germans could have argued that U.S. support for the Allies had nullified that status).

At first, the U.S. Navy helped Britain find German U-boats so British merchant ships could evade them and British warships could attack them— billing the effort publicly as reconnaissance in force. However, long before being formally at war with Germany, FDR later publicly ordered a shoot-on-sight order for American naval vessels to attack the German submarines directly. He also began confiscating Axis ships in American ports. In the early months of 1941, after the 1940 German invasions of Denmark, Norway, France, Belgium, and the Netherlands—countries that were naval launch points—Hitler had stepped up his campaign in British waters and on the high seas to shut off Britain's food and raw materials.

In the rich U.S. tradition of James Polk against Mexico and Abraham Lincoln against the South, FDR tried his best to increase soft American public support for a U.S. war against Nazi Germany. As late as the beginning of 1941, the Gallup poll found that 83 percent of Americans wanted to stay out of the war, and in August of that year the House of Representatives voted by only one vote to extend conscription. But FDR had a plan for both going around public opinion and changing it along the way. In May 1941 FDR told Lord Halifax, the British ambassador to the United States, that if the U.S. Navy's patrolling of the Atlantic led to a dustup with the German Navy, it would be welcomed. Later that month, after the British sinking of the powerful German battleship *Bismarck*, British Prime Minister Winston Churchill—who was eager to trigger a U.S.-German naval incident to bring the United States fully into the war on Britain's side—suggested that U.S. naval forces join in the pursuit of the *Bismarck*'s companion ship, cruiser *Prinz Eugen*, which they did.

Winston Churchill told his cabinet that FDR said to him, when they met off the coast of Newfoundland in August 1941, that he would "wage war" against the German Navy but "not declare it."[49] FDR told advisors Harold Ickes and Henry Morgenthau that he hoped for an incident on the high seas that would give him an excuse for using U.S. warships for convoy protection or for getting to a state of war with the Germans. Congress, in the Lend-Lease bill passed in March 1941, had banned U.S. warships from protecting convoys to avoid war with Germany in the North Atlantic. Yet FDR secretly ordered the navy to conduct such convoying and began an undeclared shooting war with German submarines.

In early September 1941 FDR got the naval incident he wanted between the U.S. and German Navies; his provocative policy of aggressively trailing German U-boats, acting as an arm of the British Navy, had worked. Southwest of Iceland, the USS *Greer*, a destroyer, hunted and pursued a U-boat for hours in compliance with U.S. policy. Despite FDR's aggressive policy, German U-boats were under orders not to start hostilities against U.S. warships. However, a British patrol plane working with the *Greer* dropped depth charges on the submarine. The U-boat, unable to learn the nationality of the ship and believing the explosive charges came from it, fired two torpedoes at the vessel, which missed their target. The *Greer* responded with depth charge attacks and further pursuit. FDR then ordered the sinking of the U-boat, with more U.S. destroyers coming from Iceland to do just that. He was unsuccessful.

FDR considered the U-boat's torpedo attack on the *Greer* "piracy legally and morally." He ordered an expansion of cooperation with the British Navy on maritime convoys. He further ordered illegal offensive shoot-on-sight attacks on German and Italian warships in the western Atlantic even if they had not attacked first. Thus, FDR unconstitutionally, and without a declaration of war, actually entered the United States into World War II months before the Japanese attack on Pearl Harbor. Publicly, FDR eagerly mentioned the attempted torpedo attack by the U-boat on the *Greer*, the expansion of convoy protection, and his retaliatory initiation of a general shoot-on-sight policy against Axis warships found in the western three-fourths of the Atlantic. Characteristically, he did not mention the earlier hostile pursuit of the submarine by the U.S. warship, which had provoked the U-boat's attack, or the known fact that the U-boat could not identify the nationality of the ship that had been aggressively following it. (Again, this episode was like other American presidents' deception before U.S. involvement in other wars—James Polk in the Mexican War, Abraham Lincoln in the Civil War, Lyndon Johnson in the Vietnam War, and George W. Bush before the U.S. invasion of Iraq.)

On November 13, 1941, less than a month before Pearl Harbor, Congress barely voted to remove the remaining Neutrality Acts, authorized the arming of American merchant ships, and the entry of U.S. warships into combat zones. FDR removed the restrictions confining to the western Atlantic U.S. warship attacks on German surface raiders; any German warship entering the Atlantic anywhere was now fair game. Yet some historians believe that FDR had concluded from the close congressional votes that not even the later attacks by U-boats on U.S. warships (for example, the destroyers *Kearny* and *Reuben James*, which killed 126 Americans) would be enough to bring the American public around to supporting a war against Germany. These historians believe he needed to provoke the Germans' Japanese ally to attack the United States for the U.S. to go to war against Germany through the back door.[50]

For in a republic in those days, the public usually needed to be convinced of a credible threat to pick up arms. FDR went to war because the madman in Berlin was disrupting the balance of power in Europe. The Nazis' human rights record, including the persecution of Jews, had not been a factor in FDR's decisions. In fact, if FDR had wanted to go to war to remedy human rights abuses in Europe, he would have gone to war alongside Nazi Germany against his future ally, the Soviet Union. Up to 1941, Stalin had killed far more people than Hitler. Hitler did not start his genocide against Jews and other groups until 1942. Because of Stalin's bloody purges in the 1930s, Americans, as late as 1937, rated Stalin above Hitler on their least-favorite leader list.[51]

Yet it is doubtful that saving the European balance of power depended on U.S. entry into the war, or that getting involved in World War II against Hitler's Germany protected U.S. security. Although some German bombers, at the end of their tether, might have been able to hit the United States, the wide Atlantic Ocean offered a huge buffer against an amphibious attack from Western Europe. The United States could have prudently, and without controversy, enhanced its defenses, including augmenting its air force and air defenses. Without air superiority, Germans had already given up on launching an amphibious attack across the narrow English Channel.

Furthermore, although the U.S., British, and Canadian amphibious assault across the channel on D-Day in June 1944 is deservedly praised as a great tactical achievement, it occurred long after the Soviets had halted the Nazis' offensive into the USSR and had them on the run back to Germany. During World War II, the Germans suffered 80 percent of their combat deaths on the Eastern front alone. Soviet manpower on the Eastern front was decisive in deciding the outcome in the European theater of war, and the Red Army would have more than likely defeated Hitler without the vaunted Allied invasion at Normandy and break out across France into Germany. Before the Japanese attack on Pearl Harbor, the Roosevelt administration thought the Soviet Union would fall to the

Nazis. However, as the war raged on, it became clear that the USSR would survive and thus allowed the United States to raise fewer forces for the fight in Europe. Overall, the U.S. Army during World War II, fighting in the European and Asia/Pacific wars simultaneously, was smaller than Germany's and less than half the size of the Soviets'. As in World War I, U.S. military casualties in World War II were lower than the other major belligerent nations. The Soviet military lost fifty times more men than did the American military during the war.[52]

Although the United States provided material support to the Soviet Union as well as to Britain through the Lend-Lease program, the Soviets had bogged down the German offensive after only about one month (end of July 1941), inflicting horrendous German losses of about 213,000, with only negligible Western assistance at that time.[53] By early December 1941, shortly before the Japanese attack on Pearl Harbor, the German offensive had collapsed before it could take Moscow, the reinforced Soviets had begun a counteroffensive, and Rostov in Russia had been recaptured, denying Caucuses oil to the Germans. As historian Justus Doenecke concluded, "The tide of battle. . . . had swung in the Soviets' favor long before American aid had arrived in quantity."

The Nazi reverses of December 1941 meant the United States was not a critical ally in Europe. In fact, opponents of the war in the United States made the cogent argument that U.S. entry would destroy the post-war balance of power in Europe between Germany and the Soviet Union. Furthermore, Senator Robert Taft astutely saw that if Hitler had failed to conquer Britain, why would he attack the United States?[54] Alternatively, the United States could have just continued to provide Lend-Lease aid to Britain and the Soviet Union without ever sending any forces to Europe. After all, FDR already correctly regarded the Soviets and British as prox-ies in the fight against fascism and assisted them. This assistance was supported by a public otherwise reluctant to go to war.

After Japan's desperate attack on Pearl Harbor and the U.S. decla-ration of war, Hitler made his second greatest mistake of the war—the first was invading the Soviet Union—by declaring war against the U.S. economic juggernaut. Hitler felt he could now attack U.S. shipping of war matériel to Britain and the Soviet Union and had little to lose, given the already undeclared war in the Atlantic vis-à-vis the U.S. Navy. Hitler also believed the Japanese could tie down the United States, which now faced a two-front war.

FDR Exceeds the Constitution in the U.S. March to War

The Atlantic Undeclared War on German Submarines

After the meat grinder of World War I, most of the American public was so against further war that the United States turned down entry into the League of Nations, the World Court, a security guarantee for France, free trade, and forgiveness of Allied war debt. The U.S. government used the Washington Naval Conference to negotiate limits to naval power with Britain and Japan and even signed the international Kellogg-Briand Pact outlawing war. In 1935, after Hitler came to power and the Japanese were fighting in Manchuria, large peace marches broke out all over the United States, pressuring Congress to pass the first neutrality act that year.[55]

After Wilson's abuse of U.S. neutrality during the early years of World War I, which led to the United States entering the war after it had been raging for almost three years, Congress decided to pass strict neutrality laws from 1935 to 1937. In a reaction to Wilson's reckless neutrality-in-name-only polices, the statutes banned munitions sales and loans to belligerent nations and required Americans to travel on foreign ships at their own risk—all to prevent a recurrence of the horrendous experience of breaking an American tradition of avoiding European wars, which had been enshrined in the Monroe Doctrine of 1823. Although politically he had to cater to the anti-war vote, which made up much of his own party, FDR—who had decided, sometime in the 1930s, that he could not live with Adolf Hitler's regime in Germany—chafed under such neutrality statutes and looked for ways to circumvent them. Long before the Japanese attack on Pearl Harbor, FDR had been trying to form an alliance with England. It took some time, but he did it later via King George, without any congressional approval, dramatically increasing the likelihood of the United States entering another European war.

By early 1939, FDR tried to reform the Neutrality Act of 1935 but failed. He argued preposterously that the reform would keep the United States out of the war. Congress saw through FDR's duplicity; instead, it put an arms embargo into the act.

In an argument foreshadowing the discredited domino theory of the Vietnam War, FDR said that assistance to the Allies would decrease the risk of the United States getting into the war by helping them defeat Hitler without U.S. participation. He exaggerated the unlikely possibility that Allied defeat in Europe would make U.S. entry into the conflict inevitable because it would motivate a triumphant Hitler to commit aggression against the western hemisphere and the United States.[56] Given the huge undertaking that the eventual Allied amphibious assault on Normandy over fifty miles of water turned out to be, it would have been impossible for Hitler to have launched an amphibious assault on the faraway United States from Europe, or on Latin America from Africa. Also, in FDR's far-fetched imagination, Hitler could have taken advantage of political instability in Latin America to install Nazi regimes there, then use the converted countries as bases to attack the United States, especially with long-range bombers. (But the U.S. would have had plenty of time to augment its defenses, including its air defenses, or attack those bases.)

After Poland fell to the Nazis in September 1939, and France and British Commonwealth nations had declared war on Germany, the Neutrality Acts bound FDR to announce U.S. neutrality. However, by November 1939, Congress relented, allowing private Americans to sell arms to the Allies, but only when they paid cash and used their own vessels to carry them (the cash and carry policy). Neither Britain nor France was to receive credit to buy arms. FDR again made the mendacious claim that selling arms only to one side in the war would keep the United States out of the war, ignoring American experience in World War I. Then in 1940, he similarly claimed that the first peacetime draft in the nation's history would keep the United States out of the European war.

In that same year, FDR was standing for an unprecedented third term and did not want to appear to be unilaterally rushing the U.S. into a war that had little public support (only a slight majority of Americans supported just sending supplies to Britain). Wendell Willkie, his Republican opponent, claimed that a vote for FDR was a vote for war. Therefore, during the campaign that same year, FDR deceptively asserted, "Your boys are not going to be sent into any foreign wars," even as he was expecting the United States to soon enter the war and was secretly working toward that goal. Like Woodrow Wilson in 1916 during World War I, FDR ran in the 1940 election on having kept the United States out of the European war, but then the next year after the poll was over, he ramped up his rhetoric and got the U.S. into the conflict.

By December 1940, the Nazi threat to Britain had lessened after the British had won the Battle of Britain, thus denying Hitler the air superiority needed to carry out his planned amphibious assault on the island. Yet, the Germans had sunk more than five hundred merchant ships, and

Britain was almost bankrupt. In December 1940 Churchill informed FDR that Britain could no longer afford to pay cash for supplies and ships to carry them. Instead of taking advantage of Britain's having won the Battle of Britain to reassert U.S. neutrality, FDR—now reelected and inaugurated to an unprecedented third term—instead successfully pushed Congress approve the Lend-Lease Act in March 1941. The act delegated to him the immense power to lend, lease, or give American-made military equipment and food to Britain, Free France, China, and the Soviet Union, thus effectively circumventing the neutrality laws of the 1930s and bringing the United States another step closer to war. Correctly assessing that the United States was shedding its neutrality, Hitler regarded Lend-Lease as U.S. economic warfare against Germany, and his advisers told him to expect the United States to get into the shooting war soon.

While he could have waited to see what happened in Europe, FDR instead, by executive order, expanded the patrolled area in the Atlantic by U.S. warships and announced that the U.S. would notify British ships of the location of German naval vessels, though initially it would not supply escorts for British merchant ships carrying American-made war matériel and supplies. The mere expansion of the area of the Atlantic patrolled by U.S. ships, however, expanded the possibility of a German submarine attacking a U.S. ship. In September 1941, FDR's order for U.S. warships to escort convoys of British merchant ships as far as Iceland and his shoot on sight order against even nonattacking German submarines and warships in the vastly expanded western Atlantic region further escalated the probability of a hostile encounter between the two navies. Both orders violated international law. In November of 1941, Congress removed most of the last vestiges of U.S. neutrality laws by allowing American ships into the war zone.

FDR's policy orientation was clear even if he was typically devious in its implementation. Without anything close to a formal declaration of war, FDR was paying for and shipping war matériel to informal allies, having U.S. warships escort vessels carrying the war matériel across the Atlantic, shooting at nonhostile German submarines or warships, and secretly conducting joint planning with the British military for a Europe-first war effort.[57] Most of those activities were illegal or unconstitutional as the founders would have understood them. And acts of war, as Hitler would have seen it.

As a former U.S. Navy official who was quite familiar with the history of the Spanish-American War and World War I, FDR knew the value of using naval incidents to spark wars. In May 1941 he informed his cabinet that he was "not willing to fire the first shot". In August 1941, after meeting shipboard with FDR off the coast of Newfoundland, Churchill reported to his war cabinet that Roosevelt had told him that "he was skating on pretty thin ice in his relations with Congress" and that "if he were to put the issue of peace and war to Congress, they would debate it for three months." Demonstrating his contempt for Congress's constitutional war power, FDR said that instead "he would wage war, but not declare it, and that he would become more and more provocative. If the Germans did not like it, they could attack American forces.... Everything was to be done to force an 'incident' ... which would justify him opening hostilities."[58]

Thus, after Lend-Lease passed in March 1941 and long before the Japanese attack on Pearl Harbor, FDR—to help ensure that the American arms and food safely reached Britain and to provoke a war with Germany—started his aggressive, undeclared, and therefore unconstitutional war to find and attack German U-boats in the North Atlantic.

More evidence of FDR's activities in the Greenland-Iceland-United Kingdom (GIUK) gap maritime choke point—two strategic passages between those three islands into the North Atlantic Ocean from the North Sea, the Norwegian Sea, and the Greenland Sea—further demonstrated his desire to have the U.S. enter the European war. In April 1940, Germany had invaded and occupied Denmark, which exercised sovereignty over both Iceland and Greenland, making both unoccupied territories of the Third Reich. The idea was: if the Germans occupied Greenland, they could bomb New York.

Therefore, to forestall an invasion of Greenland—not by Germany but by Britain or Canada—FDR's administration, without congressional authorization, assumed Greenland's defense, sent U.S. troops to occupy the island, dispatched U.S. Coast Guard ships to conduct antisubmarine patrols in its waters, and agreed with Greenland's governing authorities to build U.S. air bases there. In the spring of 1941, the United States began setting up several military installations in Greenland before formally entering the war at year's end. Meanwhile, the FDR administration continued to deny that the U.S. Navy was engaged in convoy operations and was patrolling farther east in the Atlantic than the American public was aware.

The Questionable Domino Theory

As a precursor to the domino theory of the Cold War, FDR was concerned that if Britain fell to the Nazis, they then could capture Iceland by sea and use it as a stepping-stone to the United States. Because Iceland was near the convoy routes from America to Britain, possessing it was becoming critical to keeping Britain in the war. If the United States were to supply effective support to Britain across the Atlantic, it would need to control Iceland. The island was east of Greenland and not considered to be in the western hemisphere—until FDR, who had justified his maritime actions in the Atlantic by claiming hemispheric defense—included it (an early 1940s version of Donald Trump's famous altering of a FEMA map of severe weather with a Sharpie marker).[59]

In July 1941, months before the United States formally entered the war, the defense of Iceland shifted from Britain to the United States. The United States sent Marines without public knowledge or FDR obtaining advanced congressional approval for this military deployment. This unapproved military deployment to a war zone, which generated criticism in Congress, was like James Polk's deployment of U.S. Army forces to disputed territory on the U.S.-Mexican border, intending to provoke a war with Mexico. FDR realized that his unilateral sending of forces to Iceland was far more than the announced hemispheric defense; it was helping a belligerent in a European conflict. Also, he knew from history that the fait accompli of unauthorized and provocative military deployments would not be nixed by Congress—as it hadn't for Thomas Jefferson in the first Barbary War, Polk in the Mexican War, Abraham Lincoln in the Civil War, and Woodrow Wilson in his Latin American interventions. FDR's belated announcement of the arrival of the Marines in Iceland avoided the issue of whether the U.S. Navy would be convoying to keep sea-lanes open to the island, and newspapers faced censorship when reporting on the issue.[60]

With troops securing Iceland, FDR could begin sending and defending maritime convoys of supplies through the western Atlantic, with Iceland as a transshipment point. However, Admiral Harold Stark, U.S. Chief of Naval Operations, considered FDR's sending Marines to Iceland to be "practically an act of war."[61] (Senator Robert Taft agreed and complained about the executive's usurpation of congressional powers.) Stark and Rear Admiral Richmond Kelly Turner, the director of the Navy's war plans division, opposed the deployment to Iceland and believed the limited escorting of convoys in the western Atlantic to Iceland would be useful only in provoking a maritime incident with the Germans, leading to a U.S. excuse for entry into the war—which is one reason why FDR was so enthusiastic about conducting the escorts.

Despite FDR's redefinition of the western hemisphere, the deployments of troops to Iceland was the first outside it since World War I. These U.S. national commitments and military deployments to Greenland and Iceland without congressional approval, before any declaration of war against Germany and Japan, eroded Congress's power to declare war and thus were of questionable constitutionality, especially in an increasingly tense world facing an ongoing global conflagration.

In short, by July 1941 FDR, with no congressional nod, had agreed to defend much of the North Atlantic—past U.S. territorial waters, beyond neutrality limits, and across the midpoint of the Atlantic on the threshold of Europe. FDR unilaterally had committed the United States to control much of the Atlantic and risked war—or invited it—with Germany to do that mission.[62]

In 1940 and 1941, before the U.S. formally entered the war by congressional declarations of war, FDR—by his U.S. destroyers-for-British bases trade with Britain absent congressional approval, unilateral commitments to defend other nations, decision to escort war supply convoys to Iceland, and shoot-on-sight orders against Axis vessels that had not attacked U.S. warships—had set another precedent for executive usurpation of the power to initiate war, as delegated to Congress in the Constitution. He stretched the meaning of self-defense from defending the United States—as intended by the founders—to include ensuring the security of other nations (the concept of collective defense).[63]

FDR's Military Leadership Less than Stellar

Although FDR during World War II managed his generals more competently than Abraham Lincoln did in the Civil War—FDR mostly chose good military commanders from the start—he still made some key mistakes during the war.

Moving the Pacific Fleet to Hawaii

In the spring of 1940, FDR moved the Pacific fleet from the U.S. West Coast to Pearl Harbor, Hawaii, believing that it would better deter Japanese expansion in East Asia. When Admiral James Richardson, commander in chief of the U.S. fleet, protested that it would only make the Navy's ships more vulnerable to attack, FDR fired him. A further problem with the redeployment was that Washington was five thousand miles from Hawaii and communications between the two locations were then rudimentary. At a minimum, FDR could be blamed for endangering the U.S. Pacific Fleet by moving it to more vulnerable Hawaii. At worst, he could be accused of deliberately inviting or failing to forewarn of an imminent Japanese attack on Hawaii to persuade a reluctant American public to enter the war.

During the 1944 election for an unprecedented fourth term, FDR was horrified to learn that an army officer had told the aides of Thomas Dewey, his Republican opponent, that before the Pearl Harbor attack, FDR and his military chiefs had read intercepted Japanese diplomatic traffic revealing that Japan was going to strike Hawaiian island bases. In the campaign, Dewey was going to exploit this information to accuse FDR of deliberately allowing the attack to occur to get into the war. George Marshall, the army chief of staff, sent Dewey a written warning that if he went public with his Pearl Harbor secrets, he would be helping the enemy by revealing that the U.S. had broken the Japanese diplomatic codes. A dejected Dewey backed off from using the issue in the campaign.[64]

A Sub-Optimal War Strategy

In 1942, having decided that the Allied armies were not ready for a cross-English Channel invasion of Europe, Anglophile FDR let Winston Churchill suck him into a diversion of U.S. military resources to save the British Empire. The United States invaded northern Africa in 1942 and then Italy in 1943. These diversions wasted valuable resources that could have been better used for an earlier invasion of France in 1943. But part of FDR's strategy was waiting for the Soviet Red Army to finish off Hitler's forces on the eastern front and push toward Berlin.

In the Pacific, FDR let both the Army and Navy/Marines have their seats at the war strategy table. To please both services, he used a less efficient two-pronged strategy: he first focused on the Navy/Marines island-hopping across the central Pacific toward the Japanese home islands. Then he allowed General MacArthur and the Army to conduct a slower trek from Australia to New Guinea back to the Philippines. In July 1944 FDR met with his two combat commanders—Admiral Chester Nimitz and prima donna General MacArthur. The president's staff and Nimitz suggested that the Philippines, heavily defended by the Japanese, be hopscotched. MacArthur would have none of it. Having loudly proclaimed that he would return to the Philippines when ordered to evacuate early in the war under Japanese attack, MacArthur bluntly told the president he would suffer at the polls if the U.S. Philippine colony was not freed. FDR, always the politician, allowed the two-pronged inefficiency to continue. Predictably, the Japanese Army on the Philippines conducted a delaying action in the mountains and jungles of the archipelago, which resulted in a costly U.S. operation that contributed little to the final Japanese defeat.[65] Nevertheless, MacArthur became a war hero due to his theatrics of returning to the islands.

FDR Demanded Unconditional Surrender

The American economic colossus could vastly outproduce the Axis countries combined. Even when the Americans did not have the best technology, such as in tanks, they simply outproduced their enemies. America was besting Japan in the Pacific and in late 1944, coming from the west after the Normandy landings in France, finally relieved pressure on Soviet forces closing in on Germany from the east.

FDR demanded the unconditional surrender of Germany and Japan—making both nations fight harder and longer. Japan was stubbornly reluctant to surrender on FDR's terms because it meant removing its sacred emperor. FDR may have borne in mind Teddy Roosevelt's extremely hawkish criticism of Wilson's armistice with Germany in World War I, which may have driven this ambitious unconditional demand. Since the United States was bringing most of the resources to the war, Winston

Churchill agreed with FDR's demand for unconditional surrender though he also feared it would make their enemies fight to the end. By that point, Churchill was concerned that even more war destruction would hinder Germany's postwar ability to stand up to Soviet military power.[66]

FDR Avoided Congressional Oversight

After the fighting started, FDR showed he had learned from the foibles of Woodrow Wilson during World War I. He communicated to Congress and the American public his strategy to win the war and the conflict's progress. However, like Wilson, he managed to deflect, albeit more privately and diplomatically, congressional pressure for a special committee to investigate the war effort—which had been a necessary burr in Lincoln's saddle during the Civil War.

Atomic Bombs and Other Forms of Mass Incineration

Unlike World War I, civilians would suffer the most from World War II—as belligerents waged unrestrained warfare on each other's populations. Although Allied democracies—the United States and Britain—did not kill as many civilians in the war as did the Axis powers, they still engaged in the unnecessary, ineffective, and mostly counterproductive and barbaric bombing of enemy cities. Hundreds of thousands of Germans and a staggering million Japanese died from aerial bombardment. Yet, even during the heaviest bombing, German economic output tripled from 1941 to 1944, and German willingness to fight on only increased. The British, more honest in their war crimes than the Americans, even called the deliberate bombing of civilians what it was—terror bombing. Curtis LeMay, who had been in charge of U.S. bombing of Japan, admitted that if the United States had lost the war, the architects of the bombing would have been tried for war crimes.[67] Tragically, as in the U.S. Civil War, late in the conflict and with exhaustion and anger, even as it became more likely that ultimately the they would be victorious, the Allies increased their assaults on civilians.

The decision of Harry Truman, FDR's successor after he died in April 1945, to drop two atomic bombs on the two Japanese cities of Hiroshima and Nagasaki ushered in a new age of armaments of historic and unparalleled power of mass destruction. In World War II, the new bombs simply made the ongoing mass slaughter of enemy civilians more efficient. FDR had begun a heavy bombing campaign against German and Japanese cities to bring these nations to heel using incendiary weapons (firebombing). Before the United States entered the war, FDR had sanctimoniously urged all belligerents to follow the never-ratified 1923 Hague Rules of Air Warfare. In 1940, FDR characterized the Nazi bombing of Rotterdam in the Netherlands as "inhuman barbarism that has profoundly shocked the conscience of humanity."[68]

However, once the United States entered the war, FDR changed his tune. In Japan, the United States used incendiary weapons because most Japanese had houses of paper and wood, thus destroying cities by spreading fire. Beginning in February 1945, FDR launched this monthslong firebombing campaign of Japanese cities, rendering 40 percent of the urban areas of the cities uninhabitable and destroying the homes of millions.[69] More people—greater than one hundred thousand—were killed in incendiary bombing raids against Tokyo than by Truman's two atomic bomb (A-bomb) raids over Hiroshima on August 6, 1945 (sixty-six thousand deaths), and Nagasaki on August 9 (thirty-nine thousand deaths).[70] General Curtis LeMay said of the Tokyo fire bombings of civilians: "There are no innocent civilians. It is their government, and you are fighting a people, you are not trying to fight an armed force anymore. So, it does not bother me so much to be killing the so-called innocent bystanders."[71] Killing civilians for political purposes is usually the modern definition of terrorism. A primary difference between the firebombing campaign of Tokyo and the atomic bombings of Hiroshima and Nagasaki was that the destruction of the last two cities was by one bomber each, while the Tokyo campaign involved hundreds of bombers. From a moral point of view, little difference existed between FDR's firebombing and Truman's use of more efficient atomic bombs.

Even today, more than seventy-five years after their use, Truman's dropping of the atomic bombs is controversial. His apologists insist that an invasion of mainland Japan would have cost one million U.S. military deaths, given how tenaciously the Japanese fought earlier battles in which their homeland was not at stake. Some even make the argument that the use of the bombs saved Japanese lives that would have perished in any U.S. invasion. Yet, at the time, the overwhelming majority of U.S. military leaders were skeptical of any of these "dropping the bomb would save lives" arguments. General Dwight Eisenhower said, upon hearing the bomb would be dropped, "I had . . . a feeling of depression and ... voiced ... my grave misgivings, first on the basis of my belief that Japan was already defeated and that dropping the bomb was completely unnecessary, and secondly because I thought that our country should avoid shocking world opinion by the use of a weapon whose employment was ... no longer mandatory ... to save American lives."[72]

However, strikingly, the White House did not consult U.S. military leaders. If it had, the president and staff would have learned there was an overwhelming view that military considerations did not call for the use of the A-bombs. Several military leaders notably recoiled at their use against cities. Truman's lack of consultation with the military indicates that use of the powerful new weapons was not based on military necessity. According to Admiral William D. Leahy, chief of staff for Presidents Roosevelt and Truman: "The use of this barbarous weapon at Hiroshima and Nagasaki was of no material assistance in our war against Japan. The Japanese were already defeated and ready to surrender because of the effective sea blockade and the successful bombing with conventional weapons. In being the first to use it, we had adopted an ethical standard common to the barbarians of the Dark Ages."

Astonishingly, even the extremely hawkish General Curtis LeMay, under whose command the military dropped the atomic bombs, said at a press conference a month and a half after dropping them: "The war would have been over in two weeks without the Russians and without the atomic bomb. The atomic bomb had nothing to do with the end of the war at all."[73]

The argument in favor of dropping the A-bomb is based on dubious assumptions, which are rarely questioned, despite such assessments by the military. The foremost shaky assumption in the argument is that, to achieve a Japanese surrender, the United States needed to invade Japan. By fall of 1945, the United States had achieved overwhelming naval superiority by destroying the Japanese Navy; after the Battle of Leyte Gulf, U.S. surface warships and submarines had gone a long way toward cutting off the trade of Japan's home islands with the world, including oil for the Japanese military. As Fleet Admiral Chester Nimitz noted, the Japanese were already short on food. As a result, Japan—an island nation—was quite vulnerable to being sealed off completely from the world by a tightening naval blockade.

According to Rear Admiral Richard Byrd, "Especially it is good to see the truth told about the last days of the war with Japan . . . I was with the fleet during that period; and every officer in the fleet knew that Japan would eventually capitulate from . . . the tight blockade. I too felt strongly that it was a mistake to drop the atomic bombs, especially without warning."[74]

This testimonial alone shoots down the argument that bombing the Japanese atomically would save them by preventing even more civilian casualties in any U.S. invasion of the home islands. To avoid substituting the wanton slaughter of Japanese by starvation instead of aerial nuclear bombardment, until they surrendered, a basic level of food and medicine could have been allowed through the blockade, so that the Japanese could live but not thrive. Yet a continued U.S. naval blockade does not appear to have been seriously considered, although the Navy proposed it. Truman later wrote, "Let there be no mistake about it, I regarded the bomb as a military weapon and never had any doubt that it should be used."[75]

Even if an invasion of the Japanese home islands was somehow deemed necessary, the estimate of a million U.S. casualties was very soft. The invasion plan presented to Truman by the top generals did no in-depth analysis of the matter.[76] General Marshall's informal estimate of U.S. invasion casualties was 63,000 while Admiral Leahy's was 268,000.

The perceived need to invade Japan arose from the American goal of total victory over its wartime opponents, expressed in FDR's aim for the unconditional surrender of Germany and Japan. General Ulysses S. Grant started this trend by demanding it of the Confederates during the American Civil War. Yet most wars in world history and many in American history did not result in total victory, but instead in a negotiated settlement among the belligerents—for example, the War of 1812, the Mexican War, the Spanish-American War, and World War I. However, politically, Truman was afraid the American public would roast him alive politically if he dropped the unconditional surrender demand.

When the A-bombs were dropped, the Japanese were already trying to surrender through the Soviet Union, and the Americans knew it through intercepted Japanese communications. Even if the United States was concerned that the Soviets would want part or all of Japan, Americans still could have controlled the country through the naval blockade.

The U.S. demand for unconditional surrender (UC) in World War II made both Germany and Japan fight harder to avoid national humiliations. In the case of Germany, the United States achieved UC, because Soviet and Allied forces conquered German territory and its capital Berlin from two directions but had to engage in fierce combat to do so. UC to the Japanese meant that their emperor must go. However, even after dropping two atomic bombs, the United States did not achieve UC. To get a Japanese surrender, the United States had to agree to let Japan keep its emperor. Truman could have and should have offered this concession before dropping the A-bombs to see if the Japanese would have surrendered without added loss of life.. General Douglas MacArthur believed that Japan would have surrendered if Truman had made this concession before dropping the A-bombs. In fact, by June 1945, the Japanese, at the urging of their emperor, had reached out to propose peace—as long they could keep the emperor. But Truman lacked the political courage to accept this condition until absolute necessity forced him to do so.

That said, Germany and Japan killed many more innocents in World War II than did the United States and its allies, but why lower the "fight for freedom" to their level by the mass slaughter of civilians, especially for no sound military reason? Some analysts have doubted Truman's veracity. They argue that his claims of military necessity were less vital to him than the desire to try to impress and intimidate Stalin.

If Truman believed he needed to bomb the Japanese into submission, he could have just continued with conventional fire-bombing raids. Instead, he kept delaying the Potsdam Conference with Stalin and Churchill until the atomic bomb test in New Mexico had been completed. According to Joseph E. Davies, U.S. Ambassador to the Soviet Union, Truman told him that he did not want the summit to take place until July because the atomic bomb test had been delayed until then—the test was held on July 16 and the summit began on July 17. Dean Acheson, Truman's secretary of state, later recorded that Truman "wore the bomb ostentatiously on his hip" at the conference to shock, awe, and intimidate Stalin—then an ally but likely a future adversary, Truman believed, once Japan had been defeated. However, since Stalin's spies had infiltrated the U.S. Manhattan Project, which designed and built the atomic weapons, he already knew about them and was unfazed at the summit. Before the successful test of the atomic weapon, Truman had thought he might need Soviet entry into the Pacific war to draw Japanese military resources away from U.S. forces. However, now that he had the powerful new weapon, he believed he could win the war without the Soviets getting any of the East Asian spoils.[77]

This explanation for U.S. use of atomic bombs is quite plausible. Truman would soon prove to be far more aggressive in dealing with Stalin than FDR had been, launching a global crusade against communism that turned into a forty-plus-year Cold War. If Truman did use the A-bombs against civilians in a futile attempt to impress and intimidate Stalin, it was morally reprehensible, although no more so than FDR's unneeded firebombing of German and Japanese cities at the end of the war.

Truman was politically too timid to remove the UC requirement to let the Japanese keep their emperor. He had feared that the American public would have his political head for abandoning the traditional American UC demand, especially after the policy's success against Nazi Germany. Thus, Truman dropped the A-bombs to hasten Japanese surrender, fence the Soviets out of Japan, and intimidate the USSR with the destructive new technology. As David Model convincingly asserts, Truman committed some of the same war crimes the Nazis were accused of at the post-war Nuremberg trials: "War crimes: ill-treatment of civilian population . . . wanton destruction of cities, towns, or villages, or devastation not justified by military necessity," and "Crimes against Humanity: namely, murder, extermination . . . of civilian population."[78] Although the Nazis and Imperial Japanese committed unspeakable crimes on a grander scale, FDR and Truman were culpable too. But only losers in wars are prosecuted for horrendous depredations.

Unconstitutional Acts at Home

The most horrendous and shameful breach of the U.S. Constitution during World War II was FDR's executive order interning in U.S. prison camps 110,000 Japanese residents and American citizens of Japanese heritage (about 70 percent of the total), neither of whom were threats to U.S. security. FDR knew this because his White House staff had reached this conclusion. Far worse, in many cases, the internees had sons who were fighting for the United States in Europe.

However, Earl Warren, later receiving accolades as chief justice of the U.S. Supreme Court for his progressive rulings, did not act so liberally as a politician when governor of California. Being on the West Coast, California had a large ethnically Japanese population, and public pressure—based solely on racial hatred and economic gain—pushed Warren to do something about a nonexistent problem. Warren in turn pressured master politician FDR. Although Francis Biddle, FDR's attorney general who was far more concerned about wartime civil liberties violations than the president, did not tell him ethnic Japanese incarceration was unconstitutional, he tried unsuccessfully to dissuade his boss from doing it. But then Biddle noted that Japanese removal and confiscation of their property, oftentimes good farmland, would help white Californians in agricultural competition with ethnic Japanese. Arguing to the contrary, but later, Harold Ickes, a trusted presidential advisor and secretary of the interior, thought that internment had just needlessly created an embittered population on U.S. soil. Even J. Edgar Hoover, director of the FBI, who was himself a notorious violator of civil liberties, was against Japanese incarceration because it derived from public pressure rather than the facts.[79]

FDR knew the facts very well but nonetheless took the politically advantageous route to enact a scandalous violation of human rights. Fearing he might lose California in the 1944 election, FDR refused to rescind his executive order—freeing the ethnic Japanese in December 1944, only after the election was well over.[80]

The incarceration of ethnic Japanese in the United States began after the very limited threat of a Japanese attack on the West Coast had all but evaporated, with the outnumbered U.S. aircraft carriers having nonetheless defeated the Japanese at the Battle of Midway in June 1942. Further demonstrating that the Japanese American threat was bogus, the large ethnic Japanese population of Hawaii—which FDR had unilaterally made a war zone—was never interned in prison camps and faced less severe restrictions that ethnic Japanese in California, 2,500 miles away from the war zone. A further indication of blatant racism was the different treatment of ethnic Japanese compared to that of ethnic Germans and Italians living in the United States, who neither had their property confiscated nor were held in prison camps.

Congress backed FDR's monstrous breach of the civil liberties of ethnic Japanese on the West Coast by passing a law making it illegal for the Japanese to resist relocation to the prison camps. In 1942, in the *Hirabayashi* case, the Supreme Court cruelly ruled that it could not overrule military judgments. Similarly, in the *Korematsu* case of 1944, even when the war was looking much better for the Allies, the court said that government mass incarceration of citizens and residents despite no crimes being committed was constitutional. During World War II, no ethnic Japanese individual in the United States was charged with sedition, treason, sabotage, or espionage. *Korematsu* is one of the worst Supreme Court decisions in American history.

In 1942, authorities caught eight alleged German saboteurs—including two U.S. citizens—and tried them, via FDR's executive order, in unconstitutional military tribunals. Such tribunals have lax procedural safeguards for defendants compared to civilian trials, thus making conviction much easier. In the case of *Ex Parte Milligan*, the Supreme Court—in 1866 after the Civil War had ended—had ruled that the Constitution prevented the president, even during a massive war on U.S. soil, from bypassing functioning civilian courts in favor of using kangaroo military commissions to try civilians. In other words, Abraham Lincoln too had violated the founding document by nonetheless using such military tribunals for that purpose.

The Constitution guarantees everyone a civilian trial for the commission of crimes, except for U.S. armed forces personnel during wartime, who get court-martialed for alleged injurious behavior. Yet, even given the earlier Supreme Court ruling, FDR held military tribunals for the alleged saboteurs anyway. He made it clear to the Supreme Court of 1942 that he would not give up the defendants to the civilian justice system and even hinted he would execute the Germans, no matter how the Supreme Court decided.

The generally pro-civil liberties Attorney General Francis Biddle argued that the men, no matter what their aims, had committed no crimes. Yet Biddle agreed to try the saboteurs in the military commissions because of the difficulty of proving the government's case in a civilian court. Obviously, such venue shopping that drastically eases the rules for conviction defeats the entire purpose of a fair justice system. The Supreme Court did not interfere with FDR's use of military tribunals and their verdicts. All eight alleged saboteurs faced conviction in a kangaroo fashion; most were dead within six weeks of arrest. Unlike Lincoln during the Civil War, however, FDR did not impose an unconstitutional general suspension of habeas corpus (defendants' right to challenge their detention in court).[81]

The segregation of military units, in addition to its moral bankruptcy, was inefficient and impeded the war effort. Nevertheless, FDR, always the politician first, felt he needed to keep southern white Democrats in his coalition at election time. Therefore, he did nothing to integrate military units or allow black soldiers to vote.[82] As happened in World War I, some white southerners lynched black soldiers coming home in uniform from World War II.

On other issues of civil liberties, however, the Roosevelt administration during World War II was generally better than the Wilson administration had been during World War I. It was not that FDR was more conscientious about civil liberties than Wilson; his racist treatment of ethnic Japanese disproves that thesis. Instead, because once a major direct attack had occurred on U.S. soil to start World War II—which did not happen in World War I—the American people were far more united in support of a war against the horrific Nazis and Imperial Japanese than they had been against the milder Kaiser Wilhelm's Germany. Therefore, FDR felt that he did not need to ask that Congress legislate new general strictures on public speech or the press to stifle anti-war dissent, as had Wilson. Also contributing to FDR's general moderation on civil liberties during World War II was the adverse public reaction to Wilson's draconian censorship and repression of dissent during World War I. Yet, copious public racism against ethnic Japanese and African Americans prevented outrage when their liberties were severely violated during World War II.

Despite the Supreme Court's ruling that warrantless surveillance was illegal, FDR secretly allowed J. Edgar Hoover to illicitly surveil and investigate anti-interventionist dissidents, communists, fascists, congressional critics, and political opponents, including Wendell Willkie, his 1940 election opponent. Also, in an abuse of the Internal Revenue Service, FDR illegally had his foes' tax returns investigated.

With technological advances during World War II, presidents began to make the dubious case that total war required the president to be commander in chief on the home front, as well as top commander of U.S. forces during battle—the narrower role that the nation's founders had envisioned when they wrote the Constitution. At the time of World War II, some bombers flying from Europe could reach the United States at the end of their range. This led to concerns about civil defense. However, the founders' original constitutional framework had allowed the president to conduct self-defense of the country in dire situations when the Congress could not meet to declare war.

Continued technological advances in weapons and the vast scale of the production needed to fight World War II meant that the entire American society was mobilized as never before, including industrial-scale production of arms and other items. (This phenomenon began in World War I, but the United States only entered in the last year and a half of that conflict.) These needs encouraged FDR and later presidents to believe they needed to expand the narrow constitutional role of commander in chief to one that included domestic industrial production and civil liberties. In late May 1941, for example, more than six months before the attack on Pearl Harbor and the U.S. declaration of war, FDR announced an unlimited national emergency that gave the president sweeping extra-constitutional powers over trade, transportation, aliens, communication, and public utilities.

Suspicious of excessive executive power, the nation's founders did not write emergency presidential powers into the Constitution. Only Congress could temporarily suspend habeas corpus (the power of individuals to challenge their detention by the government) in times of rebellion and invasion and provide for calling out the militia to enforce the laws, repel an invasion, and put down rebellion. But FDR questionably seized an airplane factory in California to pre-empt a labor strike from disrupting military aircraft production. After the Japanese attack on Pearl Harbor, he seized other private factories.[83]

Government Penetration of the Economy Exceeds That in WWI

WWI had brought about the most government penetration of the American economy during any war in American history to date. However, World War II involved higher technology and was fought on an even grander scale than the First World War. And government intrusion into the private market was also far greater in the second conflict.

A commonly heard but fallacious contention is that World War II finally brought the U.S. economy out of the Great Depression. But many other industrial countries had recovered from that large economic downturn much sooner than the United States—for example, the British per capita GDP had recovered by 1934, long before strong war winds swept the European continent.

In contrast, because of the economic drag of FDR's big-government New Deal policies, the Great Depression did not really end in America until 1945—when World War II was over and vast amounts of resources returned to the private sector. Although the U.S. economy (expressed in GDP) grew rapidly during the war, that expansion was an artificial war prosperity caused by huge increases in military spending. By 1945, defense spending alone made up more than 40 percent of the American economy.[84] Rationing of certain foodstuffs and other consumer items was instituted so that societal resources could be used by the military. Thus, the nondefense sector of the American economy grew during the war at even slower rates than during the prior Great Depression. War-induced prosperity was an illusion.

In addition, war nearly always causes price inflation at home because production shifts from commercial items to military weapons and supplies, which civilians do not consume. Yet many people work in war-related industries, thus generating more income, but there are fewer consumer goods to buy. Inflation results when too much money chases too few goods in the consumer market. Thus, many times in war, governments impose price controls to slow or stop price inflation; the controls rarely are successful and distort the domestic economy. During World War I, price controls were informal and indirect, but in World War II they were formal and direct. The more formal and direct the controls, the greater the economic distortion.

To assert widespread control over the domestic wartime economy, FDR threatened to invoke his authority as commander in chief to flout the high congressional farm price ceiling contained in the Emergency Price Control Act of 1942 in favor of a lower one allegedly designed to fight inflation. Some Republicans likened the threat to that of a dictator, and even some Democrats were concerned about its constitutionality. FDR made the far-fetched claim that the multifront war overseas made it more critical that he control the domestic economy. However, his threat worked; not wanting the president to exert such broad commander-in-chief powers, Congress capitulated by legislating greater presidential authority to fight inflation—even though price controls can still have earthshaking collateral long-term ill effects on society and the economy.

If too much money chasing too few goods is the cause of inflation, one way to battle it is to raise taxes, thus taking money out of consumers' pockets. Although this further distorts the economy, it is better than financing the war by worse methods—heavy borrowing that increases debt, and worst of all, by printing money. FDR believed Woodrow Wilson had financed World War I with too much borrowing, debt accumulation, and inflation. Thus, FDR wanted after-tax income limits on Americans, prohibitively elevated income tax rates, new taxes on upper-income people, and excess-profits taxes to prevent defense profiteering.

During wartime, taxing the wealthy minority exorbitantly is politically crafty because war efforts survive on a majority of the populace continuing to support them; thus, drastically higher taxes on ordinary people can be avoided. However, Congress balked at even taxing the well-heeled, so FDR again—as he did by using executive authority to set price ceilings—threatened flagrantly unconstitutional action to get Congress to approve higher taxes to fund the war. FDR's most flagrant abuse of the Constitution during the war was his threat to unilaterally set tax levels, one of the most important core functions of the legislature in a republic. Although FDR taxed the wealthiest people the most to fund the war, the conflict was so large and expensive that this gambit would not cover all the costs. Another way to finance the war was converting the income tax, which had been confined to the highest incomes during pre–World War II years, into a mass tax applied to all citizens. Before the conflict, the percentage of the workforce paying income taxes was only 7 percent; after the war it had increased to 64 percent. Before the war, the income tax was never more than 1.5 percent of GNP; since, it has rarely dipped below 7 percent.

The government's withholding of money from citizens' paychecks throughout the year to pay the income tax—which began in 1943 in the middle of the war—was even worse than expanding the income tax to the lower incomes. It began, ironically, with the help of Treasury official Milton Friedman, a future advocate of smaller government and lower taxes. Before the war, people simply paid their tax bill in a lump sum after the tax year was over. Advance withholding helped with tax compliance, but piecemeal tax payments of money workers never saw hid elevated levels of taxation and focused citizens' attention on any year-end refunds rather than on their total tax bill. Corporate taxes also increased to fund the war. This radically new and remunerative tax structure would fund a lavishly large federal government from the end of the war to the present. World War II also institutionalized the Keynesian revolution in economics' pernicious rationale for big government: full employment. But the federal budget deficits used to achieve it caused a fateful shifting of the goals and the methods of economic management in the postwar economy.[85]

During World War II, with millions of civilian workers drafted into the military and many others transferred from commercial to defense work, the supply of labor in commercial industries effectively declined, thus raising wages. To stanch this increase, the government imposed wage controls (controlling the price of labor). Thus, businesses competing for scarce labor had to offer more fringe benefits instead of wage hikes. They began to supply healthcare for their workers and the modern American healthcare system was born. Thus, during the war, healthcare coverage became dependent on a person's job—an inefficient way to supply healthcare and potentially catastrophic if an employee was laid off or fired. Also, the federal government's involvement in supplying public housing came about because of housing shortages near key defense plants as war production ramped up.

Summary of FDR's Wartime Expansion of Executive Power

In short, during World War II, the powers of the presidency were expanded by FDR's abuse of the president's constitutional role as commander in chief and by his use of public and secret unilateral executive orders and agreements. Such abuse was fueled by the Supreme Court's questionable opinions in the *United States v. Belmont* case, where the court discovered "inherent" powers of the presidency not listed in what was supposed to be a Constitution of strictly enumerated powers, and in the *United States v. Curtiss-Wright* case where, despite the Constitution's grant of many more enumerated powers to Congress than to the executive in foreign policy and national security, the court decided that the president was the "sole organ" of U.S. foreign policy.

Before the United States entered the war, FDR undertook questionable unilateral actions to trade U.S. destroyers in exchange for British military bases in the Caribbean, move troops to Iceland and Greenland without proper congressional approval, and provoke a shooting war at sea with Nazi Germany without legislative sanction. During the war, he established illegal military tribunals, violated the rights of ethnic Japanese by confiscating their property and throwing them in prison camps without due process of law, seized industries for war production, and threatened unconstitutional executive action to coerce Congress to give him power to control prices and raise taxes.

However, despite all these legally dubious threats and acts, FDR carefully avoided directly defying Congress using his commander in chief power or other alleged inherent or implied Article II authorities. Yet the war had altered the balance of power among governmental branches dramatically toward the president and away from Congress, which the Founders intended to be the dominant branch of government.[86] Now the executive branch was clearly the first among equals in the government. Later Cold War executives would begin regularly claiming such unconstitutional inherent and implied powers to act unilaterally, as what historians would come to call imperial presidents.

Following the republican custom of the revered George Washington, no president had ever served more than two terms. That is, until Americans elected FDR to a third term in 1940 with U.S. entry into World War II on the horizon, and then to a fourth term in 1944 as U.S. troops conducted large-scale global combat missions. Unnerved by FDR's aggrandizement of executive power, Congress passed, in 1947, the 22nd Amendment that limited presidents to two terms, which completed ratification in 1951.

Birth of the Military-Industrial-Congressional Complex

Some academic research alleges that there is no military-industrial-congressional complex (MICC). This argument would be a hard sell to officials or former officials in the defense industry or government, including this author, who has seen the cozy relationship private weapons and defense equipment producers have with the military bureaucracies and Congress to the point that in many cases, defense firms are wards of the state. Not much competition exists in the defense market because excessive government requirements, specifications, and regulation keep out potential competitors. Defense budgets are excessively high because of inordinate political pressure rather than because they are needed for U.S. national security; and the public often receives for its tax dollars defense equipment that is overpriced, of poor quality, and years behind schedule in delivery.

For most of American history, when the United States engaged in war, commercial industries converted to making war articles during the conflict and then reconverted to production for consumers after peace was reestablished. According to Murray L. Weidenbaum, as late as World War I, 80 percent of the military equipment fielded by armies was derived from products manufactured in civilian factories.[87] This conversion regularly happened because in the nation's founders' constitutional system, Congress—representatives of the public, who would be sacrificing their lives and tax dollars during any war—controlled the decision for war and the raising and funding of military forces. Congress was eager to reduce such costs after any war ended. Furthermore, the nation's founders had instilled in the system the fear of a permanent military establishment, especially of a large peacetime army run unilaterally by a kinglike executive. Even business organizations like the U.S. Chamber of Commerce and the National Association of Manufacturers (NAM) had distrusted a large peacetime standing military establishment. Yet during World War II, the conversion of the Chamber of Commerce and NAM to support for a standing army was, at least in part, because preparedness increased profits for many of their members.[88]

During and after World War II, the normal industrial conversion and post-war reconversion did not happen. During the conflict, a dedicated defense industry formed, lingered after the war ended, and has since become a politically powerful behemoth. In *The American Warfare State: The Domestic Politics of Military Spending*, Professor Rebecca U. Thorpe challenged the conventional wisdom in academia about the lack of a MICC and demonstrated that it first developed during World War II.[89] She showed that the largest war in world history was so massive—and the demand for military production so vast—that the U.S. military establishment, for the first time, issued contracts to firms outside major American cities. These suburban, semirural, and rural areas had little other economic sustenance besides such defense contracts. When the war ended in 1945, those areas needed continuing defense contracts for their undiversified regional economies to stay afloat. And since the defense industry had a monopsony buyer—the governmental defense bureaucracy—these outlying regions lobbied their members of Congress to continue to shovel peacetime defense contracts to the companies found in those areas. Research from the beginning of the Cold War into the twenty-first century shows that defense contracting has spread farther and farther geographically, replacing commercial industry as an economic development tool in more and more regions of the country.

Going forward, costs for American wars were shifted to a minority of the population who chose to fight in them and risk their lives (conscription was eventually replaced by volunteer military participation to stanch future anti-war protests), to foreign countries in which the wars occurred, and to future generations of taxpayers by large government budget deficits accumulating into massive national debt. High defense spending and overseas military interventions serve narrowly distributed economic and political needs at home. If political majorities regard themselves as unaffected or less affected adversely by such expenditures or force projections, insofar as tax increases are dispersed among hundreds of millions of taxpayers, U.S. leaders can get away with pursuing them. Despite the wide geographical spread of the defense industry, the benefits are not widely distributed among the population but concentrated among a few politically powerful interest groups. The famed branch of public policy and economics, public choice theory, firmly predicts that concentrated beneficiaries usually triumph politically over dispersed and less organized taxpayers.

Today's dedicated defense industries produce very few consumer products, cannot convert to commercial production if international threat levels fall, and resist any such conversion plans. In fact, conversion plans might impair the industries' argument to Congress to shovel more money their way to "support the defense industrial base" or "support local economies that depend on defense spending."[90] This insulates captive, increasingly oligopolistic, defense markets from the need to rapidly acquire the latest technology, from competitive capitalism, and from effective democratic control because of defense industry lobbying and sizeable contributions to congressional and presidential campaigns. In practice, the MICC privatizes profit and socializes risk from quasi-private companies toward the taxpayer.[91]

The aftermath of wars usually results in larger permanent defense spending than existed at prewar levels (a ratchet effect). However, during the massive World War II, a dedicated MICC was born—contributing to perennially excessive U.S. defense spending beyond what is needed for the nation's security and to a nontraditional, globe-girdling, and interventionist American foreign policy during the Cold War and beyond to justify such excessive spending. Because Congress—fueled by local economic concerns at home—supported and funded this peacetime MICC, it gave the president the permanent resources and mechanism (funding, weapons, and military forces) needed to wage war independently of that very legislature, thus eroding Congress's constitutional war powers. Instead of James Madison's "ambition countering ambition" conception of the constitutional checks and balances between Congress and the executive, since World War II and spurred on by local economic dependency on defense contracts, Congress has facilitated the president's imperial ambitions overseas. This outcome was something the founders had feared but erroneously thought they had controlled through the framework of checks and balances.

Alternative Outcomes Without U.S. Entry into World War II

In the Pacific theater of World War II, instead of taking a hardline stance against the Japanese, FDR could have tried to negotiate a limit to Japanese expansion by rolling back their incursion into Indochina in return for a resumption of U.S. oil and scrap metal exports; a U.S.-facilitated end to the Japanese quagmire in China could have been exchanged for a partial Japanese withdrawal from there. Such an outcome could have saved the civilian government in Japan and prevented the attack on Pearl Harbor. Although China was the big prize for Japan, the desperate Japanese, from 1937 to 1941, had suffered a half million casualties trying to subdue the large and populous nation.

Alternatively, a stronger, but safer, policy that avoided the risky draconian attempt to strangle the Japanese military with an oil embargo might have been for FDR to ramp up aid to the Chinese Nationalists to further bog down the Japanese occupiers. By doing this, FDR could have lessened the risk that Japan would have taken advantage of the German attack on the western USSR to attack Siberia or elsewhere in the East Asian region to grab Soviet territory. Yet another option, and arguably the smartest, could have been for the United States to realize that the fool's gold of what had been a disappointing Chinese market for U.S. trade was not critical to U.S. security. FDR could have agreed to end aid to the Chinese nationalists in exchange for a Japanese guarantee to stay away from U.S. possessions in East Asia.

Even if one grants that Germany was an implacably evil adversary, FDR, as the president of a republic, still needed to prove his case for war to the American people. Any major, or indeed minor, war must be vetted in full by open congressional and public debate before the Congress takes any steps toward entry into the conflict.

Americans were justly skeptical of entering another European war after Woodrow Wilson's fiasco during the Great War. Even after Adolf

Hitler had overrun most of Western Europe in 1940, Americans over-whelmingly opposed U.S. entry into the European conflict. Instead of ramping up an effort to publicly convince the public otherwise, FDR took unilateral unconstitutional actions by trading U.S. destroyers for Britain's military bases, sending U.S. forces to Iceland and Greenland without congressional approval, and attacking German U-boats in the Atlantic Ocean to unsuccessfully provoke Hitler into declaring war. In taking these actions, FDR sometimes used deception to maneuver the American public into war. Many historians excuse FDR's behavior because of the perceived necessity and nobility of helping to vanquish the evil Nazi Germany, fascist Italy, and Imperial Japan. In republics, war puts exces-sive strain on any constitutional system.

However, going against conventional wisdom, it remains an open question whether the United States needed to enter World War II against Hitler's Germany. Instead of sending troops to Europe, the United States could have quickly augmented its home defenses, including improved air defenses. Furthermore, the U.S., British, and Canadian amphibious assault across the channel on D-Day in June 1944 occurred long after the Soviets had stopped the Nazis and had them on the run back to Germany. During World War II, the Germans suffered 80 percent of their military casualties on the eastern front alone. That is, the eastern front was deci-sive in deciding the outcome in the European theater of war, and the Red Army under the circumstances likely would have defeated Hitler without the vaunted Allied invasion at Normandy and break out across France into Germany. Although the United States supplied material support to the Soviet Union through the Lend-Lease program, the Soviets had begun to thwart the Germans before that assistance, slow to start, really kicked in with significant amounts. Also, the United States could have provided such aid, and even ramped it up, without sending any U.S. forces to Europe. Furthermore, at its peak, only 10 percent of U.S. Lend-Lease aid went to the Soviets. The imbalance of sacrifice made Stalin angry and spurred his repeated complaints about delays by the other Allies in open-ing a second front in France, which accounted for much of the animosity in the alliance of convenience during the war. Ironically, the United States used the invasion of Normandy in 1944 (it had broken its promise to Stalin to invade France in 1943) to justify a cut in Lend-Lease aid to the Soviets by 60 percent.[92]

On the other hand, if the United States had not entered the war against Germany and Italy, and Britain and the Soviet Union, even with U.S. Lead-Lease aid, were not able to emerge victorious, a negotiated settlement restoring a balance of power in Europe might have been achieved between the exhausted Soviets and Germans. Such a balance of power would have obviated the need for the United States to deploy troops in Europe after the war to defend a prostrate Germany and Western Europe against a dominant Soviet victor.

SECTION IV.
COLD WAR CONFLICTS

>> CHAPTER 10 <<

THE COLD WAR: A SYNOPSIS

U.S. Hegemony in Guise of Anti-Communism

Did the United States or the Soviet Union win the Cold War (lasting from 1945 to the fall of the Soviet Union in 1991)? The best answer is both countries lost it. The Soviet Union lost because its communist economic and political systems proved unworkable and collapsed. Americans lost for economic reasons too. Strongly anti-communist after the 1917 Bolshevik Revolution, Americans fell prey to their government's exaggerated fear of communism. Eventually, this paranoia led to their sending valuable economic resources everywhere on a global anti-communist crusade. This in turn led to costly permanent U.S. military protection of what would later become wealthy allies who could have paid for their own security. This subsidy allowed these allies to divert resources from military spending into civilian research, development, and production, enabling them to compete with U.S. companies starved of resources through higher taxation to pay for the global military presence. By the 1960s, European countries and Japan, long recovered economically from World War II but still nestled comfortably under the U.S. security umbrella, began to take markets away from American firms. Thus, in the 1970s, the United States began its Cold War economic decline.

With added spurts of U.S. defense spending in the early 1980s and in the 2000s after the 9/11 attacks, the decline of U.S. civilian industry deepened while new competitors from the developing world (some of them protected allies) appeared—inter alia China, Taiwan, South Korea, and India. The United States is not unique in suffering economic decline from an excessively expansionist and overly militarized foreign policy. Historian Paul Kennedy has famously noted this trend among dominant powers since the 1500s.

The chief driver of this exaggeration of the Soviet threat after World War II was the U.S. government's attempt to mask its drive for global hegemony built on an integrated world economy—with a U.S. military guarantee of the needed "stability" for commerce to flourish. Of course, an integrated world economy could have evolved naturally since it was in the interest of everyone to exchange goods and capital. Thus, the expansive military policing by the U.S. military was unnecessary.

The U.S. government had commandeered great sectors of the American economy to fight World War II. These sectors were never fully demilitarized. Militarization quickly recurred to fight the Korean War—or as some contend, the Korean war was necessary to save what had become a military-based economy. In its aftermath, the modern defense industry had been born. The American economy grew to be dependent on this peacetime military-industrial-congressional complex. Defense contractors and subcontractors had spread throughout the country, ensuring continued political support for the Cold War. On occasion, this policy of being the world's policeman sucked the United States into large military quagmires, such as those in Asia. There were also smaller "stabilization" missions in many strategically unimportant developing countries. This further diverted resources from the pockets of Americans.

U.S. hegemony required interventionism, alliances, military bases, covert action by the CIA, and foreign military and economic aid to countries under "threat from communism"—all of which cost Americans great sums of money.

The Cold War was unique in world history insofar as it coincided with the nuclear age: a period of high tension for more than four decades between two rival powers deterred by the threat of nuclear annihilation. Yet the two superpowers continued to joust through negotiations, diplomacy, espionage, covert operations, military and economic aid to client states or guerrilla movements, and proxy wars. Yet on certain occasions one of the powers would get directly engaged in larger, longer wars with clients of the other government. In the case of the Soviet Union, it was against U.S.-assisted Afghan mujahideen. For the United States, it was against North Korea and China in the Korean War and against North Vietnam and the South Vietnamese Vietcong insurgency in the Vietnam War.

The virulent anti-communism governments and businesses had instilled in American public opinion prevented many later presidents from improving relations with adversaries during the Cold War—especially after Stalin died in 1953 and was replaced by Soviet leaders seeking co-existence. Domestic anti-communism had come about as FDR's World War II propaganda portrait of "Uncle Joe" Stalin as a benevolent ally against the Nazis rapidly gave way to the anti-communism promoted by FDR's successor, Harry Truman, via an exaggerated caricature of an aggressively expansionist Soviet red menace. American politicians, and Truman in particular, soon found that being anti-Soviet was good domestic politics. Before the 1948 election, which the pundits predicted Truman would lose, top aides James T. Rowe and Clark Clifford told him, "There is considerable political advantage to the Administration in its battle with the Kremlin. . . . The worse matters get . . . the more is there a sense of crisis. In times of crisis, the American citizen tends to back up his president."[1] The new propaganda line was fueled both by Truman's own hardline anti-communist views (compared to those of FDR) and his desire to stay ahead of the anti-communism espoused by the opposition Republican Party, especially when they tried to make political hay off his "loss" of China to the communists in 1949. Dean Acheson, Truman's secretary of state, later admitted they purposefully embellished the Soviet threat.

Yet the politicians did not need to try as hard as they did to rev up anti-communist sentiment in the United States. The American government, business, and public, long accustomed to freewheeling capitalism and individualism, had a visceral dislike of communism from its start in 1917 during the Bolshevik Revolution. This natural hatred was demonstrated early on by American society, which had just been put through the meat grinder of the Great War, tolerating Woodrow Wilson's invasion of Russia (1918–1920), in an unsuccessful attempt to strangle the Bolshevik baby in the cradle during the Russian civil war, and the post–World War I Red Scare of 1919 in the United States. Thus, the post–World War II American interventionist politicians and political appointees from both parties found they could sell their quest for U.S. global hegemony best by draping it in exaggerated anti-communist rhetoric.[2] For example, Will Clayton, Truman's third-ranking official in the State Department, even admitted, "The United States will not take world leadership effectively unless the people of the United States are shocked into doing so."[3]

Democratic President Harry Truman, Republican Joe McCarthy, and other red baiters drove the inflated anti-communist rhetorical train for their own purposes. The U.S. government's anti-Russian propaganda and policies have overwhelmed American life and culture from the end of World War II until the present day and sometimes have resulted in Russian responses that created a self-fulfilling reality.

Because the U.S. government exaggerated the threat of the Soviet Union—known derisively at the Pentagon as "Upper Volta with missiles" because of its dysfunctional economy—some analysts have concluded that the Cold War was only a cover for a not-so-hidden project of U.S. mercantilist world hegemony.[4] During the Cold War, the United States was always, by far, the strongest superpower—with nuclear superiority through much of the Cold War and, more important, a vast economic advantage over a creaking Soviet economic system. Lending credence to this view is that after the Berlin Wall fell, the Soviet Union collapsed and the Cold War ended, defense spending remained high, the informal American overseas empire of alliances and military bases was still there, and U.S. military interventions in the world increased with no Soviet enemy to counter them.

During the Cold War, the U.S. government wanted to hold sway not only over the Soviet Union but also postwar allies—inter alia Britain, France, Germany, and Japan—and the developing world. U.S. policymakers believed that a now exaggerated threat of Soviet power would keep the allies, especially Germany and Japan, under the U.S. military umbrella so that their economies would revive and become consumers and producers in a U.S.-led integrated global economy. Although the United States quickly reduced the size of its army in 1945 and 1946, it remained the greatest military and economic power on earth—with continued naval supremacy, leadership in long-range strategic air power, a monopoly on atomic weapons, and 50 percent of the world's economic power. Also, anti-communism would prevent a resurgence of traditional isolationism at home.

Ironically, even in their virulent ideological opposition to Soviet communism, U.S. officials continued to believe in the old overproduction theory of capitalism popular among American imperialists around the turn of the century and adopted by Vladimir Lenin. American imperialists and Lenin believed that capitalist economy produced too many goods for domestic absorption and would inevitably need overseas markets. Military power supposedly kept overseas markets open and prevented domestic recession or depression. A committee formed in 1947 by the State, War, and Navy Departments concluded, "It is inescapable that, under present programs and policies, the world will not be able to continue to buy United States exports at the 1946–1947 rate."[5] Thus, American foreign policy would need to become more expansionist.

U.S. officials believed that the two world wars, the Great Depression, and the communist revolutions in China and Russia were caused by political and economic nationalism. Being one of the few major countries at the end of World War II with no war damage, the United States accounted for half of the world's economic production. Thus, U.S. companies, grown large with the economies of scale of a huge internal market, would benefit most from a single integrated world economy—with free-flowing trade, capital, currencies, people, and ideas—secured with U.S. political and military hegemony to enforce international rules and create stability so that the global market could be created and maintained.

Concomitantly, the United States would set up U.S.-dominated international financial organizations, such as the World Bank, which would help recovering and integrating Western European economies (and later those of developing countries) that adopted the U.S. model of economic internationalism instead of nationalism, and the International Monetary Fund (IMF), which would stabilize and manage the value of nations' currencies by interconvertibility based on the value of the dollar as the new world reserve currency.

To help U.S. companies, the U.S. government pushed the world's nations into adopting policies that freed up their economies to foreign trade and capital. Many likely would have done this anyway without American aid because of its economic benefits. The full recovery of Japan and Western Europe was key to an integrated international economy. However, in the years after the war, both areas had a dollar gap—that is, insufficient dollars to buy U.S. exports. The White House Council of Economic Advisers concluded that Europe's dollar gap and the resultant contraction of the European market for U.S. businesses would impose stark changes on the U.S. economy. To address this problem, the United States created the Truman Doctrine, the Marshall Plan, and the North Atlantic Treaty Organization (NATO).

In 1947, the U.S. government decided to provide aid to Greece and Turkey to fight communist encroachment, implicitly taking over from financially exhausted Britain its costly imperial commitments to security in that region.[6] In his speech announcing it, however, President Harry

Truman went further and committed the United States to a grandiose and unnecessary worldwide crusade against communism, which lasted more than forty years until the collapse of the USSR.

To help Western Europe buy American exports, the U.S. government provided aid via the Marshall Plan. Sold as an anti-communist measure, the Marshall Plan enabled the subsidizing of American business. In a rational world, paying people to buy your products is silly—unless the U.S. taxpayer is paying for the government aid, and American business is reaping the benefit through increased sales to Europe. Thus, big business and big labor in the United States eagerly supported the aid plan. To receive the aid, the Europeans had to adopt U.S. advice to create a greater European common market. France, understandably nervous about a reindustrialized Germany, was more willing to accept that outcome if the Germans were part of a larger Europe-wide economy. By mid-1949 the Ruhr-Rhine industrial core of Western Europe, the prize of Western military strategy during World War II, was politically and economically integrated into the West.[7]

U.S. military intelligence in November 1945 had concluded the war-exhausted Soviet Union could not attack Western Europe till 1960. Moreover, the policy planning staff of George Kennan's State Department discounted the likelihood of any attack after 1954, even though by that time the Soviets would have a substantial number of nuclear weapons and delivery vehicles. Nevertheless, in 1949 the United States created the NATO alliance, pledging to defend Western Europe, hem in an eventually reindustrialized and remilitarized Germany, and make sure Germany and other Western European nations were not tempted by neutrality or friendliness toward the Soviet Union. However, NATO's design also served to enhance European security so U.S. overseas capital would be safe, Europe's capital would come back home, and new domestic European investment would happen. The American nationalist right was convinced to support NATO by obviously questionable promises that creating the alliance would not require the rearming of Germany or large numbers of U.S. forces in Europe.

A free, integrated world market was highly desirable, particularly for the dominant American economy, and did have some benefits for companies and nations around the globe. It could have been self-creating and self-sustaining—and thus decoupled from any need for U.S. global political and military dominance, which was bound to be costly and unsustainable. In fact, the American global hegemony element in the package had raised fears of "capitalist encirclement" in the Soviet Union, thus hardening Soviet policy toward the United States.

Being the world's policeman and banker led to excessive state-subsidized military research, development, and production—helping the military-industrial-congressional complex at home and leading to American overinvestment overseas in the 1970s and 1980s, where U.S. hegemony allowed American capital to obtain favored returns. This situation resulted in starving the American civilian economy of research and development and capital spending, leaving it undercapitalized, less innovative, and therefore less competitive globally. Even by 1961, 65 percent of American high-tech research and development funds came from the government, and 85 percent of those went to the military sector. Many of the best American scientists were diverted from the commercial sector to military research and development. Supporting Japan and Western Europe's defense and even providing them with military aid compounded the U.S. global competitiveness problem by allowing those nations to redirect resources to their civilian technology and production, which then competed with American industrial sectors that had previously led the world. The United States confirmed Paul Kennedy's thesis by going down the same path of all leading powers since the 1500s: spending ever increasing amounts of their GDPs defending their expansive empires, and thus declining economically relative to their rivals, which instead chose to use their resources to modernize their domestic economies and infrastructures.[8] Following this line of reasoning, both superpowers lost in the Cold War while other rising powers, with far less military spending, gained from it—Japan, European Union countries (especially Germany), and China.

Causes of the Cold War

Most Western historians reflexively blame the Soviet Union for the start of the Cold War because totalitarian communism is a much harsher and less desirable form of government than is Western democracy. Among American historians, nationalism also subtly runs toward an "our team is better than your team" mentality. However, the harshness of internal government does not always correlate to an aggressive foreign policy, nor does the reverse. For example, the British and French Empires often had a more benevolent and democratic government at home but treated their colonies brutally. The republican United States treated Native American nations and Philippine colonial subjects ruthlessly when they rebelled against U.S. rule.

Joseph Stalin's more mature Soviet Union during the early years of the Cold War was even more vicious internally but had much less ideological zeal for spreading communism globally than did Vladimir Lenin's new and revolutionary USSR during the 1920s. After the cataclysmic Second World War had devastated the western USSR and killed between twenty-five to thirty million Soviet citizens, Stalin was most of all concerned with setting up a buffer of friendly states along the West's historical invasion route into his country. In addition to its postwar devastation, the Soviets had a battered army, no strategic air command, no atomic bomb, no modern navy, a poor transportation system, and technological backwardness, including the Red Army's continued use of horses. In November 1945, U.S. military intelligence concluded, even before the partial demobilization of the Red Army in 1946, that the Soviets would not be ready for a substantial war until 1960.[9]

Truman More Hawkish Than FDR

Historian Gar Alperovitz saw an immediate hardening of U.S. policy toward the Soviet Union at the end of World War II. Franklin Delano Roosevelt, more inclined to cajole his Soviet wartime ally, died on April 12, 1945, and was replaced by the inexperienced, hawkish Harry S. Truman. Eleven days later, on April 23, 1945, the newly installed President Truman bluntly hectored Soviet Foreign Minister Vyacheslav Molotov about Truman's belief that the Soviets were not keeping their promises related to Eastern Europe from the Yalta Conference, especially involving Poland. The new president found himself surrounded by hard-line advisers, especially Dean Acheson, who wanted a confrontation with the Soviets over their behavior in Eastern Europe.

Alperovitz argued that from May to mid-August 1945, the new U.S. hard line toward the USSR came from anticipation that the atomic bombs to be used against Japan would give the United States an advantage over the Soviets in Eastern Europe. Truman even bragged that "if it explodes, as I think it will, I'll certainly have a hammer on those boys." He also crowed that the bomb gave him "an entirely new feeling of confidence."

Secretary of State James Byrnes bluntly admitted that atomic bombs dropped on a defeated Japan that was seeking surrender terms "might well put us in a position to dictate our own terms" and "make Russia more manageable in Europe." Truman refused Churchill's requests to have another Big Three meeting with Stalin until after the successful bomb testing in the Nevada desert. He bragged about it to Stalin at the eventual Potsdam Conference, beginning in the latter part of July 1945, and postponed discussion of all the important issues involving Eastern Europe to a subsequent foreign ministers' conference after the bombs had been dropped on Japan.[10] At the Potsdam Conference, the hawkish Dean Acheson reported that Truman had worn the freshly tested bomb (but not yet dropped) ostentatiously on his hip. Thus, the Cold War could be dated to Truman's ascension to office and the success of the Manhattan Project.

In August 1945, at the Potsdam conference, Truman wrote his wife after his first meeting with Stalin, saying, "He is straightforward, knows what he wants and will compromise when he can't get it."[11] Yet in late 1945, Truman abruptly terminated Lend-Lease aid to its former ally, and by then, the United States had acquired air bases close to Soviet borders.[12] If the Soviets had done the same in Mexico or the Caribbean, the U.S. security establishment would have been apoplectic—as it was in 1962 when the Soviets installed nuclear missiles in Cuba, even though those weapons were not believed by JFK and Robert McNamara, his secretary of defense, to alter measurably the favorable nuclear balance between the United States and the USSR. As part of a general hardening of U.S. policy on postwar Germany, Eastern Europe, and the Middle East in 1946 that included a seeming U.S. violation of the Yalta agreement, Truman declared that the Yalta pact was only a wartime "interim agreement" that needed a change because of the realities of postwar power redistribution. In any renegotiation, Truman showed that he would be tough by growling in January 1946: "I am tired of babying the Soviets."[13]

In fact, Eric Alterman summarized his belief about how the Cold War started by summarizing what Truman did to FDR's Yalta agreement of February 1945: "The vicious killer atop the Soviet evil empire honored the deal; the Americans and their British allies reneged. And that's how the Cold War began."[14] Like Woodrow Wilson at Versailles after World War I, who gave up too much to his allies to win adoption of the eventually failed League of Nations, FDR had to give up much to Stalin to get him to agree to the idealistic United Nations. FDR had agreed to a Soviet sphere of influence in Poland and Eastern Europe, which he had never revealed to the American people. Stalin wanted Poland—located on one of the traditional invasion routes into Russia—to have a friendly (that is, communist) government. At Yalta, FDR promised Stalin, "I hope that I do not have to assure you that the U.S. will never lend its support in any way to ... a government in Poland that would be inimical to your interests."[15]

FDR had no choice but to agree to this demand because the massive and battle-hardened Red Army—which had swept west into central Europe during the war, being the principal hammer breaking Nazi Germany— would inevitably decide the future political systems of Eastern European nations. According to Alterman, FDR, a chronic dissembler, lied to the public, Congress, and even his closest advisers about his deal with Stalin at Yalta. Truman, dealing with the fallout, then accused the Soviets of violating the agreement and launched a public relations campaign back home to defend against the accusation that his government had sold out U.S. interests to communism in Eastern Europe. The idealistic American public, ignorant of the necessary realpolitik, was appalled by brutal Soviet actions across Eastern Europe. The failure of the Yalta agreement thus contributed to the immediate souring of mutual trust, and U.S.-Soviet relations, after the war.

Because of Poland's key geographic position on a flat historic invasion route into western Russia, and because of Polish hostility to the Russians from past conflicts between the two countries, that nation was key to the entire Eastern European theater. Stalin was adamant to have a friendly, pro-Soviet government there, not just whatever might result from free elections, because he had just dealt with yet another invasion of Russia that had caused so much destruction and astronomical Soviet deaths. Averell Harriman had noted that FDR had "very little interest in eastern European matters except as they affect sentiment in America." (Read: the Polish ethnic lobby in Chicago and other places.) The Yalta communique made no mention of the Polish government in exile in London but did say that the Soviet-backed Lublin government was the "present government of Poland." The agreement's text had no promises of replacing the existing Lublin government with persons from the London government in exile—it only spoke of the current government being "reorganized on a broader democratic basis with the inclusion of democratic leaders from Poland itself and from Poles from abroad." The accord called for elections in Eastern Europe but had no mechanism to ensure their fairness. The Soviets diluted an early U.S. draft calling for "free and unfettered" elections jointly administered by the Soviet Union, the United States, and Britain to require only "consultation" among the three powers, "looking toward" free elections at an unspecified date. This wording change alone made it clear that the Allies knew what they were agreeing to: Soviet dominance of Eastern Europe. Admiral William Leahy, FDR's chief of staff, even verbalized the issue, complaining upon leaving Yalta that the accord's language on Poland was "so elastic that the Russians can stretch it all the way from Yalta to Washington without ever technically breaking it." FDR replied, "I know, Bill. I know it. But it is the best I can do for Poland at this time."

Nevertheless, after the conference at Yalta, according to Alterman, U.S. and British diplomats in Moscow tried to pressure Stalin for a new Polish government that included London Poles, leading Stalin to correctly accuse the West of violating the elastic accord. The hawkish Truman ordered the U.S. military and the State Department to make a list of Soviet violations of the Yalta accord; they could only find Soviets taking advantage of "technicalities."[16]

Yet even before going to Yalta, FDR had told congressional leaders that the Soviets had the power in that region, and the best he could do was to mitigate it. Similarly, before leaving for the conference, Winston Churchill had said to an aide that the entire Balkans, except Greece, would be "Bolshevized." In fact, by his own admission, Churchill had met with Stalin in October 1944 and divided up Eastern Europe; because the U.S. had traditionally stayed out of European affairs, FDR was merely honoring their informal agreement at Yalta. The U.S. and Britain had not consulted the USSR when negotiating the armistice after they defeated fascist Italy in 1943 (or would not after the United States occupied Japan in 1945), so they could not, and did not, expect to be full partners in Soviet "liberated" Eastern Europe.

Even the hawkish Dean Acheson and other high-level U.S. and British officials agreed—at least for a while—to a Soviet sphere of influence in Eastern Europe. Britain had a security sphere of influence in the Low Countries of northwestern Europe and the Suez Canal, and the United States had one in Central America, the Caribbean, and the entire western hemisphere under the Monroe Doctrine. Furthermore, after World War II, the United States would dominate industrial Japan and the richer part of Europe (the entire western side) and, given the vastly superior U.S.

economy, would have much greater influence in the rest of the world than would the USSR. The typically outspoken Truman, however, was less inclined to appreciate the Soviet need for a security sphere of influence in Eastern Europe and thus did not accept the informal Churchill-Stalin agreement or its fine-tuning at the Yalta Conference in February 1945.

Even Alterman concedes that the Cold War could still have happened even if the Allies had not violated the Yalta agreement, but he argues that Truman's actions were the cause of it. Stalin did not secure his East European sphere of influence until 1947—long after the U.S. procurement of military bases near Soviet territory and the dropping of U.S. atomic bombs in Japan, both occurring in early August 1945. In fact, in 1946 Stalin partially demobilized his Red Army in occupied Eastern Europe to concentrate on post-conflict domestic economic reconstruction. Alterman concludes, based on evidence emanating from Soviet archives made public after the Cold War ended, that although he regards Stalin as the most bloodthirsty dictator in human history, Stalin was a foreign policy realist—more concerned with Soviet state interests than spreading communism around the globe and prepared to deal with superior U.S. military and economic power pragmatically, even cooperatively.[17]

The Truman Doctrine

Although the Cold War seems to have started earlier, many Western historians date the beginning of it to 1947, with Harry Truman giving aid to the governments of Greece and Turkey, though some might try to blame the Soviet Union for helping Greek anti-monarchist revolutionaries in the first place. Stalin had promised not to aid the revolt and did not do so appreciably. However, Marshall Josip Broz Tito, the ruler of Yugoslavia, a small communist country independent of the Soviet bloc, did supply significant help to the Greek insurrection. In 1947, when the British, financially exhausted after the war, told Truman that they could no longer foot the aid bill for Greece and Turkey, the United States jumped at the opportunity to replace Britain in the region.

As for the Soviet dustup with Turkey, it involved the centuries-old regional dispute over control of the Turkish straits, which connected the Black Sea to the Mediterranean Sea through Turkish territory. Typically, great powers like to control key water choke points they regard as strategic—for example, the United States vis-à-vis the Panama Canal and

Britain vis-à-vis the Suez Canal. The Soviets felt the same way about the Turkish straits and had some credible historical claims on the nearby territory. During World War II, Turkey had allowed warships from Nazi Germany and fascist Italy to pass through the straits, despite Soviet displeasure. The Soviets also were unhappy about a visit to Turkey by the American battleship USS *Missouri* in April 1946. In August 1946, the USSR wanted Turkey to revisit the treaty governing its management of the waterway—which was the only practical way for Soviet shipping to access the Mediterranean—to allow Soviet traffic to flow freely through the straits, but Turkey resisted. Such interests put in perspective why the Soviets chose a naval show of force to induce the Turks to let their ships pass freely though the straits.

Truman did not care that the Turkish straits were critical to Soviet maritime security. President Harry Truman had initially agreed at the Potsdam conference to a revision of the treaty concerning management of the straits but then said that the two countries should iron out the issue between themselves. However, after the Soviets built up naval forces near the Turkish coast in the summer and fall of 1946 to intimidate Turkey into compliance, Turkey appealed to the United States for assistance. Truman changed his mind and sent a naval task force to Turkey, fearing that the straits or all of Turkey would fall into Soviet hands. The U.S. military wanted Allied control of faraway Turkish territory and the straits for operations against the Soviet Union in case of war. Fancifully, the Truman administration saw communist dominoes falling everywhere: Turkey, Greece, then in the Near and Middle East (Iranian and other Persian Gulf oil falling to the Soviets), and after that Africa, Europe, and even distant India and China.

After Truman sent out the naval task force and reaffirmed U.S. support for Turkey in October 1946, the Soviets dropped their demand for a treaty revision and withdrew their intimidating naval forces. However, this incident was the deciding factor in the issuance of the Truman Doctrine, which turned the regional issue of the potential spread of communism into Turkey and Greece into a questionable worldwide U.S. crusade against the spread of communism.

The United States had few direct security interests in the Soviet neighborhood, which was halfway across the world. Truman and the State Department did not want Turkey to go communist or even be unduly influenced by Stalin—a reasonable goal but one not vital to U.S. security, nor one that needed a global crusade against any communist inroads in any country on any continent. However, Truman and the U.S. security elite had developed an imperial mindset, convinced that because the United States emerged from World War II as the most powerful country on earth—a quantum leap above the war-devastated and economically dysfunctional communist Soviet Union—U.S. prestige would be irreparably tarnished if even one country went communist.

Furthermore, the domino theory—originated by the hawkish Dean Acheson and eventually discredited after the Vietnam War—predicted that if one country went communist, it could be used as a base to overthrow the government in a neighboring nation or at least have a demonstration effect on other countries, thus initiating a series of nations falling like dominoes all around the world. U.S. officials saw Soviet Union's actions near Turkey as the first time it had tried to expand its influence outside Eastern Europe and believed that if not stopped, the communist dominoes would start falling everywhere.

Truman told Congress that "it must be the policy of the United States to support free peoples who are resisting attempted subjugation by armed minorities or by outside pressures," thereby proclaiming the Truman Doctrine that globalized the Monroe Doctrine. Even high U.S. officials in the Truman administration, including Secretary of State George Marshall, thought his speech "overstated the case a bit," because the communist threat to Greece and Turkey had not recently spiked, but Truman had nevertheless exaggerated the threat to convince Congress to cough up the aid money. Truman argued that because totalitarian regimes suppressed free peoples, they automatically were a danger to international peace and the security of the United States—which was not necessarily true.

The Truman Doctrine set a precedent for assisting anti-communist governments around the world, even if they had autocratic tendencies, which aptly described the regimes in Greece and Turkey at the time.[18] Though exasperated with the undemocratic rulers in Greece he was supporting, Truman included them in the "free peoples who are resisting attempted subjugation" category in his speech; the authoritarian Turkish government did not qualify for this category either. Ironically, the Truman Doctrine was an obverse reflection of Vladimir Lenin's doctrine, expounded in 1915, of "raising revolts against the capitalists, and coming out even with armed force if necessary," ignoring the fact that, upon taking power in the USSR after Lenin died in January 1924, Stalin had already backed off from this doctrine of international communist expansion.[19]

The Truman Doctrine looked to "contain" the spread of communism around the world until its driving force, the communist regime in the Soviet Union, collapsed from its own contradictions. This policy, as it developed over four decades, not only entailed shoveling enormous quantities of military and economic aid into foreign countries but also covering the world with permanent formal and informal U.S.-led alliances, American military bases, and U.S. military interventions. The Cold War also generated the first large U.S. peacetime military in American history and the first huge peacetime defense budgets, both a derivative of the political power of the first dedicated and permanent defense industry, which was left over from World War II. The nation's founders would have been appalled.

The Globalization of American Containment Policy

Some historians believed that the Cold War was not only about containing Soviet expansionism; instead, the larger goal was to stamp out revolution anywhere in the world to further and secure U.S. global interests.[20] Many of these interests were economic. The U.S. State Department believed in security through the establishment of a new world economic order, which included the creation of U.S.-dominated international economic organizations—for example, the General Agreement on Tariffs and Trade (GATT), the Bretton Woods currency scheme, the International Monetary Fund (IMF), and the World Bank. The United States would be the hegemon of a more integrated worldwide market, gaining great benefit. Truman even believed "if it [the United States] did not act decisively, the world capitalist system would flounder."[21] Because international commerce is mutually beneficial, however, it happens naturally without militaries protecting it or superpowers directing it. The same could not be said of imperial commerce, rooted in domination and exploitation.

Later events may have proved these scholars correct. After the collapse of the East Bloc and Soviet Union, the United States kept its informal global empire of military bases and elevated defense spending, expanded and strengthened its alliance systems, increased its military interventions worldwide, and continued to dominate international economic organizations in protection of its economic interests.

The core of the Western case alleging that the Soviets started the Cold War depends on three pillars: (1) the coup in Czechoslovakia in 1948, which gave the communists total power in that country; (2) the Berlin Blockade beginning in late June 1948; and (3) the Korean War beginning in 1950. Yet the Cold War was in full swing long before these events occurred.[22]

Even the standard view—that the Cold War began in 1947 over communist activities around Greece and Turkey—is probably wrong. In 1918, the last year of World War I, Allied nations, including the United States, invaded the Soviet Union to intervene in the raging civil war between the Reds (communists) and the Whites (non-communists) a year after the 1917 Bolshevik Revolution.[23] The Allies not only wanted to defeat the Bolsheviks, who had withdrawn Russia from the European war but also to hold the eastern front to prevent Germany from taking Russian resources. Churchill said the Allied invasion was to "strangle the Bolshevik baby in its cradle." Despite the Allies' intervention not going well, they did not withdraw their forces until 1920.

This Western invasion of the Soviet Union cemented the many lasting Bolshevik suspicions of the West, including of the United States. Because of its communist ideology, the United States had immediate suspicions of Vladimir Lenin and the Bolshevik Party when they grabbed power in 1917. As a result, it took sixteen years for the United States to recognize Bolshevik rule in the Soviet Union, only doing so in 1933—the year Hitler and the Nazis took power in Germany. The early frost of the Cold War with the Soviet Union thus began at the start of the Bolshevik regime.

George Kennan was the senior State Department official who developed the vague policy of communist containment[24] until the Soviet Union fell from its "internal contradiction." Kennan recognized the Soviet danger to Western capitalism and argued that any appeasement of the USSR would get the same result as had Neville Chamberlain with Adolf Hitler; only a tough pushback at its outer limits would "contain" Soviet expansion. Kennan believed that in foiling Soviet expansionism, the USSR would eventually collapse, be overthrown, or mellow. Yet Stalin had given up the Leninist zeal for worldwide revolution in favor of "socialism in one country" and had rejected communist radicalism—as in Maoist China, Tito's Yugoslavia, and the Greek insurgency—unless it pledged fealty to Moscow.[25] After FDR, U.S. officials lacked any empathy for the Soviet need for legitimate security buffers on its borders.

However, Kennan was correct about the dysfunction and fragility of the communist system, which, having abolished private property, thus offered few positive incentives for productivity from the population. He believed it would eventually collapse as Soviet citizens experienced a dearth of consumer goods and political and entrepreneurial freedoms. Before and during the failed Vietnam War, however, Kennan complained that the government had militarized and globalized his containment policy, which he said he had intended mainly as one of political and economic containment. Despite his apprehension about the Soviet Union, Kennan did not believe in the U.S. taking military actions, including accumulating a large arsenal of nuclear weapons, which would provoke a "paranoid" USSR into a hostile reaction. The Truman Doctrine in 1947, which turned communist actions toward Greece and Turkey into a U.S. global crusade against Soviet communism, was just such an ill-advised U.S. move. After the Berlin Wall finally fell, Kennan reclaimed his doctrine and argued that it had brought down communism.

A bigger problem with the U.S. containment strategy was that, in practice, the global policy set few priorities about which regions or countries in the world were vital to U.S. security and which were not. For example, after Cuba—an island in the western hemisphere only ninety miles from American shores—had a communist revolution in 1959, the CIA sponsored an invasion in 1961 by ragtag, incompetent exiles who had almost no chance of reversing the revolution instead of sending U.S. ground and air forces. On the other hand, the United States ended up sending huge ground and air forces to faraway, nonstrategic developing countries in Asia—Korea and Vietnam—to reverse communist gains.

Thus, a more focused Cold War–Lite strategy would have been better at bringing down the Soviet empire much more cheaply in terms of American lives and treasure and maybe even more quickly than the four decades taken by the full Cold War strategy. The containment doctrine the United States adopted should have limited its top priority to safeguarding the areas of economic power and technology that, if conquered by the Soviet Union, could have improved its ability to harm the United States. At the end of World War II, besides North America, those areas were Western Europe and Japan. At first, the United States did an excellent job of using this strategy. For example, in 1948 when the USSR, which occupied eastern Germany after the war, closed all land access routes into the western part of Berlin (which was in the eastern sector of Germany), Truman launched a massive air resupply of the city until the Soviets lifted the blockade. However, the original cause of the Soviet blockade, which was the adoption of the Deutsch Mark as the common currency for the western occupation zones (British, French, and American) of West Berlin and West Germany, is often lost. This move toward a unified currency revealed the U.S. intention to unite those zones and leave out the Soviet zones in East Berlin and East Germany. A divided Germany into East and West was the outcome. The Soviet blockade had more to do with the maneuverings of Walter Ulbricht, the East German leader, than it did with a Soviet long-term strategy of expansion in Europe.[26]

NATO

U.S. containment went too far in creating the entangling NATO (North Atlantic Treaty Organization) alliance in 1949. The United States wanted to revive Germany as a bulwark against the Soviet Union, but this alarmed France, which now feared both the Germans and the Soviets. As Lord Ismay said, the design of NATO was to keep the United States in (Europe), the Soviet Union out, and the Germans down (under a form of military control). The Marshall Plan—massive U.S. postwar aid to Western Europe—was not only to help those countries recover economically and stabilize them politically; it was also intended to increase European wealth and enable them to buy American products, including weapons. In this way, it was an indirect subsidy to American business interests.[27] Although at the time exports were less than 10 percent of U.S. GNP, key sectors of the American economy—steel, autos, and agriculture—were heavily dependent on them. In addition, the United States imported critical materials for its military-industrial-congressional complex from Europe's imperial possessions, which helped the Europeans maintain their empires in the wake of rising nationalism. According to historian Melvin Small, the globalization of U.S. containment policy had a great deal to do with perceived postwar American economic vulnerabilities.[28] Yet, just after World War II, the undevastated United States was the envy of the world.

From the creation of NATO until the present, this alliance has been the crown jewel of the informal global American empire, which American politicians today claim "won the Cold War." Yet even at the time of the alliance's birth in 1949, the consensus of historians now is that Soviet military behavior was not directed toward aggression against Western Europe. More important, the world's policymakers at the time knew Stalin did not want further war and did not think the Soviets would invade westward.[29] The Soviet Union itself had just been devastated by the worst scorched-earth invasion in history and was unlikely to attempt a conquest of Western Europe. In 1945, no one in the Truman administration or Clement Atlee's government in Britain took this direct Soviet aggression scenario seriously. The primary fear was that an also-exhausted Western Europe could succumb to communist expansion through indirect Soviet intimidation, domestic revolutions, or demoralization, although the National Security Council concluded that the Soviets had little chance of conquering this region.

The cost-benefit ratio for the Soviets of an invasion was too unfavorable for it to have been contemplated. Any war would have certainly escalated to American nuclear strikes on the Soviet homeland. Obtaining Western trade, capital, and technology through détente, which did not happen until the 1970s, was a preferable option. According to Robert H. Johnson, the former National Security Council and State Department official, "Even without the American forces deployed in Western Europe, a Soviet attack was extremely unlikely. With them, it was wholly improbable."

Thus, NATO had been created in 1949 mainly to reassure U.S. allies, lift their morale, and keep an eye on the possible trends toward communism in Western Europe, rather than to deter any unlikely and irrational Soviet invasion of the region. By 1960, the Allies, flush with economic recovery from World War II, could have deterred—with or without the United States—what little chance there was of a Soviet attack.[30] While for most of the last two centuries, the Russians had kept large ground forces, they never had started a war with a great power. The size of the ground forces did not equate to the probability of aggression, as some in the West assumed. Most Western analysts believed that the Soviets had to win early or not at all and needed a large force against superior Western logistics, naval power, and even industrial power. (Logistics has never been a Soviet/Russian strong suit, as the invasion of Ukraine in 2022 demonstrated.)

The Western military alliance had worried Kennan. The main justification for the alliance was the American fear of Western European demoralization or that war could start by miscalculation or Soviet fear that its regime was threatened. U.S. officials seemed oblivious to the fact that the creation of NATO itself increased Soviet anxiety and thus the chance of Kremlin miscalculation,[31] just as American officials would later be oblivious to Russian legitimate objections to expanding NATO eastward after the Cold War ended.

>> CHAPTER 11 <<

THE KOREAN WAR

North Korea's Invasion of the South Fuels the Cold War

North Korea's invasion of South Korea in 1950, the year after NATO's creation, created an irrational panic among U.S. officials of Soviet expansion around the world. Some thought Korea was a diversionary attack presaging a major Soviet attack on Europe. Yet evidence from the opened Soviet archives and other sources show that the initiative for the North Korean attack came from Pyongyang, not Moscow. U.S. intelligence sources at the time reported that the Soviets did not send supplies or trainers after the invasion began, nor did they stir up diversionary attacks by leftist groups or client states around the world. North Korean leader Kim Il Sung wanted to spur a communist revolution in South Korea; he was apprehensive that Syngman Rhee, the aggressive South Korean leader, might invade the North. The more aggressive Rhee and his generals had been engaging in provocative raids over the border into North Korea, according to American General William L. Roberts, chief of the Korean Military Advisory Group (KMAG). Allied and international observers were worried that South Korea was chomping at the bit to attack the North. Yet the United States tolerated those aggressive South Korean generals.[1]

Stalin approved North Korea's attack on South Korea because he did not think the United States would intervene. Dean Acheson had declared the South outside the U.S. defense perimeter in Asia and at the same time Congress cut the supplemental aid package for South Korea. Previously, the cautious Stalin had rejected North Korean leader Kim Il Sung's aggressive pressure to invade the South. He changed his mind about the risks of war with the United States in the wake of Acheson's speech; even then, Stalin warned that if Kim got into trouble, the Soviet Union would not bail him out. Also, Stalin did not want China's new radical communist regime (as of 1949), jumping ahead of him in backing any such invasion.[2]

The exaggerated U.S. reaction to the North Korean attack on a then-poor South Korea was more of an excuse to implement a greater defense buildup pushed by the famous NSC 68 document promulgated by the National Security Council to militarize the Cold War. It had envisioned the immediate Soviet threat to Europe as political and psychological, not military. According to historian Paul Seabury, the permanent U.S. conventional military buildup in Europe after 1950, triggered by the outbreak of the Korean War, exceeded what was required for conventional deterrence of the Soviets.[3] The war also provided an excuse for sending nuclear weapons to Europe and the eventual rearmament of Germany and Japan.[4] The buildup of American military forces envisioned in NSC 68—according to its primary author, Paul Nitze[5]—was primarily intended, like the creation of NATO, as a morale booster for U.S. allies. During the Korean War, from 1950 to 1953, the U.S. defense budget quadrupled. Exhibiting the ratchet effect—that is, not returning to prewar levels—that budget during most of the rest of 1950s was kept at three to three and a half times prewar levels. A priority of the NSC-68 was developing and deploying a large stock of thermonuclear weapons (H-bombs), and a draft was instituted, which later led to the first permanent large peacetime standing army in American history.[6]

Finally, during the Korean War, Truman asserted the power as commander in chief to deploy more U.S. divisions to Europe without congressional approval and to keep them there for as long as he wanted, even if the public and Congress wanted them brought home. Furthermore, his secretary of state made the astounding claim that Congress could not regulate the direction of the armed forces, which were under the command of the president—irrespective of the Constitution's text and past cases since the beginning of the republic, which went unacknowledged.[7] These assertions of executive deployment power would set as bad a precedent as Truman's pursuit of war against the Democratic People's Republic of Korea (DPRK) without congressional support, a first for a major U.S. war.

As for the Soviet threat at the time of the Korean War, Stalin's commitment to the development of communism in one country—contrary to the pursuit of an international communist revolution, as sought by Trotsky—made Stalin one of the most conservative statesmen in the world—at that time avoiding significant assistance to communist governments in China (Mao Zedong) and Yugoslavia (Josip Broz Tito)[8] and to communist movements in Greece, France, and Italy.[9] After the Berlin Wall and the USSR fell, Soviet archives were mostly opened, confirming that Stalin had little interest in fomenting a worldwide communist revolution. He set up communist governments in Eastern Europe only as a security buffer against the possibility of a resurgent Germany conducting yet another invasion of Russia. Most Cold War scholars worldwide have reached the conclusion that new evidence found in those archives contradicts several assumptions of U.S.-slanted Cold War orthodoxy.[10] In 1980, David Holloway concluded that during the Cold War, the United States, Britain, and France used force more than did the Soviet Union, which tried to avoid a conflict with the West.[11] In a memoir, Nikita Khrushchev, Stalin's longtime aide and successor as ruler of the USSR, wrote that Stalin "trembled" and "quivered" at the thought of war with the United States. Khrushchev believed that "he was afraid of war. Stalin never did anything to provoke a war with the United States. He knew his weakness."[12] In fact, the USSR used force only reluctantly within its sphere of influence, and outside of it only to support already existing friendly regimes.[13] In the developing world, where most of the post–World War II military conflict occurred, the United States used force much more than the Soviet Union.[14]

The North Korean attack on the South made possible costly U.S.-dominated alliances around the world, along with military and economic aid to such allies. Realistically, many of the places the new U.S. alliances were meant to defend against communism were not strategic to the United States; some were even poor, developing countries. Yet assessments of the strategic worth of these countries, and the threat to U.S. security if they fell to communism, were ignored in the anti-communist hysteria of the time and by what had become the dominant imperial view that a communist advance anywhere was an encroachment on U.S. preeminence and demonstrated its weakness. In fact, in every region of the world, the American superpower—secure with two vast oceans as moats—was more worried about the expansion of communism than U.S. friends and allies who lived in those regions. NATO allies feared Soviet expansionism in Europe less than the United States did. The same was true of the People's Republic of China's expansion by East Asian allies; communist expansion in Southeast Asia by SEATO (Southeast Asia Treaty Organization) allies; and Leftist/Marxist expansion in Chile, the Dominican Republic, El Salvador, and Nicaragua by Central and South American allies.[15] The difference in perspective may have been that those countries all over the world who depended on America's security umbrella, which included both nuclear and conventional forces, had less of a military-industri-al-congressional complex to keep nourished with new weapons contracts than did the United States.

The Defense Industry Becomes the Driver of Wars

In World War II, the U.S. military's purported needs became so vast that a permanent private defense industry had to be created for the first time in American history; during the war, that new Military-Industrial-Congressional Complex (MICC) expanded as far as better than 40 percent of the American economy.[16] During earlier U.S. wars, a portion of civilian industry was converted to military productions and then reconverted to commercial production after the conflict ended. In the five years between the end of World War II and the beginning of the Korean War, the American economy went into a significant post-war recession, which deeply worried U.S. policymakers.[17] When the Korean War began in 1950, defense producers had not yet fully reconverted to commercial manufacture. They were never to do so again.

Of sociologist Anthony H. Richmond's categorization of the causes of wars—underlying causes, intervening variables, and precipitating events—he moved the vested interests of defense contractors from an intervening variable to an underlying cause of wars after World War II,[18] thus indicating that the MICC had become an enduring cause of U.S. conflicts.

The private defense contractors were so agile that they even began to crowd out the sluggish government-owned and operated weapons produc-tion facilities. However, over time private defense contractors also came to be sluggish, as they came to depend on the Department of Defense, a monopsonist (single) buyer with copious and Byzantine regulations, for more of their business. Many lost the desire and even the ability to play in the kind of fierce competition evident in commercial markets. In short, competition in the defense industry had become a façade as contracts were increasingly handed out on a sole-source basis to the politically most influential companies and to the districts and states of the politically most powerful members of Congress.[19]

Thus, presidents of both parties, members of Congress, defense industries, and the foreign policy and defense bureaucracies in Washington all had an incentive to cooperate in exaggerating the communist threat to justify to Congress and the American people continued unnecessary American interventionism around the world that would require high defense spending. For example, Republican Senator Arthur Vandenberg, a former isolationist turned interventionist hawk, told President Truman in 1947 that he had to "scare the hell out of the country" about the communist threat. Truman obliged, according to hardline Dean Acheson, his secretary of state, who later admitted that the administration made the Soviet threat "clearer than the truth." Histrionic anti-communism and exorbitant military spending were used by the Democratic Truman administration to get Republicans to buy into its worldwide Soviet containment project, which pushed American military and political dominance and management of a globally integrated economy.

Although Eisenhower ended the Korean War and spoke eloquently in his farewell address in early 1961 about the dangers of the military-industrial-congressional complex, it had become permanently entrenched during peacetime on his watch. Throughout the Cold War, because of the political pressure of that powerful complex, more bipartisan agreement was found on defense spending than on the issues of foreign aid or trade.

Such threat exaggeration led to wasted American lives, treasure, and distortions of American society and its political system.[20] After the Cold War ended, in reports done in 1992–1993, the U.S. General Accounting Office (now the Government Accountability Office), a nonpartisan investigative arm of Congress, concluded that the Defense Department during the Carter, Reagan, and Bush administrations constantly overestimated Soviet strategic nuclear capabilities to make the case for modernization of such U.S. weapon systems.[21]

Another Red Scare

A second Red Scare at home fueled by the Korean War (the first one started in 1919 from the xenophobia induced by World War I and the Bolshevik Revolution in Russia) has been blamed on Republican Senator Joe McCarthy, a fraudulent demagogue who ruined the careers of many innocent people and whom the Senate eventually censured. Blaming McCarthy is deserved, but Democratic President Truman, who wanted to look tough on communism, had contributed to the anti-communist hysteria by demanding loyalty boards of dubious due process for U.S. government employees starting in 1947—and it was this development that gave McCarthy, whose nefarious efforts began in February 1950, ammunition, legitimacy, and a permission structure. The next year, in 1948, Truman's administration prosecuted the U.S. Communist Party on phony charges. In addition, from 1946 to 1950, several high-profile spying scandals in North America and Britain involving domestic communists who stole classified material, including atomic bomb secrets, eventually fueled Truman's and McCarthy's threat inflation concerning domestic communist subversives and the Soviet Union.

Then in late June 1950, North Korea invaded South Korea. The U.S. government's strange about-face from publicly writing off the then-poor South Korea as inevitably falling under nearby Soviet sway to sending substantial forces to beat back the communist attack was driven in part by pressure on Truman from domestic anti-communist hysteria, stoked by him in the beginning and then by Joe McCarthy in the months before the invasion.

Especially stinging was McCarthy's unfair and false accusation that Truman had "lost" China to communism in 1949 because of subversion by domestic communists in the U.S. State Department. As during the Quasi-War with France (1798–1800), "disloyalty" was a lever used against political opponents.

In the summer of 1950, at a cabinet meeting in which the congressional elections topped the agenda, Truman, with an eye on voters, decided to be more anti-communist, albeit less prudent, by announcing his fateful decision to allow General Douglas MacArthur's army to go north of the 38th parallel, thereby expanding America's war aims to unite all of Korea.[22] McCarthy's criticism, MacArthur's optimism about the outcome of invading North Korea after his successful amphibious landing at Incheon that had rolled back the North Korean invaders, and public demand for action pushed Truman into ill-fated mission creep.

Truman later criticized McCarthy's activities, but other Republicans in addition to McCarthy also believed Truman had lost China because of communists in the State Department. Although a few communists were indeed working in the department and other government agencies, many more government analysts, who were not communists but did not believe in hardline anti-communism, were forced to leave the government. In contrast, President Dwight Eisenhower, Truman's successor, found it politically harder to publicly criticize McCarthy, a fellow Republican, instead hoping he would self-destruct, which he eventually did by going after alleged communists in the U.S. Army.

However, McCarthyism—pitching an excessive threat at home and abroad—survived McCarthy's demise. The hearings of McCarthy and other demagogues in Congress searching out alleged communist sympathizers in other areas of public life hardened U.S. foreign policy by making current and future political appointees and career bureaucrats leery of doing anything that critics might call "appeasement" or "sympathy" with the "reds." In contrast to the exaggeration of the communist threat in the United States, ironically, countries protected by the new Pax Americana alliances that spanned the world mostly downplayed it. As a benefit, those nations could spend less on defense, using the saved resources first to recover from World War II and later to gain a competitive advantage over U.S. companies.[23]

During the Korean War era, Congress and the Supreme Court also got into the red-baiting game. In 1950, Congress passed the McCarran Internal Security Act over Truman's surprising veto, which made all communists register with the federal government. In 1951, the Supreme Court, in a lopsided ruling, upheld the Smith Act, which removed the First Amendment rights of freedom of speech and assembly from Communist Party members. The U.S. government had exaggerated the threat to the United States from Soviet and Chinese communism, but the actual threat from communists at home was almost nonexistent. Yet Soviet and Chinese communist reaction to the U.S. hype then heightened the American public's anxiety, creating a self-escalating loop throughout the Cold War. Since the Bolshevik Revolution, the American public had been very resistant to the faux alure of communism. Thus, the Communist Party had been small; out of a U.S. population of 150 million in 1950, the communist party had only 30,000 members. During the Korean War and early Cold War era, government harassment and prosecution had reduced the party to a measly 5,000 members by 1957. However, the FBI, under J. Edgar Hoover, ruined the reputations of many innocent people. Even Truman had become afraid of the FBI, worried that they had become a secret police.[24]

The goal of the U.S. containment policy—to "contain" Soviet expansion until the USSR fell because of its dysfunctional economic system—might have been achieved earlier if its fragile communist system had been further stressed by dumping more resources into communist revolutions in less vital parts of the world, such as the then-poor South Korea. With restrained U.S. resistance to less-threatening, nonstrategic communist expansion, Soviet overreach and bankruptcy might have happened earlier. However, vested interests in the United States made a smarter Cold War–Lite strategy difficult.

Many Cold War historians now believe that the ideological pull of a free and prosperous America—versus a totalitarian, oppressive, and economically stagnant Soviet Union—was a more potent weapon in the Cold War than U.S. military power.[25] However, the United States instead chose to send troops to defend faraway developing countries of little strategic value. The first of those was South Korea in 1950.

Entering the Korean War

Few in American policy circles, including the joint chiefs of staff, believed that the impoverished Korean Peninsula was strategic for the United States in any Cold War with the USSR.[26] U.S. cold warriors did believe, however, that Japan, the industrial heartland of East Asia, needed raw materials from and markets for finished Japanese goods in China, Manchuria, and Korea—all of which were in danger of slipping into communist hands. Thus, they then looked to Southeast Asia to supply these things to Japan. Yet revolutionary nationalist movements were afoot in French Indochina and the Netherlands East Indies. In the end the U.S. occupation government did not need to overmanage Japanese economic resurgence because that renaissance came about by Japan massively exporting goods to the United States instead.[27] Thus, in 1950, Korea was less economically important to Japan than U.S. occupiers of the islands thought.

During World War II, Korea had been a Japanese colonial possession and was treated quite badly. After World War II, the Soviet Union and the United States split the Korean peninsula into North and South, managed by each superpower respectively. Because of South Korea's perceived nonstrategic nature and because of other global U.S. commitments in the face of postwar troop demobilization and budget reduction, the National

Security Council wanted to withdraw U.S. forces from there "as soon as possible with a minimum of bad effects." The dominant belief was that the peninsula would eventually fall under Soviet sway because of its location near the USSR, so the United States decided to withdraw its occupation forces, build up the South Korean armed forces, and continue aid to give the South Korean government "at least an even chance of survival." Yet because of South Korea's limited military capability, the corruption of the South Korean government, and other U.S. obligations, the U.S. military and the State Department did not want to include South Korea within the U.S. Asian defense perimeter. The U.S. Army was especially anxious to exit the peninsula and withdrew all forces by June 1949; the Soviets also withdrew their forces from North Korea the same year.

American officials refused to give Syngman Rhee, the aggressive U.S. client ruler of South Korea, many heavy weapons, because they feared he would attack the North. The North Koreans took notice of all these developments and of U.S. Secretary of State Dean Acheson's open declaration in January 1950 that South Korea was outside the U.S. defense perimeter in Asia. They consulted with Stalin in the USSR and Mao in China and got a green light to invade the South.[28]

However, after North Korea invaded South Korea in late June 1950, President Truman and the U.S. government panicked and decided that they had to defend South Korea. Without congressional approval and before the United Nations had authorized collective defense of the South, Truman, reminded of Neville Chamberlain's "appeasement" at Munich, rushed air and naval units into the Korean civil war.

The U.S. government's belated actions to defend South Korea showed that it implicitly believed—erroneously—that the then-poverty-stricken country was somehow important strategically. If Korea had indeed been that important, they would have tried to deter a North Korean attack rather than scramble to defend against one that materialized.

The United States may have succumbed to the "turbulent frontier" thesis, which notes that when countries expand their area of control, they then begin to worry about stabilizing adjoining areas, leading to further (and perhaps endless) expansion. After World War II the United States had occupied Japan. One factor in the belated U.S. decision to defend South Korea was that South Korea, being just across the Sea of Japan (East Sea) from the Japanese islands, needed stability to safeguard the new U.S. investment in stabilizing Japan. Then-Assistant Secretary of

State Dean Rusk even argued that if the communists took South Korea, it would be "a dagger pointed at the heart of Japan."[29] Yet Soviet territory was even closer to Japan than was South Korea. The Kremlin could have easily used its proximity to launch an (improbable) amphibious assault on Japan. Also, the United States wanted "free" (non-communist) areas in Northeast and Southeast Asia to supply raw materials and markets for a Japanese economy then recovering from the devastation of World War II. Strangely, this American pro-Japan vision resembled a milder version of the Japanese Empire's Greater East Asia Co-Prosperity Sphere that had helped cause that massive World War II in the first place.

Yet this explanation does not entirely explain the abrupt about-face between the military judgment that South Korea was not strategic to the United States and Truman's frantic defense of it after North Korea attacked it. A more likely explanation is that Truman was already under attack from the Republicans for having "lost China" the year before in 1949. According to most historians, Truman had withdrawn U.S. commitments to the nationalists under Chiang Kai-shek because his administration believed supporting them would be costly and futile—only starting to worry when the communists under Mao Zedong then drove them into Taiwan, and American public pressure built to defend the island sanctuary. In addition, a 1948 communist coup in Czechoslovakia and the Soviet 1949 acquisition of the atomic bomb had added to public fears in the 1950 congressional election year, in which Truman's popularity was at one of its lowest levels since he took office in 1945. When North Korea invaded South Korea, the United States—in addition to defending the South—committed to a security agreement to defend the nationalist regime in Taiwan and to do so, moved the U.S. seventh fleet into the Taiwan Strait during the Korean War.[30]

Domestic anti-communism was an important driver in Truman's abrupt turnabout and rush to defend the small, impoverished countries of South Korea and Taiwan that were of no strategic concern for the United States. Before the North Koreans invaded South Korea, U.S. policymakers had left the South outside the U.S. defense perimeter in Asia, had made no security pact to defend Taiwan, and were on the verge of recognizing communist China. After the attack, in addition to the seventh fleet interposed between China and Taiwan, the United States signed security pacts with Taiwan and other East Asian nations, set up a program of worldwide military aid to fight communism, and accelerated the integration of Japan and Germany into the West. By this expansion of an earlier defined Asian defense perimeter, the United States became involved in disputes between China and Taiwan over the islands between them in the 1950s and in the war in Indochina in the 1950s, 1960s, and early 1970s.[31]

If Truman had stuck to the original goal of liberating South Korea from the communists, the outcome of the war would have been a notable success. However, General Douglas MacArthur, a prima donna war hero from World War II, hatched a brilliant plan to launch an amphibious assault to liberate South Korea at Incheon, which was near Seoul, South Korea's capital and close to the North-South border. The assault was successful so Truman, under pressure from MacArthur, changed the aim of the war to liberate North Korea from communism as well. Newly communist China kept warning the United States not to allow its forces to get too close to the Yalu River, the border between China and North Korea, fearing a unified American client state on its border, complete with U.S. military bases for gathering intelligence and maybe attacking it. Because Republicans were already criticizing Truman for losing China, the Chinese were legitimately concerned that he might intervene in the Middle Kingdom again, using the U.S. fleet in the Taiwan Strait and a unified Korean Peninsula as a springboard.[32]

The United States paid little heed to Chinese warnings. In early November 1950, as U.S. and allied troops neared the Yalu River border, the nervous Chinese launched a massive invasion to take back North Korea, throwing U.S. and South Korean forces back. Republicans charged that Truman was trying to stifle news of the Chinese invasion and heavy U.S. casualties, keeping voters in the dark before they voted—for good reason, the American people quickly turned against the war.

The Democrats took a bath in the election on November 7, losing five seats in the Senate and twenty-eight in the House. In January 1951, a Gallup poll showed that by 49 vs. 28 percent, Americans thought Truman had made a mistake even in defending South Korea; 66 percent wanted to pull out U.S. troops at once; and Truman was given an approval rating of only 36 percent.

Lyndon Johnson later thought Truman had made a huge mistake by not getting public buy-in through a congressional vote before sending troops to Korea (so LBJ got at least got some congressional approval in the Gulf of Tonkin Resolution before escalating the Vietnam War). Throughout American history, the America people usually initially support the president when troops are sent into harm's way but can turn against a war if they think the it is not critical to national security and high casualties result or the fighting drags on. In this case, public opinion reversed with lightning speed.

Acheson told Truman that the United States needed to "get out with honor. . . . We can't defeat the Chinese in Korea—they can put in more than we can."[33] For once, Acheson was right, but that imperial phraseology, "get out with honor," would morph into the similar "peace with honor" during the even more protracted Vietnam War. The United States would have kept more honor by never getting entangled in these costly and unneeded (except by the MICC) brushfire wars in the first place.

The front then stabilized around the original North-South border in mid-1951—after a year of seesaw war. The stalemate continued for two more years, senselessly costing the United States another sixteen thousand casualties (a whopping 45 percent of the total loses for the war) for little gain and depriving Truman of a chance for another term in office. By the time Dwight Eisenhower signed an armistice during his first year in office in 1953, the United States had lost thirty-seven thousand Americans defending the nonstrategic nation of South Korea and failing in the expanded goal of liberating North Korea from communism.

According to Thomas J. McCormick, the most crucial decision the Americans made in the war was to turn down a Soviet peace initiative in late June 1951, just after the front stabilized after a year of rapid and tumultuous back-and-forth changes of fortune. The Soviets proposed an armistice line at the 38th parallel, close to what is now the Demilitarized Zone (DMZ) between North and South Korea, which was popular with the American people. Yet the United States turned down this Soviet proposal. Close to same settlement was accepted two years later by Republican Dwight Eisenhower in 1953. The reason Truman did not bite on the Soviet offer, which would have saved countless American and Korean lives, was because in June 1951, he hoped to run and win another term in the 1952 election in seventeen months. Truman's "loss" of China to communism haunted his entry into the Korean War and now prevented him from getting out of the bog. According to McCormick, Truman would have had to settle for a peace without victory and thus would have been open to Republican charges of appeasing communists during an election season. Ironically, the newly elected Eisenhower, a Republican World War II hero with a Republican Congress, was able to agree to the same deal without facing a similar charge.

Another reason Truman delayed the war settlement was that his administration needed time to implement the increases in military spending that the White House's NSC-68 document had proposed. Ending the war in mid-1951 would have destroyed the justification for the large military force the United States sought for the building of a global informal political and economic empire under the guise of "containing" communism. And that policy in turn justified a policy of military Keynesianism—massive government subsidization of military research, development, and procurement designed to help the U.S. civilian economy recover from the 1949 recession by artificial stimulus, which also would be helpful at election time. However, Truman's stalling of the armistice boomeranged, making him the unpopular overseer of a stalemated war. He lost the New Hampshire primary in March 1952 and shortly thereafter dropped out of the race for another term.

The Korean War also allowed the remilitarization of Europe, triggering a massive buildup of U.S. forces there. West Germany then went on the road to rearmament. Prior to the war, a Soviet peace offensive had played on French fears of German revanchism by proposing a reunified but demilitarized Germany. This outcome was exactly what U.S. policymakers wanted to avoid. They feared that with détente, the Soviets could entice West Germany into neutrality by the lure of reunification and entry into Eastern European markets. However, North Korea's invasion of South Korea allowed those officials to blame the Soviets for instigating the aggression (Soviet archives opened after the Cold War showed it instead to be North Korea's brainchild) and to scare Europeans by alleging that the Korean invasion was a smokescreen to obscure that Western Europe was the USSR's major target. The invasion in Korea gave a certain plausibility to this argument. It frightened the Europeans and allowed the United States to uncover its plan to remilitarize West Germany, secretly approved in NSC 68 back in 1950 just before the Korean War started.

The war put West Germany on the trajectory of remilitarization and NATO membership which, coupled with the economic integration of Western Europe, would anchor it in the U.S.-dominated sphere and lessen chances of Soviet enticement. The Europeans were even more unnerved by the Soviet response to the militarization established in NSC-68—increasing the size of the Red Army by 100 percent, hiking the USSR's defense budget by 50 percent, and testing an H-bomb (much more powerful than the A-bomb) in early 1953.[34]

During the war, although the communists were certainly no model citizens, the United States and its South Korean ally also ran a scorched-earth policy. In this smaller war, more bombs landed on the Korean Peninsula than in the Pacific theater during the more expansive World War II. Bombs were dropped on North Korean dams to flood crops and induce starvation among civilians. In addition, on the ground, to achieve the same effect, irrigation systems were attacked. U.S. and South Korean troops also destroyed thousands of villages.[35]

The Domestic Impact of the Korean War

The Korean War, like the Spanish-American War, was a forgotten war with big implications at home. The first one was positive: it reaffirmed the republican principle of civilian control of the military. The White House ordered MacArthur to refrain from giving his opinions about the war to the media that differed from Truman's exploration of peace. MacArthur wanted to wage total war against the Chinese, which included expanding the war into China with the use of nuclear weapons on Chinese cities, blockading China's coast, and opening a second front by employing the Nationalist Chinese from Taiwan. He kept talking to the media about his contrary views on the failing war, which Truman wisely wanted to keep limited, not wanting a bloody long war with China. Furthermore, the Soviet Union had gotten the A-bomb in 1949, and he did not want a nuclear war with Moscow.

MacArthur would not stop publicly criticizing Truman, and the president justly fired him for insubordination, even though MacArthur was quite popular with the American people, and he was not. It was a courageous decision. Truman was able to make it stick, in part because the generals on the joint chiefs of staff backed him. Civilian control over the military was reaffirmed.

George Kennan, the father of the containment doctrine, had helped write NSC-68, before he fell out with Secretary of State Dean Acheson for his less-hawkish views and was exiled to academia.[36] NSC-68 alarmingly predicted that with the Soviet acquisition of nuclear weapons in 1949, a new Soviet adventurism would threaten the world order based on an American nuclear monopoly. The document therefore advocated a massive increase in U.S. defense spending. NSC-68 was sitting on the shelf when North Korea invaded the South in 1950. After that event, the document became operationalized in a general buildup of the U.S. military, which became permanent during peacetime even after an armistice brought an end to hostilities on the Korean peninsula.

Secretary of State Acheson later euphemistically acknowledged that NSC-68 had exaggerated the Soviet threat by making its statements "clearer than the truth" to convince the average American of the danger. Paul Nitze, the State Department's chief policy planner and lead author of NSC-68, also later acknowledged the deliberate overstatement of threat to sell militarization of the Cold War to a fiscally conservative Congress. Acheson and Nitze intentionally exaggerated the Soviet threat to "bludgeon the mass mind" of top government officials to enlarge the U.S. military force. This chronic overestimation of the Soviet threat—by the CIA and even more by the U.S. military, which had a conflict of interest in both analyzing the threat and developing weapons to combat it—would continue throughout the Cold War.

Although the NSC-68 was a top-secret document designed to convince the president, the secretary of defense, and the Bureau of the Budget about the severity of the threat, Acheson went on a nationwide speaking tour in the spring of 1950, warning of a preposterous scenario of the communists winning in Europe and Asia without firing a shot, thus leaving the United States isolated.[37] When North Korea invaded South Korea in late June 1950, Acheson seemed to be a prophet, and the exaggerated threat assessment in NSC-68 put the United States on the road from republic to garrison state. Relieved, Acheson later said, "Korea came along and saved us."[38] Truman quadrupled the defense budget and started a plan that would augment the American nuclear force to twenty thousand nuclear warheads by 1960 and thirty-two thousand by 1966—gross overkill by any standard.[39]

Another major domestic ill effect of the Korean War was the dramatic expansion of executive power at the expense of the Constitution's stipulated congressional powers. Before the war broke out, because of the wider Cold War, Congress delegated more institutional power in national security to the president. The National Security Act of 1947 set up a new National Security Council bureaucracy within the White House, strengthened the president's control over the military by creating a new Department of Defense that controlled the military services, and gave the president a new intelligence agency—the CIA—independent of the military.

In addition to the augmentation of the institutional presidency, Truman usurped a significant constitutional power of Congress—the power to initiate war. From the beginning of the constitutional republic up through FDR, presidents tried to defuse altercations between Congress and the executive over war powers. After Truman secured election in his own right in 1948, he began brazen grabs of executive power. Other Cold War presidents followed suit, not because the threat to U.S. security had worsened but because American power had drastically increased after World War II. An informal global American empire, arising from victory in World War II and developed during the Cold War, led to an imperial presidency.

In 1950, for the first time in a major American conflict, Truman—who jealously guarded and even wanted to expand presidential power—unilaterally took the country into a major war in Korea without asking Congress for a declaration of war beforehand. Congress could have insisted that one be passed but it did not, thus abdicating its constitutional power to declare war—one of its most important under the Constitution. While William McKinley had begun significant military actions without congressional approval both in the counterinsurgency against Filipino independence fighters and the suppression of the Boxer Rebellion in China, both after the Spanish-American War, the Korean War was the first major war in American history that Congress did not declare.

Truman instead argued that he had asked the United Nations Security Council for authority to take military action, but the congressionally passed United Nations Participation Act of 1945, which governed U.S. participation in the new organization, nonetheless required that the executive get approval from Congress before supplying U.S. military forces to the world body. (Truman later showed that he had little regard for the Security Council resolution when he tossed it away to invade North Korea, which it had not authorized.)

Constitutionally, Congress's declaration of war was much more important than any UN approval. Yet Truman crowed, "I certainly never would have asked for anything. It was none of Congress's business."[40] The Constitution's framers would have vehemently disagreed. According to Louis Fisher and John Hart Ely, among scholars who often argue about the "original understanding" of the Constitution, there is remarkable agreement that the Constitution's framers specifically and intentionally broke with monarchical precedents to give Congress, not the president, the power to initiate all hostilities against other countries—big or small, declared or undeclared wars.[41]

Politically, later presidents have realized that it helps to get a congressional buy-in to spread the blame if any major war goes badly. That said, presidents since Truman have asserted that legally, they do not need congressional approval to take the nation to war. The nation's founders would have been horrified because they believed that no single person should be enabled to make such a monumental decision affecting the nation's population—as the kings did in Europe at the time of the nation's founding.

The Truman administration cited a list of eighty-five instances throughout American history of the president unilaterally using force without any congressional approval, but it neglected to mention that most of those instances involved minor uses of force to protect Americans and their property abroad from lawless mobs, island dwellers, pirates, or weak governments—not to undertake a major war involving the defense of another entire country. FDR's main spokesman in Congress had cited the same eighty-five cases when Roosevelt deployed U.S. forces to Iceland in July 1941, before U.S. congressionally sanctioned involvement in World War II began. But even many of these eighty-five cases may not have adhered to the founders' original concept of allowing executive action without congressional approval only for self-defense. Also, a difference between the Icelandic and Korean cases was that FDR's congressional defender had acknowledged that only Congress could make war; in the Iceland case, unlike the Korean one, the president was deploying troops into what was only a potentially hostile environment (even this was dubious without congressional approval) rather than inserting them into a major hot war.

Later, Dean Acheson said Truman had the direct "constitutional authority to do what he did." Then he modified that by blurting out that Truman, never much on exhibiting constitutional leadership or abiding by the principles of a republic, did not seek congressional approval because he wanted to avoid "the possibility of endless criticism" and was adamant "to pass [the presidency] on unimpaired by the slightest loss of power or prestige."[42] He did not achieve the former goal but his attainment of the latter was off the charts—converting an American presidency, already puffed up by FDR to a "first among equals" branch, into an full-blown imperial office.

A bad precedent was set because the United States has not declared war in any of its major wars since then. Even the nation's founder most susceptible to the stretching of executive power, Alexander Hamilton, likely would have disputed Truman's precedent. Hamilton had stated, "It is the peculiar and exclusive province of Congress, when the nation is at peace, to change that state into a state of war" and that the president's authority as commander in chief "would amount to no more than the supreme command and direction of the military and naval forces, as first General and Admiral of the Confederacy; while that of the British king extends to the declaring of war."[43]

The argument arose that during the Cold War—with the advent of nuclear weapons that could rapidly inflict horrific damage—the president had to have the increased ability to respond swiftly to dangerous situations, nuclear and nonnuclear, without the requirement of slow congressional deliberation and approval. Truman made this argument even during his nonnuclear response to North Korea's invasion of South Korea. The entire argument sounded reasonable but was without merit. Under the founders' conception of the war power, the executive had the authority to rapidly conduct genuine self-defense measures after a sudden attack. Even during the Cold War's extreme case, if an adversary nation launched nuclear weapons at the United States and the president needed to launch U.S. nuclear weapons before they were destroyed, the founders' original scheme would have allowed that to happen. Thus, in such an instance, the president did not need to claim any non-existent inherent power outside the constitutional scheme, including as commander in chief, to wage defensive nuclear war. Furthermore, the nature of the Cold War did not erode the ability of the president to execute constitutional self-defense against sudden conventional attacks on the United States.

The founders' original conception would not have allowed any use of military force beyond defense of the United States without congressional approval—for example, helping with the defense of another nation or an offensive U.S. attack; these uses of force still should have needed a declaration of war or other congressional approval.

Furthermore, during the Cold War and beyond, unlike during the founding period in the late eighteenth century, Congress is in session all year—instead of only a few months per annum based on a schedule driven by the then-dominant agricultural sector—and could be reconvened quickly if on recess, given the much better modern transportation and communication methods. If war is afoot, the modern Congress can act quickly.

In both the Korean War and the Vietnam War, the argument was made that defending countries important to the United States, whether formal allies or not, was just like defending the United States—thus severely stretching the founders' concept of self-defense and supposedly obviating the need for a declaration of war in these cases.[44] In both wars, Congress complained about the usurpation of executive power but then funded the wars and the conscription machinery needed to get people to fight them—the exception being the general congressional funding cutoffs at the end of the Vietnam War. With his unilateral war in Korea, Truman's flagrant flouting of the Constitution would have long-lasting and harmful effects on the ability of Congress to carry out one of its most vital constitutional duties—deciding on war and peace.

Another unilateral presidential action that most certainly would not have won the approval of the Constitution's framers was new president Dwight Eisenhower's nuclear threats in 1953 to try to intimidate the North Koreans and Chinese to reach a peace agreement in the Korean War. The North Koreans and Chinese did not attack the United States directly and did not even have nuclear weapons in 1953. As noted, as Truman had bypassed the requirement for Congress to declare war against a major adversary, now Eisenhower was threatening to launch an unauthorized offensive nuclear strike in a war that had not been approved by Congress. Richard Nixon, Ike's vice president, believed the myth that the nuclear threat had led to peace on the Korean peninsula and tried the same gambit to prod the North Vietnamese into a settlement when he was chief executive during the Vietnam War. In fact, the thaw in U.S.-Soviet relations with Stalin's death in March 1953 was more important than Ike's nuclear threats in ending the long Korean stalemate. Also, Eisenhower largely accepted the 38th latitudinal parallel as the dividing line between the Koreas, which the Soviets had proposed two years before that Truman had rejected.

With the augmentation of the institutional presidency by the National Security Act of 1947, the increased defense budgets giving the executive more tools of military intervention, and his ignoring of Congress in unilaterally taking the country into the Korean War, Truman became the first imperial president. Historian Arthur Schlesinger Jr. coined the term later to describe the presidency of Richard Nixon during the Vietnam War, but Truman fit Schlesinger's definition long before the historian applied the moniker to Nixon. Schlesinger correctly believed that the presidency had taken advantage of international crises to expand its power beyond constitutional bounds and then turned this augmented power inward to act illegally at home. Yet Truman had used the Cold War and the Korean War to do this same thing almost two decades before Nixon took office.

Truman's Stretching of Presidential Power

Truman overtly disparaged what he called weak wartime presidents, such as James Madison, and praised strong presidents, such as James Polk and Abraham Lincoln. In short, Truman imitated presidents willing to wield expansive executive tools—powers that stretched the Constitution and were unwritten for the executive in the founding document but were found useful during "emergencies." Also, in his development of a world-wide militarized crusade against communism, Truman admired Woodrow Wilson's idealism and clearly his interventionism abroad.[45]

Thus, during the Korean War, as per Schlesinger's later analysis, Truman questionably tried not only to stretch the Constitution to find "inherent" (unwritten) powers as commander in chief but also to use them in the domestic sphere. Yet, to limit the scope and power of the new federal government, the framers clearly intended the Constitution as a document of specifically enumerated federal powers. The founders intended the president's commander-in-chief powers to be narrow. During the Korean conflict, Truman tried to use the commander-in-chief powers to end a steel strike—which he claimed was impeding war production— by seizing and nationalizing (socializing) privately owned steel mills in direct violation of a congressionally passed law. He caused a tumult when asked at a news conference if his power as commander in chief also would allow him to seize newspapers if needed to win the war; he would not say no. He even threatened to draft striking workers to serve in the war. Truman's heavy-handed tactics, including the attempt to institute socialism in an industry, lent credence to the adage that "during war, we become a little more like our enemies."

Fortunately, in the Youngstown Steel case (1952), the Supreme Court disallowed his power grab, ruling that when Congress had spoken through the law, the executive could not unilaterally overturn congressional will. In Justice Robert Jackson's famous majority opinion, he wrote that nothing could be "more sinister and alarming" than a future president sending the U.S. military into "some foreign venture" to expand his power at home.[46]

Wars, both cold and hot, tend to fuel intolerance of any dissent at home. The government usually believes that people must agree with the herculean team effort of war, no matter how foolish a conflict may be for achieving U.S. interests or how damaging it may be to the American way of life at home.

At the start of the war, Congress passed, over Truman's veto, the draconian McCarran Internal Security Act of 1950, which required communist organizations to register with the attorney general, authorized the government to investigate people for subversive activities and promoting a totalitarian dictatorship, and contained an emergency detention provision that allowed the government to detain persons for whom there was only a "reasonable ground" to believe they would engage in espionage or sabotage (less than the usual higher constitutional standard of arrest that requires "probable cause" that individuals had committed a crime). The exaggerated fear was that communists would try to sabotage the war effort at home.

>> CHAPTER 12 <<

THE CUBAN MISSILE CRISIS

The Roots of the Crisis

The United States got nuclear weapons first, but after the Soviets also got them, the U.S. government wanted to enhance its force, not only to deter a Soviet attack on Western Europe but also to have nuclear superiority so that the Soviets could not challenge any U.S. military operations anywhere in the world—a shield of sorts for U.S. military actions against foreign nations worldwide.

Nevertheless, Soviet/Russian strategic bombers and long-range missiles armed with nuclear warheads had been the only existential threat to the United States in its history to date. In October 1962, during the Cuban Missile Crisis, the two superpowers came the closest to global thermonuclear war. (Other notable close calls were during the Yom Kippur War in the Middle East in 1973; Ronald Reagan's nuclear Able Archer command and control exercise in 1983, which caused the Soviets to elevate the alert levels of their nuclear forces; and when a Norwegian scientific rocket launched in 1995 was mistaken by the then decrepit Russian early warning system for an incoming American nuclear attack.)

After the harrowing Cuban Missile Crisis, the two superpowers slowly began cooling down the Cold War for a while, negotiating what eventually would become limitations on, and then even later reductions of, nuclear weapons. Yet most of this thaw took place after JFK had been assassinated because, as a Democrat, he feared Republicans labeling him "soft on communism"—a legacy of Truman's alleged loss of China in 1949.

In the American public mind, the Soviets, unprovoked, caused the Cuban Missile Crisis by brazenly installing nuclear missiles only ninety miles from U.S. shores in Cuba, which John F. Kennedy (JFK) nixed by bold action, thus gloriously "winning" the day. Unfortunately, the facts reveal that JFK unnecessarily risked global thermonuclear Armageddon, not for any national security reason, but to repair his image of weakness so that his party would do better in the upcoming congressional elections in November 1962. Furthermore, instead of "winning" the confrontation, when a secret agreement that he made with Soviet Communist Party Chairman Nikita Khrushchev regarding the missiles' removal eventually came out much later, one could conclude that the Soviets certainly held their own or even transactionally got more out of the settlement than did the United States.

The roots of the crisis came in the preceding Eisenhower administration, when the CIA developed a plan to sponsor Cuban exiles to overthrow Fidel Castro, a leftist who had taken power in a revolution in early 1959. Since the Spanish-American War, the United States had dominated the Cuban economy. Castro was a direct threat to American business interests on the island, and they exerted political pressure on the U.S. government to do something about him. The Eisenhower and Kennedy administrations had blocked vitally needed International Monetary Fund lending and instituted a draconian trade embargo, especially on Cuba's principal crop—sugar. Unsurprisingly, Castro turned to the Soviet Union.

In the 1960 presidential campaign against Republican Richard Nixon, JFK hawkishly ran against an Eisenhower administration that was allegedly weak, having let leftist Fidel Castro take Cuba and having allowed the United States to fall behind the USSR in satellites, bombers, and long-range missiles (the latter two accusations were grossly untrue). When the inexperienced but competitive JFK succeeded Ike in 1961, caught by his own hyperbolic campaign rhetoric, he foolishly let the CIA talk him into executing a plan to oust Castro, which had little chance of overthrowing the popular leader. Castro had been tipped off to the planned Cuban-exile invasion by spies and even U.S. press reports. Furthermore, JFK approved only a limited use of the U.S.-provided, exile-piloted air force, thus leaving the exile army in harm's way on the beach of invasion. Unbelievably, after this public humiliation, the Kennedy administration doubled down on ousting Castro—it continued to aid the exiles, sabotage Cuban industry, launch paramilitary raids, collude with American mafia in multiple efforts to assassinate Castro, plan for another attempt at regime overthrow, and conduct Pentagon contingency planning for a future U.S. military invasion of the island. The Soviets and Cubans were aware of much of this plotting.

The Bay of Pigs fiasco in April 1961 not only left egg on JFK's face but, according to material from Soviet archives mostly opened after the Cold War, it motivated the Soviets to decide to take a large risk and deploy short- and mid-range nuclear weapons in Cuba to deter another such U.S.-sponsored or conducted invasion.[1] In addition, in that same year, JFK had declined to intervene militarily against the communist insurgency in Laos, instead wisely reaching an agreement for regime neutrality between East and West. Furthermore, the blustering Soviet leader had bested Kennedy at a superpower summit held in Vienna in June 1961. In mid-August 1961 East Germany, a Soviet client state, began building the Berlin Wall to keep its citizens in dreary East Berlin from fleeing to vibrant West Berlin. In short, during the off-year election of 1962, JFK and the Democrats, always vulnerable to "soft on communism" attacks, looked hapless and weak. Also, JFK's domestic New Frontier had stalled in Congress. Because a rabid fear of communism among the American people still prevailed, not only the 1962 congressional election but also JFK's 1964 re-election bid could have been affected badly by this perceived flaccidity against the exaggerated communist threat. He would need all the electoral help he could get, because he had won extremely narrowly against Nixon in 1960, and even then with allegations of fraud and vote stealing.[2] This dismal reality initially motivated JFK to take a potentially cataclysmic hard line during the missile crisis in the fall of 1962.

In September 1962, U.S. intelligence picked up unusual Soviet military activity in Cuba. The CIA concluded that "the main purpose of the present [Soviet] military buildup in Cuba is to strengthen the Communist regime there against what the Cubans and the Soviets conceive to be a danger that the U.S. may attempt by one means or another to overthrow it."[3] A State Department analysis after the crisis ended concluded in early and mid-1962 that the Soviets and Cubans had been concerned about another U.S. invasion attempt. Given U.S. shenanigans in Cuba, even after the U.S. humiliation in the failed Bay of Pigs fiasco, Soviet and Cuban fears were hardly misplaced. The Soviets were also trying to counter U.S. deployments of Jupiter nuclear-capable missiles in their neighborhood in Turkey and Italy.

Yet JFK had been assured by the Soviets several times that they were not installing offensive nuclear missiles in Cuba and would not embarrass him with such a gambit during an election year. The former promise was a lie, but the Soviets genuinely did not want to embarrass JFK with an election coming up. Khrushchev wanted to keep the missiles in Cuba a secret till after the American congressional elections were over in early November, but U.S. intelligence found them before then.

However, before the discovery, with the sham Soviet guarantee in his pocket, Kennedy decided to do a little political swaggering for the 1962 election. He gave a public statement on September 4, two months before the election, saying that the Soviets had promised him they were only installing defensive antiaircraft systems in Cuba, but if the Soviets placed offensive nuclear ground-to-ground missiles in Cuba, it would be the "gravest" threat to U.S. security. Then on October 14, 1962, U.S. intelligence discovered that the Soviets were installing such offensive nuclear missiles.[4] Such missiles were a useful deterrent to any U.S.-sponsored or direct invasion of the island.

By "strutting and flexing" for political purposes, Kennedy had boxed himself into a corner to take military action if Khrushchev double-crossed him. Eric Alterman points out that to avoid such a trap, JFK, in his statement, could have just said that there was no way that the small island of Cuba could threaten the most powerful nation on earth. Kennedy did not take this precaution. Therefore, he could not tolerate politically even a strategically meaningless Soviet action, admitted by JFK and U.S. high-level security officials. Publicly, there could be no deal or tradeoff for removing any Soviet missiles in Cuba.[5]

The Crisis Unfolds

At the time, White House recordings and records show that JFK; Robert McNamara, his secretary of defense; McGeorge Bundy, his national security adviser; and others in the administration believed the Soviet missiles in Cuba did not alter the overall nuclear balance. They did not pose a new strategic threat to U.S. security. Kennedy himself admitted that if he had not made his swaggering statement, he would not have had to do anything about the Soviet missiles on the island. McNamara initially pooh-poohed the Soviet missiles in Cuba as a "domestic political problem." The other security advisers agreed.[6] In his later speech to the American people on October 22 that revealed the Soviet missiles and announced the U.S. naval quarantine around Cuba, JFK admitted that the American people were accustomed to living in the bullseye of Soviet nuclear missiles on land and at sea. The new missiles in Cuba did not measurably change this threat. They only shortened the time for nuclear annihilation, given that no reliable missile defenses existed at that time in history.[7]

Although the strategic nuclear balance might not have figured in JFK's actions during the crisis, it was at least a factor in Moscow's decision to place nuclear missiles in Cuba. Looking at Soviet archives after the Cold War, historians have reached the conclusion that Soviet long-range nuclear forces were much weaker than even the U.S. believed at the time. Ironically, if Soviet missiles had been allowed to remain on the island, the nuclear balance would have been made more stable by eliminating any Pentagon temptation to launch a preventive nuclear first strike to take out Soviet missiles before they could be launched from the USSR.[8] At the time of the crisis, the vast nuclear superiority of the United States included 1,500 atomic bombs and 3,000 aircraft capable of carrying them versus 50 to 100 Soviet missiles and 200 Russian long-range bombers; both sides had enough intercontinental missiles to destroy each other many times over.[9]

In fact, U.S. Jupiter missiles, which had been installed on the Soviet border in Turkey and were becoming operational in 1962, were useful only in such a first strike scenario. JFK, on a White House recording about Soviet missiles in Cuba, complained, "It's just as if we suddenly began to put a major number of MRBMs [medium-range ballistic missiles] in Turkey. Now that'd be goddam dangerous, I would think." McGeorge Bundy replied, "Well, we did, Mr. President."[10]

This conversation would have been an amusing anecdote indicating presidential incompetence in not knowing the status of U.S. nuclear forces if it had not been so scary. It was only in the fall of 1962, during this nail-biting crisis, that JFK had become aware that the Jupiter missiles in Turkey were a concern to the Soviets. However, JFK had to be aware that since early in the Cold War, the U.S.-dominated NATO alliance had encircled Soviet territory with bases having nuclear weapons.

After getting himself into a politically induced, dangerous nuclear standoff with the Soviet Union, JFK knew the awful risks. At first, he did not request congressional approval to take military action during the crisis. He had in fact claimed unilateral authority to take the country to war. However, when Congress insisted on approving the use of force, Kennedy acquiesced, finding it "useful."[11] An executive committee

(EXCOM) of the National Security Council was set up to consider the options of invading Cuba, conducting air strikes on the Soviet missile sites, or imposing a naval quarantine of the island. However, the eleven-member committee was unanimous that some type of force needed to be employed. The disastrous Bay of Pigs fiasco had led to uncomfortable questions about American credibility as the world's policeman. Kennedy had yet to answer these questions. The Soviets, having installed the missiles in the Caribbean as JFK knew, raised the issue of enforcing the Monroe Doctrine.[12]

However, instead of letting his aggressive advisers, including the U.S. military, push him into an invasion of Cuba or other lethal military action on the island, he quarantined the island instead. Kennedy ordered the U.S. Navy to prevent more missiles and any supporting material from arriving on the island. In his October 22 speech announcing what amounted to a naval blockade, he euphemistically used the word "quarantine" because a naval blockade was traditionally regarded internationally as an act of war. However, by the time he threw the quarantine around Cuba, the Soviets already had installed thirty-six offensive medium-range nuclear warheads and 158 short-range tactical nuclear warheads for the island's defense.

After his famous October 22 speech revealing the Soviet missiles and his naval quarantine of Cuba, in a recorded meeting with Robert Kennedy—his attorney general and brother—JFK did not talk about the perilous national security situation or the blockade. Instead, JFK feared showing weakness toward the Soviets and believed he had to show toughness—otherwise he would be impeached, and the Democrats would lose many congressional seats. Leading up to the 1962 election, Republicans had been eager to return the favor of criticizing Kennedy over Cuba, because he had done the same to Nixon in the 1960 presidential election.

During the crisis JFK estimated the chances of nuclear war "as between one out of three and even" and believed that the Soviets keeping missiles in Cuba reduced U.S. security only slightly. However, he astoundingly took such huge risks for his own political gain and that of his party. That JFK and his top advisers were talking about showing strength for domestic political purposes, when the stark threat of thermonuclear war loomed, likely means that those baser knee-jerk political reactions have infected the decision-making of other U.S. political leaders during wars and other "security crises" of lesser importance—that is, probably in almost every other such crisis in American history.

It was extremely lucky for the world that JFK chose the blockade over harsher military measures. Unbeknownst until much later when the Soviet archives were opened, in addition to the longer-range missiles installed in Cuba, the USSR had installed tactical nuclear weapons on the island. The Kremlin had authorized field commanders to use them in any U.S. invasion. Their use could have obviously escalated into a full-blown nuclear war between the superpowers. Also, other incidents during the crisis could have sparked a U.S.-Soviet war: a U.S. spy plane had been shot down, and a Soviet submarine commander did not fire a nuclear torpedo at a U.S. Navy destroyer, which had launched what looked like a depth charge at his ship.

Fortunately for the world, JFK eventually negotiated his way out of the crisis. Officially, he pledged to respect Cuba's territorial integrity (a no-invasion pledge) if the Soviets would withdraw all nuclear missiles from Cuba. However, in secret, he also agreed to withdraw U.S. Jupiter nuclear missiles that the United States had in Turkey, near the Soviet border, and Italy. Astoundingly, JFK could have proposed this deal before the crisis became acute, thereby avoiding the considerable risk of global nuclear Armageddon. At the beginning of the crisis, Adlai Stevenson II, U.S. ambassador to the United Nations, had suggested to JFK a compromise like the one finally reached. This was never seriously considered early in the confrontation. Instead, JFK risked war through a U.S. naval blockade around the island. He hoped Khrushchev would back down. Khrushchev did withdraw the missiles, but in the end, JFK had to give him something, which Stevenson had told Kennedy he would need to do early in the crisis.

Given it was an election year, JFK felt he had to keep the Jupiter deal a secret. If the deal had been made public, the view of a Soviet "win" in the crisis might have arisen, or with greater certainty, the opportunity to project the image of JFK boldly forcing the Soviets to back down would have been missed. The removal of the Jupiter missiles in Turkey was so secret that Kennedy refused to put anything down on paper. JFK only promised to pull the missiles after the crisis was over. Privately, Robert Kennedy, referring to himself in the third person, said, "Someday—who knows?—He might run for president and his prospects could be damaged if this secret deal about the missiles in Turkey were to come out."[13]

Secretary of Defense McNamara blatantly lied to a secret session of the House Armed Services Committee in 1963 when he said that there was no connection between the Soviet removal of nuclear missiles from Cuba and the U.S. withdrawal of Jupiter missiles from Turkey and Italy.

To this day, the mistaken public belief is that the Soviets "blinked" in the crisis and that Kennedy, through his brilliance, prevailed. Happily for JFK, this distorted belief helped his party make a stronger showing than expected in the 1962 congressional elections, which was what JFK cared most about in the entire artificial but potentially dire crisis.

Unlike Kennedy, who controlled the narrative, Khrushchev did not fare so well politically from the crisis. Although he had lied at first to JFK about installing offensive nuclear missiles in Cuba, he kept the U.S. Jupiter deal secret even within the Kremlin—to his own peril. Within two years, a coup ousted him from power. While domestic factors played a role in his ouster, a document from the Soviet archive says he faced scathing criticism at a Politburo meeting for his failure to get much in return for removing the missiles from Cuba; he apparently kept the secret even then.

According to U.S. Ambassador Averell Harriman, who had post-crisis meetings with Khrushchev, the Soviet leader had a greater goal. He wanted to use the crisis to negotiate a mutual limitation or reduction in defense budgets with the United States, enabling him to transfer the savings into Soviet agriculture. The Democratic Kennedy administration, always afraid of appearing weak to the domestic anti-communist hysteria, declined (it did, however, agree to a limited bilateral ban on testing nuclear weapons). As a result of JFK's intransigence, the Soviets then started a massive arms race in nuclear and conventional forces to reach parity with the United States, so they would never be so publicly humiliated again in the future. The United States responded in kind, thus blowing a chance to take advantage of a harrowing crisis to reduce tensions and cut spending on the instruments of war.[14] Thus, the only real winner in this crisis was the military-industrial complexes of the two countries.

>> CHAPTER 13 <<

THE VIETNAM WAR

Origins of the War

Historian Melvin Small, who authored *At the Water's Edge: American Politics and the Vietnam War*, concluded, "The more I studied the anti-war movement, the media, and the decision-makers, the more I was persuaded that the key to understanding American policy in the Vietnam War was American domestic politics." That conclusion could apply to most, if not all, American wars, but it applies especially to the Vietnam War. Although other wars in American history were either unpopular from the beginning (the War of 1812) or became unpopular during protracted fighting (the Spanish-American War during subsequent Philippine insurgency, the Mexican War, Korean War, and the second Iraq war), or became unpopular later (World War I), the Vietnam War became unpopular because of conscription and because it happened after the full telecommunications revolution that placed few restrictions on media coverage. It became the first "living room" war.[1] It was the first chance for the greater public pierce through the propaganda and begin to understand the horrific realities of war and the dubious U.S. role in them.

Overall, the turbulent frontier thesis applies to Southeast Asia and helps to supply some strategic, although unconvincing, rationale for the United States trying to keep the region free of communism. A major aim of America's post–World War II global strategy was the recovery of industrial Japan from the war and its integration into a U.S.-dominated integrated world economy—with the American economy as the major beneficiary. The Truman administration envisioned a milder U.S. version of Imperial Japan's colonialist Greater East Asia Co-Prosperity Sphere in Asia. Under both the Imperial Japanese and later U.S. government strategies, the smaller economies in East Asia, including those in Southeast Asia, would send the resource-starved Japan food and raw materials.

Japan would then export finished goods back to those markets. To alleviate its "dollar drain," Japan needed to buy its raw materials from countries other than the United States. It was now the U.S. military that would supply the force needed to ensure those nations were friendly to Japan. Also, U.S. officials lamely argued that Southeast Asia was along a major (but not the only) route for Japan's supplies of oil from the Persian Gulf.

In 1955, after the colonial French withdrew in defeat from Indochina, Eisenhower slyly took over their anti-communist role in Vietnam. The U.S. joint chiefs of staff best summarized American official thinking:

> [Japan's cooperation with the United States] will be significantly affected by her ability to retain access to her historic markets and sources of food and raw materials in S.E. Asia. Viewed in this context, U.S. objectives with respect to S.E. Asia and U.S. objectives with respect to Japan would appear to be inseparably related.... The loss of S.E. Asia to the Western world would inevitably force Japan into an eventual accommodation with the Communist-controlled areas in Asia.[2]

Therefore, Southeast Asia was of little direct importance to the United States but was rather only important to Japan, albeit Japan was thought vital to the American hegemonic aim of facilitating and managing a globally integrated free market economy. Not only was managing a set of free but integrated economies worldwide a manifest contradiction, it was a fragile strategy resulting in needless effort, inefficiency, excessive cost, and many failures. The ridiculousness of needing a vast U.S. military commitment to hold the entire U.S.-dominated system in place was demonstrated by the specious domino theory. If Vietnam fell to the communists, the argument went, then the rest of Indochina would be next (Laos and Cambodia), then the Philippines and Indonesia, and finally Japan.

The key problem the United States faced in Southeast Asia was that countries there still regarded historic and continuing Western imperialism as a bigger threat than communism. They wanted to industrialize rather than supply food and raw materials for Japan and then buy industrial products from it. More important, without American military policing or economic planning, market systems—if left unencumbered by excessive imperial management—would have provided the most efficient and prosperous type of economic organization possible.

Likely, the United States would have only had to lead by example. Even as the Vietnam War raged, the United States solved the original problem of Japan's getting new markets by negotiating, in the Kennedy Round of GATT (General Agreement on Tariffs and Trade) in the 1960s, an opening to the U.S. market, on which Japanese exporters gleefully seized. And although some of the countries in Southeast Asia trod down the wrong path economically, they were not strategic to U.S. interests and might have come around by experiencing the failures of managed economies. Yet the U.S. neo-imperial mindset prevailed. As in the Cuban Missile Crisis, the "credibility" of the United States to guarantee the security of its many allies around the world was perceived to be at risk—this time if Vietnam and Southeast Asia were "lost."

During World War II, Ho Chi Minh led a nationalist guerrilla movement for independence against the Japanese, who had taken over as colonial master of Indochina from the French. After World War II, the French refused to accept Ho's quest for independence and tried to reassert dominance over their colonial possession in 1949 by installing the client government of dictator Bao Dai. The next year, Harry Truman began the long American quagmire in Vietnam by backing French colonialism instead of national self-determination for the Vietnamese. After "losing" China in 1949, Truman did not want to do likewise by allowing the Viet Minh movement under Ho Chi Minh to succeed.[3] Even though Ho had brandished the American Declaration of Independence at the post–World War I Versailles peace conference in 1919 to petition for national self-determination—which President Woodrow Wilson had idealistically promised to countries of the developing world—Wilson ignored Ho. Instead he let his wartime allied empires resort to raw power politics to divide up the spoils of war, despite the objections of local peoples.

Yet Ho was an advocate of Vietnamese independence rather than being subservient to the Soviets or the Communist Chinese. He was sort of an Asian Tito—a nationalist first and a communist second. He took the support of the larger communist countries out of necessity in order to be able to fight for his cause. By fighting such a brutal war against Vietnamese independence, the United States acted more like a neocolonial empire than a republic of which the founders might have been proud. Also, during the Cold War, by supporting the efforts of colonial powers to regain their empires, America effectively renounced the principle of the Atlantic Charter (1941) to "respect the right of all peoples to choose the form of government under which they will live," just as it had reneged on Wilson's earlier promise of self-determination.

That said, President Dwight Eisenhower allowed the mostly U.S.-funded, formal French recolonization attempt to fail at the Battle of Dien Bien Phu in 1954. Ike contemplated conventional air strikes to save the French but met with media and bipartisan congressional opposition to any U.S. intervention. He had finally settled the Korean War stalemate the year before, and the public had no appetite for getting involved in another potential quagmire—this time in Southeast Asia. Ironically, both then-Senators John F. Kennedy and Lyndon B. Johnson did not want to help a colonial power re-yoke its colony, even if it were to stop communism. JFK even said that no amount of military aid to the French colonialists could beat an enemy that had the implicit support of the country's population. In private, Ike agreed with these congressional sentiments and used congressional pushback at first to avoid U.S. escalation. Shamefully, these three men would shortly forget their cogent objections to wading deeper into what would become a U.S. Southeast Asian bog.

Ike backtracked and refused to abide by the Geneva Accords of 1954 that had ended France's colonial war with the Viet Minh guerillas. The United States would not sign the document to allow elections in all of Vietnam within two years. Eisenhower knew that Ho would win a legitimate unified election and then control all of Vietnam. He parried by dividing the country into North and South, allowing a fraudulent election in South Vietnam in 1956, and sending American combat "advisers" to help local autocrats in the South fight an insurgency. If Eisenhower had wanted to take over the French burden in Indochina, logically he should have publicly done so before Dien Bien Phu fell in 1954.

Ike said he feared the falling dominos of other countries to communism. However, in addition to Southeast Asian raw materials and markets being important to Japan after China fell to the communists in 1949, U.S. economic policymakers also thought they had some importance for the United States. By 1956 Senator John Kennedy was changing his tune and spoke of a U.S. "finger in the dike" in South Vietnam that kept communism from drowning that country.[4]

Later Democratic Presidents John F. Kennedy and Lyndon B. Johnson would fear, like Harry Truman before them, being ridiculed for the loss of yet another non-strategic (to the U.S.) East Asian country to communism. Truman's loss of China in 1949 had cast a long shadow over Democratic Party policies.

The War Was Lost Before It Was Escalated

Under JFK and LBJ, U.S. involvement in the backwater of Southeast Asia, especially Vietnam, significantly deepened. The sharp increase in U.S. "advisers" in Vietnam from 685 during the Eisenhower administration to 16,000 under Kennedy was due, like JFK's reckless behavior during the Cuban Missile Crisis, to a fear of looking weak in fighting communism. JFK's 16,000 "advisers" were doing much more fighting than publicly acknowledged, including flying secret combat missions. Against the advice of the U.S. military, JFK had lost even the slim chance to win the Vietnam War in 1963, before LBJ even escalated it in 1965, by supporting a miliary coup against Ngo Dinh Diem, the leader of South Vietnam. Although Diem was far from perfect, he was better than the subsequent corrupt South Vietnamese military leadership that followed.

Diem was murdered shortly before Kennedy's own assassination. JFK allowed the fateful coup because he was frustrated with Diem's inability to win the war and congressional Republican criticism of Kennedy for that; that is, Diem's alleged failures became Kennedy's failures too. JFK feared the turmoil in South Vietnam and its ramifications at home would adversely affect his 1964 reelection campaign, which would begin in six months.[5] He did not want to run for reelection in 1964 as the president who lost Vietnam. (After he died, this nightmare would also haunt LBJ for the 1964 and 1968 elections, and Richard Nixon in the 1972 election).

Yet JFK was as pessimistic about the outcome in Vietnam, as LBJ would later be even before dramatically escalating the war. Kennedy admitted, "These people [the Vietnamese] hate us. They are going to throw our asses out of there at almost any point. But I can't give up territory like that to the Communists and then get the American people to reelect me."[6] Always afraid that Republicans would call him "soft on communism," JFK refused entreaties from dovish advisers to negotiate with North Vietnam to make way for treaty-promised Vietnam-wide elections.

In counterinsurgency (COIN) warfare, a government's political legitimacy is much more important in battling rebels than is its military strength. The coup replaced the corrupt Diem, who had at least some political legitimacy, with even more venal South Vietnamese military leaders. In the end, the Vietnam War had been lost even before LBJ escalated it after JFK's assassination. The communist-nationalist insurgency simply had more legitimacy than the corrupt military rulers of South Vietnam. That a foreign occupier backed these autocrats eroded their legitimacy even further.

Just before he died in November 1963, JFK had authorized the withdrawal of a thousand forces, and some aides and a congressional ally claimed that he had said he was waiting until after the election in 1964 to make a full withdrawal of U.S. forces from South Vietnam. Most historians are skeptical of these claims made by Kennedy apologists. The thousand troops were mostly engineers who had finished their missions. JFK had also given a speech saying that it would be a mistake to withdraw.

Like JFK, his successor LBJ had his eye on the 1964 and 1968 elections and his Great Society domestic agenda. Like other Democrat presidents during the Cold War, LBJ too feared looking soft on communism and "losing" unimportant countries to communist subversion or insurgency. Shortly after taking power after JFK's assassination, LBJ told Henry Cabot Lodge Jr., U.S. ambassador to South Vietnam, "I am not going to lose Vietnam. I am not going to be the president who saw Southeast Asia go the way China went [in 1949]."[7]

Alleged Attacks in the Gulf of Tonkin; Congress's War Resolution

In June 1964, before any congressional approval for war in Southeast Asia, the U.S. Air Force was already bombing targets in South Vietnam and Laos.[8] On August 2 and 4, 1964 (before the American presidential election), North Vietnamese torpedo boats off North Vietnam's coast allegedly twice launched attacks on U.S. warships—attacks which LBJ and his hardline advisers were trying to provoke to save a rapidly deteriorating South Vietnamese regime. American warships had encroached inside the twelve-mile boundary that the North Vietnamese claimed as their territorial waters. The only evidence of the first attack was one bullet hole in one U.S. ship. The second attack was unlikely to have occurred at all, but the appearance of it was likely caused by severe weather affecting U.S. naval radars. Commander Jack Cowles, in the navy's war room on August 4, wrote Senator J. William Fulbright, Chairman of the Senate Foreign Relations Committee, that the navy patrols off the North Vietnamese coast were designed to provoke attacks. He also wrote that the second North Vietnamese attack on August 4 was unlikely to have occurred. His basis for reaching that conclusion was that the North Vietnamese torpedo boats alleged to have attacked the two navy destroyers on that date had later been captured and their crews knew nothing of the attacks. In 1995 and 2003, LBJ's Secretary of Defense Robert McNamara finally admitted that the August 4 attack never occurred and that many U.S. actions and goals in the Vietnam War were "wrong, terribly wrong," but he did not admit to misleading the American people and Congress about the war, which he surely did.[9]

At the time, even LBJ had privately expressed skepticism about the second attack having occurred, yet he did not convey that skepticism in his briefing to congressional leaders or correct it for Congress or the American people. At the time, he was so eager to take advantage of the alleged incidents to hold his own against the North Vietnamese and appear strong, without starting a full-blown war before the election. His opponent, Republican Barry Goldwater, had already criticized him for being soft on communism. Thus, LBJ did not bother to wait for all the facts to come in, as the commander of one of the U.S. warships urged. Instead, he quickly announced the alleged North Vietnamese torpedo boat attacks against U.S. ships and his hasty, over-the-top retaliatory U.S. air strikes on targets in North Vietnam,[10] even as he promised to "seek no wider war."[11] McGeorge Bundy poohed-poohed consternation over whether the second North Vietnamese attack was legitimate, because it was all "show business" anyway. The show business achieved LBJ's short-term goal, because after LBJ's air strikes and congressional passage of the Gulf of Tonkin Resolution, Goldwater had been forced to tone down his attacks on Johnson's Vietnam War policy for the rest of the campaign.

In fact, LBJ was so eager to get on prime-time television to announce the retaliatory bombing of the North that he announced the U.S. air raids one hour and forty minutes before they even happened.[12] Unfortunately, the North Vietnamese military listened to his broadcast and was ready when the air raids actually arrived, resulting in U.S. airmen being killed or captured over North Vietnam.

In announcing the alleged North Vietnamese attacks and retaliatory U.S. air strikes, LBJ neglected to mention that the U.S. warships were hardly innocent bystanders just passing by the North Vietnamese coast.

They rather were deliberately violating claimed North Vietnamese territorial waters in support of U.S. armed, trained, and directed amphibious sabotage raids (Operation 34-A raids) on North Vietnam by the South Vietnamese military. The amphibious raids had been designed to turn on North Vietnamese radars so the U.S. warships could map them, making U.S. bombing runs safer.

There had been two Operation 34-A raids just before the first North Vietnamese torpedo boat retaliated on the USS *Maddox* on August 2. LBJ surmised that the North Vietnamese patrol boats were responding to such U.S. provocations.[13] The CIA also had been conducting secret sabotage operations against North Vietnam for almost three years. As Eric Alterman concluded, given all these factors and coupled with its unnecessarily hasty response, the evidence for a deliberate provocation by the United States in the Gulf of Tonkin is powerful. As in the Mexican War, the Civil War, the Spanish-American War, and World War II, unheralded provocative U.S. actions led to war with an adversary. That traditional trick is often needed in a democracy—at least the American one—to build support for war. Logically, however, as in many of those prior wars of choice, the incident that provoked the conflict was hardly worth fighting a large war over—especially so in this instance.

On the day after the second alleged "unprovoked" North Vietnamese attack on U.S. naval forces on August 4, LBJ immediately used the incidents to get Congress to pass the broad and open-ended Gulf of Tonkin Resolution to authorize U.S. military action in Southeast Asia. LBJ chose this option rather than asking for the constitutionally required declaration of war. Ever the master of Congress, LBJ deliberately held the vote on the resolution just months before the election so that members of Congress up for reelection would be afraid to vote against it, and skeptical members of his own party would need to put party unity first. (George W. Bush used the same legislative trick to win approval in October of 2002 of his egregious invasion of Iraq.)

When the Vietnam War eventually went noticeably wrong, some in Congress complained that they had voted for the Gulf of Tonkin Resolution only because they did not think a massive military escalation was going to occur. In fact, members of Congress—including J. William Fulbright, Chairman of the Senate Foreign Relations Committee, who sold the resolution for the administration in Congress—alleged that the administration had told them no such escalation would happen.

However, the resolution was so broad that it was Congress's fault for not narrowing it to prevent any president from running wild in Southeast Asia. Fulbright claimed that LBJ and other high-level administration officials hoodwinked him but at the time, Fulbright told one senator "there is nothing in the resolution ... that contemplates" sending large land armies to Asia, but that the resolution "would not prevent it." Another senator asked Fulbright if Congress was giving the president the advance authority to do whatever needed doing to defend South Vietnam. Fulbright replied, "I think that is correct." Democratic acquiescence to giving LBJ such a blank check in Vietnam likely was explained by their allowing the president to appear strong before the 1964 election, because the prospect of a conservative Goldwater presidency struck fear into their hearts. According to one White House official, the resolution "was sold to the Democrats on the basis that it would help with the election ... we mustn't let Goldwater get a free ride out of this."[14] And the precedent for such broad advance congressional resolutions for the use of armed force had been given during the Eisenhower administration for East Asia and the Middle East.

The war resolution said that "Congress approves and supports the determination of the President, as Commander in Chief, to take all necessary measures to repel any armed attack against the forces of the United States and to prevent further aggression," as well as determine when "peace and security" in Southeast Asia was achieved. The resolution also promised that the United States would take all needed actions, including the use of force, at the president's discretion, to help any state in the Southeast Asia Collective Defense Treaty requesting defense help.[15] LBJ was pleased with the resolution, saying that "like grandma's nightshirt—it covered everything." His aim was to keep Congress on board the war train when the going got tough later, which he knew it would.

Fulbright, who would later become a public critic of the Vietnam War, sold the Gulf of Tonkin Resolution as a moderate measure "calculated to prevent the spread of war." That statement was far from LBJ's intention. However, like other presidents in the American republic, he had to get the enemy to attack first, because the American public naively likes to believe its government does not start wars. Most Americans initially support the president when the nation goes to war, regardless of the suspicious circumstances surrounding a conflict's origin. Like James Polk had done before the outbreak of the Mexican War, the Johnson White House, before provoking a minor attack by a foreign country, had drawn up a draft war resolution and had it ready to go.

In mid-1964, the situation in South Vietnam did not look good, and the only alternatives LBJ had was negotiating with the enemy after winning the election or escalating direct U.S. intervention. In May 1964, months before the alleged North Vietnamese patrol boat attacks, the White House had a war resolution ready, but LBJ held on to it so he could first provoke a North Vietnamese attack. He then broadened the resolution and sent it to Congress. When challenged in Congress that the North Vietnamese attacks were "unprovoked," Robert McNamara lied in congressional testimony, saying that the U.S. Navy had played no role in and was not aware of South Vietnamese coastal commando operations before the North Vietnamese attacks,[16] though the U.S. warships were supposed to draw the North Vietnamese torpedo boats away from the area of the South Vietnamese amphibious raids.[17]

In the 1964 election—like his Democratic predecessors Woodrow Wilson and FDR—LBJ ran on staying out of war and, after he had won the election, he then conducted full-blown war. Politicians like to posture as being strong against adversary countries, especially before elections, but often shrink from starting massive ground wars then, for fearing of losing large numbers of votes.

During the campaign, LBJ ran an ad of a little girl with a flower engulfed in an atomic mushroom cloud, implying that his hawkish Republican opponent Barry Goldwater would incinerate the planet. This ad was effective. It had been only two years since the Cuban Missile Crisis (1962). Barry Goldwater had publicly advocated all-out bombing of North Vietnam, mused about what would have happened if Eisenhower had used an atomic weapon in Vietnam at Dien Bien Phu in 1954, and advocated using low-yield nuclear weapons to defoliate the South Vietnamese border to destroy the Vietcong's vegetative cover.

LBJ Hides Escalation

After LBJ won the 1964 election in a landslide at a time when two-thirds of Americans were not paying attention to developments in Vietnam, he escalated the war surreptitiously because he knew Congress would be reluctant to pass his massive domestic Great Society program while also paying for an expensive ground war in Asia. After he left office,

LBJ asserted that he knew that the sound of the bugle put an immediate end to the hopes and dreams of the best reformers: the Spanish-American War drowned the populist spirit, World War I ended Woodrow Wilson's New Freedom (progressivism), and World War II brought the New Deal to a close. Once the war began, then all those conservatives in Congress would use it as a weapon against LBJ's Great Society.[18]

Because presidents tend to lose congressional seats in off-year congressional elections, Johnson believed he would lose some of his legislative majority in the 1966 election. Therefore, he knew he had to get his Great Society program through Congress in 1965 and 1966. However, the situation in South Vietnam was deteriorating so fast that LBJ had begun escalation quietly in 1965. He made the decision to escalate bombing in February and to send large numbers of ground forces in July 1965 but consistently publicly low-balled the number of U.S. troops sent to Vietnam, so that Congress would not find out how rapidly he was escalating the war.[19]

However, LBJ's gradually escalating bombing campaign was not achieving the goal of pressuring the communists to the negotiating table, and the insurgency was making gains against the South Vietnamese government. LBJ did not ask for a declaration of war to supplement the Gulf of Tonkin congressional resolution because he felt it would harm the enactment of the Great Society and create public pressure to escalate even more, including a naval blockade of North Vietnam. Before the 1964 election, LBJ feared escalating the war might cost him votes; after the election in 1965, when he began escalating, he feared the opposite: being pushed by the segments of the public into extreme escalation that would lead to problems with the communist great powers. A blockade might prompt Soviet or Chinese military intervention, the fear of which haunted the United States from the Korean War. Thus, he never went to the American people to tell them why he thought U.S. security required such escalation in Vietnam, which undermined public support for the war later.[20]

And when Johnson's undersecretary of state claimed that the Gulf of Tonkin Resolution was the functional equivalent of a declaration of war, LBJ slapped him down. He said even that resolution was not needed for military action in Southeast Asia, implying he had the unilateral constitutional authority as commander in chief to conduct the war alone.[21]

Why did LBJ manufacture a reason to go to war in a small, non-strategic country and then massively escalate military action? According to Jack Valenti, Johnson's special assistant, LBJ was not a gung-ho warrior. War decisions during the Johnson years had been made with no delusion about the chances of success. In late May 1964, even before he sent in substantial numbers of U.S. ground troops, LBJ made many pessimistic predictions about the outcome of the war in Southeast Asia. For example: "It's damned easy to get in a war but it's gonna be awful hard ever to extricate yourself if you get in,"[22] and "I stayed awake last night thinking of this thing. . . . It looks to me like we're getting into another Korea. . . . I don't think we can fight them 10,000 miles away from home. . . . I don't think it's worth fighting for and I don't think that we can get out. It's just the biggest damned mess that I ever saw."[23] Also, in the same month, he mused that public pressure would not be intense to win in Vietnam—he did not "think the people of the country know much about Vietnam and I think they care a hell of a lot less"—but nevertheless he *irrationally* feared impeachment if he did not escalate the war, perhaps at the hands of the MICC and Republican hawks. LBJ was certainly right that the public was not pushing escalation. In early 1965, 81 percent of Americans wanted LBJ to hold a conference with Southeast Asian nations and China to seek peace. Thousands of academics advocated the obvious solution of neutrality for the region.

As he was escalating the war in late June 1965, LBJ complained to McNamara that he was very depressed about it because "I see no program from either Defense or State that gives me much hope of doing anything, except just praying and gasping to hold on . . . and hope they'll quit. I don't believe they're ever going to quit. And I don't see . . . any . . . plan for victory militarily or diplomatically."[24]

Oddly enough, even though LBJ had been skeptical of winning the war, he got rid of or sidelined officials who recommended that he withdraw from Vietnam. Eventually, even McNamara turned against the war, so LBJ exiled him to the World Bank. Hubert Humphrey, his own vice president, urged him not to escalate the war, contending that if LBJ did so, he would not get the Democratic nomination in 1968—and even if somehow he did that, he would not win the general election. As a message to stifle other war dissenters in his administration, LBJ then refused to let Humphrey attend National Security Council meetings.[25] Thus, LBJ actively took measures to get information and advice that told him only what he wanted to hear about the war—a sure route to policy failure under threat of electoral failure.

Once again, the history of domestic political trauma for the Democrats caused by Truman "losing" China appeared to have governed the actions of Truman and later Democratic presidents, including LBJ. Johnson fretted "that if we let Communist aggression succeed in taking over South Vietnam, there would follow an endless national debate—a mean and destructive debate—that would shatter my Presidency. . . . I knew that Harry Truman and Dean Acheson had lost their effectiveness from the day that the Communists took over China. . . . And I knew these problems would be chickenshit compared with what might happen if we lost Vietnam."

Although LBJ's reasoning might have been flawed—Vietnam was not as important as China, and Truman's presidency and chances for reelection were harmed more by the stalemated quagmire of the Korean War than by the loss of China—it shows how domestic anti-communist hysteria about an exaggerated national security threat can be galvanized by parties that have varying but vested interests. Also, during the Cold War, U.S. "credibility" as guardian of the free world influenced presidential credibility at home. Unfortunately for Johnson's presidency, his credibility went the same direction as Truman's did: given his further pursuit of an intractable war, he became so unpopular that he did not run for another term

LBJ had disingenuously assured Americans, during the 1964 election campaign against hawkish Republican Barry Goldwater, that he would not "send American boys nine or ten thousand miles away from home to do what Asian boys ought to being doing for themselves," while secretly leaning toward escalating the war and choosing bombing targets in North Vietnam before the election.[26] Like FDR in the 1940 election, he assured the country that peace would be maintained while the deteriorating situation abroad led to planning for war. Throughout the summer and fall election season in 1964, LBJ continued to promise "we seek no wider war."

After he won the election over Goldwater and the American right in a landslide with 61 percent of the vote—a record in modern American history—and his party won huge majorities in both houses of Congress, LBJ exploited the open-ended Gulf of Tonkin Resolution to pour more than a half million troops into Vietnam. Instead, he should have taken the advice of Hubert Humphrey, his vice president, who astutely told him that it was always tough to cut losses, but that after his massive political strength was shown in the 1964 election, 1965 was the year of minimum risk to do so.

Initially, memories of the Chinese military intervention in the Korean War and the Cuban Missile Crisis haunted the Vietnam War. LBJ wanted the limited bombing of North Vietnam and its gradual escalation to avoid bringing China into the war and prevent escalation to nuclear war with the Soviet Union. LBJ then used a Vietcong attack on an American airfield in South Vietnam to escalate a strategic bombing campaign in February 1965 against North Vietnam and the Vietcong infiltration in the South. Even as he did so, he was pessimistic about the outcome of a war he was escalating: "Now we're off to bombing these people. We're over that hurdle. I don't think anything is going to be as bad as losing, and I don't see any way of winning."[27]

The bombing campaign lasted eight years, morphing into the even more brutal carpet-bombing of North Vietnam under President Richard Nixon and more bombs dropping on North and South Vietnam than in all of World War I, World War II, and the Korean War combined. And like the strategic bombing of World War II, it did not achieve its objectives—in this case, bringing North Vietnam and the Vietcong to the negotiating table by ruining their morale, bucking up the confidence of the South Vietnamese forces, and reducing U.S. casualties.[28] In one way or another 415,000 Vietnamese *civilians* were killed during the Vietnam War.

To this day, some at the Pentagon, looking back, have told the author that the U.S. military could have won the war if the politicians had just turned them loose. That would have been true only if the United States vaporized Southeast Asia with nuclear weapons. Although the United States won every battle of the Vietnam war against the South Vietnamese Vietcong insurgency and the North Vietnamese army, it lost the long war and 58,000 American lives over a country of no strategic significance to the United States.

However, this Pentagon reasoning only shows that many in the U.S. military still do not understand counterinsurgency (COIN) warfare. Unlike conventional warfare, COIN warfare is overwhelmingly political. Insurgents, the weaker party, usually realize that the center of gravity for the stronger party is public opinion back home, especially in the case of a democracy. Thus, the rebels use hit-and-run ambush attacks on isolated units of the stronger army, then melt back into a supportive local population. The insurgents willingly give up territory but try to exhaust the stronger force, thus trading space for time. They play the long game of wearing down public support at home in the stronger nation for prosecuting the war abroad. Reasonably popular insurgents did so successfully in the Vietnam, Afghanistan, and second Iraq Wars. Also, the communists' long war against the illegitimate South Vietnamese government could be maintained over time because of South Vietnam's long, porous land border—easily breached with communist fighters and Soviet and Chinese supplies flowing from sanctuaries in North Vietnam, Laos, and Cambodia.

Support for the War Deteriorates

In the Vietnam War the insurgents had an easier time affecting the war's center of gravity in the United States, given the mass protests in the United States and around the world. These protests condemned a war that eventually carpet-bombed North Vietnam; mined Haiphong harbor; used napalm (liquid fire) and defoliates to devastate North and South Vietnam, Laos, and Cambodia; and employed a euphemistic "strategic hamlet" program to remove peasants to concentration camp–like conditions similar to the way the Native Americans had been removed and eventually settled on squalid reservations in the 1800s. The North Vietnamese could take heart from TV and newspaper reports of the large American protests and just waited for American public opinion to force U.S. withdrawal. The large domestic demonstrations arose, in part, from Americans watching TV and seeing unfiltered bloody images in what was called a "living room war." In later wars, the U.S. military was careful to impose greater restrictions on media coverage to avoid the same dismal outcome of the Vietnam War. Inter alia, there were to be no ceremonies marking the return of deceased American soldiers.

In the most protested war in American history, young men from the politically powerful middle class with promising civilian careers fueled the demonstrations, afraid of being shanghaied to fight in an endless war that seemed unnecessary to U.S. security. At the same time, the draft was unfair, enabling college attendees to get deferments and foisting much of the burden of fighting to men from poorer classes, who also protested the conflict. In the end, many in the American populace had a better grasp of the strategic necessity—or lack thereof—of the war than did Presidents

Johnson and Nixon and the U.S. foreign policy and defense elites, while the need to feed the MICC could not be mentioned.

Undersecretary of State George Ball, LBJ's token Vietnam War critic in his administration, warned in the summer and fall of 1964 that the Vietnam War, popular but initially less popular than the Korean War had been when it started, would become even more unpopular the longer it went on. During the Korean War, by mid-1951—a year into the con-flict—the public had started demanding the return home of U.S. service personnel. Douglas MacArthur, the U.S. commanding general in Korea, offered both Kennedy and Johnson similar prescient, but dismal, advice about the likely long-term unpopularity of the conflict in Vietnam.[29] Historically, wars with casualties mounting and little perceived value to national security grow unpopular over time, especially when there is conscription at home.

In late October 1967, thirty-five thousand youthful anti-war protest-ers showed up at the Pentagon, rattling LBJ. He then started an ambitious public relations campaign in November and December designed to show Americans that he was winning the Vietnam War. The turning point in the war came in late January 1968 with the Tet Offensive, a massive North Vietnamese and Vietcong invasion of South Vietnam. U.S. and South Vietnamese forces eventually beat back the offensive and claimed to have destroyed the Vietcong as a fighting force. Indeed, LBJ and General William Westmoreland, the U.S. commander in Vietnam, had been telling the American people that the United States was winning the war, only to have the enemy muster up enough strength to invade the South and put Vietcong fighters inside the South Vietnamese presidential palace and the U.S. embassy in Saigon (now Ho Chi Minh City). The American people did not believe Tet was a defeat for the communists or Johnson's claim that the United States was winning the war. After Tet, leading news anchor Walter Cronkite went to Vietnam and reported to the nation that the war was not going well, and no end was at hand. Johnson was dev-astated, saying that if he had lost Cronkite, he had lost the country. Tet turned public opinion in the United States against the war. However, after the claimed militarily successful beatdown of Tet, hawks at the Pentagon wanted more than two hundred thousand more troops sent to Vietnam. This action would have required calling up the reserves—a haven for middle-class kids trying to avoid serving in Vietnam—and fueled more war opposition from a politically powerful class of Americans. In late

March 1968, LBJ made the decision to limit the bombing, avoid further escalating the war, and abandon his run for reelection.[30]

LBJ ended up dropping out of the race because of low popularity ratings. In the March New Hampshire primary, one of the reasons that LBJ was unpopular was how he had financed and fought the war. LBJ reluctantly hiked taxes significantly to fund both the war and his Great Society while running a government surplus—thus actually decreasing debt as a portion of GDP—unlike George W. Bush, who would fund the second Iraq war by deficit spending (tax cuts alongside spending increases) and thus massive government borrowing and debt accumulation. However, the all-volunteer military allowed Bush to mute opposition during the second Iraq War, aware of the extent to which the draft had made the Vietnam War extremely unpopular.[31]

Before he left the presidency, however, LBJ tried to negotiate a peace deal, hoping that if an agreement with North Vietnam seemed near by the August 1968 Democratic National Convention, his party might reembrace him as a peacemaker and renominate him again as its candidate for president. As time passed that year and his fanciful hopes did not pan out, he continued talks with the North Vietnamese to salvage his own legacy and to help Vice President Hubert Humphrey, the eventual Democratic nominee, run against Republican Richard Nixon in the election.

The Nixon Era in Southeast Asia

Richard Nixon, in a near-treasonous act to improve his chances of election victory, pulled arguably the most underhanded trick of his entire infamous political career. Publicly, Nixon initially backed LBJ's peace proposal, but public opinion polls showed the Republican's lead over Humphrey dwindling, and Nixon feared news of peace negotiations would throw Humphrey over the top to an election win. Through an intermediary, candidate Nixon secretly asked South Vietnam to stall LBJ's peace initiative, claiming that country would get a better deal after he won. LBJ learned of Nixon's treachery and ordered the FBI to illegally wiretap Nixon and also bug the South Vietnamese embassy in Washington. The South Vietnamese did boycott peace negotiations in expectation of Nixon winning the election.

The South Vietnamese stonewalling of peace talks did cause the momentum in the election to swing back toward Nixon and away from anti-war Humphrey. LBJ, a political brawler to the end, wanted to release the telephone taps to the American public to show Nixon's skullduggery, but Humphrey refused to exploit the information. Nixon won an election squeaker over Humphrey by less than one percent of the popular vote, with early analyses concluding the Republican's election dirty tricks had had a sufficiently significant effect to bring his ticket into the White House.[32]

While Nixon's victory in November 1968 only delayed South Vietnam's inevitable loss (the decisive turn of the war against the United States had come in early 1968 with the communists' Tet Offensive), it led to another twenty-one thousand American deaths and countless more Vietnamese deaths on both sides—until Nixon finally reached a peace deal more than four years later. Nixon, inaugurated in early 1969, took another four years to get a peace deal he could have gotten right after the inauguration. Disingenuously, Nixon had promised during his campaign to end the war by giving the United States "peace with honor," which really meant he wanted to delay the inevitable defeat until after he was safely reelected in 1972. He heeded Henry Kissinger's warning that if he withdrew U.S. forces in 1971, South Vietnam would quite likely fall to the communists in 1972, his reelection year. He delayed reaching a peace deal until early 1973—after he had been safely reelected and inaugurated to a second term. Like LBJ, Nixon needlessly sacrificed American and Vietnamese lives for his own political gain.

The four U.S. presidents presiding over the Vietnam War— Eisenhower, JFK, LBJ, and Nixon—seemed obsessed with the imperial goal of not losing in Vietnam to retain U.S.—and their own—credibility as an effective free world leader. In the end, these presidents raised the stakes in Vietnam, stayed too long in a failing effort, and ended up undermining the credibility of both. In early 1965, John McNaughton, a key advisor to LBJ's secretary of defense, laid out U.S. objectives for the war just after the United States began its escalation by bombing North Vietnam: "70% to avoid a humiliating U.S. defeat (to our reputation as guarantor), 20% to keep SVN [South Vietnam] (and the adjacent territory) from Chinese hands, 10% to permit the people of SVN to enjoy a better, freer way of life."[33]

During this war, as in others, national credibility became fused with presidential credibility. In 1961, JFK's first decisions on Vietnam were colored by his need not to appear weak in the wake of a series of largely unfavorable events—his reaching a neutrality agreement in Laos (instead of intervening to subdue the communist insurgency), the failure of the Bay of Pigs invasion of Cuba, his embarrassment at being hectored by Nikita Khrushchev at the Vienna Summit, and the communists' building of the Berlin Wall.

Similarly, Nixon's later attacks on Cambodia and Laos, his mining of ports in North Vietnam, and the saturation "Christmas bombing" of Hanoi in 1972 are seen as a needed toughening of his image to counter his pursuit of détente with the USSR, withdrawal of ground troops from Vietnam, and U.S. general military retrenchment worldwide. To take the wind out of the growing anti-war movement at home by lessening the need for draft call-ups, Nixon began a policy of withdrawing U.S. ground forces and replacing them by trained South Vietnamese troops (Vietnamization); ratcheting up air support for South Vietnamese forces; and carpet-bombing of the North (a war crime)—all designed to also make the North Vietnamese more willing to negotiate peace on U.S. terms. At all costs, Nixon wanted to delay South Vietnam's collapse until he was safely reelected in 1972.

At the same time, Nixon escalated the broader war in Southeast Asia against communist sanctuaries in and South Vietnamese Vietcong supply routes through Cambodia and Laos, launching secret bombings and then a U.S. invasion of Cambodia in 1970 and supporting anti-communist forces in Laos with U.S. air power in 1971. Nixon initially decided to keep such side escalations secret because he did not believe Congress would support an expansion of the war in Southeast Asia after his campaign promise to end the war honorably for the United States. Nixon was warned of increased congressional assertiveness as its shame wore off about alleged legislative "isolationism" before World War II; as Congress's early deference weakened to unilateral executive military action after the dawn of the nuclear age; and as bipartisan Cold War anti-communism eroded. When Nixon's war in Cambodia became public, the anti-war protest movement became more active, and Congress became even more uncooperative. It passed the Cooper-Church Amendment, which limited the air war in Cambodia and prohibited land combat there, prompting Nixon to withdraw troops from Cambodia by the law's deadline.[34] When the clandestine war in Cambodia was publicly exposed, Nixon illegally authorized the FBI to spy, without a warrant, on the sources of the leaks.

Congress Tries to Push Back on the Imperial Presidency

Although opponents of the war screamed that Nixon was running an unauthorized secret war in Cambodia, the overly broad and open-ended Gulf of Tonkin Resolution seemed to allow such dangerous acts. Therefore, Congress in the same year repealed the Gulf of Tonkin Resolution. But then the unscrupulous Nixon went completely lawless, unconstitutionally continuing the war solely under a nonexistent "inherent" power as commander in chief.

In the spring of 1972, now thinking ahead to the period after his reelection, Nixon began a murderous aerial assault on Hanoi and Haiphong, Hanoi's port, to hasten a peace settlement during his second term. After being reelected by a landslide in November 1972, Nixon then ordered the Christmas bombing obliteration to try to induce North Vietnam to pursue a final peace agreement. Like LBJ, Nixon's goal had never been to win an unwinnable war but only to bludgeon the enemy to the peace table.

In 1973, after he had safely been reelected and started his second term, Nixon reached a face-saving peace accord with North Vietnam. In a key concession to gain the return of American prisoners of war, he agreed to let North Vietnamese soldiers stay in South Vietnam after the ceasefire, whom he knew could then help take over South Vietnam, sealing the sad fate of the South Vietnamese regime. He just wanted the communist takeover to be done at a "decent interval" after the U.S. withdrawal.

Nixon's Vietnamization, geographic widening of the war, and the brutal bombing of North Vietnam, Laos, and Cambodia only delayed the inevitable loss of Southeast Asia. Yet the tragic political reality was that all this death and destruction, inflicted on that poor region was so that Nixon would not "lose Vietnam" before he was safely reelected in 1972. Ironically, as a candidate in 1968, Nixon nefariously had used the South Vietnamese to get elected and then pulled the rug out from under them in 1973.

Congress waited until after the peace accord to pass laws in June and July of 1973, cutting off funding for any combat in the Southeast Asian theater. By this time, the Democrat-controlled legislature's trust in Nixon was zero. Congress knew that Nixon intended to find violations of the peace accord by the North Vietnamese—which did come—and begin more bombing campaigns in the North. The Nixon administration had secretly promised the South Vietnamese such martial enforcement of the peace accords to get them to sign it. It was for this reason that Congress passed such funding cutoff laws for combat in all of Indochina—and did so over Nixon's objections. Again, Congress had made a president stop military action in an area before he was ready to do so (the first had been the Cooper-Church legislation, which had led to U.S. withdrawal from Cambodia). Undoubtedly, without congressional intervention, Nixon's peace agreement would not have ensured America would have had peace.

By spring 1975, after Nixon had resigned in disgrace over the Watergate scandal, the North Vietnamese stepped up violations of the peace accord, and Gerald Ford, Nixon's successor, tried unsuccessfully to get Congress to pass new military aid to South Vietnam to "save" that country. But Ford feared taking unilateral military action, as Nixon often had, because of a resurgent Congress's undoubted wrath. Now distrustful of presidential power and fearful Ford would try to restart the war, Congress even refused to approve a large military evacuation of Americans and South Vietnamese who had helped the United States during the war, leaving Ford to settle for a smaller evacuation of mostly Americans.

Although Republicans would try to blame the inevitable fall of South Vietnam on Congress's funding cutoff, the war was lost long before Nixon's cynical "decent interval" peace accord. But Congress had no obligation to fund military actions to execute a secret agreement that Nixon, unbeknownst to the legislature, had made with the South Vietnamese to violently enforce the peace agreement.[35]

Democrats rethought their advocacy of constitutional flexibility concerning presidential war power when they moved into opposition after Republican Richard Nixon succeeded LBJ as president and continued the war. Republicans, on the other hand, were beginning to see the expansion of executive war power in a more favorable light.

In 1973, to further constrain presidential warmaking, a Democrat-controlled Congress passed the War Powers Resolution, which said that the president could unilaterally use the U.S. military only when the country or its armed forces had been attacked. This part of the resolution comported well with the founders' original constitutional scheme of Congress declaring war, with an exception in a dire emergency for presidential action for the country's self-defense. (However, the resolution expanded the founders' conception by adding another exception for executive self-defense against an attack on U.S. armed forces, which since World War II have been stationed all over the world.) Yet this clever language in the resolution's preamble by a cautious Congress had no legal effect. Thus, the legally binding main part of the resolution contented itself with an attempted legislative control of the president's actions *after* he had already committed the armed forces to hostile or potentially hostile situations. The resolution required the president to withdraw U.S. forces within sixty to ninety days unless Congress passed a declaration of war or authorized their use in the hostilities beyond those timelines.

Presidents have since disputed the resolution as being unconstitutional. It supposedly restricts their declared "inherent power" as commander in chief unilaterally to take the country to war, which is nowhere to be found in the Constitution. They have disagreed with both the preamble and the requirement that the president seek congressional approval for keeping forces in a hostile zone for more than sixty or ninety days. Presidents have even claimed that the resolution does not apply to situations in which they have committed forces to clearly hostile situations.[36]

In light of the Constitution's text and debate at the Constitutional Convention, the preamble of the resolution is mostly constitutional but not legally binding. (As a rule, preambles of laws and constitutions— introductions that explain the purposes and intentions of laws—are not legal binding.)[37] As it stands now, the resolution itself is unconstitutional only because it allows the president to unilaterally send U.S. forces into hostilities in scenarios in which the United States itself is not under attack—thus enabling the executive to nullify Congress's constitutional power to declare war by presenting the legislature with a fait accompli. The president's emergency self-defense of the country is the only legitimate exemption from the Constitution's requirement for congressional approval for war in advance of hostilities.

Later presidents have flouted the War Powers Resolution using many excuses, and Congress has supinely not done much about it. In 1975, Ford tried to say he followed that constitutional self-defense exemption when using military force to try to rescue the ship *Mayaguez* from Cambodian communists. However, Congress criticized him for informing it of the military action rather than consulting with it. In future decades, the situation went downhill from there, as should be expected when Congress willingly gives up its constitutional power to take the country from war to peace.

Vietnam War at Home

Demonstrating Arthur Schlesinger's point about the imperial presidency turning inward, Nixon administration leaks surrounding the Vietnam War and invasion of Cambodia indirectly led to the Watergate scandal at home. The *Pentagon Papers*—an internal Department of Defense study that revealed the lies told by the government about the Vietnam War and, worse, Pentagon analysts' conclusion the war was unwinnable—were leaked to the press without authorization. Before the papers had been published, the Nixon administration tried to prevent it, but importantly the Supreme Court ruled that the First Amendment prevented "prior restraint" of the publication of even classified government national security material. In a like manner, Nixon's secret invasion of Cambodia was exposed.

To stop such unfavorable press stories by expressly criminal means, Nixon ordered the organization of a dirty tricks (surveillance and sabotage) squad of "plumbers" to plug leaks in the administration. The plumbers broke into the office of the psychiatrist of Daniel Ellsberg, a Pentagon analyst who had leaked the *Pentagon Papers*, trying to get dirt on Ellsberg to discredit him. Although the *Pentagon Papers* were about the LBJ years in Vietnam, Nixon erroneously thought Ellsberg also had papers about the Republican president's escalation in North Vietnam, Cambodia, and Laos and his threats of nuclear war to get the North Vietnamese to the peace table, giving rise to the break-in.[38] He also wanted the plumbers to break into the progressive Brookings Institution, which he feared had evidence on his sabotage of LBJ's peace negotiations during the 1968 election campaign, but this break-in never happened. In short, the *Pentagon Papers* did not stop the Vietnam War, but they did in the end force Nixon to resign.

The plumbers team then moved to Nixon's heavily favored reelection campaign and turned to domestic political dirty tricks—spying on and sabotaging potential Democratic presidential challengers and breaking into the Democratic Party headquarters at the Watergate Hotel in Washington, DC. The plumbers' dirty tricks had led to dissension in the Democratic Party and helped to torpedo the candidacy of at least one of the stronger Democratic candidates, Edmund Muskie. They were finally caught by security at the Watergate Hotel before they could break into the headquarters of Democratic Senator George McGovern, Nixon's eventual opponent in his 1972 reelection battle. Ironically, all those Republican political dirty tricks were largely overkill because his antiwar views made McGovern a weak candidate.

To avoid the exposure of his many illegal activities, Nixon and his henchmen then tried to cover up the Watergate break-in by getting the CIA to call off the law enforcement investigation by saying that the burglary was a national security operation, which the agency refused to do. The Supreme Court eventually ruled that Nixon had to turn over White House tapes, which had recorded his illegal machinations, to Congress and the Watergate Special Prosecutor. To his credit, Nixon complied and sealed his own doom. One of the tapes, the "Smoking Gun" tape, recorded Nixon talking about getting the CIA to call off the law enforcement dogs in the Watergate investigation. This attempt at obstruction of justice was enough for the House of Representatives to start impeachment proceedings against him.

When Nixon resigned in disgrace, his successor Gerald Ford then unconstitutionally pardoned him, allegedly to heal the nation's wounds. However, Ford primarily did so in order that a high-profile Nixon criminal trial would not suck the oxygen out of Ford's policy agenda and pollute his own election chances during the 1976 presidential campaign. Some even alleged that Ford pardoned Nixon to get him to resign and give Ford the presidency.

While the Constitution says that presidents can pardon people for "crimes," Nixon had not been convicted of any crimes. What is notable here is that, even if Ford's stated rationale for the pardon was justifiable, the principle that even presidents are not above the law had been sacrificed to sooth the alleged public exhaustion over Watergate. Thus, the pardon created a double standard for future presidents, a precedent that might encourage future illegal behavior.[39] In the end, Ford's questionable pardon was unpopular with the American people and was one leading reason he did lost to Jimmy Carter in the 1976 election.

The necessity of criminal behavior became central to Nixon's conception of executive power. The paranoid Nixon best summed his philosophy of governance in 1971: "We're up against an enemy, a conspiracy. They're using any means. We are going to use any means." After resigning in disgrace, in a 1977 interview with British journalist David Frost, Nixon shockingly asserted that his mistake was not flouting the law but in not destroying evidence of his doing so. He tried to vindicate his actions with regard to Watergate and the imperial presidency by saying, "When the president does it, that means it is not illegal."[40]

Nixon argued that other presidents had wiretapped foes and examined their tax records for political purposes. In fact, although Nixon was known for his paranoia about his opponents trying to get him, some of his angst was not based on imagination. Nixon claimed his nefarious activities had to be done to his opponents because they were doing the same to him. For example, as president, LBJ had his opponents' (including Nixon's) taxes audited and had wiretapped Nixon's campaign plane, discovering Nixon's underhanded indirect dealings with the South Vietnamese to nix his peace deal. However, Nixon's White House plumbers, who committed illegal break-ins and other political dirty tricks, were a step beyond LBJ's illegal activities. The plumbers had been led by ex-CIA and ex-FBI officials, which made their activities much worse. In short, Nixon's criminality was over-the-top.

Civil liberties violations during wartime are the rule in American history rather than the exception. Although the JFK and Nixon administrations feared that the loss of Vietnam would create a dangerous backlash on the extreme right, the U.S. government under Democratic and Republican administrations spent more time violating the civil liberties of people on the anti-war left. During the Vietnam War, the CIA, the NSA, the army, and the FBI all illegally spied on leftist anti-war protesters. LBJ ordered the CIA, against its charter, to spy domestically on anti-war protesters because he thought the Soviets were supporting them. The FBI even infiltrated various protest groups and tried to cause internal fighting and turmoil within them. When neither the CIA nor FBI found any links to the communists among the protest groups, LBJ nevertheless tried to leak information alleging such connections to smear them. The nadir of this attempted government suppression was when the National Guard killed peaceful war protesters at Kent State University.

During the war, the unpopular draft, with unfair deferments for those attending college or exemptions for entering the National Guard with connections, tended to ensnare lower-income people and thus a disproportionate number of African Americans. The Civil Rights Movement of the late 1950s and 1960s brought increased awareness of and protest against America's legally entrenched system of apartheid (segregation). With the triggering assassinations of Martin Luther King Jr., Malcolm X and other political activists in the Black Panther Party, such racial tensions boiled over into race riots in some major cities across the country. In short, during the war, violence and turmoil at home increased, as it has during other overseas American conflicts.

The Korean War, the Cuban Missile Crisis, and the Vietnam War were the biggest highlights—actually lowlights—of the 40-plus year Cold War, which came to an end with the fall of the Berlin Wall in 1989 and the collapse of the Soviet Union in 1991.

>> CHAPTER 14 <<

THE END OF THE COLD WAR

Did Ronald Reagan Really Win the Cold War?

In the popular mind, President Ronald Reagan, the jovial anti-communist, gets credit for having had the toughness to intimidate and bankrupt the Soviet Union and its Eastern European satellite countries into oblivion. Like Eisenhower, he had said he would roll back communism rather than just "contain" it. He initially beefed-up U.S. conventional and nuclear forces to stand behind his support for anti-communist governments and movements in the developing world (for example, El Salvador, Nicaragua, Afghanistan, and Angola). Yet, the verifiable contribution he made to ending the Cold War lay in his accepting Mikhail Gorbachev as a different kind of Soviet leader and in negotiating with him—for example, reaching the Intermediate-Range Nuclear Forces (INF) Treaty limiting such weapons. However, Reagan's stubborn refusal to negotiate away his proposed pie-in-the-sky, space-based Star Wars concept—a proposed futuristic system of lasers and other technology to shoot down incoming Soviet nuclear missiles that was panned by experts—stymied breakthrough efforts by the superpowers to mutually reduce existing dangerous offensive nuclear weapons. Thus, it was left to President George H. W. Bush, Reagan's successor, to negotiate such agreements successfully.

When the communist bloc in Eastern Europe fell in 1989 and the Soviet Union collapsed about two years later at the end of 1991, people began to say that Ronald Reagan had won the Cold War, even though the most important event in the demise of communism came after Reagan had left office: Soviet President and Communist Party Chief Mikhail Gorbachev, in the summer of 1989 during the administration of George H. W. Bush, decided the Soviet Union would no longer militarily support the communist regimes of Eastern Europe. This policy change caused the collapse of those regimes because they had no popular legitimacy.

Yet yawning U.S. budget deficits from huge tax cuts and increased military spending earlier in his administration had caused Reagan to halt his military buildup by October 1985 (the start of U.S. fiscal year 1986), the same year Gorbachev took power in the USSR and long before Bush took office in January 1989.

By mid-1988 it was clear the next U.S. president would be less anti-Soviet than Reagan—whether Michael Dukakis or George H. W. Bush. Even during the spring and summer of 1989, right after his inauguration, President Bush began implementing more moderate policies: only a mild rebuke to communist China regarding the Tiananmen Square Massacre, a reduction in American military procurement, the abandonment of a successor to the U.S. Lance nuclear missile in Europe, and a reduction in funding for missile defense research and development. Thus, before Gorbachev's fateful decision in the summer of 1989, the Soviet leader could see the U.S. hardline anti-communist policies and military buildup were over.[1]

The consensus among U.S. officials during the Cold War was that totalitarian countries were naturally aggressive abroad because they willingly repressed their people at home—Adolf Hitler had been the prototype. Yet in his "long telegram" in 1946, even George Kennan analyzed Soviet behavior as not being militarily adventurist. Kennan believed the Soviets were not intent on world domination and would not risk an attack on the United States. Yet the U.S. foreign policy elite did not differentiate between totalitarian regimes. Hitler believed his regime portended a unique historical moment of destiny, which motivated him to take many risks, while Marxist-Leninist ideology was certain of communism's ultimate triumph, thus leading the Soviets to be more measured in their effort to bring it about. Furthermore, unlike Nazi Germany, the Soviet regime was a self-sufficient empire that did not need constant expansion abroad to retain power at home.

Nevertheless, the U.S. government made the mistake of paying more attention to what the Soviet Union was, ideologically, than how it behaved. Thus, American policymakers succumbed to the attribution theory of social psychology—that people tend to attribute their own actions and behavior as adaptable to the situation but when it comes to others, as immutable character traits. Furthermore, American officials—not wanting to repeat the lessons wrongly learned from Chamberlain's appeasement of the totalitarian Hitler at Munich in 1938 (lessons still taken for granted today)—were leery of negotiating with the Soviet Union during the Cold War. In short, by applying the Nazi analogy, they exaggerated the external threat posed by the Soviet Union.[2]

Americans, when asked to go to war, usually need to believe that the conflict fulfills a higher moral calling, which should work to limit the number of wars the United States enters. However, manipulative politicians and bureaucrats during the Cold War exploited this idealistic orientation to try to oversell every conflict as a moral crusade, thus gaining more support and money for their martial efforts. This chicanery usually requires the demonization of enemies who, even if of questionable character, are little threat to U.S. security. Such overselling of wars and demonization of adversaries can lead to missed opportunities for peace through negotiations, either before or during the war, or to the American people's eventual disillusionment with the conflict. The Soviet Union had been so demonized during the Cold War that even U.S. Presidents Ronald Reagan and George H. W. Bush had trouble at first believing Soviet leader Mikhail Gorbachev was serious about genuine reform at home and abroad.

Research has shown that authoritarian regimes are no less peaceable than democracies. According to historian Ronn Pineo, during the Cold War, the weaker Soviets repeatedly took numerous unilateral actions to try to end the Cold War and move to peaceful coexistence. For example, after Stalin's death, Khrushchev significantly reduced Soviet troop levels in the 1950s, the Soviets signed a peace treaty covering Austria, removed their troops from Austria and Finland, and offered arms reductions in Europe. Mikhail Gorbachev's actions to end the forty-plus-year Cold War were just more of the same. He unilaterally and drastically reduced Soviet conventional and nuclear forces and withdrew forward-deployed Soviet forces from Eastern Europe, collapsing the communist client regimes there.[3] Not only that, he negotiated money-saving arms control with the West. Gorbachev realized that the sagging Soviet economy could no longer afford such large and forward-deployed armed forces. Gorbachev even allowed a reunited Germany to join NATO in exchange for an unwritten pledge by George H.W. Bush that the alliance would not be expanded further. U.S. presidents succeeding Bush broke this verbal promise and expanded NATO into former states of the defunct Warsaw Pact and Soviet Union right up to Russia's newly truncated borders, an advance which underlies post–Cold War tensions between Russia and the

United States to this day.[4] NATO expansion was also a major underlying cause of nationalist Russian leader Vladimir Putin's rise in 1999 and invasion of Ukraine.

Some argued that Reagan's conventional and nuclear military buildup in the early 1980s so stressed the Soviet economy in its effort to keep up that it led to Soviet retraction and collapse in the late 1980s. Yet over the decades, the decrepit Soviet communist economy suffered gradually from excessive military spending, which took badly needed investment from the civilian economy, long before the Reagan military buildup of the early 1980s. According to former National Security Council and State Department official Robert H. Johnson, no correlation exists between the growth rate of U.S. military spending under Reagan and Soviet military expenditures. Thus, the Reagan defense buildup could not have caused the Soviet Union's collapse. In fact, it was not the catastrophic nature of Soviet economic problems that pushed the new Soviet leadership to reform. It was the realization that their creaking communist economic system was not working.[5]

If the USSR had merely wanted to respond to Reagan's buildup, it could have made milder adjustments in foreign policy and gone to an "empire-on-the-cheap" policy, rather than making drastic troop reductions and withdrawing from Eastern Europe. Fred Chernoff, professor of international relations at Colgate University, quantitatively examined "the claim that the U.S. military buildup stimulated increases in the Soviet military budget which ultimately bankrupted the Soviet Union and won the Cold War for the West. The study found that there is no demonstrable relationship between the U.S. buildup and the Soviet foreign policy reversal."[6]

The Soviet retraction came about because Gorbachev and the new Soviet leadership, taking power in 1985, thought their failing economic system would work better without as large a military albatross around its neck. Also, the Soviet Union's oil-based economy was put under a unique strain by Saudi Arabia's decision to tank the world's oil price to teach the OPEC cartel's cheating members a lesson. Although Gorbachev tried economic reforms (Perestroika), the economy—lacking incentives for work, productivity, or innovation—responded only slowly, ensnared by vested interests and bureaucratic resistance. To build public pressure to goose economic reform, Gorbachev instituted political openness (Glasnost), which then collapsed the entire Soviet system. Many Western

Sovietologists had predicted this would happen when trying to reform a totalitarian system. Yet U.S. intelligence, after exaggerating the Soviet threat throughout the Cold War, did not discern or admit the Soviet weakness until just before the Berlin Wall fell in late 1989.

A successful U.S. containment policy relied on the Soviets losing the Cold War through systemic economic and political dysfunction. This is what happened. Reagan's policy was only an incremental militarization of a longstanding containment policy started by Truman and carried out by every president till the elder Bush. In fact, all those presidents should get at least some credit for impeding the Soviet Union till it collapsed. The fundamental sources of change in the Soviet system came about because of the contradictions within the dysfunctional communist economic system and the advent of a new generation of Soviet leadership. Robert H. Johnson argued that if anything, Reagan's military buildup and initial hawkish anti-Soviet policies made Gorbachev's reform efforts more difficult by giving Soviet hardliners ammunition to thwart them.[7] And, the post-Cold War NATO expansion that began almost immediately may have served to vindicate some of those Soviet hawks' worries.

After the Soviet Union dissolved at the end of 1991 the Cold War was over. Yet the U.S. presidential candidates of both parties in the 1992 election pledged to keep unneeded weapons systems on the books. The now-entrenched American military-industrial-congressional complex ensured there would be resistance to troop and defense spending cuts at a time of high unemployment. During the ensuing two terms of the Clinton administration, the defense budget and military personnel levels were reduced somewhat, but a full peace dividend never came about because of the size and economic and political power of the MICC. The MICC's power made those reductions temporary, despite the drastic reduction in the external threat, and the defense budget's general upward trajectory then resumed.

The Cold War Had a Drastic Effect on the Republic

War usually leads to the centralization of power at home. In fact, it has been the greatest cause of big government in U.S. history. Such centralization inevitably entails a loss of freedom. Because tensions between the United States and the Soviet Union during the Cold War lasted more than forty years, the Cold War had a tremendous effect on the long-term size of the federal government. In this period, two large hot wars—Korea and Vietnam—and many smaller brushfire wars and U.S. military interventions added to the government's size and cost.

The Second Red Scare, launched by Harry Truman and Joe McCarthy, lasted throughout the entire Cold War, although it lessened during and after the Vietnam War. Nevertheless, increased federal government surveillance of leftist and peace groups occurred during the Vietnam era. The 1975 Senate Select Committee to Study Governmental Operations with Respect to Intelligence Activities, better known as the Church Committee, launched a major investigation of the FBI and COINTELPRO, a series of covert and illegal projects conducted between 1956 and 1971 by the United States Federal Bureau of Investigation aimed at surveilling, infiltrating, discrediting, and disrupting American political organizations that the FBI perceived as subversive. Reflective of its resurgence in the immediate aftermath of the Vietnam War, Congress then passed the Foreign Intelligence and Surveillance Act (FISA) of 1978 to curb such government spying abuses, requiring secret judicial approval of surveillance for alleged national security reasons. While most government search warrants get approved by the clandestine court, the law at least supplied some check on governmental surveillance abuse.

Equally important, within the federal government, the forty-plus years of global tension caused power to shift further to the presidency, creating the "imperial presidency," starting with Harry Truman. During World War II, FDR had increased executive power from its place in an uneasy balance among the three governmental branches—as the Constitution's framers had intended—to a "first among equals" status. The National Security Act of 1947 had increased the institutional power of the presidency in national security matters by creating a National Security Council in the White House, giving the president his own intelligence agency (the CIA) separate from military intelligence, and making it easier for the president to command the military by merging the War and Navy Departments into a Department of Defense headed by a secretary of defense. The Constitution mandated Congress to decide whether to take the nation to war. This changed with Harry Truman. He unconstitutionally expanded his commander-in-chief powers to unilaterally take the United States into the Korean War in 1950. This intervention happened without congressional approval. Congress has not declared war since then.

The first large peacetime military in the nation's history came into existence during the Cold War. Historically, after America's wars, befitting a republic, much of the armed forces demobilized. After the Korean War ended, a large force was kept in place for the first time. Thus, many men and huge sums of money were needed, so the draft lingered during peacetime, as did swollen defense budgets on virtual autopilot. This weakened Congress's constitutional authority over the military budget. Also, a large permanent defense industry—also the first in American history—was kept mostly intact after World War II and became a powerful lobbyist for excessively elevated peacetime defense budgets long after the Korean War and Vietnam Wars had ended.

Congressionally approved treaties with foreign nations, as stipulated in the Constitution, mostly became a thing of the past. For example, the Yalta agreement in February 1945 during FDR's last months and the Potsdam agreement of August 1945 under the new Truman administration, both of which reshaped the world, were made by executive agreement, not by treaty. This trend has continued down to the present day because treaties are difficult to get through Congress, requiring a two-thirds vote of approval in the Senate. If executive agreements ever become public (which many don't) or get to Congress (which many also don't), they can be approved by only a majority vote in each house of Congress.

Truman even unconstitutionally stretched his commander in chief power into the domestic sphere by trying to nationalize (socialize) the steel industry to stop a steel strike that he claimed was inhibiting defense production during the war. His action contradicted a congressionally passed law, and the Supreme Court in the Youngstown decision overruled him. However, presidents would not stop their efforts to expand the imperial presidency into the domestic sphere. For example, Nixon tried to use the CIA to head off an FBI investigation of his illegal campaign activities during Watergate, perpetrated by a White House–sponsored plumbers team of dirty tricksters, which was an egregious and illegal abuse of executive power, as was his illegal surveillance of anti-Vietnam protest groups.

SECTION V.
POST-COLD WAR

>> CHAPTER 15 <<

PERSIAN GULF WAR I

Demise of the Soviet Threat Uncorks U.S. Imperial Interventionism

The Marxist East Bloc fell in 1989, and the moribund communist Soviet Union dissolved in 1991, leaving the United States as the sole global hegemon. From 1987 to 1997, Soviet/Russian defense spending plummeted 90 percent. Yet the United States continued Cold War levels of military spending. As during the Cold War, the United States would continue the modernized imperial mercantilist quest to use its military to promote global economic integration—ensuring "stability" and "responsible" behavior by foreign governments to create environments conducive for U.S. trade, investment, and production.[1] Furthermore, the informal American Empire, with its military overextension ironically eroding its economic position, continued and even expanded its role as the world's policeman—in need of new threats to justify its ever-burgeoning hegemonic activities and high defense budgets in an effort to satiate the insatiable Military-Industrial-Congressional Complex (MICC). Fortunately for the defense industry, the U.S. government, and foreign policy establishment but unfortunately for America and Americans, the threat was self-generating.

Facing no competing superpower and with the risk of nuclear escalation dissipating, the U.S. government, instead of taking advantage of the much-reduced threat environment to retract its security perimeter, did the opposite. The United States strengthened and expanded Cold War alliances and hiked its military interventions in the developing world, including stepped up policing activities in territories where it had not yet been heavily engaged —for example, in Africa. The United States strengthened alliances in East Asia and expanded the NATO alliance eastward, pledging to defend nations in Central and Eastern Europe formerly in the Eastern Bloc. This expansion changed the organization without amending its charter, from defending its European members to conducting offensive operations outside the treaty area—for example, in Bosnia, Kosovo, Serbia, Libya, and Afghanistan.

The administration of President George H. W. Bush, in office when the Cold War ended, had verbally and implicitly promised Soviet President Mikhail Gorbachev that when Germany was reunited, NATO would not expand (that is, U.S. and NATO forces would not move into East Germany). Bill Clinton, Bush's successor, was unenthusiastic about NATO expansion until he realized that the support of Polish Americans in the Midwest and Americans of Eastern European heritage could be quite helpful to his reelection in 1996. NATO first expanded eastward of the now united Germany to include the former Eastern Bloc nations of Poland, the Czech Republic, and Hungary. The inclusion of Poland along the traditional invasion route toward Russia raised serious concerns in Moscow, but the post–Cold War Russians were too weak to do much about it at the time.

Another key area of U.S. post–Cold War expansion was in the Middle East. Until 1970, the British Empire had been policing the region, traditionally getting its oil from Iran. However, that empire, in rapid decline since 1945—exhausted financially despite being on the winning side of two destructive world wars—finally turned over regional security to the United States. In addition to Israel, the United States relied on the oil states of Iran and Saudi Arabia as security pillars in the region. All that changed in 1978 with the Islamist revolution in Iran, converting the country from a U.S. friend into an adversary. This dramatic change, coupled with the Soviet invasion of Afghanistan—which then-President Jimmy Carter had provoked by aiding radical Islamist fighters there—prompted him to issue the Carter Doctrine in 1980. The doctrine declared that the United States would use military force to defend its national interest, then mostly oil, in the Persian Gulf.

So the focus of U.S. security policy had shifted from defending Western Europe to also guaranteeing the Western world's access to Persian Gulf oil. This new military commitment was unnecessary because the cheapest way to get oil is to let the worldwide market provide it. Any supply disruption because of war or instability might raise the worldwide price temporarily, but that elevated price would then spur other producers to fill any lost output from the turmoil. P. N. Haksar, the Indian diplomat who had been principal secretary to India's prime minister, Indira Gandhi, summed it up best:

> In our view there is a persistent falsity in the perception of geo-strategists of the West that control over the oil riches of West Asia [the Persian Gulf] is necessary for the peace, stability and prosperity of the western world. The western dominance of West Asia has generated, from time to time, serious explosions in this area.[2]

The added conflict in the region caused by this counterproductive interventionist U.S. policy undermines any goal of obtaining the cheapest oil for the Western world.

Even before the recent oil fracking boom raising oil production in the United States, the U.S. government did not need to undertake the huge military expense needed to station military forces in and around the Persian Gulf to ensure that adequate oil supplies at reasonable prices flowed to America or the West when the world market could have provided it much more efficiently and cheaply. Thus, one can only conclude that what the United States wanted was to indirectly control oil supplies to other consuming nations

After the Cold War ended, George H. W. Bush, bereft of the Soviet adversary that he was even more unwilling to give up than Ronald Reagan had been, developed a new rationale for keeping American global military hegemony: promoting an international rules-based "new world order." The first test of this new justification for U.S. hegemony was Iraqi dictator Saddam Hussein's invasion of Kuwait, his small Persian Gulf neighbor, in August of 1990. Happening at the end of the Cold War, Bush's military response seemed designed to demonstrate that the United States, now the only remaining superpower, would guarantee an aggression-free new world order based on U.S.-friendly rules.[3] (Ironically, George W. Bush, H. W.'s son, would throw his father's aggression-less nirvana to the wind twelve years later, invading, for cooked up reasons, an already devastated Iraq, finally ousting Saddam.)

First Gulf War Leads to Domestic Insecurity and More Wars

A questionable war—the first Persian Gulf War—would go on to shape three decades of U.S. security policy. U.S. military intervention in the conflict set in motion a series of events that subjected the United States to the imperial blowback of terrorism at home and costly military quagmires in the Greater Middle East later, as war begot war. The United States became sidetracked and wasted too many lives and trillions of dollars for thirty years in the Middle East—to say nothing of the damaged countries that it left in its wake. For too long, the strategic significance of the Middle East has been overstated to benefit Israel and the Gulf Arab states at the expense of competing economically with the bigger future challenge: China.

No Good Reason Existed for the War

In U.S. foreign policy circles and the media, everyone knows that America gets involved in wars in the Middle East to control oil—which it might easily have accessed for its own needs via normal trade.[4] Yet, while it may now have become a common supposition, this reality is rarely mentioned. The closest that an American administration official ever came to justifying a war in non-idealistic terms was in the first Persian Gulf War. Secretary of State James Baker unashamedly admitted that one of the reasons for undertaking a huge war to compel Saddam Hussein to remove his invasion forces from Kuwait was American "jobs, jobs, jobs." Even if oil was not mentioned directly, the implication was clear. At the time of the Gulf crisis, the United States was experiencing a significant economic recession, which higher oil prices likely would have worsened.[5] In 1990, one congressional leader, fellow Republican Bob Dole, blurted out the truth, which he sometimes was wont to do, even though he dwelled among Washington spinners and dissemblers. Dole ridiculed Bush's assertion that the United States was building up troops in Saudi Arabia because of Saddam Hussein's "aggression": "We are in the Middle East for three letters—oil, O-I-L. We are there because we do not want Saddam Hussein to get his hands around our throats and jack up the price of oil, which would have a severe impact on the economy." And even he missed the bigger picture when it came to oil.

Journalists James and Molly McCartney best summarized U.S. cloaking of the real purpose of U.S. wars in the Middle East:

According to U.S. presidents, both Republican and Democratic, our country fights its now-constant Middle East warfare over moral principles. We fight, they say to promote nonaggression, build democratic nations, ensure self-determination for national groups, protect minorities' rights, or seize hideous weapons of mass destruction. Yet for these noble aims, our country has allied with military dictators and authoritarian monarchs, overthrown a democratically elected government and armed extremist, antidemocratic guerrilla fighters.[6]

The McCartneys concluded that the gap between America's rhetoric and its behavior can be explained by U.S. attempts to achieve hegemony over the region to gain control over oil.

An economic analysis done by David Henderson, former economic adviser to Ronald Reagan, showed that between the time Iraq invaded Kuwait on August 2, 1990, and the beginning of Desert Storm (the air war) on January 17, 1991, even if Saddam had invaded Kuwait, United Arab Emirates (UAE), and Saudi Arabia and taken oil off the world market to hike the price, the rise in price would have shaved only 0.5 percent off the U.S. Gross Domestic Product.

However, Saddam had special grievances against Kuwait, claiming it was illegitimately slant-drilling Iraqi oil from across the border. No evidence exists that Saddam planned to invade Saudi Arabia or UAE, despite Bush administration fears and false claims that Iraqi forces were massing on Saudi Arabia's border; a Saudi investigation and commercial satellite photos saw no such force buildup.

Before going to war with Saddam, the international community first imposed the most severe, comprehensive economic embargo on Iraq in world history, including a global price-hiking ban on most Iraqi oil exports. Furthermore, when the international coalition attacked Iraqi forces in Kuwait to liberate that country, Saddam ordered Kuwait's oil fields torched. The oil taken off the market by the international export embargo and war destruction in Kuwait totaled more than Henderson predicted Saddam would have taken off the world market if he had invaded all three nations. Ironically, the war to secure Western oil supplies did the opposite. This effect was not unusual in the Middle East. Warfare in the region usually takes oil off the market, thus raising world prices in the shorter term, while regional instability inhibits investment in oil infrastructure, thus raising world oil prices in the longer term. Thus, war and oil do not mix well, but nonetheless the international oil market over the medium to long term tends to be resilient.

Even if Saddam had achieved—through his exhausted conscript army—a net removal of Middle Eastern oil from the world market, increasing the price temporarily, other oil producers would have responded to higher prices, filling the void and then lowering the price.

Nonetheless, the idea of oil as a strategic commodity—that is, requiring governments to secure supplies—fills the psyches of generals, politicians, and bureaucrats. Ever since Winston Churchill, then first lord of the admiralty, had converted the then-dominant British Navy from coal to oil at the beginning of the twentieth century, militaries learned the value of secure supplies of oil. However, even at the time of the first Gulf War, the United States produced annually, within its borders, multiple times the amount of oil per annum needed to run the U.S. military during wartime.

Oil is not a "strategic commodity." Buying oil on the world market is the cheapest way to get it, especially when compared to keeping large standing military forces in or around the Persian Gulf region to protect against an unlikely permanent oil cutoff. Oil is lucrative to sell, and producing companies and countries will find a way to sell it through natural disasters, economic embargoes, disruption of production and transportation—and yes, even during wars. Furthermore, studies show developed industrial economies are resilient to oil price increases. On the bright side, higher prices lead to conservation, increased energy efficiency, and switching to other fuels.

However, despite these realties, in 1990—prior to the fracking boom (and even after it)—U.S. policymakers and American public officials erroneously accepted that oil was a strategic commodity because of the searing images of gas lines in the United States during the 1973 Arab oil embargo and because of production cuts at the end of the 1970s due to production disruptions from the Iranian revolution. However, those gas lines—effectively, gasoline rationing—were the result of a bungled U.S. government response to price hikes. For example, in 1973, Arab oil producers in the OPEC cartel embargoed oil to the United States and the Netherlands for supporting Israel in the 1973 Middle East war. However, Sheik Ahmed Zaki Yamani, the Saudi oil minister, later admitted that the embargo was only smoke and mirrors because in a global market, embargoed buyers can almost always buy oil from alternative suppliers in a reordered world market.

More impactful at first was that the Arab countries cut oil production in general, thus rapidly hiking the price for all oil-consuming nations, at least until non-OPEC suppliers could increase supplies. However, the most severe problem was how some governments, including that of the United States, dealt with the price rise. Japan had no gas lines because it let the price rise naturally from fewer supplies, then markets automatically sorted out the buyers most in need of fuel—or at least, those who were most willing and able to pay the higher price. In contrast, even before the Arab oil embargo, the United States had price controls on petroleum, thus impeding the natural distributing function of the price mechanism—as shown by Japan's relative success. In America, the decreased supplies and artificially low prices for those scarce supplies led to demand exceeding supply—shortages in the form of gas lines. Gas lines in the United States were to happen again in the late 1970s, during Iranian revolution–induced production decrease. While Jimmy Carter had begun to deregulate the oil market at the time, it was still not completely free of controls; Ronald Reagan, Carter's successor, would later finish the deregulation. Gas lines were again the result of government interference in the price mechanism, not from a defect in the global oil market.

Thus, specious worries about the security of U.S. oil supplies were a major economic motivator of George H. W. Bush sending hundreds of thousands of U.S. troops to the Middle East. The MICC was another major economic motivator. Now that the Soviet threat had collapsed and the Chinese threat had not yet ripened, the MICC sought a new threat for an interventionist foreign policy to combat to justify the prolonged existence of U.S. foreign military bases, a large military, and high defense spending. Historian Melvin Small best summarized the sad state of the MICC at the end of the Cold War:

> Even the simple reduction of armed-forces personnel threatened economic stability since it threw tens of thousands of young people on the job market during a time of high unemployment. Thus, the United States reached a position in the early 1990s where it had built up a massive military-industrial complex to fight an enemy that no longer existed. But that complex had become so important politically and economically that it could

not be dismantled without creating a domestic tidal wave of opposition.[7]

Fortunately, just as the Cold War wound down, as luck would have it, Saddam Hussein's indiscretion in Kuwait came gift-wrapped for the MICC. Although the Cold War was ending and George H. W. Bush had an accomplished international resume, including as former director of the CIA, he was trying to shake off the image of being a "wimp" as vice president from 1981 to 1989. (He was still trying to shake this image after he retired from the presidency by skydiving at a ripe old age.) In October of 1989, the "wimpy" President Bush did not back a coup that almost removed from power Panamanian dictator General Manuel Noriega, the former CIA asset and chief U.S. villain at the time. Noriega's drug trafficking long had been ignored, and his killing of a few American troops did not call for a full-blown invasion, so the wimp accusation seemed to be the motivator of Bush's unnecessary invasion of Panama later in December 1989.[8]

Bush now swaggered around as commander in chief of the "only remaining superpower" that was to police a "new world order." In its struggle to keep military budgets unnecessarily high as the Cold War came to a close, the MICC was enthusiastic about this NWO rhetoric. Saddam's invasion of Kuwait in 1990 came at exactly the right time. Bush declared grandiosely that "this aggression against Kuwait will not stand." (However, as vice president, Bush had supported Reagan's validation of Iraq's earlier invasion of Iran in 1980 by providing assistance to Saddam's war effort for most of the decade during the long war. This U.S. intervention culminated in the U.S. Navy conducting a naval war against Iran in 1988.[9])

Bush's bold statement snuffed out any debate among his administration on alternative nonmartial options, including attempts to induce Saddam to withdraw from Kuwait through negotiations. Brent Scowcroft, Bush's national security adviser, admitted that Bush had demonized Saddam, refusing to negotiate with him or even give him a face-saving way to withdraw his troops from Kuwait—even though the Iraqi dictator became more amenable to American demands as the crisis unfolded. Like Lyndon B. Johnson in Vietnam, Bush, Vice President Dan Quayle, and Secretary of State James Baker believed Bush's presidency would be over if he let foreign aggression against a minor country triumph. Bush also sought to divert attention from his needed tax increase to help clean up the huge budget deficits left by Reagan. Bush knew a tax increase would be needed way back in the 1988 election when he made his "no new taxes" pledge. However, a looming budget crisis in October 1990 was about to expose that need and spell the death of that pledge.[10]

As in Korea, Failure to Deter, Then Panic

Mirroring Harry Truman's actions in Korea, Bush's administration had failed to deter an attack on a minor friendly country, panicked when that invasion came, and then sent sufficient troops for a major war. Similar to Secretary of State Dean Acheson, who had excluded South Korea from the U.S. defense perimeter in Asia, a Bush administration assistant secretary of state had declared at a congressional hearing before Saddam's invasion that the United States didn't get involved in intra-Arab territorial disputes (Iraq's claim that Kuwait was slant drilling to steal from its oil fields from across the border). Saddam had known of American congressional hearings, broadcast on TV, in which experts—including senior U.S. military leaders—testified that going to war with Iraq would be a horrible error.[11]

In both the Korean and Iraqi crises, American deterrence obviously failed; foreign dictators believed the United States would not counter their invasions. The Bush administration later made April Glaspie, the U.S. ambassador to Iraq, the scapegoat, alleging that she gave Saddam the impression he had a green light for the invasion of Kuwait. Yet as the assistant secretary's earlier public testimony showed, Glaspie merely was carrying out the Bush administration's post-Iran-Iraq War (1980–1988) policy of coddling Saddam Hussein. The United States had tried to help him win that war by supplying dual-use military technology, agricultural credits, military intelligence and planning, and even precursors for biological and chemical weapons after Saddam used poison gas against the Iranians and their Iraqi Kurdish sympathizers.

Saddam Hussein was in financial trouble after the long and bitter Iran–Iraq War.[12] He wanted an immediate oil price rise and for rich little Kuwait to forgive some of his loans, After all, he had borne the burden in the war for the wealthy Sunni Arab states against Shi'i Iran. Kuwait refused to cut oil production and forgive Iraqi loans. Not only that, Iraq had traditionally claimed Kuwait as a nineteenth province and complained about the Kuwaiti slant drilling of its oil. Thus, even if Saddam had been allowed to keep Kuwait after his invasion, he would have been desperate to sell oil into the market for quick cash—not hoard it to make money off a future price rise.

After Saddam had invaded Kuwait and pillaged it terribly, the Bush administration falsely told the Saudis that the Iraqi dictator was massing troops on their border and that they could be his next victim. Bush begged them to let the United States send hundreds of thousands of forces into the Saudi desert to defend Saudi oil. However, the Saudis seemed less concerned with the possibility of an Iraqi invasion and more fearful that the presence of U.S. "infidels" in the desert kingdom, which housed the holiest sites of Islam, would cause violent internal turmoil. The Saudis nonetheless reluctantly allowed U.S. forces to come and defend them, provided Bush promised to withdraw them after the war was over, a promise he later reneged on. As during the Cold War, the United States, acting as the global policeman for the post–Cold War world, worried more about threats to countries in far-flung regions more than the countries themselves did.

Bush Usurps Congress's Power to Initiate War

Under Operation Desert Shield, Bush questionably deployed hundreds of thousands of U.S. troops to the Saudi desert without congressional approval in the latter part of 1990. In fact, in September of that year, with the massive U.S. military buildup already underway in Saudi Arabia, Secretary of State James Baker told the House Foreign Affairs Committee that the 1973 War Powers Resolution—which requires that U.S. forces deployed to a hostile situation need to return home in sixty days unless Congress consents to their remaining—was unconstitutional.[13] The actual truth was that the framers of the Constitution would have required congressional approval for such a huge military deployment to an area of potential hostilities *before* it was undertaken. The purported unconstitutionality was not because the War Powers Resolution encroached on some fanciful unilateral executive power that the commander in chief possesses to deploy forces, as Baker alleged. Rather, it was because such a unilateral presidential deployment to a dangerous area would undermine Congress's unequivocal constitutional power to decide whether to initiate war by presenting it with an executive fait accompli.

In the Mexican War, the Civil War, and the Vietnam War, Congress's failure to enforce the traditionally required approval for large and potentially dangerous military deployments allowed presidential administrations to act with too much discretion. The Gulf War case, however, concerned more than just the president making provocative U.S. force deployments to trigger an enemy attack (Iraq's attack had already happened). Here, the president was acting without proper congressional approval by sending a large army into a desert, where its readiness for battle would fast deteriorate under the harsh conditions if not used. Nor, subsequently, did the Congress approve beforehand a huge increase in U.S. forces in Saudi Arabia to seven hundred thousand, either. This reflected the key Bush decision on October 31, 1990, to undertake eventual offensive operations against Iraq. A dismayed Thomas Foley, the speaker of the House of Representatives, received notification on November 8 of a second major deployment, a full eight days after the administration made the decision to undertake it.

Bush was hell-bent on war after Saddam had invaded Kuwait. He waited, however, until after the November 1990 congressional elections before seeking congressional and United Nations approval to use force. Congress eventually authorized offensive military operations only on January 12, 1991, shortly before they began on January 17, but Bush had long since made the key decisions for war and clearly would have undertaken it, based on his authority as commander in chief of the U.S. military, even if Congress had not approved. To withdraw after sending even the first force contingent of 500,000 would have represented a major fiasco.

Such unconstitutional behavior was a direct descendent of Truman's flagrant unilateral war-making for the Korean War.[14] Like Truman, the elder Bush would rely on the United Nations Charter and Security Council resolutions demanding withdrawal of the aggressor nation and calling on UN member nations to help compel that result.[15] However, a UNSC resolution is not the same as the constitutional process of approval for war by elected representatives in touch with the American people. (In 2003, George W. Bush, would also say he, as commander in chief of the U.S. military, didn't need Congress' approval to go to war but that he would ask for it as a courtesy. And he would go on to disregard the fact that he didn't get UN approval.)

The elder President Bush had rejected the plea of General Colin Powell, his chairman of the joint chiefs of staff, to allow the most comprehensive, multilateral, and grinding economic sanctions imposed in world history more time to work—that is, continue a policy of containment of Iraq and defense of Saudi Arabia—rather than to commence offensive military operations against Iraq (converting Operation Desert Shield into Operation Desert Storm). When the elder Bush rejected Powell's entreaty, he concluded further waiting would be too slow for domestic political reasons. Secretary of Defense Dick Cheney, too, tried to stifle Powell's dissent about war with Saddam. Ironically, Powell built his reputation on a war he was reluctant to fight. The same is true about General "Stormin'" Norman Schwarzkopf, the theater commander for Desert Storm and eventual war hero, who was reluctant to move away from economic sanctions, and thought the administration was moving toward war too quickly. Secretary of State James Baker was also in this camp. Powell, Schwarzkopf, and the joint chiefs of staff were all distressed over Bush's unilateral decision on October 31 to double the number of troops in Saudi Arabia without consulting his senior generals and admirals.

To win support for the upcoming war, too many self-serving reasons given for militarily expelling Saddam from Kuwait—arresting a Hitler-like threat, creating a new world order, and saving American jobs—led to suspicions of an ulterior motive. Bush rammed through his war even though close advisers, top military men, key members of Congress, foreign leaders, and a sizable part of the public thought other options should have been considered. None seriously were.[16]

As with Bush's December 1989 invasion of Panama for scarcely a good reason, he seemed to be thirsting for a fight to counter his "wimp" image. Ironically, in the end, such overcompensation led Bush into more significant military engagements than Ronald Reagan, his macho predecessor. Also, the war—undertaken in part to give the MICC an enemy to justify the continue excessive defense spending after the Cold War ended—also unfortunately led to the triumphal end of the "Vietnam Syndrome," which had given the United States a less interventionist foreign policy for a time.

Desert Storm: A Pyrrhic Victory

Operation Desert Storm, attacking Iraqi forces in Kuwait and Iraq with 700,000 U.S. troops and 256,000 coalition forces, went exceedingly well from the air and on the ground—and even more spectacularly in the public relations arena. Saddam had an obviously outdated, outgunned army of 650,000 men, but it also had brutal combat experience against Iran (1980–1988) and recently in Kuwait (1990). However, fighting other conventional militaries using high technology was the U.S. military's forte. Saddam lost half of his army to superior U.S. combat power, while his desperate air force weirdly flew to Iran, his primary regional enemy, to avoid combat. The United States lost few men in the one-sided war. Only a small number of U.S. weapons used were new "precision" smart weapons, but the U.S. military played videos of them flying through targeted windows, which created a dazzling spectacle of American technology and power for everyone to see. Saddam's battered army made a hasty retreat from Kuwait which did not save them from being obliterated by U.S. pilots in what the latter boasted was a turkey shoot.

The U.S. military's smashing victory over what had been played up as a large and capable foreign military, even though it was vulnerable to the U.S. air force in an open desert, temporarily elevated Bush's approval rating to more than 90 percent and got rid of the so-called "Vietnam Syndrome" for good. The syndrome had served as a cautionary warning leading to a more restrained approach to U.S. military intervention in the developing world after the counterinsurgency debacle in the jungles of Vietnam. Ronald Reagan had begun to erode it by attacking small countries, such as Libya and Grenada, and oddly conducting a disastrous armed peacekeeping mission in Lebanon. Bush's triumph in the Persian Gulf in a larger war rid Americans of the syndrome.

The weakness of the Soviet Union after the collapse of the Eastern Bloc in 1989 had allowed Bush's unhindered assault on Saddam (paradoxically an ally of both the former Soviet Union and United States) in the Persian Gulf in January and February of 1991. Later in 1991, the USSR's collapse, when combined with the victory in Desert Storm, left the United States as the self-proclaimed "only remaining superpower." American triumphalism about winning the Cold War and the vanquishing of the Vietnam Syndrome via Desert Storm then led to a feverish bout of U.S. military intervention in the developing world, including in the Middle East.

At the end of Desert Storm, conservatives and other hawks criticized George H. W. Bush and Defense Secretary Dick Cheney for not going all the way to Baghdad and toppling Saddam for good. Yet Bush feared he would lose popularity at home in a longer and costlier war—a lesson taught by the Korean and Vietnam Wars (and which his son should have learned). Bush and Cheney were further blamed for letting Saddam use his remaining forces, including helicopters, to kill thousands of Kurds in northern Iraq and Shiites in southern Iraq, whom Bush encouraged to rise up after Saddam's loss in Desert Storm, hoping that they could bring him down without U.S. intervention. When they did rise up, Saddam horrifically smashed the rebellions, but Bush then offered no help—again because of fear that a longer war would significantly erode his approval ratings at home. Eventually, the United States set up no-fly zones over northern and southern Iraq to prevent Saddam from further suppression of Kurds and Shiites—thus continuing low-level combat from the end of the Gulf War in 1991 to the George W. Bush's invasion of Iraq in 2003. Bill Clinton, the Democratic president between the two Republican Bushes, continued this limited aerial warfare during the period from 1993 and 2001, as well as additional U.S. military interventions in Somalia, Haiti, Bosnia, and Kosovo. In the interim, the most comprehensive multilateral economic sanctions in world history killed an estimated half million Iraqi children, according to the United Nations; nevertheless, of the measures, Clinton's Secretary of State Madeleine Albright infamously said it was "worth it".

George H. W. Bush had sound reasons for not going all the way to Baghdad, which his son George W. Bush discovered the hard way in 2003, when he launched his own invasion of Iraq. The elder Bush's security team in 1991 did not want to remove Saddam as the principal counterweight to Islamist Iran in the Persian Gulf region.

Yet the father's limited but decisive tactical victory in Desert Storm led in 2003 to his son's ill-fated and illegal invasion of Iraq later but was itself a U.S. strategic blunder. Empires suffer opposition—often violent—from their interventions abroad. George H. W. Bush's Gulf War against Saddam in 1991 led to retribution at home in one of the few significant foreign attacks on U.S. territory in the republic's history on September 11, 2001.

CHAPTER 16

9/11 AND THE WAR ON TERRORISM

Why Osama bin Laden Attacked U.S. Targets

In 1979, during the Cold War, Zbigniew Brzezinski, Jimmy Carter's national security adviser and anti-Soviet hawk, convinced the president that he should support radical Islamist mujahideen fighters against the communist government in Afghanistan. When the Soviets invaded Afghanistan in December 1979 to shore up the government, the Carter administration then increased aid to Islamist opposition forces to snare the Soviets into their own Vietnam-style quagmire. The Soviet invasion put the last nail in U.S.-Soviet détente, with the Carter administration imposing an embargo on American grain sales to the USSR, boycotting the 1980 Olympics scheduled for Moscow, reactivating registration for the draft, and taking the first steps to create a new military command in the Persian Gulf. Carter and Brzezinski's stratagem eventually worked, but not without the help of his successor, Ronald Reagan.

Reagan easily adopted Carter's stratagem but upped the stakes. He increased military aid to the radical Islamist insurgency to beat the Soviets, instead of simply tying them down in another Vietnam. It looked like a winning idea at the time—engaging the United States' principal Cold War rival in a military bog in a backward developing Islamic country. Ultimately, however, it contributed to disastrous eventual outcomes for the United States: the rise of al-Qaeda and the 9/11 attacks on the American homeland, to say nothing of a quagmire in Afghanistan for the Americans.

The Soviets' invasion of Afghanistan, bringing them closer to the Persian Gulf oil fields, led the Carter administration to overreact. U.S. officials assumed the Soviets were maneuvering to get control of the

Iranian oil when they were simply anxious about an Islamist takeover of Afghanistan, which worryingly bordered their own Muslim regions. Such exaggerated American fears motivated Carter in early 1980 to push the Carter Doctrine, which locked the United States into the fools' errand of preserving access to Persian Gulf oil through military deployments and, if necessary, the use of force.

Militant Islamists resist non-Muslim invasions or occupations of Islamic countries. Radical Islamist Osama bin Laden, a wealthy Saudi, migrated to Afghanistan to help fight the Soviet "infidels" invading a Muslim country. He built an outsized reputation during the 1980s from his anti-Soviet activities in Afghanistan. After the U.S.-assisted radical mujahideen had evicted the Soviets in early 1989, bin Laden returned home to Saudi Arabia. After Iraq had invaded Kuwait in 1990, bin Laden begged the Saudi government to let him raise an Islamist force to defend the kingdom against any attack by the reviled Saddam Hussein, a Baathist secular dictator. Yet, in bin Laden's eyes, the Saudi government turned him down in favor of letting an apostate power—the United States—occupy his native land, home to the holiest Islamic places of worship in Mecca and Medina.

The United States government arm-twisted the Saudis to allow it to station American troops in Saudi Arabia to defend it after Saddam had invaded Kuwait. The Geroge H.W. Bush administration also promised the Saudis that U.S. forces from Desert Shield/Desert Storm would leave after the Gulf War was won. The reason that the then-secretary of defense, Dick Cheney, and a high-level U.S. delegation had to badger the Saudis to let the U.S. defend them against a possible attack from Saddam was simple: the Saudis feared internal rebellion by radical Islamists such as bin Laden far more than they feared an attack by Iraq. Yet in the end, the Saudis feared losing their informal alliance with the powerful Americans even more than they feared either Saddam or internal rebellion. And anyway, from the Saudi perspective, U.S. troops were on their way to the desert kingdom no matter what.[1]

Nor did U.S. forces leave Saudi Arabia as promised after the first Persian Gulf War ended in 1991. Instead, the United States built up their forces in other parts of the region, further enraging bin Laden. Furthermore, the George H. W. Bush, Bill Clinton, and George W. Bush administrations continued the imposition of comprehensive economic sanctions against Iraq and a no-fly zone over the country. Thus, despite the intervening years between the Cold War's end and the inauguration of George W. Bush as president, Clinton bequeathed to the younger Bush a defense budget in 2001 that was greater in inflation-adjusted terms than Cold War levels—thanks to the existence and continuing outsize influence of the Military-Industrial-Congressional Complex (MICC) driving U.S. security policy. The United States spent on defense (and still approximately does) what the next highest-spending eight countries combined did on their security.[2]

Osama bin Laden had noticed that despite the many military interventions that the United States had conducted, the American public was averse to casualties. He remembered that even the hawkish Ronald Reagan withdrew U.S. forces from Beirut in the early 1980s after U.S. 241 service personnel died in the Marine barracks bombing and concluded from that incident that inflicting a few casualties could send the U.S. forces packing. Therefore, in 1993, bin Laden helped a warlord in Somalia evict U.S. peacekeeping troops by shooting down two American helicopters and killing eighteen U.S. military personnel. That same year, the first Islamist attack on the World Trade Center took place. Furthermore, little noticed by the American public at the time, in 1996 bin Laden declared war on the United States and began planning terrorist attacks on U.S. targets, including on the U.S. embassies in Kenya and Tanzania. After these attacks in 1998, the U.S. government tried to take him out with sea-launched cruise missile attacks on Afghanistan but did not kill him. In 2000 bin Laden's organization—al-Qaeda—successfully attacked and damaged an American destroyer, the *USS Cole*, docked in the Islamic country of Yemen.

Throughout bin Laden's manifestos and video recordings, he made very clear why he was waging war against the United States: he opposed the U.S. stationing of non-Muslim U.S. forces on Saudi Arabia's holy Muslim soil, the U.S. military's killing of Muslims, the U.S.-led embargo against Iraq that the United Nations estimated killed five hundred thousand children, and U.S. support for Israel. Bin Laden's al-Qaeda group included many veterans of the U.S.-sponsored war in Afghanistan against the Soviets, who had been on the CIA's payroll at one time.[3]

W. Lies about Bin Laden's Motives for Attacking the U.S.

After the catastrophic September 11, 2001, al-Qaeda attacks on the twin towers in New York City and the Pentagon, President George W. Bush chose to ignore the reasons for bin Laden's anger, namely U.S. adventurism abroad,[4] wanting instead to portray bin Laden's motives as solely pure evil rather than blowback from U.S. overseas interventions. In ejecting the USSR from Afghanistan, the United States already had unintentionally built up the capabilities and, more importantly, the reputation of radical Islam. If it had wanted to defend Persian Gulf oil more cheaply, it could have brought forces from Europe and the United States only when needed, as it did during the First Gulf War, rather than raising Islamist hackles by their long-term stationing on Muslim soil, as it had after the first Gulf War.

With the American people in an understandably surly mood after the 9/11 attacks, George W. Bush, the politician, could not help taking advantage of the situation. He stoked the flames of anger by lying to the public about the root cause of the terrorism—interventionist U.S. foreign policy—instead opting to play the patriot card, falsely declaring that "America was targeted for attack because we're the brightest beacon for freedom and opportunity in the world."[5] (Not coincidentally, he also later claimed Saddam Hussein hated U.S. freedom too). These statements so angered bin Laden that he put out a video to debunk Bush's nonsense and set the record straight, saying that if he had wanted to attack a country for just its freedom, he could have attacked Sweden. He then reiterated that U.S. interventionism in the Middle East provoked him to attack

Instead of Killing Bin Laden, Bush Gave Us the Afghan Quagmire

The American media, also incensed by terrorist attacks on U.S. soil that killed almost three thousand civilians, was in no mood to focus on the words of what they viewed as a vile madman. Instead, the American people and media, as they usually do, rallied around the president and gave him the benefit of the doubt when war on Afghanistan began. As had the Japanese strike on Pearl Harbor in 1941, the surprise terrorist attack on 9/11 was so searing to the nation's consciousness that it quickly became politically incorrect to point to any underlying motivations for the attacks that might have cast the U.S. government in a more unflattering light. In neither case were the 1941 or 2001 surprise attacks by U.S. adversaries justified. But U.S. government officials have not added to our understanding of them by avoiding national introspection.

After 9/11, the American public awarded George W. Bush the biggest spike in the history of American polling, with his approval rising from 51 percent on September 10, 2001 to 90 percent twelve days later—not just recording the highest rating in history but also maintaining it the longest. Even John F. Kennedy during the Cuban Missile Crisis and George H. W. Bush during Desert Storm had smaller and less sustained increases in their approval rating. The younger Bush was thus able to convert that enhanced approval into rare congressional gains for his party in the 2002 off-year elections. Not since 1934 had a president's party gained seats in both houses of Congress during his first term, and not since 1882 had a non-presidential election converted a divided government on Capitol Hill into one united behind the president. This enhanced public support reflected a "patriotic" or "rally 'round the flag" effect after the 9/11 attacks, and it kept going because members of Congress and opposition presidential candidates were less willing to criticize his foreign policy moves.[6]

Unfortunately, the younger Bush exploited such soaring popularity to enlarge his war on terrorism beyond the congressional authorization, expanding his response to fight perceived enemies other than those who had attacked the United States on 9/11. Instead of adopting a limited war against the central al-Qaeda organization and the Islamist Taliban rulers of Afghanistan who had harbored al Qaeda (but offered to turn Bin Laden over to a third country if evidence of his guilt were provided), George W. Bush launched a much broader global war on terrorism (GWOT), with a view to targeting all terrorist groups having "global reach." In short, Bush took aggressive actions on several fronts instead of focusing on the perpetrators of 9/11. The outcome was that it took ten years and another president to kill Osama bin Laden. Bush's expansion beyond Congress's authorization was yet another clear and dangerous violation of Congress's intent and therefore illegal and unconstitutional. However, Congress did little about the flagrant abuse—which perhaps should raise questions as to whether Congress, in its current supine form, represents a line of defense against unnecessary wars.

Unsurprisingly, Bush's GWOT overreach was bloody but ineffective and divided the country and the world. According to a 2008 RAND study, of the 648 terrorist groups in the world between 1968 and 2006, only 7 percent were defeated by military means, whereas 40 percent were defeated by intelligence and police work and 43 percent willingly gave up violence when it was feasible to join the political processes.[7] In fact, Bush's military adventurism became an unintended recruiting magnet for Islamist terrorist response, as the number of terrorist attacks soared in Iraq and worldwide.

Similarly, the war in Afghanistan expanded well beyond ensuring that Afghanistan would not be a base again to launch a terrorist attack against the United States. The post-9/11 U.S. invasion of Afghanistan in 2001 had quickly tossed out the Taliban rulers, decimated al-Qaeda, and driven the rest of the group into the mountains of neighboring Pakistan. Yet, despite Bush's 2000 election criticism of Clinton's military interventionism and armed nation building, he turned the U.S. occupation of Afghanistan into a long nation-building war, purportedly designed to bring democracy and good governance to the country, reduce its opium exports, and bring about more rights for women in a male-dominated Islamic society. Bush could have avoided this long quagmire by negotiating a power-sharing government with the defeated Taliban. The Taliban even offered to surrender under certain conditions. However, in the American tradition of demanding unconditional surrender started by Ulysses S. Grant during the Civil War, the Bush administration refused and pursued total victory. Continued U.S. occupation by U.S. forces spurred a Taliban resurgence against the foreign occupier, leading eventually to U.S. defeat and withdrawal two decades later. In short, Bush's inept policy led to the United States snatching defeat from the jaws of victory.

The United States should have learned earlier from costly and unsuccessful U.S. nation-building efforts in Vietnam, Lebanon, Somalia, Haiti, Bosnia, Kosovo, and other countries: they rarely work. Afghanistan was, of course, no exception. Demonstrating that the MICC had a bipartisan hold on U.S. policy, in the 2000 campaign, long before the 9/11 attacks, both Bush and his opponent Al Gore advocated increases in defense spending despite the absence of any real great power threat.

Just before the 2000 election, a neoconservative group of future Bush appointees called the Project for a New American Century—which included future Vice President Dick Cheney, Secretary of Defense Donald Rumsfeld, Deputy Secretary of Defense Paul Wolfowitz, and UN Ambassador John Bolton—had concocted a plan for transforming the U.S. military and invading Iraq. They had despaired at the lack of a "new Pearl Harbor" to trigger the plan's implementation. The 9/11 attacks would supply a new day of infamy.[8] Bush used the attacks as an excuse to invade Iraq and balloon the defense budget, including buying many complex and expensive weapons not especially useful in detecting, capturing, or killing ragtag terrorists.

In his 2008 election campaign, Barack Obama made the lame promise to withdraw from what was by then an unpopular war of occupation in Iraq to accelerate the "good war" in Afghanistan. In the militarized American culture, because Obama—a progressive Democrat—was afraid of appearing weak, he added twenty-one thousand troops to an already lost cause in Afghanistan. But the generals were not appeased and waged a public campaign to sandbag the inexperienced Obama into sending even more troops, to which Obama capitulated, as he later admitted, merely to satisfy the powerful U.S. military. Then-Vice President Joe Biden, more seasoned in foreign policy, opposed sending more troops to Afghanistan and wanted to refocus U.S. efforts to the original goal of neutralizing the al-Qaeda terrorists, then in the mountains of Pakistan. Biden lost the internal battle, and Obama then allowed the military to add another thirty thousand troops to the failing effort but, thinking to pen in the generals, gave them eighteen months before he would start to withdraw the forces in 2011. However, telling a guerrilla force like the Afghan Taliban that the United States was eventually leaving just made them wait out the U.S. forces. Although after his troop surge, Obama did begin to withdraw U.S. forces from the country, he should have stood up to the generals in the first place, avoided the surge, and discretely (to the extent possible) withdrawn U.S. forces.

Obama then expanded Bush's GWOT to more nations across Central Asia and Africa by bombing or inserting U.S. forces into more countries, including inducing chaos and civil war in Libya by overthrowing dictator Muammar Gaddafi. The expansion of such interventions caused U.S. military bases abroad to increase to eight hundred bases in eighty countries.[9]

All U.S. forces did not withdraw from Afghanistan during the remainder of the Obama administration or even during the following Trump administration. Trump doubled down on Obama's mistake by signing an agreement in February 2020 with the Afghan Taliban that stipulated all U.S. forces would be out by May 1, 2021. Given that American public opinion wanted U.S. forces out of the country, Trump wanted to sign the agreement before the upcoming election. Nevertheless, telling the enemy specifically when you are leaving is even worse than telling them vaguely that it will eventually happen. The Taliban then used the interim period to negotiate with local and provincial governments and Afghan forces to surrender quickly when the U.S. pulled out. On succeeding Trump as president, Joe Biden decided to honor Trump's agreement to withdraw all U.S. forces from the country. However, because of an intelligence failure, he did not realize the Taliban would take over the country so quickly and did not begin evacuation of U.S. and U.S.-friendly Afghans soon enough, leading to a chaotic exit. However, to avoid such messy exits, the lesson—still unrecognized after Vietnam, Iraq, and Afghanistan—is to avoid getting into counterinsurgency/nation-building wars in the developing world that usually turn into quagmires.

In the twenty years of U.S. fighting in Afghanistan, progress was made on some of the ambitious U.S. social and political goals for the country, but the final U.S. withdrawal reversed most, if not all, of them. The Taliban brought back the dark ages. However, the United States could not keep its finger in the dike of a losing war effort indefinitely, and President Joe Biden wisely withdrew all American forces to finally cut American losses.

Ted Koppel, a prominent TV journalist, wrote in a *Washington Post* piece in 2010 that the 9/11 attacks had "succeeded far beyond anything Osama bin Laden could possibly have envisioned" by sucking the United States into overreacting in Afghanistan, the Global War on Terrorism, and the invasion of Iraq.[10] That is the best summary of failed post-9/11 military interventionism.

The American war on Afghanistan failed, like those in Vietnam and Iraq, because Americans cannot seem to realize that other countries do not see U.S. invaders and occupiers as benevolent—and nor, indeed, is it. The United States staying on as an occupying force after decimating al-Qaeda contributed heavily to the Taliban's resurgence and a split in the Afghan client regime itself. Foreign occupiers usually spur local inhabitants to fight fiercely for their home, honor, and religion—especially when non-Muslim interlopers invade and occupy an Islamic nation, such as Afghanistan.

At a critical early stage in the Afghan War, the Bush administration transferred critical and limited special forces troops and intelligence assets to a higher priority invasion of Iraq, and the war in Afghanistan lingered into a twenty-year "forever war." Lieutenant General Karl Eikenberry, both a general and a diplomat there during the conflict, summed up the long debacle: "In the end, we prosecuted the war in Afghanistan because we could. With no peer competitor [the Soviet Union had fallen a decade earlier], a volunteer force, and deficit spending, we had the luxury strategically and politically of fighting a forever war."[11] It was a luxury that cost more than 6,200 American lives, more than 1,100 lives from allied nations, more than 46,000 Afghan civilian lives, and $2.3 trillion dollars that added substantially to the staggering U.S. national debt.[12]

War on Terrorism's Detrimental Effects on the Republic

The Cold War was very detrimental to the republic and American civil liberties at home because it lasted more than forty years. Similarly, at this writing, the GWOT has lasted more than twenty years and has had the same effect. In addition to needlessly stretching the battlefield beyond the Afghanistan/Pakistan region to create more enemies for the United States around the world, Bush—also like Truman during the Cold War—tried to stretch his commander-in-chief powers onto the home front.

Despite that Congress, fearful of executive abuse, had avoided delegating any authority domestically to the president in the post-9/11 authorization to use military force, Bush just decided that during a national emergency, he could simply override congressionally passed laws and even the Constitution. He did so repeatedly in the areas of domestic spying, suspension of habeas corpus, the creation of military commissions, and torture of suspected terrorism suspects.

During the negotiations for the 2001 Authorization of the Use of Military Force (2001 AUMF), at the last minute, the Bush administration tried to slip in language that would have allowed the president to use "necessary and appropriate force" to combat terrorism "in the United States." The administration thought that it would need to use some types of force domestically, including surveillance, inside the United States. Tom Daschle, the then-Democratic senate majority leader, had been appalled by this gambit and rejected the language. Just as the administration had first backed down on the language of the congressional authorization for the use of force abroad and then violated it, it did so again domestically, stretching the commander in chief's authority to fight terrorism at home and ignoring congressionally passed laws. The executive claimed that just as Congress could not interfere with the commander in chief's strategic and tactical decisions on a battlefield, it had no authority during wartime to meddle with his collection of intelligence at home and detention, trial, and interrogation of prisoners, or even their torture.

This claim was nonsense because historically the president, during every war in the nation's long trajectory, had had to deal with many congressional stipulations and restrictions, sometimes even on strategic and tactical issues in battle. Under the American constitutional system, the president is supposed to execute laws passed by Congress, not ignore or override them.

Like Nixon—who outrageously asserted, after leaving office, that "when the president does it, that means that it is not illegal"—Bush, the sitting president, claimed that the president's commander-in-chief authority "could render specific conduct otherwise criminal, not unlawful." In 2005, in a statement after signing a new congressionally passed statute aiming to rein in the administration's torture of detainees by banning "cruel, inhumane, and degrading treatment or punishment," the president claimed the power to nullify the law for the above-noted reason. However, in the end, even Justice Department lawyers in the Bush administration became uncomfortable with the administration's grandiose assertions of executive power and backed off from some of them.[13]

The 9/11 attacks and Global War on Terror brought increased U.S. government surveillance of its own population, as well as of suspected terrorists overseas. Congress passed the draconian Patriot Act, which vastly expanded unconstitutional surveillance at home sometimes without the check of judicially approved search warrants. Because it contradicted the Constitution's requirement for warrants with no national security exemption, the Patriot Act was of questionable constitutionality. Furthermore, the Foreign Intelligence and Surveillance Act (FISA Act) of 1978 required an independent, but in practice a very lenient, secret court to bless executive branch requests for warrants for surveillance of suspected foreign agents and terrorists, even in time of war. The Bush administration, after 9/11, flagrantly ignored the warrant approval requirement in this law and ordered the National Security Agency to illegally spy on Americans without warrants. The administration justified this outrage on the basis that the president, as commander in chief, could ignore FISA during wartime, even though the congressionally passed law stipulated that it applied even in such instances.

In 2004, the administration became uncomfortable with flouting this FISA wartime provision and let the illegal surveillance program temporarily lapse. Yet it then tried to justify the illegal surveillance by the equally questionable argument that the 2001 congressional authorization of the use of military force (AUMF) against the perpetrators of the 9/11 attacks and those harboring them implicitly overrode the explicit FISA requirements for warrants. However, when it passed the AUMF in 2001, Congress, fearing a presidential effort to use it to subvert civil liberties at home during the War on Terrorism, explicitly left out the administration's request for language applying the authorization domestically and instead confined it only to force used overseas against 9/11 participants and enablers.

More media and public scrutiny on the domestic surveillance finally made the administration yield to FISA court authorization, review, and restrictions. Then, in a move that smacked of rank hypocrisy, Congress, which had previously complained vehemently about the illegality of the domestic surveillance program, amended FISA in 2008 to accommodate the program and make private telecommunications companies immune from legal responsibility for helping the U.S. government break the law. However, Congress's amendment of FISA may be unconstitutional because the Constitution's Fourth Amendment on illegal searches and seizures, which requires probable cause that a crime has been committed before a warrant for domestic surveillance can be issued by judge, has no exemption for national security.

Ironically after all this effort and illegality, in 2009 an internal analysis of the president's surveillance program found that it brought forth little valuable information to battle terrorism.[14] Yet the domestic surveillance program—which has had few national security benefits but has inflicted excessive harm to the nation's unique civil liberties—has continued. In 2013, Lt. Gen. James Clapper (Ret.), President Barack Obama's director of national intelligence, lied to Congress, saying the NSA was not wittingly collecting intelligence on Americans. He was forced to apologize to Congress when NSA contractor Edward Snowden revealed that the NSA was doing just that by secretly and illegally collecting the telephone and email communications data from millions of Americans.

Bush deliberately held terrorism detainees, called "unlawful combatants," offshore at the U.S. military prison at Guantanamo, Cuba, so that they would be in legal limbo. The U.S. government offered them neither prisoner of war status nor rights defendants have on American soil. Their trials would be in unconstitutional kangaroo military commissions at Guantanamo, which give defendants lesser rights. Although such military commissions were used during the Civil War and World War II, they were not strictly constitutional either then or now. But because of the precedents of use in prior wars, the Supreme Court ruled that the Bush administration's military commissions did not comport with the laws that Congress had passed and allowed their use only if the administration made changes to them enhancing defendants' rights. That said, the Constitution only allows military courts martial for U.S. service personnel; all others are guaranteed a trial by jury. In domestic terrorism cases, civilian courts, even with their better procedural safeguards for defendants' rights, have had a much better track record in achieving convictions than have the military commissions. Yet the commissions continue to disastrously slog away, often holding people indefinitely in Guantanamo without trial and conviction.

Finally, Bush flagrantly violated U.S. and international law by conducting rendition and torture of terrorism suspects, some of whom turned out to be innocent and had simply been victims of a haphazard capture on the battlefield. One of the rights prisoners of war have under the Geneva Conventions is protection against mistreatment or torture. Yet the Bush administration lawyers in the Justice Department deliberately created the category of "unlawful combatant" who are deemed as unattached to any state, claiming that therefore terrorism suspects did not fall under the Geneva Conventions. State Department lawyers later found the Justice Department's argument to be flawed and instead suggested that the U.S. officials who had engaged in torture were liable for war crimes. Justice Department lawyers, presumably the source of the Bush administration assertions, had argued that the War on Terrorism nullified all humanitarian laws, and that the president had unlimited powers as commander in chief to conduct the war as he liked. The nation's founders, including the pro-executive Alexander Hamilton, would have fainted at this perversion of the executive's constitutional power, which they had envisioned only narrowly as the role of a chief general or admiral to direct combat once Congress initiated war. The Supreme Court ruled that the administration, in its war against the stateless al-Qaeda group, had to abide by the Geneva Conventions' banning of cruel treatment of prisoners. The administration reluctantly followed the court's ruling.

Thus, the highest levels of the Bush administration, while loudly proclaiming to defend U.S. "freedoms," nevertheless authorized waterboarding, exposure to extreme temperatures, sleep deprivation, and forced nudity against terrorism suspects. Some of these techniques used at Guantanamo prison in Cuba, Abu Ghraib prison in Iraq, and CIA black sites around the world became public. Some might ask: why should the average citizen care about the rights of suspected heinous terrorists? Because a free society with genuine rule of law is required to uphold high standards, no matter what crime is involved. Even people accused of horrible crimes are to be regarded as innocent until proven guilty if a trial is to be fair. The reason is simple: to protect the innocent. Several terrorism detainees, haphazardly captured on battlefields and later tortured, were in fact innocent. The commitment to uphold even suspected terrorists' rights safeguards basic rights for everyone.

Moreover, like domestic surveillance, torture was not effective. The most seasoned interrogators argued that it was ineffective in producing good intelligence because the victim would tell the interrogators whatever they wanted to hear just to stop the severe punishment. Furthermore, the U.S. military—including General Colin Powell (Ret.), then secretary of state—was mostly against torture because of the excuse it gave adversaries to torture captured U.S. forces. Besides, torturing enemy fighters usually makes them fight harder to avoid capture, rather than surrender. Eventually Congress banned torture, but Bush, in signing the statute, wrote an unconstitutional signing statement insisting nonetheless that he could violate the law if he believed its prohibitions put U.S. security at risk.

When Barack Obama succeeded Bush, he declined to prosecute Bush administration officials' clear violations of law during the war on terrorism, probably because he did not want himself or his officials to later be prosecuted for their likely illegal behavior in the continuing Global War on Terrorism. For example, Obama's program of targeted drone killings—really assassinations—of suspected terrorists killed more people than Bush did. He also went as far as to kill U.S. citizens in an illegal (congressionally unapproved) war against Islamists in Yemen without any legal due process.[15] Also, Obama used the Espionage Act of 1917, passed during World War I but which just keeps on giving, to prosecute more government whistleblowers and leakers than all his predecessors combined in an attempt to intimidate the media. Furthermore, during his administration in 2014 the CIA broke the law by searching the computers of the Senate Intelligence Committee, which was then investigating the agency's torture of suspected terrorists during the Bush administration. Donald Trump rhetorically advocated bringing back torture and went further by rewarding such behavior by nominating Gina Haspel—who had run a CIA black (torture) site during the Bush administration—as director of the CIA.[16]

The courts, including the Supreme Court, tried to rein in some of Bush's excesses, and Congress further tried to legislate to fence him in—but both also codified some of his transgressions. In sum, the Bush administration was adept at finding legal justifications for doing criminal things, especially in domestic surveillance and torture. Bush eventually had to step back from some of his overreach, but he nevertheless made Truman look like a piker when it came to abusing commander in chief authority.

Although the 9/11 attacks were spectacularly horrific, the reality even then was that small terrorist groups, many more times than not, have neither the resources nor the ability to carry out such mass casualty attacks, whether by the conventional means used on 9/11 or using so-called weapons of mass destruction (employing nuclear, biological, or chemical weapons) on a large scale. Even after 9/11, the chances that an international terrorist would kill the average American was still less than their chance of being struck by lightning. Nonetheless, the Bush administration exploited the 9/11 attacks to conduct a costly expanded Global War on Terrorism to attack groups worldwide that had nothing to do with 9/11 but were unfriendly to alleged "U.S. interests," even if they were not focusing their efforts on striking U.S. targets.

International or domestic crises usually lead to the growth of government. This phenomenon occurs even when the government is controlled by the Republican Party—a party that always preaches the need for smaller government, but post–World War II has had presidents that have presided over increases in federal spending as a percentage of GDP even greater than those of the perceived "big-government" Democratic Party. George W. Bush enlarged the government and increased the already bloated Department of Defense budget—and not just to pay for his quagmires in Afghanistan and Iraq. In every war since World War II, taxes rose to pay for the wars; Bush instead reduced taxes, with the wars adding trillions to the already large national debt, thus exacerbating

U.S. "imperial overstretch." The two wars, together the most expensive in American history, are likely to cost as much as $6 trillion when the future disability and long-term care for military personnel and veterans is included.[17] Contributing to massive federal budget deficits, the wars helped cause the Great Recession of 2008.

Bush's defense budget increases were not just for items for fighting terrorism—such as more special forces troops, drones, and other intelligence collection methods—which are relatively cheap. He padded the budget by buying large weapon systems appropriate for use in conventional wars with other great powers, which were at that time quiescent. This waste of funds shows the powerful reach of the MICC.

Furthermore, unlike the funding for past wars, which came out of the regular Department of Defense budget, Bush got yearly "emergency" supplemental appropriations bills passed to fund the Afghan and Iraq Wars—even though these long conflicts were hardly unexpected emergencies after the first year. And sometimes the department inserted less essential non-war items in the war budgets, thus growing defense spending even more than the hikes in the department's regular budgets.

In addition, after 9/11, Bush at first rejected Democratic calls for a new Department of Homeland Security (DHS) but then proposed his own version of the legislation. Disparate government agencies were merged into the new department, and a new departmental bureaucracy imposed on top of all such agencies. That department has become one of the most bloated and inefficient in Washington. Similarly, because of coordination problems between the FBI and CIA that hampered the U.S. response to the 9/11 attacks, Bush decided to add an office of the Director of National Intelligence (DNI) to coordinate the already sprawling then-sixteen agency intelligence community, hardly solving the original interagency coordination problem; adding yet another organization multiplied it. Also, because the DNI does not have control over the budgets for the individual intelligence agencies, its authority over the intelligence community is weak.

Nonetheless, Congress acquiesced and created the bloated DHS and ineffectual DNI to fight terrorism—even though terrorist groups, unlike nation-states, act quickly and nimbly, thus requiring a more agile government reaction. Adding another layer of bureaucracy to these two already slothful and expansive security communities hardly made the government more agile. To better combat terrorist groups, the number of government bureaucracies combating them needed to be streamlined instead of ballooning. However, expanding the government during a crisis attempts to show the public that something is being done about a problem, regardless of whether the expansion enhances or impedes government effectiveness in resolving it. In this instance, Bush's post-9/11 effort to show he was doing something about terrorism—especially the creation of DHS after earlier rejecting Democrats' proposals to do the same—deflected attention away from congressional hearings in the summer of 2002 about his administration's intelligence failures that allowed the horrific attacks to happen, which the independent 9/11 Commission later deemed "preventable."[18]

Finally, Bush took advantage of the angry mood of the American public after 9/11 by preposterously, yet successfully, linking the Islamist Osama bin Laden to the corrupt secular Saddam Hussein to finish what his father started by invading Iraq and this time toppling the Iraqi leader from power.

>> CHAPTER 17 <<

U.S. INVASION OF IRAQ (GULF WAR II)

Why Did George W. Bush Invade Iraq?

Many analysts have said that planning for the 2003 invasion of Iraq caused the Bush administration to transfer valuable special forces personnel and intelligence assets from its invasion and occupation of Afghanistan (which had begun in late 2001), thus impairing that earlier effort. Although true, the reality was that the 9/11 attacks and U.S. retaliation in Afghanistan had interrupted Bush's intense desire to take out Iraq's Saddam Hussein. In the first National Security Council (NSC) meeting after being inaugurated in late January 2001, more than eight months before the 9/11 attacks, according to Bush's Secretary of the Treasury Paul O'Neill and other sources,[1] Bush told the gathering that he wanted them to find him a rationale to overthrow Saddam. O'Neill is quoted as saying, "The president kept saying, 'Go find me a way to do this." If nothing else, this may confirm the well-known top-down acquiescence to the whims of an impetuous president rather than a rational decision. One might well ask: what is the point of having extensive military and intelligence capacities and understandings, if their input is only to serve the whim of an all-powerful commander rather than chart a wise course for the nation?

A cynic might point to the threat that Saddam posed to the oil interests of the Bush family and Vice President Cheney. One might see a desire to use the U.S. military to secure substantial Iraqi oil and war reconstruction contracts to well-connected Western companies, especially Republican-leaning ones. The vice president had headed a prominent oil services and reconstruction company and still held stock options in it.[2]

Evidence exists for this desire to control the world's second largest oil reserves. As early as February 2001, the Bush administration discussed plans for war against Iraq and the distribution of its oil resources. The Defense Intelligence Agency was mapping Iraq's oil fields and indicating which Western companies might be interested in exploiting those assets. O'Neill concluded that dividing up Iraq's oil was irresistible to the administration.[3] And indeed, this exploitation was carried out after American forces invaded and conquered the country. Political scientist David A. Lake concludes: "As the Iraq case demonstrates, domestic actors played an important role in driving the United States and Iraq to war. Indeed, popular discourse often implied that oil companies or the military-industrial complex in the United States was a major cause of the turn to violence. An extension of bargaining theory and an examination of the case suggest that particularistic interests such as these can—and likely did—increase the belligerency of the United States."[4] Other administration skeptics have noted that because Bush won the 2000 election without a popular vote plurality, he leaped at the opportunity the 9/11 attacks gave him to be a "war president" by invading Afghanistan—it was the supposed location of Osama bin Laden, after all—and then invading Iraq (the diversionary theory of war),[5] framing his response as the Global War on Terrorism so that it could include Iraq.

Bush was invoking the old Washington adage "never fail to take advantage of a crisis"—this installment using the tragedy of 9/11 to divert military efforts to invade the unrelated Saddam-led Iraq. In a very telling statement, Secretary of Defense Donald Rumsfeld, on the afternoon of the 9/11 attacks implicitly referring to this adage, advocated military action to attack Saddam as well as bin Laden. Rumsfeld urged, "Go massive. Sweep it all up. Things related and not."[6] A wide swath of Bush administration officials have gone public saying that Rumsfeld, Cheney, and others in the administration were trying to use the 9/11 crisis to go after Iraq.

Bush too got on board if he was not there already. As early as September 17, six days after the 9/11 attacks, according to journalist Bob Woodward, Bush said, "I believe Iraq was involved."[7] Political scientists Amy Gershkoff and Shana Kushner Gadarian charitably took Bush at his word that he really believed the Saddam-9/11 connection.[8] However, even if he did, his belief was without evidence; yet most of the administration snapped into line with the president's thinking. In his book *Plan of Attack*, Bob Woodward reported that on the day before Thanksgiving in 2001, Bush approached the already convinced Rumsfeld, saying, "What have you got in terms of plans for Iraq? What is the status of the war plan? I want you to get on it. I want you to keep it secret."[9]

Moreover, the president personally continued to pressure Richard Clarke, his counterterrorism chief in the National Security Council, to tie Saddam to those terrorist strikes, even after Clarke protested that only bin Laden had committed the acts.[10] Clarke implied to the 9/11 Commission that Bush administration officials, especially Iraq hawks Vice President Dick Cheney and Paul Wolfowitz, the deputy secretary of defense, purposefully exploited the 9/11 crisis, manipulated intelligence, and exaggerated the threat to U.S. security posed by Saddam to justify invading Iraq.[11]

Despite Clarke's protest, the major reasons Bush gave for the United States committing a wanton act of aggression against Saddam's Iraq—all lame—were its alleged but much exaggerated ties to terrorism; its "undoubted" possession of weapons of mass destruction that would likely be given to terrorists; and the especially implausible argument that its democratization by force would lead to a domino effect of new democracies in the Middle East. All such excuses did not pan out. According to Karlyn Kohrs Campbell and Kathleen Hall Jamieson, experts on presidential war rhetoric, exaggeration or fabrication in such rhetoric is not a novelty; instead, strategic misrepresentation is standard fare when war is afoot. By design, such disingenuity stifles dissent and unifies the nation for the upcoming clash of arms, whether justified or not.[12] However, George W. Bush's dissembling prior to his invasion of Iraq was second to none in American history.

No evidence existed that al-Qaeda and Saddam Hussein had collaborated on the 9/11 attacks or had any "cooperative operational relationship" at all, according to the 9/11 Commission.[13] It was an unlikely scenario in the first place because Osama bin Laden and al-Qaeda were fervent Islamists who detested corrupt, secular dictators, such as Baathist Saddam Hussein.

However, political scientists Amy Gershkoff and Shana Kushner Gadarain claim that nonetheless more than 70 percent of Americans initially supported the war because the Bush administration successfully framed the invasion of Iraq as part of the war on terrorism, which was a response to the 9/11 attacks. Their analysis of Bush's speeches concluded that he repeatedly connected Iraq with terrorism and al-Qaeda, even though he never explicitly accused Saddam of perpetrating 9/11 or linked him to bin Laden. The only time a member of the Bush administration explicitly said that the war in Iraq was an extension of its response to 9/11 and the global war on terrorism was when Colin Powell in his speech to the United Nations justified military action against Iraq. Also, he fallaciously claimed that the United States had ironclad evidence that Saddam had WMD, especially biological and chemical weapons, which threatened the United States and the world. Vice President Cheney chimed in with "there is no doubt that Saddam Hussein now has weapons of mass destruction; there is no doubt he is amassing them to use against our friends, against our allies, and against us."[14]

Preparing the ground for invading Iraq, Bush, in his State of the Union Address in January 2002, predicted the war on terrorism had to be enlarged to disarm the cartoonish "axis of evil" (the rogue states of Iraq, Iran, and North Korea), which were hardly a real "axis." In mid-August and September of 2002, about a year after the 9/11 attacks, astoundingly majorities of Americans believed Saddam was personally responsible for the 9/11 attacks. According to political scientists Scott L. Althaus and Devon M. Largio, this mistaken belief came about because in April 2002, about seven months after the attacks, the Bush administration made a blatant attempt to replace bin Laden with Saddam as the nation's foremost villain by linking the Iraqi dictator to the war on terrorism. Althaus and Largio found that mention of bin Laden all but vanished from Bush's public statements while mention of Saddam increased. (Gershkoff and Kushner Gadarian find the same phenomenon, yet date it a little later—to Bush's taking advantage of his first anniversary of 9/11 speech on September 12, 2002, at the United Nations, to tie together the Saddam-9/11 connection.)[15] Yet according to Althaus and Largio, the American people were ready and willing to believe that Saddam was involved in the 9/11 attacks right from the start. The Bush administration merely took advantage of an existing climate of public opinion that was predisposed to believe their deception. These authors also point out that a poll taken in late February 2001, about seven months before the 9/11 attacks, showed that 73 percent of Americans thought it was very or somewhat likely that Saddam would organize terrorist attacks on U.S. targets in retaliation for U.S. and British air strikes on his country to enforce the no-fly zones over Iraq, which had been going on since the first Gulf War in 1991.[16] At the time of 9/11 and since the first Gulf War in 1990–1991, Saddam, not bin Laden, had been enemy number one in the United States for more than a decade. Thus, the

Bush administration's false linking of Saddam to bin Laden and 9/11 was easy.

After laying the groundwork for the implicit Saddam-9/11 connection, Bush wisely held the congressional vote on going to war in October 2002, just before the November congressional election. After the searing effect on American public opinion of the 9/11 attacks the year before, the Democrats and media response was shamefully meek in disputing this preposterous claim of a popular president; between September and December of 2002, Bush's approval rating remained between 60 and 70 percent.

After all, neither did the Democrats want to look weak before the election. They had seen some of their Democratic predecessors fail to get reelected for opposing Bush the elder's first Gulf War in 1991. John Zaller, a scholar who has developed a theory of public opinion, notes that when the policy elite forms a consensus on a course of action, the public usually agrees with the one-sided approach. However, when the elite is fractured, so is the public, running to their respective ideological camps.[17] In this case, the public got a one-sided information flow because the Democrats were cowed into submission, muting their criticism of Bush's invading another Muslim country that had nothing to do with the 9/11 attacks—thus implicitly or explicitly endorsing Bush's aggressive preventive war policy against Iraq. Nevertheless, anti-war demonstrations did break out but they were less intense and widespread than during the Vietnam War because of a dearth of elite opposition to Bush's invasion, the absence of conscription shanghaiing unwilling young middle-class people to fight the war, and later, the war's financing by deficit spending rather than higher taxes.

Analogous to Bush's warlike policy toward Iraq would be if the United States, after the Japanese struck Pearl Harbor, invaded Thailand, while putting a lower priority on defeating Japan. Only in the Iraq case, Bush's invasion was worse than this hypothetical example because he doubled down on the policy that had caused the 9/11 terrorist attacks in the first place—non-Muslim U.S. military forces stationed or fighting on Islamic soil. Predictably, the U.S. invasion of Iraq caused a spike in terrorist attacks in that country against U.S. occupation forces and later around the world.

Why the younger Bush really targeted Saddam is still the subject of debate. Saddam had already been neutralized as an offensive threat in the Persian Gulf by the heavy destruction his military took in the first Gulf War, to say nothing of the incessant air strikes that followed under Clinton along with what was effectively a stringent blockade of needed goods causing widespread deaths. In fact, after that war, Iran became a bigger threat to Gulf oil than Saddam's Iraq. And Bush did not need a "demonstration effect" of U.S. toughness after the 9/11 attacks because he had just invaded Afghanistan in retaliation for them.

Personally, the younger Bush's intense desire for more war could have been in part because he believed Saddam had tried to kill his father, mother, and wife when the elder Bush traveled to the Persian Gulf in 1993 on a first Gulf War victory lap after he left office. He had asserted that Saddam had "tried to kill my dad."[18] That Saddam was behind the foiled assassination attempt, however, is disputed. Another possible explanation is that he wanted to one up what his un-reelected "wimp" father had failed to do—topple the dictator from power.

It is arguable, however, how much W's comments had to do with the actual formulation of U.S. policy. More generally, for decades, U.S. policy in the Middle East has revolved around three main pillars—ardent support for Israel continuing to acquire and incorporate more Arab land, controlling the region's oil supplies, and feeding the MICC at home with ever more lucrative defense contracts. These pillars all have domestic roots. First, W's administration, laden with neoconservatives, had no problem going to war to support the strong Zionist lobby in Washington,[19] which included evangelical Christian organizations whose beliefs about the holy land featured Jewish rebuilding of their Temple on the site of the Al Aqsa mosque and the second coming of Christ. The Republican Party was becoming increasingly dependent for political support and funding from both of these interest groups.[20] Notably, neo-conservatives Paul Wolfowitz, deputy secretary of defense, and Douglas Feith, also a political appointee at the Pentagon, were the two main drivers of the invasion at the working level, promoting the military aggression that clearly took out one of Israel's major adversaries. As Jeffrey Sachs, in a recent address to the Council of Europe, put it: "That war was directly concocted by Netanyahu and his colleagues in the U.S. Pentagon. I'm not saying that it was a link or mutuality. I'm saying it was a war carried out for Israel. It was a war that Paul Wolfowitz and Douglas Feith coordinated with Netanyahu."[21]

Second, as for oil being the driver to war, as earlier noted, the idea of oil insecurity being a serious concern for the U.S. government was always fallacious and even more so after the fracking boom in the United States. Furthermore, had the U.S. needed oil, it could simply have purchased it. The invasion, in part, may have been to gain U.S. or Western control of the huge oil reserves in the country. Also contributing to the illegal aggression against Iraq might have been a U.S. desire to shore up the petrodollar, which required countries to hold dollar reserves to purchase oil. Indeed, Saddam's threat to sideline that requirement via an oil bourse may have contributed to a desire for his demise.

Third, once again, the interests of the MICC undoubtedly played a part. After the Cold War ended, the post 9/11 Great War on Terror had not required the use of heavy weapons of conventional war, and an excuse was needed to continue to spend dollars on those more costly systems, which could be justified only by invading countries with large conventional forces—read Iraq and maybe even Iran.

The Dishonest Road to War

By mid-2002, the chief of British intelligence concluded that the Bush administration had decided on war (which would not start till March 2003) and that the intelligence on Iraqi involvement with terrorism and weapons of mass destruction was being tailored around the desired policy rather than the reverse.[22] Political Scientist David A. Lake concluded: "There is no doubt that the Bush administration disregarded evidence suggesting that Iraq's WMD programs were either dismantled or significantly inhibited over the 1990s and used intelligence not to guide policy but to market it."[23] The Bush administration did not want to hear any evidence contradictory to its case for war. Cheney and Rumsfeld tried to intimidate U.S. intelligence agencies with a personal visit by Cheney to the CIA and by setting up a competing ad hoc intelligence agency, the Office of Special Plans in the Pentagon directed by neoconservative Abram Schulsky, a scholarly expert in the works of the political philosopher Leo Strauss, to review "stove-piped" preferred intelligence on Iraq. Few outside experts on Iraq or the Middle East from academia or private organizations were consulted before the invasion. The CIA succumbed to the pressure and tailored intelligence reports to the policy preferences of

Bush and his senior officials, even though key CIA analysts doubted that Saddam had weapons of mass destruction.

One example of the administration manipulating intelligence relates to a justification for war: Iraq's alleged reconstitution of its WMD programs. The CIA sent Ambassador Joe Wilson—whose wife, Valerie Plame, was a covert operative for the agency—on a mission to check out the claim that Saddam was trying to buy uranium from Niger. He found no evidence to support the accusation. The administration kept using the claim nonetheless, ignoring three different negative reports on the Iraq-Niger connection, and continued to manipulate intelligence to exaggerate the threat from Iraq. After the U.S. invasion, Wilson wrote an op-ed in the *New York Times* exposing the Bush deception and asserting that the United States had gone to war on false pretenses. In retaliation, the Republican administration—which had implied that anyone who opposed the war was unpatriotic—violated the law by exposing Valerie Plame as a CIA covert asset, thus endangering her life.[24]

"Scooter" Libby, Cheney's chief of staff, was found to have lied to the FBI in the case. Bush and Cheney parted ways because Cheney campaigned relentlessly for a presidential pardon for the convicted Libby while Bush suspected Libby took the fall to protect Cheney. Bush refused a pardon but commuted Libby's prison sentence. Republican President Donald Trump later pardoned Libby.

Although secondary to implicitly and falsely linking Saddam to Al Qaeda terrorism and 9/11, according to Gershkoff and Kushner Gadarian, Bush tried another justification for war: since Iraq still had WMD, Saddam could *give them* to terrorists.[25] Yet scholars continue to disagree on the main cause of the war. As David A. Lake notes,

"The issue in dispute between the United States and Iraq is not obvious to scholars, and perhaps not even to political leaders on either side. Although Iraq's supposed WMD programs were the casus belli, they were the precipitant, not the underlying issue, and are better thought of as one source of bargaining failure."[26]

The United Nations and agencies of the U.S. intelligence community, except for the State Department's Bureau of Intelligence and Research, believed that Saddam would do, and was capable of doing, anything to get WMDs—nuclear, biological, or chemical weapons—despite that all his unconventional weapons programs had been dismantled after he lost the Persian Gulf War in 1991. Moreover, comprehensive worldwide

UN economic sanctions had been imposed to prevent him from getting materials and technology needed to reconstitute them. In fact, because of the intense scrutiny of the international community after the first war, Saddam had decided to lay low and not resume those programs until the international heat was off him. However, he did not reveal this decision to the world, because he did not want to ruin his deterrence vis-à-vis Iran, his next-door neighbor and mortal enemy, or internal enemies; he erroneously believed they were all a bigger threat to him than was the United States.[27]

Iraq had admitted the UN weapons inspectors in 2002, but Bush had refused their request for more time to finish the most intrusive such inspection ever conducted—a suspicious refusal if Bush really wanted to find WMDs or even such unconventional weapons programs. In fact, shutting down the inspections before they were completed showed, even before the U.S. invasion, either that the Bush administration had already made up its mind that Iraq had those weapons or programs, or that this was not the reason for the invasion (the latter being most likely). Thus, while international inspectors reported that they had so far found no such weapons programs, this fact did not stop Bush's march to war.

Although the U.S. itself had given Saddam biological and chemical weapons for use against the Iranians, few people asked whether these weapons (almost no one thought that Saddam had nuclear weapons) were a threat to the United States. Even if Iraq had reconstituted its nuclear, biological, and chemical programs from their dismantled state after the first Gulf War, North Korea, Iran, and Libya were known to have more advanced programs that would have been more of a threat to the United States in 2003. Also, as with these other countries, it is an odd view that Saddam somehow would have been undeterred from using WMDs against American targets by the ability of the more powerful United States to obliterate Iraq.[28] Former Bush administration official Richard Haass later admitted that there was a "complete lack of evidence of any imminence of hostile attack by Iraq."[29]

Furthermore, Senator Bob Graham, then-Chairman of the Senate Intelligence Committee and skeptic of the need for another war with Iraq, had a summary of the intelligence community's findings declassified that destroyed this specific Bush administration rationale for war. The intelligence concluded that even if Saddam had biological or chemical weapons, he would be unlikely to initiate an attack with them against the

United States, but might take the extreme step of giving or selling them to terrorists only if the American military attacked Iraq and made him desperate—exactly what Bush was planning to do to purportedly take the weapons out.[30] (Developing WMDs is expensive and transmitting them to unpredictable terrorist groups could have gotten Saddam into conflict with the world's most powerful nation if traced back to Iraq, which, unlike the terrorists, had a home address.) Shockingly, the intelligence summary was a two-day news story that failed to create even a speed bump on the invasion road that Bush was traversing.

When no operational link had been found between Saddam, al-Qaeda, and the 9/11 attacks and no weapons of mass destruction were found in Iraq, the administration dragged out the laughable argument that a neocolonial superpower democratizing Iraq by force would compel other autocratic Middle Eastern nations to democratize too. Of course, this depended on postwar Iraq becoming a model democracy and either the rulers or ruled in other Middle Eastern autocratic nations—most of which had little experience with democracy—suddenly becoming enlightened by (or terrified into following) Iraq's precedent. The thinking became even more far-fetched when neoconservatives in the administration implausibly claimed that democratizing Iraq would create a path toward making Arab states less hostile to Israel, but which made many pro-Israel groups in the United States happy.

The Unexpected Outcome of Iraq War II

The dysfunctional democracy that resulted from the U.S. illegal aggression on Iraq was not a model for any country to emulate. Rather, Middle Eastern peoples and governments took note that democracy imposed from the top-down by a neocolonial superpower using force—which had violated international law and bypassed the UN Security Council—was a disaster.

Moreover, as with the Spanish-American War, the conventional war ended successfully but the lengthy counterinsurgency effort to pacify the country led to a quagmire. Although Saddam had killed hundreds of thousands of Iraqis in his more than a decade of rule, both U.S. wars against Iraq and its occupation after the second one also killed hundreds of thousands more.[31]

As in the Philippines after the successful Spanish-American War, a more lethal insurgency broke out against U.S. occupation forces in Iraq. Both Sunni and Shi'i insurgencies developed in Iraq to continue the fight against American occupation forces after U.S. troops had quickly overrun Saddam's already battered and depleted conventional forces. Before the U.S. invasion, Saddam had secretly passed out guns to Sunni fighters to enable such a long guerrilla war. As the U.S. military campaign against the insurgencies bogged down, as it had in the Philippines and Vietnam, support at home for the war eroded. The Sunni insurgency lasted many years until the United States gave it money and arms to change sides to fight a more violent spinoff of al-Qaeda in Iraq: ISIS. Shi'i militias, many funded and trained by Iran, finally tamped down their violence when the Sunni groups turned their violence from them to ISIS, which the Shiite groups also hated.

The abysmal squandering of U.S. resources, both in lives and the staggering sums of money that poured into Iraq from 2003 to 2011 during the botched U.S. occupation, shows why George H. W. Bush had wisely refrained earlier from going all the way to Baghdad to remove Saddam from power during the first Gulf War. The younger Bush might have been better advised if he had taken Saddam's offer, made prior to the invasion through Egyptian ruler Hosni Mubarak's son, to go into exile if allowed to take a pile of cash with him. But Bush wanted a war of conquest; in fact, one of Bush's greatest fears was that Saddam would concede before the U.S. military got there.[32]

With Saddam's army smashed and stupidly decommissioned by the United States after the invasion, the main counterweight to Iran had been removed from the Gulf region—another reason George H. W. Bush did not go to Baghdad in 1991. Predictably, even before U.S. troops withdrew in 2011, Iran had more influence in Iraq than did the United States. With the demise of Iraq, Iran became the four-hundred-pound gorilla in the region. Finally, the younger Bush had to follow the alleged Pottery Barn rule: the United States broke Iraq and then had to buy it (and fix it).

Fortunately for the younger Bush, Iraq did not turn into the quagmire it eventually would become until after his reelection in 2004. He improved on his popular vote loss to Al Gore in 2000 by beating John Kerry, albeit with the narrowest popular vote margin (50.7 percent to 48.3 percent) of any re-elected president since Woodrow Wilson in 1916.[33] After a few years the Iraq War became very unpopular—as military quagmires usually do—in the United States and around the world. The Republicans lost control of both houses of Congress in the 2006 election because of public disillusionment with the war.

As yet another demonstration of the imperial presidency, Bush doubled down with a thirty-thousand-troop surge, a new strategy, and a new general to implement it. General David Petraeus did reduce the violence in Iraq for a time so the United States could claim victory, but it had little to do with the surge or new strategy. By 2006, here were the main factors reducing the carnage: (1) the United States bribed Sunni insurgents to switch sides from fighting U.S. forces and Shi'i militias to fighting al-Qaeda in Iraq (which would later become ISIS), (2) militant Shi'i militias, not facing as much violence from Sunnis in the civil war, unilaterally instituted a ceasefire with U.S. troops and converted to electoral politics, and (3) the violence between the Sunni, Shi'a, and Kurds decreased because mixed neighborhoods sadly had been ethnically cleansed into homogeneous enclaves in which there was less sectarian/ethnic contact. Yet the desired power sharing between the ethno-sectarian groups never materialized.[34]

In 2007, the House and Senate added a rider to war appropriation that required the administration to withdraw troops by 2008. Although Bush vetoed the bill, it spooked his White House into producing a timetable for U.S. withdrawal by 2011. The U.S. counterinsurgency quagmire continued until Barack Obama, Bush's successor, implemented his predecessor's schedule to withdraw U.S. forces in 2011.

After that, ISIS—originally created to oppose the U.S. invasion and now separated from al-Qaeda—swept across a third of Iraq and a large chunk of Syria. Many of the Sunni fighters, whom the United States bribed in 2006 to switch sides to reduce violence, had been told that they would be part of the Shi'i dominated Iraqi security forces, but this promise went unmet. They then switched sides again and fought for ISIS. Obama sent back a smaller U.S. force into Iraq and Syria to battle the group in conjunction with Kurds and Iranian-backed Shi'i militias. President Donald Trump completed the mopping-up operations. However, Iraq remains far from a stable democracy, with Iran-backed Shi'i militias still attacking remaining U.S. forces in the area and later, after October 7, 2023, attacking Israel.

Of course, the lesson learned by the ever-interventionist U.S. foreign policy community was that Obama, after an eight-year war, left Iraq too soon in 2011—not that the real mistake was invading Iraq in the first place, thus creating insurgencies by Sunni groups, Iranian-backed Shi'i groups, and the vicious ISIS regional terrorist group.

The Vietnam War, the invasion and occupation of Iraq, and the even longer war in Afghanistan proved that once the U.S. government and military get into brushfire wars, it is difficult to get out. No president, member of Congress, or senior military officer wants responsibility for losing a war, so on they go, as guarding the national honor—really, saving personal careers—becomes paramount. Because U.S. military interventions, if they do not go well, are so tough to leave, plans should be developed to exit prior to entry. Better yet, more care should be taken before sending the nation to war in the first place. That prudent caution has not been exercised after World War II, and especially since the Cold War.

Of recent major U.S. wars, George H. W. Bush's first Gulf War was probably the most significant. The war itself was unnecessary and counterproductive. It led instead—indirectly at times—to the 9/11 attacks and the twenty-year U.S. war in Afghanistan in retaliation. It also led more directly to a second Iraq war of invasion and occupation to finish the job of neutralizing an already weak Iraqi dictator. The public backlash against the quagmires of the Afghan War and the second Iraq War was a factor in Donald Trump's election.

The entire string of U.S. interventions from the 1980s to 2021 showed that once unleashed, wars lead to more wars, civil wars, and revolutions. Oil and the interests of Israel have been at the bottom of most of these wars in the Greater Middle East. As far as oil goes, economic analysis shows that instead of using expensive U.S. military power to secure petroleum supplies at inexpensive prices, the world oil market alone will best supply oil at the cheapest possible cost. The use of U.S. military power only leads to war and thus oil price spikes through constricted supply. Thus, future U.S. military interventions in the Greater Middle East should generate strong public opposition. And if they are clearly on behalf of Israel, they should create the same resistance.

CONCLUSION

CONCLUSION

A MORE RESTRAINED U.S. STRATEGY FOR A MULTIPOLAR WORLD

In his book, *The Rise and Fall of the Great Powers*, historian Paul Kennedy concluded that historically, great powers have declined because they spent more on military interventionism at the expense of their economies—what he dubbed imperial overstretch. He warned that this could happen to America too.[1] Like Kennedy, this author would argue that this has been happening with the United States since 1970. Moreover, the rapid Chinese economic growth since the 1980s, combined with its more restrained defense spending and less foreign interventionism than practiced by the United States, has allowed China to become a formidable economic competitor to America on the world stage.

However, U.S. defense spending will continue at ever higher levels to counter new inflated threats, such as an exaggerated military threat from China, and excessive U.S. military interventions will likely continue to suck U.S. taxpayers dry.

If instead, U.S. leaders could overcome the inertia of the non-traditional U.S. foreign and defense policies adopted since World War II, changing back to more traditional restrained policies, the resources saved could be plowed back into the American economy. This would clip the wings of U.S. interventionism and would ensure that America would remain a great power for the indefinite future.

A more restrained U.S. foreign policy would reduce the areas of U.S. vital interest to what they were before World War II made American leaders rulers of the world. Those areas would be the Western Hemisphere (especially the Caribbean and Central America) and the western Atlantic and eastern Pacific maritime approaches to the United States. The United States could use as a permanent model what President Franklin D. Roosevelt envisioned for an interim realist arrangement between great powers to manage the post-war world. He called it the Four Policemen concept, with the victors of World War II—United States, Russia, Britain and China—dividing the world into clearly defined spheres of influence for policing, thus reducing great power conflict and enhancing their cooperation.

The concept could be brought up to date by adding at least Germany, Japan, and India to the UN Security Council. The worldwide spheres of influence, in addition to the one just mentioned for the United States, would entail: Britain / the European Union could manage European security; Russia could manage Central Asian security; China and Japan could divide up East Asian spheres of influence; India could manage South Asia; and the resources of the Middle East and Africa could be governed principally by the free market, backed up by collective great power action only in dire circumstances. Because the spheres of influence would be clearly delineated and agreed to in advance, less friction should occur between great powers, reducing the chances of major wars and even nuclear conflict. The UN Security Council could peacefully resolve any minor boundary issues concerning great powers' spheres. Any major aggression by one great power into another's sphere would be obvious and should result in a united push back on that country by the other great powers. Finally, the Security Council could deal with transnational issues, such as air and sea transportation, seabed resource rights, climate change, water management, and other environmental problems.

Great powers go out of their way to insist rhetorically that spheres of influence are "so yesterday." Yet they behave as if they do have them—and have had them for centuries in international politics. A realist might argue that the spheres should be openly acknowledged and managed. Perhaps, under the new Trump administration, this is already in train, with its rapprochement to Russia and Secretary of State Marco Rubio's admission of the present existence of a multipolar world.

Since World War II, the United States has sought to advance its unacknowledged claim to police the entire world. But if one thinks hard about the role of the United States as global policeman, it is absurd to believe that such grand policing can be done competently—it hasn't been—or to think it is even needed for the well-being of an intrinsically secure United States distant from the world's primary conflict zones.

One sure way to reduce—and maybe even eliminate—great power wars is to adopt and modernize FDR's Four Policemen concept to manage the world but drop the name. After all, great powers might soon realize (no guarantees) that they can get more by managing their spheres of influence with "sugar rather than vinegar"—as the United States found during the 1930s when Herbert Hoover and FDR adopted the "Good Neighbor" policy toward Latin America. Rather than "spheres of influence," FDR liked the term "spheres of [great power] responsibility." That term best encapsulates the idealistic end goal of this realist proposal to dampen major wars around the globe. Indeed, the extraordinary lethality and costliness of modern militaries should convince thoughtful policymakers that there is little other choice.

ABOUT THE AUTHOR

IVAN R. ELAND is a Senior Fellow at the Independent Institute and Director of the Independent Institute's Center on Peace & Liberty. Dr. Eland is a graduate of Iowa State University and received an MBA in applied economics and a PhD in public policy from George Washington University.

He was previously Director of Defense Policy Studies at the Cato Institute, and he spent sixteen years working for Congress on national security issues, including stints as an investigator for the House Foreign Affairs Committee and as a Principal Defense Analyst at the Congressional Budget Office. He also has served as Evaluator-in-Charge (national security, intelligence, and international commerce) for the U.S. General Accounting Office (now the Government Accountability Office). He has testified on the military and financial aspects of NATO expansion before the Senate Foreign Relations Committee, on CIA oversight before the House Government Reform Committee, and on the creation of the Department of Homeland Security before the Senate Judiciary Committee. He was awarded a medal by the president of Italy for his work on international affairs.

Dr. Eland is the author of many books, including the forthcoming *U.S. Defense Policy in a New Multipolar World: Less Military Intervention Brings More Security with Fewer Costs*. Some of his eight previously published books have won publishing awards. He is a contributor to numerous other books and the author of forty-five in-depth studies on national security issues.

His articles have appeared in *American Prospect, Arms Control Today, Bulletin of the Atomic Scientists, Emory Law Journal, The Independent Review, Issues in Science and Technology (National Academy of Sciences), Mediterranean Quarterly, Middle East and International Review, Middle East Policy, Nexus, Chronicle of Higher Education, American Conservative, International Journal of World Peace, The National Interest,* and *Northwestern Journal of International Affairs.*

Dr. Eland's popular writings have appeared in such publications as the *Los Angeles Times, San Francisco Chronicle, USA Today, Houston Chronicle, Dallas Morning News, New York Times, Chicago Sun-Times, San Diego Union-Tribune, Miami Herald, St. Louis Post-Dispatch, Newsday, Sacramento Bee, Orange County Register, Washington Times, Providence Journal, The Hill, Daily Caller, Inside Sources, DC Journal, Responsible Statecraft, The Tribune News Service,* and *Defense News.*

He has appeared on ABC's *World News Tonight,* NPR's *Talk of the Nation,* PBS, Fox News Channel, CNBC, Bloomberg TV, CNN, CNN-fn, C-SPAN, MSNBC, Canadian Broadcasting Corp. (CBC), Canadian TV (CTV), Radio Free Europe, Voice of America, BBC, TRT World, CGTN, RT, Asharq TV, Al Arabiya, al Ghad, al Qahera, RTVi, and other local, national, and international TV and radio programs.

ENDNOTES

CHAPTER 1

1 Melvin Small, *Democracy and Diplomacy: The Impact of Domestic Politics on US Foreign Policy, 1789–1994* (Baltimore and London: Johns Hopkins University Press, 195), xviii.

2 Bruce Bueno de Mesquita and Alastair Smith, *The Spoils of War: Greed, Power, and the Conflicts that Made Our Greatest Presidents* (New York: PublicAffairs, 2016), 232–234, 238.

3 Bruce Bueno de Mesquita, "Domestic Politics and International Relations," *International Studies Quarterly* 46, no. 1 (2002): 1–9.

4 Melvin Small, *Was War Necessary?: National Security and US Entry into War* (Beverly Hills, California: Sage Publications, 1980), 14–15, 16–17.

5 Small, *Was War Necessary?* 17, 23–24.

6 Stephen Berry, "The Future of Civil War Era Studies," *Journal of the Civil War Era* 2, no. 1 (March 2012).

7 Melvin Small, *At the Water's Edge: American Politics and the Vietnam War* (Chicago: Ivan R. Dee, 2006), ix.

8 Alastair Smith, "Diversionary Foreign Policy in Democratic Systems," *International Studies Quarterly* 40, no. 1 (March 1996): 134–135.

9 Melvin Small, "The Domestic Side of Foreign Policy," *OAH Magazine of History* 8, no. 3 (Spring 1994): 15.

CHAPTER 2

1 Gregory E. Fehlings, "America's First Limited War," *Naval War College Review* 53, no. 3 (Summer 2000): 132.

2 Tom Schachtman, *How the French Saved America: Soldiers, Sailors, Diplomats, Louis XVI, and the Success of a Revolution* (New York: St. Martin's Press, 2017), 288–289.

3 William Stinchcombe, "Talleyrand and the American Negotiations of 1797–1798," *The Journal of American History* 62, no. 3 (December 1975): 575.

4 Melvin Small, *Democracy and Diplomacy: The Impact of Domestic Politics on US Foreign Policy, 1789–1994* (Baltimore and London: Johns Hopkins University Press, 1995), 7.

5 David J. Barron, *Waging War: The Clash Between Presidents and Congress, 1776 to ISIS* (New York: Simon and Schuster, 2016), 40–45.

6 Robert Scigliano, "Politics, the Constitution, and the President's War Power," in *The New Politics of American Foreign Policy* ed. David A. Deese (New York: St. Martin's Press, 1994): 151.

7 Fehlings, "America's First Limited War," 101.

8 Barron, *Waging War*, 37–38, 52, 99.

9 The Constitutional Convention changed the draft document from "the Congress shall make war" to "the Congress shall declare war," with the record clearing showing that this wording change was designed to give the executive, as commander in chief, some liberty of action only in a situation of emergency national self-defense. Especially since 1950 in the Korean War, however, presidents have flagrantly abused their authority as commander in chief, which was designed by the founders to be narrowly construed as merely commander of US forces on the battlefield after Congress had initiated any war. It was the military equivalent of the president executing domestic laws passed by Congress. At present, chief executives regularly claim that they have the authority as commander in chief, without needing congressional approval, to deploy troops anywhere in the world, to initiate hostilities—whether for the defense of US forces abroad or to attack other nations—and to decide when they'll withdrawal forces. This claim of extraconstitutional power is a gross perversion of the founders' anti-militaristic vision of setting up a governmental checks and balances system that would slow the march toward war by taking the decision out of the hands of one person and putting into the hands of numerous representatives of the American people. Even Alexander Hamilton, the greatest advocate of executive power among the founders, wrote that "it is the peculiar and exclusive province of Congress, *when the nation is at peace*, to change that state into a state of war." Also, Hamilton wrote that the chief executive's authority "would amount to no more than the supreme command and direction of the military and naval forces, as first General and Admiral of the Confederacy; while that of the British king extends to the *declaring* of war." Alexander Hamilton, "The Federalist No. 69," in Alexander Hamilton, James Madison, and John Jay, *The Federalist: A Commentary on the Constitution of the United States* (New York: Modern Library, 1937), 448 (emphasis in the original). Finally, Hamilton commented that in a delicate case, "one which involves so important a consequence as that of war—my opinion is that no doubtful authority ought to be exercised by the President." Letter from Alexander Hamilton to James McHenry, May 17, 1798, in Henry C. Syrett, ed., *The Papers of Alexander Hamilton* , vol. 21 (New York: Columbia University Press, 1974), 462. Robert Scigliano, a professor of American Politics at Boston College, noted that he doesn't know of any early American who ever suggested that the Constitution gave the president the power to make war. Robert Scigliano, "Politics, the Constitution, and the President's War Power," *The New Politics of American Foreign Policy*, ed. David Deese (New York: St. Martin's Press, 1994) 149.

10 Fehlings, "America's First Limited War," 110–111.

11 Peter P. Hill, "Prologue to the Quasi-War: Stresses in Franco-American Commercial Relations, 1793–1796," *The Journal of Modern History* 49, no. 1 (1977): D1041, D1046–D1049, D1058–D1059; Fehlings, "America's First Limited War," 107–108.

12 Tom Shachtman, *The Founding Fortunes: How the Wealthy Paid for and Profited from America's Revolution* (New York: St. Martin's Press, 2020), 232.

13 Hill, "Prologue to the Quasi-War": D1057–D1058.

14 Stinchcombe, "Talleyrand and the American Negotiations," 576–577, 581, 588.

15 Lance Banning, "John Adams, 1797–1800," in *Presidential Misconduct: From George Washington to Today*, ed. James M. Banner (New York: The New Press, 2019), 22–23.

16 Shachtman, *The Founding Fortunes*, 234.

17 Fehlings, "America's First Limited War," 126. In the 1804 case *Little v. Barreme*, the Supreme Court ruled that, in the Quasi-War, the executive had ordered military action that exceeded the authority given him by Congress. Congress had authorized US vessels to intercept ships going to French ports, so the court frowned on Adam's executive order ordering their interception going both to and from those ports.

18 Fehlings, "America's First Limited War," 101, 106, 110–111, 114–115, 124–125.

19 Small, *Democracy and Diplomacy*, 7; Barron, *Waging War*, 55.

20 Shachtman, *The Founding Fortunes*, 239; Small, *Democracy and Diplomacy*, 8.

21 Banning, "John Adams, 1797–1800," 23–26.

22 Fehlings, 117–118, 129–130.

23 Shachtman, 220.

24 Michael Kitzen, "Money Bags or Cannonballs: The Origins of the Tripolitan War, 1795–1801," *Journal of the Early Republic* 16, no.4 (Winter 1996): 602–603.

25 Shachtman, 222, 233.

26 Kitzen, "Money Bags or Cannonballs," 612.

27 Kola Folayan, "The 'Tripolitan War': A Reconsideration of the Causes," *Africa: Revista Trimestrale di Studi e Documentazione dell'Istituto Italiano pe l'Africa e l'Oriente* 27, no. 1 (Marzo 1972): 617–624.

28 Kitzen, "Money Bags or Cannonballs," 623.

29 Kitzen, 617, 624.

30 Robert McColley, "Review: *Empire of Liberty: The Statecraft of Thomas Jefferson* by Robert W. Tucker and David C. Hendrickson," *Georgia Historical Society* 75, no. 2, Religion and Society in Georgia and the South (Summer 1991): 426.

31 Scigliano, "The President's War Power," 160.

32 Shachtman, *The Founding Fortunes*, 253–254.

33 Scigliano, 160.

34 Shachtman, 254.

35 Scigliano, 151.

CHAPTER 3

1 Michael Beschloss, *Presidents of War: The Epic Story, From 1807 to Modern Times* (New York: Broadway Books, 2018), viii, 4–5.

2 Quoted in Beschloss, 93.

3 Daniel A. Sjursen, *A True History of the United States: Indigenous Genocide, Racialized Slavery, Hyper-Capitalism, Militarist Imperialism, and Other Overlooked Aspects of American Exceptionalism* (Lebanon, New Hampshire: Steerforth Press, 2021), 135.

4 Tom Shachtman, *The Founding Fortunes: How the Wealthy Paid for and Profited from America's Revolution* (New York: St. Martin's Press, 2020), 262, 264, 268, 279–280.

5 J. C. A Stagg, "James Madison and the Malcontents: The Political Origins of the War of 1812," *William and Mary Quarterly* 33, no. 4 (October 1976): 564.

6 Melvin Small, *Was War Necessary?: National Security and US Entry into War* (Beverly Hills, CA: Sage Publications, 1980), 33–34, 44–45, 47, 56–57.

7 Stagg, "James Madison," 557–558.

8　Small, *Was War Necessary?*, 39–40, 71.

9　Shachtman, *The Founding Fortunes*, 266.

10　Andrew J. B. Fagal, "American Arms Manufacturing and the Onset of the War of 1812," *New England Quarterly* 87, no. 3 (September 2014), 533.

11　Beschloss, *Presidents of War*, 19.

12　Shachtman, *The Founding Fortunes*, 268–269.

13　Small, *Was War Necessary?*, 33.

14　Richard W. Maass, *The Picky Eagle: How Democracy and Xenophobia Limited US Territorial Expansion* (Ithaca, New York: Cornell University Press, 2020), 92.

15　Small, *Was War Necessary?*, 47, 52–56.

16　Small, *Democracy and Diplomacy*, 10–11.

17　Small, *Was War Necessary?*. 42, 65.

18　Bueno de Mesquita and Smith, *The Spoils of War*, 65–66.

19　Small, *Democracy and Diplomacy*, 11; Small, *Was War Necessary?*, 58.

20　Beschloss, *Presidents of War*, 62–63.

21　Bueno de Mesquita and Smith, *The Spoils of War*, 68–73.

22　Bueno de Mesquita and Smith, 63–64.

23　David J. Barron, *Waging War: The Clash Between Presidents and Congress, 1776 to ISIS* (New York: Simon and Schuster, 2016), 86.

24　Ronald Hatzenbuehler, "The War Hawks and the Question of Congressional Leadership," *Pacific Historical Review* 45, no. 1 (February 1976): 2–3, 6–7.

25　Small, *Was War Necessary?*, 59–60.

26　Shachtman, *The Founding Fortunes*, 284–285.

27　Bueno de Mesquita and Smith, *The Spoils of War*, 59–60.

28　Beschloss, *Presidents of War*, 55–56.

29　Julius Pratt, *Expansionists of 1812* (New York: The Macmillan Company, 1925), 12–13; Lawrence B. A. Hatter, "Party Like It's 1812: The War at 200," *Tennessee Historical Quarterly* 71, no. 2 (Summer 2012): 95–96.

30　James M. Banner, "Thomas Jefferson, 1801–1809," *Presidential Misconduct: From George Washington to Today*, ed. James M. Banner (New York: The New Press, 2019): 35–37; Robert Scigliano, "Politics, the Constitution, and the President's War Power," in *The New Politics of American Foreign Policy*, ed. David A. Deese (New York: St. Martin's Press, 1994), 151; and Hatzenbuehler, "War hawks," 19.

31　Small, *Democracy and Diplomacy*, 9.

32　Tom Shachtman, *How the French Saved America: Soldiers, Sailors, Diplomats, Louis XVI, and the Success of a Revolution* (New York: St. Martin's Press, 2017), 119, 122.

33　Sjursen, *True History*, 132.

34　Reginald Horsman, "On to Canada: Manifest Destiny and the United States Strategy in the War of 1812," *Michigan Historical Review* 13, no. 2 (Fall 1987): 8, 15, 20.

35　Beschloss, *Presidents of War*, 44–47, 53–54.

36　Both men quoted in Bueno de Mesquita and Smith, *The Spoils of War*, 80.

37　Barron, *Waging War*, 86–87.

38　Bueno de Mesquita and Smith, 72–74.

39　Sydney Howard Gay, *James Madison* (New York: Houghton Mifflin, 1898), 297–298.

40　Roger H. Brown, *The Republic in Peril: 1812* (New York: W.W. Norton,

1964), 44–46.

    41 Beschloss, *Presidents of War*, 5; Hatzenbuehler, "War Hawks," 2, 21–22; Stagg, "James Madison," 583–584.

    42 Stagg, 560–561.

    43 Ronald L. Hatzenbuehler and Robert L. Ivie, "Justifying the War of 1812: Toward a Model of Congressional Behavior in Early War Crises," *Social Science History* no. 4 (Autumn 1980): 464, 473–475.

    44 Barron, *Waging War*, 85.

    45 Small, *Was War Necessary?*, 61.

    46 Shachtman, *The Founding Fortunes*, 285.

    47 Barron, 87.

    48 Beschloss, *Presidents of War*, 57–58.

    49 Barron, 83–84.

    50 Beschloss, 54–55, 61.

    51 Bueno de Mesquita and Smith, *The Spoils of War*, 82–84.

    52 Beschloss, 60–62.

    53 Shachtman, *The Founding Fortunes*, 287–288.

    54 Hatter, "Party Like It's 1812," 102–103.

    55 Bueno de Mesquita and Smith, *The Spoils of War*, 87–88.

    56 Beschloss, *Presidents of War*, 89–91.

    57 Beschloss, 3–4, 79.

    58 Barron, *Waging War*, 94–97.

    59 Barron, 84.

    60 Barron, 89–90.

    61 Bueno de Mesquita and Smith, *The Spoils of War*, 85–86.

    62 Shachtman, *The Founding Fortunes*, 277–278.

    63 Mayhew, "Wars and American Politics," 475–476.

CHAPTER 4

    1 Melvin Small, *Was War Necessary?; National Security and US Entry into War* (Beverly Hills, CA: Sage Publications, 1980), 76, 107, 111.

    2 Norman A. Graebner, "The Mexican War: A Study in Causation," *Pacific Historical Review* 49, no. 3 (August 1980): 405, 407, 411–412, 416–417, 419–420.

    3 H. W. Brands, *Dreams of El Dorado: A History of the American West* (New York: Basic Books, 2019), 96–97, 99–100.

    4 Daniel A. Sjursen, *A True History of the United States: Indigenous Genocide, Racialized Slavery, Hyper-Capitalism, Militarist Imperialism, and Other Overlooked Aspects of American Exceptionalism* (Lebanon, New Hampshire: Steerforth Press, 2021), 173–177.

    5 Bryan Burrough, Chris Tomlinson, and Jason Stanford, *Forget the Alamo: The Rise and Fall of an American Myth* (New York: Penguin Press, 2021), 3–4.

    6 Carrie Gibson, *El Norte: The Epic and Forgotten Story of Hispanic North America* (New York: Atlantic Monthly Press, 2019), 191–200.

    7 Brands, *Dreams of El Dorado*, 105–107, 129–130.

    8 Small, *Was War Necessary?*, 103–104.

    9 Melvin Small, *Democracy and Diplomacy: The Impact of Domestic Politics on US Foreign Policy, 1789–1994* (Baltimore: Johns Hopkins University Press, 1995), 16–17.

10 Richard W. Maass, *The Picky Eagle: How Democracy and Xenophobia Limited US Territorial Expansion* (Ithaca, New York: Cornell University Press, 2020), 132.

11 Small, *Was War Necessary?*, 87–88.

12 Graebner, "The Mexican War," 414.

13 Sjursen, *True History*, 177.

14 Gibson, *El Norte*, 206.

15 Small, *Was War Necessary?*, 76.

16 Peter T. Harstad and Richard W. Resh, "The Causes of the Mexican War: A Note on Changing Interpretations," *Arizona and the West* 6, no. 4 (Winter 1964): 290, 297, 299–301.

17 Maass, *The Picky Eagle*, 137.

18 Robert W. Johannsen, "America's Forgotten War," *Wilson Quarterly* 20, no. 2 (Spring 1996): 98; Small, *Was War Necessary?*, 84.

19 Michael Beschloss, *Presidents of War: The Epic Story, From 1807 to Modern Times* (New York: Broadway Books, 2018), 108–109.

20 Graebner, 410–412, 419.

21 Small, *Was War Necessary?*, 92–96.

22 Johannsen, "America's Forgotten War," 97.

23 Gibson, *El Norte*, 186.

24 Small, *Was War Necessary?*, 91; Graebner, "The Mexican War," 420.

25 H. W. Brands, *The Man Who Saved the Union: Ulysses Grant in War and Peace* (New York: Anchor Books, 2012), 21; Brands, *Dreams of El Dorado*, 222–223.

26 Graebner, "The Mexican War," 422.

27 Johannsen, "America's Forgotten War," 96.

28 Maass, *The Picky Eagle*, 133.

29 Nicholas Lawrence, "'This Boa-Constrictor Appetite of Swallowing States and Provinces': Anti-Imperialist Opposition to the US/Mexican Review," *South Central Review* 30, no. 1 (Spring 2013): 59.

30 Beschloss, *Presidents of War*, 115–116.

31 Small, *Was War Necessary?*, 97–98.

32 Robert Scigliano, "Politics, the Constitution, and the President's War Power," in *The New Politics of American Foreign Policy*, ed. David A. Deese (New York: St. Martin's Press, 1994), 151.

33 Beschloss, *Presidents of War*, 119–120.

34 Small, *Was War Necessary?*, 92.

35 Lawrence, "'This Boa-Constrictor Appetite,'" 78.

36 Lawrence, 58.

37 Quoted in Small, *Democracy and Diplomacy*, 17–18.

38 Lawrence, 58 (emphasis in original).

39 "The Mexican War Speech of Mr. Corwin of Ohio," *Congressional Globe*, Senate, 29th Congress, 2nd Session, 11 February 1847, in *A Century of Lawmaking for a New Nation: US Congressional Documents and Debates, 1774–1875*, Library of Congress, 211 (emphasis in original).

40 Sjursen, *True History*, 180–181.

41 Brands, *The Man Who Saved the Union*, 33, 40.

42 Lawrence, "'This Boa-Constrictor Appetite,'" 78.

43 Small, *Was War Necessary?*, 99–100.

44 Quoted in Small, *Democracy and Diplomacy*, 17–18.

45 Quoted in Gibson, *El Norte*, 214.

46 David J. Barron, *Waging War: The Clash Between Presidents and Congress 1776 to ISIS* (New York: Simon and Schuster, 2016), 102–103.

47 Lawrence, 58.

48 Clayton C. Kohl, *Claims as a Cause of the Mexican War* (New York: New York University Press, 1914), 77–79; Graebner, "Mexican War": 408–420.

49 Maass, *The Picky Eagle*, 134–135.

50 Small, *Democracy and Diplomacy*, 16.

51 Small, *Was War Necessary?*, 84–86.

52 Maass, 104–107.

53 Johannsen, "America's Forgotten War," 96.

54 Maass, 137–144; Gibson, *El Norte*, 214–215.

55 Sjursen, *True History*, 186–187, 250–251.

56 Small, *Was War Necessary?*, 108–109.

57 Graebner, "The Mexican War," 424–425.

58 Brands, *Who Saved the Union*, 41.

CHAPTER 5

1 Heather Cox Richardson, *How the South Won the Civil War: Oligarchy, Democracy, and the Continuing Fight for the Soul of America* (New York: Oxford University Press, 2020), 43.

2 Drew Gilpin Faust, "'We Should Grow Too Fond of It': Why We Love the Civil War," *Civil War History* 50 (December 2004): 368–383.

3 Thomas J. DiLorenzo, *The Problem with Lincoln* (Washington, DC: Regnery History, 2020), 64–66.

4 Quoted in Dominic Erdozain, *One Nation Under Guns: How Gun Culture Distorts Our History and Threatens Our Democracy* (New York: Crown, 2024), 72.

5 Letter from Abraham Lincoln to Horace Greeley, August 22, 1862, in Abraham Lincoln, *The Collected Works of Abraham Lincoln*, ed. Roy Basler (New Brunswick, New Jersey: Rutgers University Press, 1953), vol. 5, 389.

6 Abraham Lincoln's to Horace Greeley, August 22, 1862, 389.

7 Quoted in Bruce Bueno de Mesquita and Alastair Smith, *The Spoils of War: Greed, Power, and the Conflicts that Made Our Greatest Presidents* (New York: PublicAffairs, 2016), 129–130.

8 Abraham Lincoln, First Inaugural Address, delivered March 4, 1861, accessed via https://avalon.law.yale.edu.

9 Frank Towers, "Partisans, New History, Modernization: The Historiography of the Civil War's Causes, 1861–2011," *Journal of the Civil War Era* 1, no. 2 (June 2011): 255.

10 Michael E. Woods, "What Twenty-First-Century Historians Have Said about the Causes of Disunion: A Civil War Sesquicentennial Review of the Recent Literature," *The Journal of American History* 99 (September 2012): 419.

11 Towers, "Partisans, New History, Modernization," 253.

12 Gerald Gunderson, "The Origin of the American Civil War," *The Journal of Economic History*, 34, no. 4 (December 1974): 926.

13 Woods, "The Causes of Disunion," 430.

14 James Oakes, *The Crooked Path to Abolition: Abraham Lincoln and the Antislavery Constitution* (New York: W. W. Norton and Company, 2021), xx–xxi, xxv.

15 Woods, "The Causes of Disunion," 421, 424.

16 DiLorenzo, *The Problem with Lincoln*, 12–14.

17 Daniel A. Sjursen, *A True History of the United States: Indigenous Genocide, Racialized Slavery, Hyper-Capitalism, Militarist Imperialism, and Other Overlooked Aspects of American Exceptionalism* (Lebanon, New Hampshire: Steerforth Press, 2021), 190–192.

18 Oakes, *Crooked Path*, xxi.

19 Gunderson, "The American Civil War," 919.

20 David J. Barron, *Waging War: The Clash Between Presidents and Congress: 1776 to ISIS* (New York: Simon and Schuster, 2016), 115.

21 Woods, "The Causes of Disunion," 428.

22 Bueno de Mesquita and Smith, *The Spoils of War*, 101–103, 120–121.

23 Doris Kearns Goodwin, *Team of Rivals: The Political Genius of Abraham Lincoln* (New York: Simon and Schuster, 2006), 296.

24 Sjursen, *True History*, 201.

25 Towers, "Partisans, New History, Modernization," 245.

26 Gunderson, "The American Civil War," 933–934.

27 US Constitution, article 4, section 3.

28 Bueno de Mesquita and Smith, *The Spoils of War*, 114–118, 120–122, 130; John Minor Botts, *The Great Rebellion: Its Secret History, Rise, Progress, and Disastrous Failure* (Charleston, SC: Nabu Press, 2010), 196; and H. W. Brands, *The Man Who Saved the Union: Ulysses Grant in War and Peace* (New York: Anchor Books, 2012), 113.

29 Woods, "The Causes of Disunion," 428.

30 DiLorenzo, *The Problem with Lincoln*, 31–33.

31 David R. Mayhew, "Wars and American Politics," *Perspectives on Politics* 3, no. 3 (September 2005), 476.

32 Quoted in Bueno de Mesquita and Smith, *The Spoils of War*, 96.

33 Bueno de Mesquita and Smith, 96.

34 Noah Feldman, *The Broken Constitution: Lincoln, Slavery, and the Refounding of America* (New York: Farrar, Straus, and Giroux, 2021), 134–135.

35 Fergus M. Bordewich, *Congress at War: How Republican Reformers Fought the Civil War, Defied Lincoln, Ended Slavery, and Remade America* (New York: Knopf, 2020), 50.

36 Beschloss, *Presidents of War: The Epic Story, From 1807 to Modern Times* (New York: Broadway Books, 2018), 173.

37 Michael Beschloss, *Presidents of War*, 173, 176.

38 Towers, "Partisans, New History, Modernization," 253.

39 Howard Cecil Perkins, *Northern Editorials on Secession* (Gloucester, Massachusetts: Peter Smith, 1964).

40 Feldman, *The Broken Constitution*, 142–145.

41 http://teachingamericanhistory.org/library/document/the-war-with-mexico-speech-in-the-united-states-house-of-representatives/.

42 Barron, *Waging War*, 119–121, 126–129.

43 Feldman, 135.

44 Abraham Lincoln, First Inaugural Address, delivered March 4, 1861.

45 Beschloss, *Presidents of War*, 164, 166.

46 Bueno de Mesquita and Smith, 122–124.

47 Feldman, *The Broken Constitution*, 271–275.

48 DiLorenzo, *The Problem with Lincoln*, 4–5, 9–11.

49 Oakes, *Crooked Road*, 37, 135–136, 144–145.

50 US Constitution, article 1, section 8.

51 Feldman, *The Broken Constitution*, 261.

52 Feldman, 260–265.

53 Sjursen, *True History*, 213.

54 Bordewich, *Congress at War*, 156–157, 253–254.

55 Bordewich, 167–168.

56 Beschloss, *Presidents of War*, 208–210.

57 Bordewich, *Congress at War*, 275–278.

58 Feldman, *The Broken Constitution*, 306–307.

59 Beschloss, 226.

60 Bordewich, 337, 339–340.

61 Sjursen, *True History*, 205.

62 Quoted in Bordewich, *Congress at War*, 178, 188, 192.

63 Bordewich, *Congress at War*, 101–105, 371.

64 D. Scott Bennett and Allan C. Stam III, "The Duration of Interstate Wars," *American Political Science* Review 90 (June 1996): 239–257; Bueno de Mesquita and Smith, *The Spoils of War*, 110–111.

65 DiLorenzo, *The Problem with Lincoln*, 5.

66 Harry S. Stout, *Upon the Altar of the Nation: A Moral History of the Civil War* (New York: Viking, 2006), 381.

67 Beschloss, *Presidents of War*, 225.

68 Brands, *The Man Who Saved the Union*, 198–200, 215–220.

69 Miller, 484.

70 Beschloss, *Presidents of War*, 156.

71 Bordewich, 61–63.

72 DiLorenzo, *The Problem with Lincoln*, 78, 86, 90–91.

73 Quoted in Bueno de Mesquita and Smith, *The Spoils of War*, 93.

74 DiLorenzo, *The Problem with Lincoln*, 78, 86, 90–91.

75 Quoted in Sjursen, *True History*, 217.

CHAPTER 6

1 Ned Blackhawk, *The Rediscovery of America: Native Peoples and the Unmaking of U.S. History* (New Haven, Connecticut: Yale University Press, 2023), 50.

2 Gibson, *El Norte*, 94; Captivating History, *The Indian Wars*, 6, 30.

3 Daniel A. Sjursen, *A True History of the United States: Indigenous Genocide, Racialized Slavery, Hyper-Capitalism, Militarist Imperialism, and Other Overlooked Aspects of American Exceptionalism* (Lebanon, New Hampshire: Steerforth Press, 2021), 53–55.

4 Bill Yenne, *Indian Wars: The Campaign for the American West* (Yardley, Pennsylvania: Westholme Publishing, 2008), 10.

5 Gibson, *El Norte*, 121–122.

6 Sjursen, *True History*, 93.

7 Richard W. Maass, *The Picky Eagle: How Democracy and Xenophobia Limited US Territorial Expansion* (Ithaca, New York: Cornell University Press, 2020), 66–68.

8 Quoted in Gibson, *El Norte*, 151.

9 Peter Cozzens, *The Earth Is Weeping: The Epic Story of the Indian Wars for the American West* (New York: Vintage Books, 2016), 13–14.

10 Maass, *The Picky Eagle*, 71.

11 Maass, *The Picky Eagle*, 70–72.

12 Quoted in Joseph J. Ellis, *American Creation* (New York, Vintage Books, 2007), 232–233.

13 Cozzens, *The Earth Is Weeping*, 13–14.

14 Cozzens, 4–7.

15 Blackhawk, *The Rediscovery of America*, 322–327.

16 Cozzens, 7.

17 Yenne, *Indian Wars*, 177–231.

18 Yenne, 285–294; Brands, *Dreams of El Dorado*, 433–440.

19 Yenne, 301–307.

CHAPTER 7

1 Quoted in Alexis Heraclides and Ada Dialla, *Humanitarian Intervention in the Long Nineteenth Century* (Manchester, UK: Manchester University Press, 2015), 204.

2 Daniel A. Sjursen, *A True History of the United States: Indigenous Genocide, Racialized Slavery, Hyper-Capitalism, Militarist Imperialism, and Other Overlooked Aspects of American Exceptionalism* (Lebanon, New Hampshire: Steerforth Press, 2021), 268–269.

3 Louis Perez Jr., "The Meaning of the Maine: Causation and the Historiography of the Spanish-American War," *Pacific Historical Review* 58, no. 3 (August 1989): 317.

4 Melvin Small, *Democracy and Diplomacy: The Impact of Domestic Politics on US Foreign Policy, 1789–1994* (Baltimore: Johns Hopkins University Press, 1995), 26.

5 Heraclides and Dialla, *Humanitarian Intervention*, 199.

6 H. W. Brands, *The Man Who Saved the Union: Ulysses Grant in War and Peace* (New York: Anchor Books, 2012), 459–460.

7 Small, *Democracy and Diplomacy*, 28–29.

8 Richard W. Maass, *The Picky Eagle: How Democracy and Xenophobia Limited US Territorial Expansion* (Ithaca, New York: Cornell University Press, 2020), 173–174.

9 Melvin Small, *Was War Necessary?: National Security and US Entry into War* (Beverly Hills, CA: Sage Publications, 1980), 117–118.

10 Heraclides and Dialla, *Humanitarian Intervention*, 203.

11 H. W. Brands, *Dreams of El Dorado: A History of the American West* (New York: Basic Books, 2019), 455–456.

12 Quoted in Sjursen, *True History*, 273.

13 Maass, *The Picky Eagle*, 174–175.

14 Small, *Democracy and Diplomacy*, 30.

15 David Gompert, Hans Binnendijk, and Bonny Lin, *Blinders, Blunders, and Wars: What America and China Can Learn* (Santa Monica, CA: RAND, 2014), 53–55, 60.

16 Michael Beschloss, *Presidents of War: The Epic Story, From 1807 to Modern Times* (New York: Broadway Books, 2018), 249–250.

17 Carrie Gibson, *El Norte: The Epic and Forgotten Story of Hispanic North America* (New York: Atlantic Monthly Press, 2019), 270.

18 Gompert, Binnendijk, and Lin, *Blinders, Blunders, and Wars*, 58.

19 Sjursen, *True History*, 270.

20 Small, *Was War Necessary?*, 135–136.

21 Pierro Gleijeses, "1898: The Opposition to the Spanish-American War," *Journal of Latin American Studies* 35, no. 4 (November 2003): 691.

22 Beschloss, *Presidents of War*, 245–246, 252–259.

23 Gibson, *El Norte*, 269.

24 Beschloss, 241.

25 John D. Long, *The New American Navy* (London: G. Richards, 1904), 1–141.

26 Nick Kapur, "William McKinley's Values and the Origins of the Spanish-American War: A Reinterpretation," *Presidential Studies Quarterly* 41, no. 1 (March 2011): 33–34.

27 Kapur, "William McKinley's Values," 28–29.

28 Gleijeses, "1898," 712.

29 Robert H. Ferrell, *American Diplomacy: A History*, 2nd ed. (New York: W. W. Norton and Company, 1969), 389.

30 Quoted in Kapur, "William McKinley's Values," 25.

31 John L. Offner, *An Unwanted War: The Diplomacy of the United States and Spain over Cuba, 1895–1898* (Chapel Hill: University of North Carolina Press, 1992), cf, ix, 234. Richard F. Hamilton, *President McKinley, War and Empire*, vol. 1 (New Brunswick, NJ: Transaction Publishers, 2006), 118.

32 Perez, "Meaning of the Maine," 308–309.

33 Quoted in Small, *Was War Necessary?*, 139.

34 John L. Offner, "President McKinley and the Origins of the Spanish-American War," (PhD diss. Pennsylvania State University, 1957), 286, 375–377.

35 Heraclides and Dialla, *Humanitarian Intervention*, 206.

36 Justin Rex, "The President's War Agenda: A Rhetorical View," *Presidential Studies Quarterly* 41, no. 1 (March 2011), 99.

37 Gleijeses, "1898," 708–710, 713.

38 Rex, "The President's War Agenda," 103–104.

39 Julius K. Pratt, "American Business and the Spanish-American War," *Hispanic American Historical Review* 14 (May 1934): 163–201.

40 Nancy Lenore O'Connor, "The Spanish-American War: A Re-Evaluation of Its Causes," *Science & Society* 22, no. 2 (Spring 1958): 138.

41 Gleijeses, "1898," 685–686, 702.

42 Small, *Was War Necessary?*, 140–142.

43 Stephen Kinzer, *The True Flag: Theodore Roosevelt, Mark Twain, and the Birth of American Empire* (New York: Henry Holt, 2017), Kindle Location 38.

44 Maass, *The Picky Eagle*, 172–173, 179–180.

45 Small, *Was War Necessary?*, 144–145.

46 Beschloss, *Presidents of War*, 262–263.

47 Sjursen, *True History*, 278–280.

48 Beschloss, *Presidents of War*, 264, 279.

49 Jon G. Sproat, "William McKinley, 1897–1901," in *Presidential Misconduct: From George Washington to Today*, ed. James M. Banner (New York: The New Press, 2019), 189–192.

50 Maass, *The Picky Eagle*, 196.

51 Sjursen, *True History*, 266, 286.

52 Gibson, *El Norte*, 273–274; Gleijeses, "1898," 717–718.

53 Beschloss, *Presidents of War*, 288–289, 291–292.

54 Quoted in Sjursen, *True History*, 272.

55 Gibson, *El Norte*, 274–279.

56 Beschloss, *Presidents of War*, 285–286.

57 Quoted in Sjursen, *True History*, 280–282.

58 David J. Barron, *Waging War: The Clash Between Presidents and Congress, 1776 to ISIS* (New York: Simon and Schuster, 2016), 190–198.

59 Robert Scigliano, "Politics, the Constitution, and the President's War Power," in *The New Politics of American Foreign Policy*, ed. David A. Deese (New York: St. Martin's Press, 1994), 153.

60 Beschloss, *Presidents of War*, 285.

CHAPTER 8

1 Jim Powell, *Wilson's War: How Woodrow Wilson's Great Blunder Led to Hitler, Lenin, Stalin, and World War II* (New York: Crown Forum, 2005), 292.

2 David C. Gompert, Hans Binnendijk, and Bonny Lin, *Blinders, Blunders, and Wars: What America and China Can Learn* (Santa Monica, CA: RAND, 2014), 72–73, 75–76.

3 Adam Tooze and Ted Fertik, "The World Economy and the Great War," *Geschichte und Gesellschaft* 40 Jahrg., H. 2 (April–June 2014): 217–219.

4 Melvin Small, *Was War Necessary?: National Security and US Entry into War* (Beverly Hills, CA: Sage Publications, 1980), 156–158.

5 John Milton Cooper, "World War I: European Origins and American Intervention," *Virginia Quarterly Review* 56, no. 1 (Winter 1980): 5.

6 Walter Laqueur, *Weimar, A Cultural History 1918–1933* (London: Phoenix Press, 1974), 3.

7 Powell, *Wilson's War*, 2.

8 Powell, *Wilson's War*, 91.

9 Tooze and Fertik, "The World Economy," 220–222, 226.

10 Benjamin O. Fordham, "Revisionism Reconsidered: Exports and American Intervention in World War I," *International Organization* 61, no. 2 (Spring 2007): 286.

11 Quoted in Powell, *Wilson's War*, 90.

12 Small, *Was War Necessary?*, 177–186.

13 Powell, 98.

14 Small, 187.

15 Melvin Small, *Democracy and Diplomacy: The Impact of Domestic Politics on US Foreign Policy, 1789–1994* (Baltimore, MD: Johns Hopkins University Press, 1995), 46–47.

16 Quoted in Small, *Was War Necessary?*, 193.

17 Small, *Was War Necessary?*, 192.

18 Beschloss, *Presidents of War*, 305–306.

19 Beschloss, 306–308.

20 Livermore, *Woodrow Wilson*, 10–11.

21 Powell, *Wilson's War*, 2.

22 Powell, 95.

23 Quoted in Justus D. Doenecke, *Nothing Less Than War: A New History of America's Entry into World War I* (Lexington, KY: The University of Kentucky, 2011).

24 Gompert, Binnendijk, and Lin, *Blinders, Blunders, and Wars*, 75.

25 Cooper, "World War I," 11–12.

26 Fordham, "Revisionism Reconsidered," 287, 295–307.

27 David J. Barron, *Waging War: The Clash Between Presidents and Congress, 1776 to ISIS* (New York: Simon and Schuster, 2016), 210.

28 Livermore, *Woodrow Wilson*, 12–13.

29 Fordham, "Revisionism Reconsidered," 278.

30 Barron, *Waging War*, 205–206.

31 Small, *Democracy and Diplomacy*, 42–43.

32 Puong Fei Yeh, "The Role of the Zimmermann Telegram in Spurring America's Entry into the First World War," *American Intelligence Journal* 32, no. 1 (2015): 63.

33 Tooze and Fertik, "The World Economy," 228, 230.

34 Yeh, "The Zimmermann Telegram," 63.

35 Fordham, "Revisionism Reconsidered," 278.

36 Cooper, "World War I," 15.

37 Small, *Democracy and Diplomacy*, 47.

38 Gompert, Binnendijk, and Lin, *Blinders, Blunders, and Wars*, 71–72.

39 Yeh, "The Zimmermann Telegram," 61.

40 Tooze and Fertik, "The World Economy," 226.

41 Cooper, "World War I," 17.

42 Small, *Was War Necessary?*, 155.

43 Cooper, "World War I," 2.

44 Quoted in Beschloss, *Presidents of War*, 342–343.

45 Barron, *Waging War*, 224–225.

46 Powell, *Wilson's War*, 136–137, 159, 161, 226, 238–245.

47 Quoted in Powell, 8–10.

48 Quoted in Powell, 11.

49 Quoted in Small, *Was War Necessary?*, 153.

50 Beschloss, *Presidents of War*, 324–325.

51 Barron, *Waging War*, 214–215, 223–224.

52 Daniel A. Sjursen, *A True History of the United States: Indigenous Genocide, Racialized Slavery, Hyper-Capitalism, Militarist Imperialism, and Other Overlooked Aspects of American Exceptionalism* (Lebanon, New Hampshire: Steerforth Press, 2021), 305–312.

53 Small, *Democracy and Diplomacy*, 48.

54 John W. Chambers, "Woodrow Wilson, 1913–1921," in *Presidential Misconduct: From George Washington to Today*, ed. James M. Banner (New York: The New Press, 2019), 238–241.

55 Paul A. Koistinen, "The 'Industrial-Military Complex' in Historical Perspective: The InterWar Years," *Journal of American History* 56, no. 4 (March 1970): 819–820, 822.

56 Sjursen, *True History*, 295.

57 William E. Leuchtenburg, "The New Deal and the Analogue of War," in *Change and Continuity in Twentieth-Century America*, eds. John Braeman, Robert H. Bremner, and Everett Walters (Columbus, Ohio: Ohio State University Press, 1964), 81–143.

58 Koistinen, "InterWar Years," 824–825.

59 Robert D. Cuff, "An Organizational Perspective on the Military-Industrial Complex," *Business History Review* 52, no. 2 (Summer 1978): 264–267.

60 Tooze and Fertik, "The World Economy," 214–216, 223, 232–233.

61 David R. Mayhew, "War and American Politics," *Perspectives on Politics* 3, no. 3 (September 2005): 477.

62 Quoted in Beschloss, *Presidents of War*, 344–347.

63 Gompert, Binnendijk, and Lin, *Blinders, Blunders, and Wars*, 76–79.

64 Barron, *Waging War*, 225–226.

65 Mayhew, "War and American Politics," 484–485.

66 Fordham, "Revisionism Reconsidered," 278–287.

67 Paul A. Koistinen, "The 'Industrial-Military Complex' in Historical Perspective: World War I," *Business History Review* 41, no. 4 (Winter 1967): 379.

68 Koistinen "World War I," 286, 307.

CHAPTER 9

1 Melvin Small, *Was War Necessary?: National Security and US Entry into War* (London: Sage Publications, 1980), 217.

2 United States Holocaust Museum, "Voyage of the St. Louis," Holocaust Encyclopedia, https://www.ushmm.org/wlc/en/article.php?ModuleId=10005267.

3 Daniel A. Sjursen, *A True History of the United States: Indigenous Genocide, Racialized Slavery, Hyper-Capitalism, Militarist Imperialism, and Other Overlooked Aspects of American Exceptionalism* (Lebanon, New Hampshire: Steerforth Press, 2021), 367–368.

4 Angelo M. Codevilla, *America's Rise and Fall among Nations: Lessons in Statecraft from John Quincy Adams* (New York: Encounter Books, 2022), 86.

5 John M. Schuessler, "The Deception Dividend: FDR's Undeclared War," *International Security* 34, no. 4 (Spring 2010): 145, 151.

6 Warren F. Kimball, "Franklin D. Roosevelt and World War II," *Presidential Studies Quarterly* 34, no. 1(March 2004): 84.

7 Ralph Zuljan, "Allied and Axis GDP," in *Ralph Zuljan Archive*, https://www.zuljan.info/articles/0302wwiigdp.html#google_vignette.

8 Franklin Delano Roosevelt, Annual Message to Congress, January 6, 1941, www.ourdocuments.gov. Click on President Franklin Roosevelt's Annual Message (Four Freedoms) to Congress (1941).

9 Melvin Small, *Democracy and Diplomacy: The Impact of Domestic Politics on US Foreign Policy, 1789–1994* (Baltimore: Johns Hopkins University Press, 1995), 62.

10 Waldo Heinrichs, *Threshold of War: Franklin D. Roosevelt and American Entry into World War II* (New York: Oxford University Press, 1988), 4.

11 Heinrichs, *Threshold of War*, 13–15.

12 Heinrichs, 83–84.

13 Codevilla, *America's Rise and Fall*, 86.

14 Bruce Bueno de Mesquita and Alastair Smith, *The Spoils of War: Greed, Power, and the Conflicts that Made Our Greatest Presidents* (New York: PublicAffairs, 2016), 155–157.

15 Heinrichs, *Threshold of War*, 5.

16 James K. Galbraith, "The Unbearable Costs of Empire," *American* Prospect,

November 6, 2002, https://prospect.org

17 Small, *Democracy and Diplomacy*, 73.

18 Quoted in Irving H. Anderson Jr., *The Standard-Vacuum Oil Company and United States East Asian Policy, 1933–1941* (Princeton, NJ: Princeton University Press, 1975), 175.

19 Michael Beschloss, *Presidents of War: The Epic Story, From 1807 to Modern Times* (New York: Broadway Books, 2018), 381–382.

20 "Pearl Harbor: Did Roosevelt "Let" It Happen? FDR Library and Museum, fdrlibrary.org

21 David Model, *Lying for Empire: How to Commit War Crimes with a Straight Face* (Monroe, Maine: Common Courage Press, 2005), 44.

22 Codevilla, *America's Rise and Fall*, 86.

23 Memo of conversation, August 8, 1941, FR Japan, 2:550–551; Tokyo to Washington, August 7, 1941, #12, "MAGIC" Background, 3A: 8–9; Tokyo to Washington, August 9, 1941, #21, #22, 14.

24 Cordell Hull memo, August 16, 1941, FR Japan, 2:553–554.

25 Kimball, "Franklin D. Roosevelt," 95–96.

26 Heinrichs, *Threshold of War*, 7, 136, 154–155, 207–209, 213–214.

27 Small, *Was War Necessary?*, 238–239, 242, 244.

28 Jeffrey Record, *Japan's Decision for War in 1941: Some Enduring Lessons* (Carlisle, PA: Strategic Studies Institute, US Army War College, 2009), 21.

29 Schuessler, "The Deception Dividend," 160.

30 Richard Law minute, FO 371/27984, F10456/1299/23, PRO; Harvey diary, 40.

31 Heinrichs, *Threshold of War*, 183–184.

32 Domei quoted in Heinrichs, *Threshold of War, 202*.

33 Heinrichs, *Threshold of War*, 202–205.

34 Small, *Was War Necessary?*, 245.

35 Model, *Lying for Empire*, 46.

36 Quoted Beschloss, *Presidents of War*, 382.

37 Kimball, "Franklin D. Roosevelt," 97.

38 Justus Drew Doenecke, *Storm on the Horizon: The Challenge to American Intervention, 1939–1941* (Lanham, MD: Rowman & Littlefield, 2000), 317.

39 Beschloss, *Presidents of War*, 383.

40 Small, *Was War Necessary?*, 256–257.

41 David Reynolds, *From Munich to Pearl Harbor: Roosevelt's America and the Origins of the Second World War* (Chicago: Ivan R. Dee, 2001), 163.

42 Quoted in Sjursen, *True History*, 377–378.

43 Quoted in Robert E. Sherwood, *Roosevelt and Hopkins: An Intimate History*, rev. ed. (New York: Harper and Brothers, 1950), 428, 431.

44 Schuessler, "The Deception Dividend," 162.

45 Ralph Raico, "On the Brink of World War II: Justus Doenecke's 'Storm on the Horizon,'" *The Independent Review* 6, no. 4 (Spring 2002): 610.

46 Marks, "Origin of FDR's Promise," 458–459.

47 Quoted in Sjursen, *True History*, 368–369.

48 Small, *Was War Necessary?*, 221–222.

49 War cabinet minutes from Britain, cited in Thomas A. Bailey and Paul B. Ryan, *Hitler vs. Roosevelt: The Undeclared Naval War* (New York: The Free Press, 1979), 166.

50 John M. Schuessler, "Correspondence: FDR, US Entry into World War II, and Selection Effects Theory," *International Security* 35, no. 2 (Fall 2010): 184.

51 Small, *Democracy and Diplomacy*, 66.

52 Sjursen, *True History*, 383–384.

53 Heinrichs, *Threshold of War*, 137–141, 150.

54 Doenecke, *Storm on the Horizon*, 115, 225.

55 Sjursen, *True History*, 362–363.

56 Dan Reiter, "Correspondence: FDR, US Entry into World War II, and Selection Effects Theory," *International Security* 34, no. 4 (Spring 201): 177–178.

57 Small, *Was War Necessary?*, 233.

58 Quoted in David Reynolds, *The Creation of the Anglo-American Alliance, 1937–1941: A Study in Competitive Cooperation* (Chapel Hill: University of North Carolina Press, 1982), 214–215.

59 Michael T. Corgan, "Franklin D. Roosevelt and the American Occupation of Iceland," *Naval War College Review* 45, no. 4 (Autumn 1992): 38–42.

60 Corgan "American Occupation of Iceland," 46, 48–50.

61 Beschloss, *Presidents of War*, 380.

62 Heinrichs, *Threshold of War*, 60–91.

63 Robert Scigliano, "Politics, the Constitution, and the President's War Power," 154–155, 160.

64 Beschloss, *Presidents of War*, 361, 382–384, 386–387, 426–427.

65 Sjursen, *True History*, 401, 404–405.

66 Schuessler, "The Deception Dividend, 141.

67 Sjursen, 390–393.

68 Quoted in Sjursen, 390.

69 Model, *Lying for Empire*, 58.

70 James Fallows, "The Military-Industrial Complex," *Foreign Policy*, no. 133 (November–December 2002): 46.

71 Quoted in Sjursen, *True History*, 390.

72 Quoted in Sjursen, 415.

73 Military leaders quoted in William D. Leahy, *I Was There* (New York: Whittlesey House, 1950), 441 and Gar Alperovitz, *The Decision to Use the Atomic Bomb* (Toronto: Random House of Canada, 1995), respectively.

74 Model, *Lying for Empire*, 76.

75 Quoted in Sjursen, *True History*, 414.

76 Sjursen, 59.

77 Sjursen, 64–65.

78 Sjursen, 78.

79 Beschloss, *Presidents of War*, 396–398, 409.

80 Bueno de Mesquita and Smith, *The Spoils of War*, 169–170.

81 David J. Barron, *Waging War: The Clash Between Presidents and Congress 1776 to ISIS* (New York: Simon and Schuster, 2016), 258–267.

82 Bueno de Mesquita and Smith, *The Spoils of War*, 167–168.

83 Barron, *Waging War*, 254.

84 Bueno de Mesquita and Smith, *The Spoils of War*, 146, 162–163.

85 David Mayhew, "Wars and American Politics," *Perspectives on Politics* 3, no. 3 (September 2005): 473, 478–479, 488.

86 Barron, *Waging War*, 284.

87 Murray L. Weidenbaum, *The Economics of Peacetime Defense* (New York:

Praeger, 1974), 134.

88 Small, *Was War Necessary?*, 227.

89 Rebecca U. Thorpe, *The American Warfare State: The Domestic Politics of Military Spending* (Chicago: University of Chicago Press, 2014), ix, 3–23, 180.

90 Melman, "Ten Propositions," 317.

91 Michael A. Bernstein and Mark R. Wilson, "New Perspectives on the History of the Military-Industrial Complex," *Enterprise and Society* 12, no. 1 (March 2011): 2.

92 Sjursen, *True History*, 384, 386–387.

CHAPTER 10

1 Quoted in Melvin Small, *Democracy and Diplomacy: The Impact of Domestic Politics on US Foreign Policy, 1789–1994* (Baltimore: The Johns Hopkins University Press, 1995), 87.

2 James McCartney and Molly Sinclair McCartney, *America's War Machine: Vested Interests, Endless Conflicts* (New York: St. Martin's Press, 2015), 77.

3 Quoted in Small, *Democracy and Diplomacy*, 81, 84.

4 Thomas J. McCormick, *America's Half-Century: United States Foreign Policy in the Cold War and After*, 2nd edition (Baltimore, MD: Johns Hopkins University Press, 1995), xiii–xv, 6, 47.

5 Quoted in Daniel A. Sjursen, *A True History of the United States: Indigenous Genocide, Racialized Slavery, Hyper-Capitalism, Militarist Imperialism, and Other Overlooked Aspects of American Exceptionalism* (Lebanon, New Hampshire: Steerforth Press, 2021), 422.

6 McCormick, *America's Half-Century*, 74–78.

7 McCormick, 78–81.

8 Small, *Democracy and Diplomacy*, 107–108.

9 McCormick, 48.

10 Gar Alperovitz, *Atomic Diplomacy: Hiroshima and Potsdam* (New York: Vintage Books, 1967), 106, 227, 229.

11 Melvyn Leffler, "Cold War and Global Hegemony, 1945–1991," *Organization of American Historians Magazine of History* 19, no. 2 (March 2005): 65.

12 Brian Thomas, "Cold War Origins, II," *Journal of Contemporary History* 3, no. 1 (January 1968): 187.

13 Quoted in McCormick, *America's Half-Century*, 65.

14 Eric Alterman, *When Presidents Lie: A History of Official Deception and Its Consequences* (New York: Viking, 2004), 23–28.

15 Quoted in Sjursen, *True History*, 426–427.

16 Quoted in Sjursen, 32–38, 43, 65.

17 Sjursen, 43–45.

18 Michael F. Hopkins, "Continuing Debate and New Approaches in Cold War History," *The Historical Journal* 50, no. 4 (December 2007): 926.

19 Thomas, "Cold War Origins, II," 196.

20 David Horowitz, *The Free World Colossus: A Critique of American Foreign Policy in the Cold War* (New York: Hill and Wang, 1965), 413. Horowitz agreed with Arnold Toynbee that the United States led a global anti-revolutionary movement to protect vested interests. Horowitz has since become a neoconservative.

21 Quoted in Leffler, "Cold War and Global Hegemony," 67.

22 Thomas, "Cold War Origins, II," 193.

23 D. F. Fleming, *The Cold War and Its Origins, 1917–1960* (New York: Taylor & Francis, 1961).

24 Thomas F. Berner, "Who Won the Cold War?" *Strategic Studies Institute, US Army War College* (2009), 5–6, 11.

25 McCormick, *America's Half-Century*, 66–68.

26 Ron Pineo, "Recent Cold War Studies," *The History Teacher* 37, no. 1 (November 2003): 82.

27 Hopkins, "Continuing Debate," 919.

28 Small, *Democracy and Diplomacy*, 86.

29 Leffler, "Cold War and Global Hegemony," 66.

30 Edward A. Nordlinger, "America's Strategic Immunity: The Basis of a National Security Strategy," in *Soviet-American Relations After the Cold War*, eds. Robert Jervis and Seweryn Bialer (Durham, NC: Duke University Press, 1991), 250.

31 Robert H. Johnson, *Improper Dangers: US Conceptions of Threat in the Cold War and After* (New York: St. Martin's Press, 1997), 70–71.

CHAPTER 11

1 A. B. Abrams, *Immovable Object: North Korea's 70 Years at War with American Power* (Atlanta, GA: Clarity Press, Inc., 2020), 43–47, 52, 57.

2 Michael Beschloss, *Presidents of War: The Epic Story, From 1807 to Modern Times* (New York: Broadway Books, 2018), 444–445.

3 Paul Seabury, "Cold War Origins, I," *Journal of Contemporary History* 3, no. 1 (January 1968): 173.

4 Abrams, *Immovable Object*, 48–49.

5 "Record of the Meeting of the State-Defense Policy Review Group," *Foreign Relations of the United States, 1950*, vol. 1 (February 27, 1950): 170–171.

6 Abrams, *Immovable Object*, 48.

7 David J. Barron, *Waging War: The Clash Between Presidents and Congress, 1776 to ISIS* (New York: Simon and Schuster, 2016), 304–305.

8 Thomas, "Cold War Origins, II," 189.

9 Leffler, "Cold War and Global Hegemony, 1945–1991," 65.

10 Pineo, "Recent Cold War Studies," 82, 84.

11 David Holloway, "Military Power and Political Purpose in Soviet Policy," in *Soviet Foreign Policy in a Changing World*, eds. Robbin F. Laird and Erik Hoffmann (New York: Aldine De Gruyter, 1986), 251.

12 Quoted in McCartney and McCartney, *America's War Machine*, 77.

13 Michael MccGwire, *Military Objectives in Soviet Foreign Policy* (Washington, DC: Brookings Institution Press, 1987), 350–353, 375.

14 Johnson, *Improper Dangers*, 131–154.

15 Nordlinger, "America's Strategic Immunity," 252.

16 Dinah Walker, "Trends in Military Spending," Council on Foreign Relations, July 2014, cfr.org

17 Abrams, *Immovable Object*, 49–50.

18 Anthony H. Richmond, "Does War Lead to More War?" *Peace Research* 35, no. 2 (November 2003): 11–13.

19 Harvey Sapolsky, Eugene Gholz, and Allen Kaufman, "Security Lessons from the Cold War," *Foreign Affairs* 78, no. 4 (July–August 1999): 81–82.

20 Johnson, *Improper Dangers*, 7.

21 Johnson, 36.

22 Small, *Democracy and Diplomacy*, 83, 93–94.

23 Sapolsky, Gholz, and Kaufman, "Security Lessons," 80.

24 Sjursen, *True History*, 448–456.

25 Leffler, "Cold War and Global Hegemony," 69.

26 Melvin Small, *Was War Necessary?: National Security and US Entry into War* (Beverly Hills, CA: Sage Publications, 1980), 278–279.

27 Leffler, "Cold War and Global Hegemony," 68.

28 Russell D. Buhite, "'Major Interests': American Policy Toward China, Taiwan, and Korea, 1945–1950," *Pacific Historical Review* 47, no. 3 (August 1978): 425–426, 440, 442, 444–447, 449.

29 Quoted in Beschloss, *Presidents of War*, 446.

30 Buhite, "Major Interests," 425, 431, 440.

31 Johnson, *Improper Dangers*, 206–207.

32 Sjursen, *True History*, 443–444.

33 Beschloss, *Presidents of War*, 467–470, 473.

34 McCormick, *America's Half-Century*, 106–107.

35 Sjursen, *True History*, 447.

36 Berner, "Who Won the Cold War?" 5.

37 Johnson, *Improper Dangers*, 39–40.

38 Quoted in McCormick, *America's Half-Century*, 98.

39 McCartney and McCartney, *America's War Machine*, 77.

40 Beschloss, *Presidents of War*, 459–460, 464.

41 Louis Fisher, "Unchecked Presidential Wars," *University of Pennsylvania Law Review* 148, no. 5 (May 2000): 1657–1658.

42 Robert Scigliano, "Politics, the Constitution, and the President's War Power," in *The New Politics of American Foreign Policy*, ed. David A. Deese (New York: St. Martin's Press, 1994), 154–155.

43 Alexander Hamilton, "The Federalist No. 69," in Alexander Hamilton, James Madison, and John Hay, *The Federalist: A Commentary on on the Constitution of the United States* (New York: Modern Library, 1937), 448, emphasis in original.

44 Scigliano, "The President's War Power," 160–161.

45 Beschloss, *Presidents of War*, 440–441.

46 Beschloss, 482–483.

CHAPTER 12

1 Pineo, "Recent Cold War Studies," 83.

2 Mark I. Gelfand, "John F. Kennedy, 1961–1963," in *Presidential Misconduct: From George Washington to Today*, ed. James M. Banner (New York: The New Press, 2019), 347.

3 Central Intelligence Agency, "The Military Build-Up in Cuba," no. 85-3-62, CIA records; Thomas L. Hughes to acting secretary of state, "Daniel's Conversation with Castro," December 13, 1963, box 23-F-1-2F.

4 Bruce Bueno de Mesquita and Alastair Smith, *The Spoils of War: Greed, Power, and the Conflicts that Made Our Greatest Presidents* (New York: PublicAffairs, 2016), 228–232.

5 Alterman, *When Presidents Lie*, 124–125.

6 Alterman, 94.

7 Bueno de Mesquita and Smith, *The Spoils of War*, 231–232.

8 Pineo, "Recent Cold War Studies," 83.

9 Sjursen, *True History*, 466, 483.

10 Philip Zelikow, Timothy Natali, and Ernest May, eds., *The Presidential Recordings: John F. Kennedy: Volumes 1–3, The Great Crises* (New York: W. W. Norton and Company, 2001), 451.

11 Scigliano, "The President's War Power," 157.

12 McCormick, *America's Half-Century*, 144–146.

13 Quoted in Alterman, *When Presidents Lie*, 106.

14 Alterman, 132–133.

CHAPTER 13

1 Melvin Small, *At the Water's Edge: American Politics and the Vietnam War* (Chicago: Ivan R. Dee, 2005), x.

2 McCormick, *America's Half-Century*, 111–118.

3 Eric Martel, "Gulf of Tonkin," *Organization of American Historians Magazine of History* 7, no. 2, History of US Foreign Policy (Fall 1992): 36.

4 Small, *At the Water's Edge*, 6–9.

5 Small, *At the Water's Edge*, 19–22.

6 Quoted in Small, *Democracy and Diplomacy*, 115–117.

7 Quoted in Small, *Democracy and Diplomacy*, 493.

8 Adam Roberts, "The Fog of Crisis: The 1964 Tonkin Gulf Incidents," *The World Today* 26, no. 5 (May 1970): 213.

9 Alterman, *When Presidents Lie*, 225–226, 234.

10 Martel, "Gulf of Tonkin," 36–37.

11 Beschloss, *Presidents of War*, 514.

12 Roberts, "The Fog of Crisis," 212.

13 Beschloss, *Presidents of War*, 494–495.

14 Quoted in Small, *At the Water's Edge*, 28–32; quoted in Scigliano, "The President's War Power," 158.

15 Gulf of Tonkin Resolution, Enacted by Congress, August 10, 1964, www.ourdocuments.gov, Click on "Tonkin Gulf Resolution (1964)."

16 Martel, "Gulf of Tonkin," 37–38.

17 Roberts, "The Fog of Crisis," 214.

18 Quoted in Small, *At the Water's Edge*, 23.

19 The Committee for the Republic, "'The Most Dangerous Man in America' Salon: Defender of Liberty Award: Daniel Ellsberg," June 30, 2021.

20 Small, *At the Water's Edge*, 38–51, 54, 76–77.

21 Scigliano, "The President's War Power," 157.

22 Bueno de Mesquita and Smith, *The Spoils of War*, 175, 184.

23 Michael R. Beschloss, *Taking Charge: The Johnson White House Tapes, 1963–1964* (New York: Simon and Schuster, 1997), 238.

24 Alterman, *When Presidents Lie*, 168–170, 219.

25 The Committee for the Republic, "Most Dangerous Man," June 30, 2021.

26 McCormick, *America's Half-Century*, 152.

27 Quoted in Beschloss, *Presidents of War*, 528.

28 McCormick, *America's Half-Century*, 153.

29 Small, *Democracy and Diplomacy*, 122.

30 Small, *Democracy and Diplomacy*, 121, 123.

31 Bueno de Mesquita and Smith, *The Spoils of War*, 178.

32 Kathryn S. Olmsted and Eric Rauchway, "Richard Nixon, 1969–1974," in *Presidential Misconduct: From George Washington to Today*, ed. James M. Banner (New York: The New Press, 2019), 372–373.

33 Quoted in Johnson, *Improper Dangers*, 157–158, 161.

34 Barron, *Waging War*, 318, 321, 329–331.

35 Barron, 343–358.

36 Scigliano, "The President's War Power," 158–159.

37 Kent Roach, "The Uses and Audiences of Preambles in Legislation," *McGill Law Journal*, Vol. 47, 2001, p. 129.

38 The Committee for the Republic, "Most Dangerous Man," June 30, 2021.

39 Joan Hoff, "Gerald Ford, 1974–1977," in *Presidential Misconduct*, ed. James M. Banner, 389–390.

40 Olmsted and Rauchway, "Richard Nixon, 1969–1974," in *Presidential Misconduct: From George Washington to Today*, ed. James M. Banner (New York: The New Press, 2019), 371, 374–386.

CHAPTER 14

1 Fred Chernoff, "Ending the Cold War: The Soviet Retreat and the US Military Buildup," *International Affairs* 61, no. 1 (January 1991): 118, 124.

2 Johnson, *Improper Dangers*, 53–55.

3 Pineo, "Recent Cold War Studies," 83–84.

4 Sjursen, *True History*, 584.

5 Johnson, 4–5.

6 Chernoff, "Ending the Cold War," 111–112, 118–126.

7 Johnson, 4–5.

CHAPTER 15

1 George Leaman, "Iraq, American Empire, and the War on Terrorism," *Metaphilosophy* 35, no 3 (April 2004): 235, 237.

2 P. N. Haksar, "Gulf War I: Need for Probe," *World Affairs: The Journal of International Issues* 3 (December 1991): 16.

3 Robert Scigliano, "Politics, the Constitution, and the President's War Power," in *The New Politics of American Foreign Policy*, ed. David A. Deese (New York: St. Martin's Press, 1994), 161.

4 Abdulkhaleq Abdulla, "Gulf War: The Socio-Political Background," *Arab Studies Quarterly* 16, no. 3 (Summer 1994): 6–7.

5 Steve A. Yetiv, "Groupthink and the Gulf Crisis," *British Journal of Political Science* 33, no. 3 (July, 2003): 428.

6 James McCartney and Molly Sinclair McCartney, *America's War Machine: Vested Interests, Endless Conflicts* (New York: St. Martin's Press, 2015), 106–107, 112.

7 Melvin Small, *Democracy and Diplomacy: The Impact of Domestic Politics on US Foreign Policy, 1789–1994* (Baltimore: The Johns Hopkins University Press, 1995), 155–156.

8 Small, *Democracy and Diplomacy*, 156; Daniel A. Sjursen, *A True History of the United States: Indigenous Genocide, Racialized Slavery, Hyper-Capitalism, Militarist Imperialism, and Other Overlooked Aspects of American Exceptionalism* (Lebanon, New Hampshire: Steerworth Press, 2021), 584–585.

9 Haksar, "Gulf War I: Need for Probe," 14–15.

10 Yetiv, "Groupthink and the Gulf Crisis," 428–429.

11 Small, *Democracy and Diplomacy*, 158.

12 Abdulla, "Gulf War," 7.

13 Testimony of James A. Baker, III, before the Committee on Foreign Affairs, US House of Representatives, in *Crisis in the Persian Gulf*, Hearings and Markup, September 4, 1990, 101st Congress, 2nd Session (Washington, DC: Government Printing Office, 1990), 4, 82.

14 Yetiv, "Groupthink and the Gulf Crisis," 423.

15 Scigliano, "The President's War Power," 161.

16 Yetiv, "Groupthink and the Gulf Crisis," 433–434, 442.

CHAPTER 16

1 Abdulla, "Gulf War," 9.

2 William Hartung, "Eisenhower's Warning the Military-Industrial Complex Forty Years Later," *World Policy Journal* 18, no. 1 (Spring 2001): 40.

3 Sjursen, *True History*, 606–607.

4 Carol Winkler, "Parallels in Preemptive War Rhetoric: Reagan on Libya; Bush 43 on Iraq," *Rhetoric and Public Affairs* 10, no. 2 (Summer 2007): 325.

5 Quoted in Gregory Britton, "September 11, American 'Exceptionalism' and the War in Iraq," *Australasian Journal of American Studies* 25, no. 1 (July 2006): 131–132.

6 Marc J. Hetherington and Michael Nelson, "Anatomy of a Rally Effect: George W. Bush and the War on Terrorism," *Political Science and Politics* 36, no. 1 (January 2003): 37–42.

7 Cited in McCartney and McCartney, *America's War Machine*, 12–13.

8 Sjursen, *True History*, 618–619.

9 Sjursen, 634, 642.

10 Sjursen, 118.

11 Quoted in Robert Burns, "Analysis: How Afghan War Showed Limits of US Military Power," *Associated Press*, July 17, 2021.

12 Watson Institute for International and Public Affairs, "Human and Budgetary Costs to Date of the US War in Afghanistan, 2001–2022," Brown University, https://watson.brown.edu

13 Barron, *Waging War*, 392–403, 422–424, 425.

14 Kathryn S. Olmstead and Eric Rauchway, "George W. Bush (2001–2009)," in *Presidential Misconduct: From George Washington to Today*, ed. James M. Banner (New York: The New Press, 2019), 453–456.

15 Christopher M. Faulkner and Jeff Rogg, "Ten Years After the Al-Awlaki Killing: A Reckoning for the United States' Drone Wars Awaits," Modern War Institute, September 27, 2021, mwiwestpoint.edu.

16 Olmstead and Rauchway, "George W. Bush," 459–463.

17 Linda Bilmes, "The Financial Legacy of Iraq and Afghanistan: How Wartime Spending Decisions Will Constrain Future National Security Budgets," *M-RCBG*

Faculty Working Paper No. 2013-01, Harvard Kennedy School.

18 Sue Lockett John, David Domke, Kevin Coe, and Erica S. Graham, "Going Public, Crisis after Crisis: The Bush Administration and the Press from September 11 to Saddam," *Rhetoric and Public Affairs* 10, no. 2 (Summer 2007): 198.

CHAPTER 17

1 Ron Suskind, *The One Percent Doctrine: Deep Inside America's Pursuit of Its Enemies since 9/11* (New York: Simon and Schuster, 2007), 26; George Packer, *The Assassins' Gate: America in Iraq* (New York: Farrar, Straus and Giroux, 2006), 39.

2 Olmstead and Rauchway, "George W. Bush," 452.

3 Leaman, "Iraq, American Empire," 234–235.

4 David A. Lake, "Two Cheers for Bargaining Theory: Assessing Rationalist Explanations of the Iraq War," *International Security* 35, no. 3 (Winter 2010–2011): 8.

5 Daniel Lieberfeld, "Theories of Conflict and the Iraq War," *International Journal of Peace Studies* 10, no. 2 (Autumn/Winter 2005): 8–10.

6 Quoted in David Martin, "Plans for Iraq Attack Began on 9/11," *CBS News*, September 4, 2002, http://www.cbsnews.com/stories/2002/09/04/september11/main520830.shtml.

7 Bob Woodward, *Bush at War* (New York: Simon and Schuster, 2002).

8 Amy Gershkoff and Shana Kushner, "Shaping Public Opinion: The 9/11-Iraq Connection in the Bush Administration's Rhetoric," *Perspectives on Politics* 3, no. 3 (September 2005): 526.

9 Quoted in McCartney and McCartney, *America's War Machine*, 71.

10 Lockett John, Domke, Coe, and Graham, "Crisis after Crisis," 211.

11 Britton, "September 11," 125–126.

12 Karlyn Kohrs Campbell and Kathleen Hall Jamieson, *Deeds Done in Words: Presidential Rhetoric and Genres of Governance* (Chicago: University of Chicago Press, 1990).

13 Michael Beschloss, *Presidents of War: The Epic Story, From 1807 to Modern Times* (New York: Broadway Books, 2018), 583.

14 Gershkoff and Kushner, "Shaping Public Opinion," 525, 534; McCartney and McCartney, *America's War Machine*, 68, 70.

15 Gershkoff and Kushner, "Shaping Public Opinion," 525-537.

16 Scott L. Althaus and Devon M. Largio, "When Osama Became Saddam: Origins and Consequences of the Change in America's Public Enemy #1," *Political Science and Politics* 37, no. 4 (October 2004): 796–797, 799.

17 John R. Zaller, *The Nature and Origins of Mass Opinion* (Cambridge, United Kingdom: Cambridge University Press, 1992), 185.

18 Quoted in Michael Isikoff and David Corn, *Hubris: The Inside Story of Spin, Scandal, and the Selling of the Iraq War* (New York: Three Rivers, 2007), 115.

19 James Petras, *Zionism, Militarism, and the Decline of US Power* (Atlanta, Georgia: Clarity Press, 2008), 22–25.

20 Lieberfeld, "Theories of Conflict and the Iraq War, 8–10.

21 https://www.youtube.com/watch?v=_RNE3X41IvM

22 Lieberfeld 8–9.

23 Lake, "Bargaining Theory," 27.

24 Olmstead and Rauchway, "George W. Bush," 456–459.

25 Gershkoff and Kushner, "Shaping Public Opinion," 531.

26 Lake, "Bargaining Theory," 14.

27 Kevin M. Woods, Michael R. Pease, Mark E Stout, Williamson Murray, and James G. Lacey, *Iraqi Perspectives Project: A View of Operation Iraqi Freedom from Saddam's Senior Leadership* (Norfolk, VA: Joint Center for Operational Analysis, US Joint Forces Command, 2006); Charles Duelfer, head of the Iraq Survey Group trying to find Saddam's WMD after the war, cited in Isikoff and Corn, *Hubris*, 375.

28 Lieberfeld, "Theories of Conflict," 3–5.

29 Richard Haass, *The Opportunity: America's Moment to Alter History's Course* (New York: PublicAffairs, 2005), 94.

30 Eric Alterman, *When Presidents Lie: A History of Official Deception and Its Consequences* (New York: Viking, 2004), 298.

31 Lake, "Bargaining Theory," 16.

32 Lake, 18–20.

33 Beschloss, *Presidents of War*, 583–584.

34 Sjursen, *True History*, 620–621.

CONCLUSION

1 Paul Kennedy, *The Rise and Fall of the Great Powers: Economic Change and Military Conflict From 1500 to 2000* (New York: Vantage, 1989).

INDEX

888ok888888ok

U.S. Department of Defense, 248–249, 259, 296, 305, 336, 337
U.S. Department of Homeland Security (DHS), 337–338, 358
U.S. General Accounting Office, 249, 356
U.S. global hegemony, 4, 226–227, 231
U.S. House of Representatives, 27, 30, 34, 50, 60–61, 63, 68, 73, 85, 115, 142, 192, 255, 297, 319, 350
House Armed Services Committee, 273
House Foreign Affairs Committee, 318, 358, 381n
House Government Reform Committee, 358
U.S. Justice Department, 158, 332, 334
U.S.-Mexican War. See Mexican War
U.S. military bases, 3, 50, 122, 125, 184, 216, 226, 228, 236, 239, 255, 315, 329
U.S. national debt, 35, 37, 69, 52, 117, 214, 219, 290, 331, 336
U.S. Navy, 10, 13, 15–16, 21, 24, 33–34, 46, 48, 69, 109, 111–112, 119–120, 125, 176, 179, 184, 186–192, 195, 199–200, 203, 207, 232, 271–272, 280, 283, 316
U.S. Navy Department, 10, 13, 305
U.S. neutrality, 10, 23, 106, 130, 136–143, 146–147, 165–166, 173, 191, 193, 196–198, 201
U.S. Pacific Fleet, 119, 179, 184, 186–190, 202
U.S. Postmaster General, 158
U.S. presidency, commander-in-chief role, 212–214, 216–217, 246, 262, 264, 282, 284, 293, 295, 305–306, 316, 318–319, 331–332, 334, 336, 339, 361n
U.S. Senate, 9, 28, 30, 42, 43, 60–62, 64–65, 73, 115, 117, 118, 142, 154, 250, 255, 306, 350
Senate Foreign Relations Committee, 109, 280–281, 358

Senate Intelligence Committee, 336, 347
Senate Judiciary Committee, 358
Senate Select Committee to Study Governmental Operations with Respect to Intelligence Activities See Church Committee
U.S. Secretary of the Navy, 16, 44, 109, 111
U.S. Secretary of State, 16, 24, 32, 66, 75, 108, 139, 153, 180, 181, 233, 238, 253, 258–259, 312, 316–318, 320, 322, 356
U.S. Secretary of War, 38, 66, 77, 115, 122, 185, 188
U.S. State Department, 185, 227, 230, 235, 237, 239, 240, 243, 250, 253, 268, 303, 334
U.S. Supreme Court, 11, 13, 36, 63, 81, 121, 158, 209–211, 251, 264–265, 295, 297, 306, 334, 336, 362n
U.S. territorial expansion, 28, 30, 38–39, 43–45, 50–51, 102, 201
U.S. trade, 9, 11, 15–16, 23–25, 28, 35, 37, 43, 51, 64, 109, 117, 123, 126, 136, 138–139, 144–145, 147, 149, 162, 165–167, 171, 174–175, 178, 180, 182, 201, 206, 213, 216, 220, 229, 309, 312
U.S. Virgin Islands, 121
USS Cole, 325
USS Greer, 193
USS Maddox, 281
USS Maine, 53, 102, 104, 110–115, 117–118, 139
USS Missouri, 237,
USS Philadelphia, 18

V

Vallandigham, Clement L., 80–81
Valenti, Jack, 285
Van Buren, Martin, 93
Vandenberg, Arthur, 249
Velvet Revolution, 68
Venezuela, 133
Veracruz, 48–49